THE MEDIEVAL HOSPITAL AND MEDICAL PRACTICE

AVISTA Studies in History of Medieval Technology, Science and Art is a series produced by AVISTA (The Association Villard de Honnecourt for Interdisciplinary Study of Medieval Technology, Science and Art), and published by Ashgate. The aim of the series is to promote the cross-disciplinary objectives of AVISTA by publishing in the areas of the history of science, technology, architecture, and art. The society takes its name from Villard (Wilars) de Honnecourt, an elusive persona of the 13th century whose autograph portfolio contains a variety of fascinating drawings and descriptions of both the fine and mechanical arts.

www.avista.org

AVISTA President
Lynn T. Courtenay 2000–2005
Robert Bork 2005–present

Volume Editor-in-Chief
Barbara S. Bowers

Assistant Editors
Anne Van Arsdall, Emilie Savage-Smith
Theresa Vann, Carol Neuman de Vegvar

Review Panel
John Goodall, Piers Mitchell
John Riddle, Ellen Shortell

AVISTA Studies in the History of Medieval Technology, Science and Art
Volume 3

The Medieval Hospital and Medical Practice

Edited by
BARBARA S. BOWERS

ASHGATE

Published by
Ashgate Publishing Limited
Gower House
Croft Road
Aldershot
Hampshire GU11 3HR
England

Ashgate Publishing Company
Suite 420
101 Cherry Street
Burlington, VT 05401-4405
USA

Ashgate website: http://www.ashgate.com

British Library Cataloguing in Publication Data
The Medieval Hospital and Medical Practice. – (AVISTA Studies in the History of Medieval Technology, Science and Art)
    1. Hospitals – Europe – History – To 1500. 2. Medicine, Medieval. I. Bowers, Barbara S. II. Association Villard de Honnecourt for the Interdisciplinary Study of Medieval Technology, Science and Art
    362.1'1'094'0902

Library of Congress Cataloging-in-Publication Data
The Medieval Hospital and Medical Practice / edited by Barbara S. Bowers.
    p.   cm. – (AVISTA Studies in the History of Medieval Technology, Science and Art)
    Includes bibliographical references and index.
    1. Medicine, Medieval – History. 2. Hospitals, Medieval – History.
    I. Bowers, Barbara S. II. Series.
    R141.M48 2006
    610.9–dc22   2006005230

ISBN-13: 978-0-7546-5110-9

This book is printed on acid-free paper

Printed and bound in Great Britain by TJ International Ltd, Padstow, Cornwall.

Contents

III New Approaches to Written Sources

IV The Monastic Connection

List of Illustrations

Notes on Contributors

Renzo Baldasso
Doctoral candidate in the Art History and Archaeology Department at Columbia University. With support from the Kress Foundation, he is completing a dissertation entitled "Between Nature and Mathematics: The Role of Visual Representation in the Early Stages of the Scientific Revolution." His other art historical work engages with issues of naturalism in Renaissance Italian painting and printmaking, as well as the theory of art proposed by Filarete in the Trattato. He also continues his researches on early modern cosmology: he has recently published an article on Galileo (in the volume *Largo campo di filosofare*).

Barbara S. Bowers
Holds a PhD in somatic studies, an area of research that explores the body/mind connection. Her cross-cultural research combined the fields of anthropology, somatic studies, counseling psychology, and studio art. She is a graduate of the American Numismatic Society's Summer Graduate Program and has presented papers in the United States and Canada on topics related to image credibility in medieval art as a source for researching technology, numismatics and art psychotherapy. Having served on the AVISTA Board of Directors, she is at present AVISTA Secretary, and is pursuing studies in art psychotherapy.

James W. Brodman
Professor of History at the University of Central Arkansas and Director of the Library of Iberian Resources Online. He is a specialist in medieval Spanish history; his books include *Ransoming Captives in Crusader Spain: The Order of Merced on the Christian–Islamic Frontier* (1986) and *Charity and Welfare*: *Hospitals and the Poor in Medieval Catalonia*. Currently, he is working on a general history of religious charity in the Middle Ages.

Lynn T. Courtenay
Emerita Professor University of Wisconsin-Whitewater and Research Associate, Department of Art History, University of Wisconsin-Madison; past president of AVISTA (2000–2004). She received her MA and PhD in medieval history and art history at the University of Wisconsin-Madison. Her areas of specialization are social and ecclesiastical history and northern European architecture, particularly historic carpentry. She has published extensively on medieval timberwork and is both author and editor of *The Engineering of Gothic Cathedrals* (Ashgate, 1997) as well as a number of articles in the *Macmillan-Grove Dictionary of Art*, the *Oxford Dictionary*

of National Biography, and most recently entries in the new *Oxford Dictionary of the Middle Ages* (forthcoming).

Maria A. D'Aronco

Professor of Germanic Philology at the University of Udine (Italy). Her research and publications address Old and Middle English language and literature. In particular, in the field of Old English medicine and botany, she has studied the diffusion of medical and scientific knowledge in Anglo-Saxon England in the eighth and ninth centuries. She is the main editor of *The Old English Illustrated Pharmacopoeia* (Copenhagen, 1998).

Geoff Egan

Has worked at the Museum of London since 1976, at first directing sites, then specializing in researching medieval and later finds, especially metalwork. He lectures widely in Europe and the United States on a variety of themes within these broad interests, and is a consultant on the Jamestown Rediscovery project in Virginia. His range of publications includes leading contributions to the Medieval Finds from Excavations in London series (1991–98), the catalog *Lead Cloth Seals and Related Items in the British Museum* (1995), and most recently "Domestic Space" and several catalog entries for the Victoria & Albert Museum's exhibition on Gothic art (2003). He is currently working on the remarkable medieval finds assemblage from the sea-eroded village of Meols in north-west England, as well as material from a number of London sites, and also doing work as an adviser to the national Portable Antiquities Scheme.

Peregrine Horden

Reader in Medieval History at Royal Holloway College, University of London. He is co-author with Nicholas Purcell of *The Corrupting Sea: A Study of Mediterranean History* (Oxford, 2000), of which a second volume, *Liquid Continents*, is in progress. He has also edited a number of volumes, including *Music as Medicine: The History of Music Therapy since Antiquity* (Aldershot, 2000), and is currently completing a comparative study of health care in the early Middle Ages.

Rafaël Hyacinthe

Holds a PhD in medieval history and archaeology from the Sorbonne (2000). He has presented papers internationally at medieval congresses (Kalamazoo, Leeds and London). He has authored the first comprehensive study of the Order of Saint Lazarus, *L'Ordre de Saint-Lazare de Jérusalem au Moyen Age* (Millau, 2003). Working along with fellow scholars of the International Network on the History of Leprosy (*Historia Leprosorum)* and of the International Network for the History of Hospitals, he studies the history of assistance from the Middle Ages to modern times, especially in the southern parts of western Europe. He is currently a member of the Laboratoire de Médiévistique Occidentale de l'Université Paris I, and works in the Hospitaller records department in the archives of Montpellier.

Piers Mitchell
Based at the Wellcome Trust Centre for the History of Medicine at University College London. His research interests center on disease and medical treatment during the crusades to the medieval Middle East. He employs historical and archeological methods to investigate this topic. He is author of *Medicine in the Crusades: Warfare, Wounds and the Medieval Surgeon* (Cambridge, 2004). In 2005 he organized an international conference entitled *Medicine and Disease in the Crusades*, hosted by the Wellcome Trust Centre.

John M. Riddle
Alumni Distinguished Professor of History and Botany at North Carolina State University. He has served as President of the Society for Ancient Medicine and the American Institute for the History of Pharmacy. Author of seven books, he is currently writing a medieval history textbook. His most recent book was *Eve's Herbs: A History of Contraception and Abortion in the West* (Harvard University Press, 1997).

Bruno Tabuteau
PhD is a French medievalist and a specialist in the history of leprosy. He has published several papers on that topic in Normandy, and takes part in scientific programs and activities of academic research centers in Normandy and Picardy. He also belongs to the International Network for the History of Hospitals (UK) and the international network *Historia Leprosorum*, of which he was a co-founder.

Alain Touwaide
Historian of Sciences at the National Museum of Natural History of the Smithsonian Institution in Washington, DC. He received a PhD in Classics at the University of Louvain (Belgium) and an *Habilitation* in History from the University of Toulouse-le-Mirail (France). He has researched and published extensively on the history of medicine and pharmacy in the ancient and medieval eastern Mediterranean world.

Anne Van Arsdall
Fellow of the Institute for Medieval Studies at the University of New Mexico, where she continues research into pre-Salernitan medicine. She is editor of the *AVISTA Forum Journal*, a publication of the Association Villard de Honnecort for the Interdisciplinary Study of Medieval Science, Technology and Art. She is the author of *Medieval Herbal Remedies: The Old English Herbarium and Anglo-Saxon Medicine* (Routledge, 2002) and several articles on herbal medicine of the early medieval period.

Theresa M. Vann
Joseph S. Micallef Curator of the Malta Study Center, Hill Museum and Manuscript Library, Saint John's University, New York. She has written and presented on the history of the crusades, both east and west. Currently she is under contract with

Ashgate to publish *Hospitaller Piety and Crusader Propaganda: Guillaume Caoursin's Description of the Siege of Rhodes*.

William J. White

Curator of the Centre for Human Bioarchaeology at the Museum of London. His recent papers include "The excavation and study of human remains," in *Grave Concerns: Death and Burial in England 1700-1850* (Council for British Archaeology Research Report No. 113, 1998); "Publishing the peopling of London," *Transactions of the London & Middlesex Archaeological Society*, 50, (London, 1999); with Peter Hammond, "The sons of Edward IV: A re-examination of the evidence on their deaths and on the bones in Westminster Abbey," in *Richard III: Loyalty, Lordship and the Law* (Bury St Edmunds, 2000), and with Michael Prentice et al., "Absence of *Yersinia pestis*-specific DNA in human teeth from five European excavations of putative plague victims," *Microbiology*, 150 (London, 2004).

M.K.K. Yearl

A historian of medicine and a medievalist. She received her academic training at the now-defunct Wellcome Unit for the History of Medicine at the University of Cambridge, and at Yale University.

Preface

Barbara S. Bowers

For those unfamiliar with the work of AVISTA, the Association Villard de Honnecourt for the Interdisciplinary Study of Medieval Technology, Science and Art, as our name declares, it is our special and particular mission to promote the interdisciplinary studies. Since our founding in 1985, our activities include sponsoring sessions of papers both at the International Congress on Medieval Studies at Kalamazoo and the International Medieval Congress at Leeds, the publication of the AVISTA *Forum Journal*, and by our maintaining a web site at <www.avista.org> to provide online information, news and networking opportunities to scholars.

This third volume in the series AVISTA Studies in the History of Medieval Technology, Science and Art is the result of sessions I organized for the 36th International Congress on Medieval Studies for AVISTA. These sessions were co-sponsored by *Medica* (the Society for the Study of Healing in the Middle Ages), and the Hill Museum and Manuscript Library. The six sessions provided a significant forum for 23 scholars from Europe and the USA to meet, present the latest research on the medieval hospital and medicine and, most importantly, to exchange ideas. The wealth of expertise exchanged was most notable at the speaker round table, the grand finale that capped three very intense days of presentations.

This ambitious program would not have been possible without the very generous financial backing of The Samuel H. Kress Foundation, whose financial support made it possible to bring together such an impressive group of international researchers and to further support the publication of this volume.

I would like to express my thanks first to my assistant editors for this volume, Anne Van Arsdall, Emilie Savage-Smith, Theresa Vann, and Carol Neuman de Vegvar, who during the initial review process were instrumental in getting this book off to a solid start. Thanks too to the readers who lent their expertise in the critical review phase of preparing this text, John Goodall, Piers Mitchell, John Riddle, and Ellen Shortell. Beyond question, the editing process would have been impossible without the unflagging help and support of Marie-Thérèse Zenner, editor of the second volume in this series, who answered innumerable questions and provided clear guides and templates to follow. AVISTA's Publications Chair, Ellen Shortell, rode shotgun along the way, giving sound advice and help at every turn. And special thanks go to Mary Counter of *Counter Point*, my tech-guru who, with gargantuan effort, brought this Luddite into twenty-first-century computer technology.

My greatest expression of thanks and gratitude goes to my authors, who patiently bore with me in this, my often stumbling process of editing, and who have provided me with revised and updated versions of their original congress papers so that, with this volume, I can present the latest cutting-edge scholarship.

For my own part, I had nothing more to recommend me as the organizer and editor for this volume other than the claim that I am the daughter of probably the last practicing country doctor in Ohio, and the way of *doctoring* that this implies. What has turned out to be an enormous undertaking began by my envisioning the possibilities that the medieval hospital could have as a central organizing theme, one that could call together scholars from many diverse disciplines to focus their expertise on a single topic: the medieval hospital. As the theme evolved, it focussed on the hospital and medical practice as part of a holistic environment centering on site and setting. Eventually, this theme led to combining archaeological evidence, architectural history, textual criticism, monastic studies, and other fields of inquiry. The aim was to bridge the evidence and seek out and share new approaches to research. As this volume demonstrates, we have succeeded.

SECTION I
On Doing Medieval Medical Research

Chapter 1

Research Procedures in Evaluating Medieval Medicine

John M. Riddle

Introduction

A rainbow with clouds caused an illness that afflicted the Mikasuki Seminole Indians in Florida. In the routine course of a historian's investigation of Native American culture, one would seek to discover what the cluster of symptoms was that caused the Seminoles to recognize a disease called "the rainbow illness." The investigator experiences curiosity bordering on bewilderment when he or she learns that a fever, stiff neck, backache on one side and a twitching eyelid on the same side characterize the rainbow disease. A dream of thunder and rain may precede the onslaught of the disease.[1] These symptoms neither correspond with our understanding of nature and disease, nor do we believe (deep down, but never in print) that the Seminoles could have observed these symptoms accurately. Instead, some historians conclude that disease is culturally defined, so it is safer in research to confine oneself to description, not analysis. It follows that, if diseases are cultural, so too are therapies employed to cure them. This chapter will examine first the problems in relating ancient diseases to modern understanding, and then the methodology that can be employed in accessing medieval therapeutics.

Diseases

Historians of early medicine are all too familiar with the talent and energy given to identifying the plagues that struck Athens in 430 BCE and Constantinople in 541, but still no consensus hypotheses have emerged. One of the more recent hypotheses for the Athenian plague is the Ebola virus, and if the history of history is a predictor, many a new disease to come will be proposed as a candidate, just as in the recent past when toxic shock syndrome, influenza, typhus and Rift Valley fever were variously proposed.[2] There are two major schools of thought on this kind of

---

1   W.C. Sturtevant, *The Mikasuke Seminole: Medical Beliefs and Pratices* (PhD Dissertation, Yale University, 1955); 67–11, 355, pp. 210–11.

2   P.E. Olson, C.S. Hames, A.S. Benenson and E.N. Genovese, "The Thucydides Syndrome: Ebola Déjà Vu? (or Ebola Reemergent?)," *Emerging Infectious Diseases*, 2 (1996), 155–6. For a summary and discussion of other theories, see the summary by Jody Rubin

problem: one school says that most attempts to identify disease in our terminology are doomed to failure; the other school regards many, if not most, diseases as likely to be understood according to our medical science of today. The adherents to the former school assert that symptoms are cultural, and grouping them into patterns similar to our diseases is amorphous, impressionistic and inexact – so inexact, they argue, as to be unsuccessful. Moreover, infectious disease-causing micro-organisms alter through mutation, and the human immune system naturally builds genetically transmitted antibodies, with the result that ancient and medieval infections are quite different from our diseases.

In contrast, historians ignore or are ignorant of hard evidence when they claim that medieval medicine cannot be related to modern medical knowledge. Certainly, the Romans and medieval persons were afflicted with pneumonia (in various forms), cancer, typhus, gout (although a cluster of afflictions passed under its name), tuberculosis, pinta, yaws (the micro-organism of which eventually evolved into that causing endemic syphilis) and malaria, the latter being very prevalent and increasingly severe. Asthma and diabetes are two diseases that were not only prevalent and recognized, but also given exactly the same name in Greek and Latin as we employ in English today. This disease list is, of course, expandable, both in respect to where modern research is and what it will be in the future.

The Plague

Some historians argue that the bubonic plague of the 1340s is not pathologically the same as the similar plague today. Just the same, we are better informed about the plague's impact on the times through an understanding of the bubonic plague's complex biology. Victims experienced first hallucinations, followed by fever and fatigue. Others said there was first a sore throat and diarrhea. Near to the time of death, buboes (lumps) appeared in the groin area. Two to three days elapsed between the time of the first symptom and death. The pandemic infection in the 1340s and in the 540s (Justinian's time) was a form of bubonic plague with secondary and tertiary opportunistic infections. A second stage was pulmonary or pneumonic, and the third septicemic (infecting the bloodstream). Fleas, which prefer rats but will move to humans, spread a disease bacillus (*Yersinia pestis*). Some differences in contemporary accounts have caused some historians to question whether the plague of the sixth century was the same as the one of the fourteenth century. Two recent scientific studies reveal some new data. The first is a study that has the complete genome sequence of *Yersinia pestis*.[3] The second study of the genetic substance of

Pinault of the 13th Annual Meeting of the Society for Ancient Medicine in *SAMPh Newsletter*, 16 (1988), 5–8; "Plague of Athens," 1999 Releases, *University of Maryland Medical News*, January 1999; Rachel Finnegan, "Plagues in Classical Literature," *Classics Ireland*, 6 (1999), on the Web: <http://www.ucd.ie/~classics/99/finnegan.html>.

3   J. Parkhill, B.W. Wren, N.R. Thomson, R.W. Titball et al., "Genome sequence of *Yersinia pestis*, the causative agent of plague," *Nature*, 413 (2002), 523–7.

the micro-organism shows that there are three biovars, one of which, named *antiqua*, is postulated to be the infectious organism of the plague in the 540s, the other *medievalis* of the late 1340s.[4] Why do these laboratory studies help us understand the Middle Ages? For now, they inform us why the seemingly same plague can have differing symptoms, albeit minor differences. More important for the future, with chance archaeological recoveries of plague victims, it may be possible for precise identifications. More on this point will come later in this chapter. Let us look deeper into historical problems.

Terminology in any period is inexact. Leprosy, identified in biblical and classical texts, is not the disease known in the Middle Ages by that name. The ancients' leprosy was likely elephantiasis in most cases, but other skin afflictions as well.[5] Leprosy as it evolved in the medieval period and is still present today is an entirely different, more virulent and serious affliction. That said, the historian can read the historical data, both written and paleopathological, and make a reasonable judgment about what leprosy meant in a particular period and culture. Whatever diseases they had, the larger question for the historian is: what did medieval people know about illness and health, how and when did they know it, and what, when they knew it, did they do about it? One may add: was their therapy (regime, diet, drugs and surgery) effective by their own and by our standards of reality? Because this latter question is one of natural curiosity, one that any student might ask, we should deal with it as best we can.

New Investigations

The early and mid-twentieth-century historians, such as Henry Sigerist, Charles Singer and Thomas Cockayne, were primarily philologists whose considerable talents focussed on texts, not so much an evaluation of their contents. The image they presented of medieval medicine was negative: "dark ages," "superstitions" and "stagnant conventionalism." While acknowledging the contributions of these great scholars, we, as modern investigators, should take the next step and evaluate the historical medical lore as medicine.

Harm or Good?

The prominent medical sociologist L.J. Henderson declared that prior to 1912 a random patient with a random disease going to a random physician had no better than

---

4   Mark Achtman, Kerstin Zurth, Giovanna Morelli, Gabriela Torrea et al., "*Yersinia pestis*, the cause of plague, is a recently emerged clone of *Yersinia pseudotubuerculosis*," in *Proceedings of the National Academy of Sciences USA*, 96 (1999), 14 043–8.

5   Mirko D. Grmek, *Diseases in the Ancient World*, trans. Mireille Muellner and Leonard Muellner (Baltimore, MD, 1989), pp. 198–204.

a fifty-fifty chance of profiting from the encounter.[6] The placebo effect is proposed by a number of modern medical and scientific persons as the only possible link between medieval and modern medicine ("modern" meaning around the twentieth century, of course). This view places them with virtually the same conclusion as Sigerist and Singer. Even a recent prominent medical historian, J. Worth Estes, saw that pre-modern "therapeutic maneuvers," that is to say, medicine as applied historically, "could, at best, have provided only opportunities for wounds or illnesses to heal on their own."[7] When he examined pharmaceuticals as late as the eighteenth and nineteenth centuries, he excused his inability to identify some drugs on the grounds that they had no efficacy anyway.[8]

The Placebo Effect

Before I challenge the theory that medieval people were scientifically dim-witted, let me acknowledge the power of the placebo effect. Modern science, after numerous errors, adopted the double-blind methodology because the placebo effect is very powerful. In fact, medieval thinkers were aware of the placebo as a positive factor in therapeutics.[9] But that said, one benign or non-toxic drug is as good as another one regardless of whether the diagnosis is correct or incorrect.

Did medieval medicine "work"? Did medieval people perceive it as effective? Do we? Some historians see the latter question as Whig or Positivist history ("handing out medals to moderns"). These same historians, however, find it perfectly normal for a historian of medieval economic history to employ modern economic concepts in order to understand economic changes within the medieval period. The question of whether medieval people had an economic theory or whether it accurately described their economies is another matter. The point is that modern historians employ modern axioms for human behavior regardless of whether the people under investigation conceived the axioms. Similarly, a historian of the exact sciences, such as mathematics, physics or astronomy, has no hesitation in judging "right" and "wrong" when accessing a historical work on those subjects, even though he strives mightily to understand the cultural context that would give rise to error. If a medieval writer on mathematics makes an arithmetical error, it is an error, then and now. If, on the other hand, a medieval physician treated a broken bone as a sprained ankle (the wrong diagnosis, wrong therapy), he made a mistake. There is nothing cultural about it.

Most medical treatments in the Middle Ages (and now as well!) are for symptoms, not generic diseases – a sore throat, upset stomach, headache and so on. Diseases

---

6   B. Barber, *Drugs and Society* (New York, 1964), p. 4.

7   J. Worth Estes, *The Medical Skills of Ancient Egypt* (Canton, MA, 1989), p. 119.

8   J. Worth Estes, *Dictionary of Protopharmacology: Therapeutic Practices, 1700–1850* (Canton, MA, 1990), p. x.

9   Judith Wilcox and John Riddle, ed. and trans., "Qustā ibn Lūqā's *Physical Ligatures* and the Recognition of the Placebo Effect," *Medieval Encounters*, 1 (1995), 1–48.

are more difficult, but they can be addressed. There are a few examples of clearly identified diseases: arthritis and gout, for instance. The Greek and Latin word is *arthritis*, so, one would think, all one had to do was drop the Latin or Greek ending for a translation. No, that is not the case. The Greek's "arthritis" had a lexical range that would have included our arthritis (rheumatoid and so on) but would also have included a number of other afflictions associated with the joints. The same is true with gout.

Methodology for Addressing Therapeutics

For the early Middle Ages (before 1050), other than chance descriptions of illnesses in the annals and literary works, practically all medical sources are *antidotaria*, herbals and *receptaria*. Most manuscripts containing them are compilations of medical prescriptions, giving the name of the recipe, a list of symptoms or afflictions for which it is addressed, a list of ingredients, their quantities, and special preparation instructions. Henry Sigerist, Julius Jörimann, Gundolf Keil and Thomas Cockayne published many of these texts, and more recently Ulrich Stoll edited the *Lorsch Monastic Recipe Book* and produced a good translation in German.[10] For the most part, they remain in rather corrupt Latin or early vernaculars. Even the medical literature from approximately 1150, the period of Constantine the African, through the fifteenth century has medical recipes as therapies in more comprehensive medical writings. The method for evaluating the *receptaria* is valid for evaluating all medical therapies, regardless of the genre of literature.

An example of a single recipe, among the thousands, will be our model for evaluating, not merely describing, medieval medicine. The following recipe from the Reichenau manuscript (fol. 4 of *Reichenau Antidotarum* in Karlsruhe Bibliothek, MS Aug. 120, ninth–tenth century) conveys the problem for the historian:[11]

> Antidotum pigra optima Galieni qui facit ad diversionem stomachi, et debilitatem et qui sibi anxiant in stomachi languento, et omnen matrices causam, generaliter diuretica est. Facit hydropicis, nefriticis, epaticis, provocat et mulieribus purgationem.

---

10 *Das Lorscher Arzneibuch: ein medizinisches Kompendium des 8. Jahrhunderts (Codex Bambergensis medicinalis 1): Text, Übersetzung und Fachglossar*, Sudhoffs Archiv, Vol. 28, ed. Ulrich Stoll (Stuttgart, 1992).

11 Reichenau MS Augiensis 120, fol. 4, as published by Henry Sigerist, *Studien und Texte zur frühmittlalterliche Rezeptarien* (Zurich, 1925), p. 41; Lorsch Ms is a similar but inexact copy of the text; see Ulrich Stoll, ed., Bamberg, MS med. 1, fol. 64 v, p. 354.

Recipe hec:

aloe	50 dragmae[12]
spica nardi	3 dragmae
asaru	3 dragmae
crocu	3 dragmae
mastice	3 dragmae
xilobalsumu	3 dragmae
cassia	6 dragmae

mel quod sufficit.

Translating the Latin into modern English looks relatively easy; compared to Cicero, it is! But problems arise. Although attributed to Galen, the recipe is not found among the surviving works attributed to the Roman Empire physician who wrote in Greek. In the case of this recipe, translating plant names is relatively easy. Most pharmaceuticals are herbal, roughly 80 per cent, a figure that is fairly constant from early classical Greek medicine down to our own days, excluding synthetic drugs. Drugs derived from animals and animal products (eggs, fat, milk, suet and so on) are easily translated; minerals are more difficult, but several excellent researchers of mineral lore can assist with the more difficult ones.[13]

Plant Identifications

Whether in our time or medieval times, plant names are notoriously difficult to ascertain. For example: in the Carolinas alone there are 21 "common" and different names for black cohosh (*Cimicifuga racemosa* L.), a plant famous for treating menopause.[14] Note that in identifying the plant with the common name black cohosh, there are the binominal scientific name *and* the author of the scientific name, in this case "L." for Linnaeus. Scientific names can vary for the same plant, therefore for exactitude one must give the author's name. To a botanist, that is as important as an author's name on a journal article is to a historian. It is essential to translate plant names into modern scientific nomenclature because otherwise one cannot bring modern science to bear in understanding medieval medicine. A number of guides are essential to the translation into modern terms, such as those by Jacques André,

---

12 1 drachma = approximately 4½–6 grams.

13 Dietlinde Goltz, *Studien zur Geschichte der Mineralnamen in Pharmazie, Chemie und Mediczin von den Anfängen bis Paracelus.* Sudhoffs Archiv Series, Vol. 14 (Wiesbaden, 1972); Earle R. Caley and John C. Richards, *Theophrastus on Stones* (Columbus, OH, 1956), with translation and excellent commentary; Dorothy Wyckoff, *Albertus Magnus Book of Minerals* (Oxford, 1967), also with translation and commentary.

14 Edward M. Croom, "Documenting and Evaluating Herbal Remedies," *Economic Botany*, 37 (1983), 16–17.

Albert Carnoy, Hermann Fischer and Tony Hunt.[15] Translators of some classical and medieval texts are excellent at identifying plant names. William Thiselton-Dyer assisted A.F. Hort in his translation in the Loeb series of Theophrastus' *Enquiry into Plants* (2 vols, 1968), advised on the Liddell and Scott's *Greek–English Lexicon*, and also influenced the *Oxford Latin Dictionary*; perhaps the best interpretation of classical plant lore was Julius Behrendes' German translation of Dioscorides.[16] However, classical terms were frequently modified in the medieval centuries. Especially good are G. Frisk's translation of Macer Floridus and J.L. Mowat's edition of *Alphita.*[17] The Arabic translations into Latin altered and often confused the task of identifying plant names. Translators like Constantine and Gerard of Cremona often did not know the proper Latin term for an Arabic name, so they either guessed or they transliterated the term. There is no easy guide to solving these problems, but to start the process one should consult Fred Rosner's English translation of Max Meyerhof's French edition of *Moses Maimonides' Glossary of Drug Names*[18] and a German encyclopedic reference to drugs by Wolfgang Schneider.[19] For critical but perplexing questions about identification, the Renaissance commentators on the texts of Galen, Dioscorides, Avicenna, Pliny and Theophrastus have long, learned discussions about plant identifications just as we do. Because they lived before the Linnaean system was devised, they can be invaluable in producing a bridge between our plant identifications and ancient or medieval plant knowledge.[20]

Quantification

We all know that drug amounts (dosages) and frequencies are critical in judging the safety and effectiveness of actions. Medieval sources seldom give frequencies, but early medieval medical accounts pay more attention and give more detail to quantifications. Clearly, medieval medical dispensers were aware of what we call dosages, but qualifications are in order about quantifications. The conversion of quantities into our systems is fairly easily done with tables. The best one, at least,

---

15 Jacque André, *Les noms de plantes dans la Rome antique* (Paris, 1985); Albert J. Carnoy, *Dictionnaire étymologique des noms grecs de plantes* (Louvain, 1959); Hermann Fischer, *Mittelalterliche Pflanzenkunde* (Munich, 1929); Tony Hunt, *Plant Names of Medieval England* (Cambridge, 1989).

16 J. Behrendes, *Pedannii Dioscoridis Anazarbei De material medica libri quinque*, 3 vols (Stuttgart, 1902).

17 G. Frisk, *A Middle English Translation of Macer Floridus De viribus herbarum* (Uppsala, 1949); J.L. Mowat, *Alphita: A Medico-botanical Glossary from the Bodleian Manuscript Selden B. 35* (Oxford, 1887).

18 Max Meyerhof, ed., *Moses Maimonides' Glossary of Drug Names* (Philadelphia, PA, 1979).

19 W. Schneider, *Lexikon zur Arzneimittelgeschichte*, 7 vols (Frankfurt am Main, 1968–75).

20 Microfilm copies of the commentaries are available on inter-library loan from the National Library of Medicine USA.

the one I usually employ, was provided by Max Niedermann's translation of *De mensuris et ponderibus medicinalibus* in the edition of Marcellus.[21] Manuscript notation marks, numbers and Arabic numbers are in Cappelli's Dictionary.[22] Medieval persons performed medical quantifications similarly to those of the culinary arts: a pinch of this, a tablespoon of that. In the recipe above, the amount of aloe is far too much according to modern science. Indeed, because of the aloe amount, the pill would be greater than the size of a fist, and thus could not be swallowed. A similar recipe in a Lorsch manuscript has a slightly larger amount of aloe, therefore we can assume that the problem was not in the manuscript copying.[23] There is no indication, however, of whether the entire amount was given at once or over an extended period; almost always that detail is missing.

While the amount of aloe is too large, the saffron content is almost precisely correct for one of the actions specified. The statement *omnen matrices causam* was common circumlocution for an early-term abortifacient. Modern science states that saffron (*Crocus sativus* L.) acts an abortifacient where its dosage is 10 grams, or about the same as in the Reichenau and Lorsch manuscripts. It should be noted, however, that the lethal dosage is reported to be 20 grams.[24] Saffron is also used as a sedative, for spasms and asthma; the daily dosage is 1.5 grams.

Medical Evaluation

Understanding the recipe in modern medical terms involves more than merely translating the text. Here is a translation of the recipe above:

Galen's best purgative that is made for an unsettled and ailing stomach and helps the recovery of a weak stomach, and for all womb problems, it is generally diuretic. It is given for dropsy [generalized edema], kidney disease, liver disease, and it provokes women's purging.

---

21 Max Niedermann, *Marcellus Über Heilmittel*, 2 vols, trans. Jutta Kollesch and Diethard Nickel (Berlin, 1968) 1:10–17.

22 A. Cappelli, *Dizionario di abbreviature latine et italiane* (Milan, 1990).

23 See note 11 above.

24 *The Complete German Commission E Monographs: Therapeutic Guide to Herbal Medicines*, senior ed. Mark Blumenthal, CD-ROM edn (Copyright © 1999 American Botanical Council, Dallas, Texas).

Take thus:

Aloe vera L. + spp.	200 grams
Nardostachys jatamansi D.C.	15 grams
Asarum europaeum L.	15 grams
Crocus sativus L.	15 grams
Pistacia lentiscus L.	15 grams
Commiphora opobalsamum Endl.	15 grams
Cinnamomum cassia Blume	30 grams

mixing honey as needed.

The first assertion, as a laxative, is probably the easiest to evaluate, although nearly the same recipe in the Lorsch account gives the title as: "Recipe for Good Health."[25] Laxatives are easily verified. The Ebers Medical Papyrus of around 1150 BCE begins with a long list of laxatives. Of those laxatives that are on our over-the-counter shelves, all were employed as laxatives in early times as well, with the exception of mineral oil, a nineteenth-century discovery.[26] The mechanisms of laxative actions vary, and should be understood in modern terms. First, one needs to understand the medical aspects. The place to begin is Goodman and Gilman's periodic reference to therapeutics, with sections by various medical experts and for experts, but understandable to those with a moderate grasp of science.[27]

Two other references for natural product drugs are: James A. Duke and the German "E" Commission.[28] This German commission was established to license in Germany natural product drugs on the basis that vendors must prove that a potential product was a traditional remedy and that it does no harm. The periodic publications assembled by Mark Blumenthal are the greatest single authority on natural product actions.

---

25 See note 11 above.

26 John M. Riddle, "Fees and Feces: Laxative in Ancient Medicine with Particular Emphasis on Pseudo-Mesue," in *The Diffusion of Greco-Roman Medicine into the Middle East and the Caucasus,* ed. John A.C. Greppin, Emilie Savage-Smith and John L. Gueriguian (Delmar, NY, 1999), pp. 7–26.

27 Louis S. Goodman and Alfred Gilman, eds, *The Pharmacological Basis of Therapeutics* (New York, 2001).

28 James A. Duke, *CRC Handbook of Medicinal Herbs* (Boca Raton, FL, 1985); *The Complete German Commission E Monographs: Therapeutic Guide to Herbal Medicines,* senior ed. Mark Blumenthal, CD-ROM edn (Copyright © 1999 American Botanical Council, Dallas, Texas).

Databases

Following Duke and the German "E" Commission, one should do a data search, especially on Medline (a no-charge service sponsored by the US National Library of Medicine).[29] In 2003 there were 10 192 serial titles and 3 923 journals indexed. For pharmaceuticals, one should research by scientific name, first by trying just the generic name, because species names are too limiting.

For many journal articles, abstracts are available for download, and there is a service (sometimes involving a fee) for delivery of the full article. For broader, more intense research one should explore ChemAbstracts and Biological Abstracts, both fee-based, through research libraries.

Matching Modern to Historical Data

This exercise is critical in forming judgments. For example, in the prescription above one finds through the modern data that the recipe is truly a laxative and diuretic. For the upset, ailing stomach, mastic (the resin of *Pistacia lentiscus* L.) has recently been rediscovered to have very positive results when treating gastric and duodenal ulcers, and it has demonstrated antimicrobal actions as well.[30]

In referring to all the usages, however, the most intriguing discovery is the number of drugs in this one prescription that successfully treat diabetes. We know diabetes to be a pancreatic disorder, but pre-modern people associated it with the kidneys. Diabetes is a transliteration from the Greek meaning "to flow through," a symptom whereby a diabetic patient does not retain liquids, but allows them to flow through without a cleaning action (*dia* = "through" and *betes* = "go"). In Greek, Paul of Aegina wrote the following description of diabetes in the seventh century:[31]

> Diabetes is a rapid passage of the drink out of the body, liquids being voided by urine as they were drunk; and hence it is attended with immoderate thirst; and therefore the affection has been called *dipsacus*, being occasioned by a weakness of the retentive faculty of the kidneys, while the attractive is increased in strength, and deprives the whole body of its moisture by its immoderate heat.

---

29 See Medline: <http://www.ncbi.nlm.nih.gov/entrez/query.fcgi>. Additional Websites for scientific studies are: National Center for Complementary and Alternative Medicine <http://nccam.nih.gov/research/>; homepage for Library at the Missouri Botanical Garden <http://www.mobot.org); useful, but without much scientific basis is *Grieve's Herbal* <http://botanical.com/botanical/mgmh/mgmh.html://botanical.com/botanical/mgmh/mgmh.html>.

30 J. Koscielny et al., "The anti-atherosclerotic effect of *Allium sativum*," *Atheroschlerosis*, 144 (1999), 237–49; Mark Blumenthal, ed., *Herbal Medicine: Expanded Commission E Monographs* (Austin, TX, 2000), pp. 139–48.

31 Paul of Aegina. *Seven Books of Medicine*. 3. 45, trans. Francis Adams, 3 vols (London, 1847), Vol. 1, 547.

Although Galen and a few other Greeks employed the term "diabetes," there is only one use of the term in Latin (by Columella, a non-medical writer).[32] Even Dioscorides did not use the term. We should not conclude that because Dioscorides did not use the term, he did not know how to treat diabetes. He treated the symptoms. We should make the same assumption about early medieval physicians. A 2001 study (*Phytotherapy Research*) of the effects of aloe vera leaves on blood glucose level in type I and type II diabetic rat models shows that a pulp extract has hypoglycemic activity, and concludes that it could be useful in the treatment of non-insulin-dependent diabetes mellitus.[33] A look through recent Medline data supplies results from a number of animal and clinical studies that show aloe to be a therapeutic agent for non-insulin dependent diabetes mellitus.[34] A search of cinnamon bark and myrrh (*Commiphora opobalsamum* Endl.) shows that each is effective for diabetic conditions. A recent dissertation by Helena Paavilainen masterfully employs modern scientific research to evaluate historical therapies, in this case Avicenna's *Canon of Medicine*. Paavilainen showed that 54 per cent of Avicenna's therapies for diabetes were effective.[35]

The examination above of the Reichenau recipe was only one of hundreds of early medieval monastic recipes, many of which are for *nefriticis*, or if our analysis is correct, diabetes. Most of the recipes include aloe and myrrh. Many of the recipes have additional ingredients, two prominent ones being cumin (*Cuminum cyminum* L.) and fenugreek (*Trigonella* sp.). A 2002 study published in *Pharmacological Research* showed that cumin supplementation resulted in a significant reduction in plasma and tissue cholesterol, phospholipids, free fatty acids and triglycerides.[36] Fenugreek, on the other hand, is the subject of 27 recent scientific studies of its compound trigonelline, which is a hypoglycemic betain, considered responsible for its activity. Moreover, the herb is a traditional remedy for diabetes in Ayurvedic medicine.[37] In 2002, a survey was conducted of what herbs, if any, patients took who were hospitalized for diabetes mellitus in the Kingdom of Saudi Arabia. Five herbs

32 Columella, *De re rustica*. 3. 10. 2 (Cambridge, MA, 1967).

33 A. Okyar, A. Can, N. Akev, G. Baktir and N. Sutlupinar, "Effect of Aloe vera leaves on blood glucose level in type I and type II diabetic rat models," *Phytotherapy Research*, 15(2), 157–61.

34 For example, F. al-Awadi, H.Fatania and U.Shamte, "The effect of a plants mixture extract on liver gluconeogenesis in streptozotocin induced diabetic rats," *Diatbetes Research*, 18 (1991), 163–8; J.K. Grover, S. Yadav and V. Vats, "Medicinal Plants of India with Anti-diabetic Potential," *Journal of Ethnopharmacology*, 81 (2002), 81–100.

35 Helena Paavilainen, "Medieval Pharmacotherapy – Continuity and Change: A Study on Ibn Sina's *Kitāb al-Qānūn* and Some Medieval Commentators," submitted to the Hebrew University, Jerusalem, 2002, p. 274.

36 S. Dhandapan, V.R. Subramanian, S. Rajagopal and N. Namasivayam, "Hypolipidemic effect of Cuminum cyminum L. on alloxan-induced diabetic rats," *Phamacological Research*, 46 (2002/2003), 251–5.

37 V. Vats, S.P. Yadav and J.K. Grover, "Effect of *T. foenumgraecum* on glycogen content of tissues and the key enzymes of carbohydrate metabolism," *Journal of Ethnopharmacology*,

were commonly taken: myrrh, cumin, *helteet*, fenugreek and aloe.[38] In other words, the most commonly taken drugs for what appears to be diabetes are the same (except for *helteet*, which I cannot identify) in early medieval monastic medical recipes and in self-treated diabetic patients in modern Saudi Arabia.

Thus, through researches in modern medical sciences combined with anthropological and historical evidence, independent of the medieval period, we can safely conclude that diabetes was treated rationally. But is this sufficient to conclude that the Latin term *nefriticis* is our diabetes? I believe that the answer is "no"; however, the hypothesis is justified that the term included a spectrum of kidney afflictions, including diabetes. The recipe would help a person with a diabetic condition. So, with all of this evidence from modern medical journals and from anthropological surveys, what conclusions may we draw from the examination of this one recipe in two early medieval monastic accounts? Certainly the recipe contains plants that would be a useful therapeutic agent in the treatment of non-insulin-dependent diabetes mellitus. We are concerned, however, by the imponderables implicit in the evidence. The dosage, notably the amount of aloe, would be too high if the entire recipe were to be taken at one time. And what about the other ingredients in our sample recipe? The presence of nard, asarum and saffron indicates actions on the uterus and, in early pregnancy, causative agents for a miscarriage or abortion. Indisputably the recipe is rational as defined by modern science.

Drug Preparation

The most neglected problem in judging drug efficacy, and one impossible for us to address definitively, is preparation. For example, if a prescription names the opium poppy plant, one must assume that the prescription contained opium. However, the plant only produces opium during a few weeks of its existence, and then it has to be extracted carefully. Extraction is critical in almost all drugs derived from natural products; sometimes the difference between a latex or an alcohol extraction is the difference between an effective remedy and one with no significant effect. Not only should we know what part of the plant is employed (root, flower, seed, leaf and so on), but also the time of harvesting, and even soil and climatic conditions, all of which affect plant chemistry. Even when we know the exact species, we must assume that the preparation was done correctly. Modern scientists look down on assumptions of this sort, but the historian must look to the evidence as it exists, not only that which is created in laboratories.

---

85 (2003), 237–42; James Duke, *CRC Handbook of Medicinal Herbs* (Boca Raton, FL, 1985), p. 490. There are 27 articles cited by Medline on fenugreek and diabetes.

    38 N.A. Al-Rowais, "Herbal medicine in the treatment of diabetes mellitus," *Saudi Medical Journal*, 23 (2002), 1 327–31.

Laboratory and/or Clinical Evidence

When citing scientific evidence, one should cite a laboratory study or clinical trial. Scientists usually begin their articles with citations to previous studies; in the case of drug actions, these often include anecdotal stories, folklore and anthropological studies. An example: once I wanted to know whether a particular plant in Dioscorides' text had the medicinal action he alleged. I found a citation seemingly verifying the action in a recent review article in the *Journal of the American Pharmaceutical Association*. One would think initially that would be sufficient to say that modern science attests to Dioscorides' usage. Since the article cited another article, also in a science journal, and did not present laboratory findings, I followed the citation, which led to another citation and so forth, a total of about six, all in scientific and medical journals. Finally, at the end of the chain was a citation to Behrendes' 1902 translation of Dioscorides. It was all a circle, even though every report was written by scientists and published in scientific journals.

Ask

The historian should not hesitate to ask the numerous experts who live in our communities. No matter how clumsily a question is phrased and how silly we think we might appear, most experts are intrigued and all too happy to answer questions that shed light on problems in the field of medieval medicine. Often it means asking an expert, going back to the source material, realizing that you still do not understand, and returning once again to refine your questions. Once I found a statement about radish juice in the works of Gargilius Martialis that said in corrupt Latin syntax – so I was not absolutely sure as to the meaning – that "Egyptian kings of old" whose practice it was to examine dead bodies for the cause of death learned that radish juice prevents *phthiriasis* (meaning, "lice disease") from attacking the heart. Pliny made a similar statement.[39] I went to the chair of the entomology department in our university and asked if he had any lice experts. He did, and upon contacting the expert, he told me the infection known as louse-born typhus attacks cardiac tissue. In such cases, death can be attributed to cardiac arrest. Next question: could an ancient person have detected the change in tissue through post mortem examination without the assistance of instruments? I learned that there was an expert in Rocky Mountain spotted fever, pathologically the same as louse-born typhus, in a neighboring medical school. From this expert, I learned that the peritoneum (*praecordia* in Gargilius) was visually transformed by the infection when the disease was mortal. Just to confirm the findings, I asked a well-known pathologist who had written on the history of medicine. He said that it was impossible for the Greeks to have made such an observation. "You should see how medical students fumble around with cardiac tissue," he said. Thus there was a contradiction between two

---

39 John M. Riddle, "Gargilius Martialis as a Medical Writer," *Journal of the History of Medicine and Allied Sciences*, 39 (1984), 414–17.

experts. Going back to the Rocky Mountain spotted fever expert, he showed me the differences in the tissues and persuaded me that, indeed, the Greeks at Alexandria could have seen the difference. Research in the ancient descriptions (Galen, Caelius Aurelianus) of the symptoms of *phthiriasis* persuaded me that the disease was truly our typhus. I learned that in ancient Egypt the practice was for a physician to testify, for all unnatural deaths, as to the cause of death. Surviving are two papyri of such inquests; one case involved a knife-stabbing, and the other a young man who fell from an upper-story window while leaning out "to see the dancers." Neither would have involved deep post mortem examinations. Medical historians have not found evidence within the fragments of Erasistratus or Herophilus, where one would have expected it, for routine deep autopsies. Going to other experts in entomology and in plant chemistry, I learned that radishes contain saponins that prevent lice infestation. A person who applied radish juice to hairy regions, especially the groin area, would not have *phthiriasis*. One cannot conclude absolutely that ancient medicine was so clever as to have discerned these causal relationships, but on the other hand, how can one explain Gargilius' and Pliny's statements? One needs to ask experts in chemistry, pharmacy, anatomy, biochemistry, microbiology, medicine and all tangential areas of science to help understand what medieval peoples understood.

Historical Methodology

The historical data is not the equivalent of the scientist's hard evidence. The laboratory data carefully controls and certifies each aspect of the trial, and to be doubly sure, there is a control cohort and the process is double-blinded. Historical analysis cannot produce these opportunities. For example, there is no way of knowing the growing conditions or exact harvesting and preparation procedures for the drugs even when their identification is fairly certain. The historian cannot be a scientist (even though the subject is science); the weight of evidence is the same as that applied by the lawyer, not the scientist. Historians and lawyers alike ask this question: given the evidence, derived from all the sources possible bearing on the subject, what is the reasonable conclusion to make? If all these prescriptions were random, out of the half-million or so higher plant species, would there be found such a preponderance of effective drugs?

Conclusion

A number of studies by scholars of the generation or two since Charles Singer challenge the retrogressive theory about early medieval medicine. Anne Van Arsdall's book on early Anglo-Saxon medicine is an excellent example of the new scholarship.[40] Through keeping up with the discoveries in science, such as the

---

40 Anne Van Arsdall, *Medieval Herbal Remedies: The Old English Herbarium and Anglo-Saxon Medicine* (New York, 2002).

genetic code for the plague virus, we have a good prospect of learning in the future for sure about the nature of these infections simply by finding chance-preserved soft tissue of a plague victim. At the same time, historians have an opportunity to contribute to science. No longer should the historian be satisfied merely with finding and translating medical texts.

We must seek to learn what they knew and to understand how they organized and applied their experiences. In the process we shall learn more about the Middle Ages, gain a greater understanding about modern science, and perhaps make a contribution both to medieval studies and to modern science.

Chapter 2

The Archives and Library of the Sacra Infermeria, Malta

Theresa M. Vann

Introduction

The Sacra Infermeria was the great hospital built in the sixteenth century by the Knights of Malta in Valletta, Malta. The Knights of Malta, also known as the Knights of the Hospital or the Hospitallers, were a military religious order established in Jerusalem before the First Crusade (1095–99). The Order, despite its military associations, has a long tradition of medical charities that continues to the present day. Its eighteenth-century medical archives and library are housed today in the National Library of Malta in Valletta. This chapter provides an introduction to the archives and the medical library of the Order of the Hospital.[1]

Historical Background: The Medical Traditions of the Order of the Hospital

Some time in the eleventh century, Amalfite merchants established a hospice to care for Christian travelers to Jerusalem. This became the Order of the Hospital by the early twelfth century. Although the Order militarized in the mid- to late twelfth century, the needs and requirements of the Jerusalem hospice remained at the center of the Order's Rule and economic planning. The Hospitallers' internal organization

---

1 For the medical history of the Order of the Hospital, see Anthony Luttrell, "The Hospitallers' Medical Tradition: 1291–1530," in *The Military Orders: Fighting for the Faith and Caring for the Sick*, ed. Malcom Barber (Aldershot, 1994), 64–81; also, for the Order's Rhodian period, see Fotini Karassava-Tsilingiri, "The Fifteenth-century Hospital of Rhodes: Tradition and Innovation," in Barber, *The Military Orders*, 89–96; for the Order's early period in Malta, see Ann Williams, "*Xenodochium* to sacred infirmary: The changing role of the Hospital of the Order of St John, 1522–1631," in Barber, *The Military Orders*, 97–102; see also Roger Ellul-Micallef, "Sketches of Medical Practice in Sixteenth-century Malta," in *Karissime Gotifride: Historical Essays presented to Professor Godrey Wettinger on his Seventieth Birthday*, ed. Paul Xuereb (Malta, 1999), 103–20. Paul Cassar, *Medical History of Malta* (London, 1964), is essential for the history of medical practice on Malta, including the *Sacra Infermeria*. Charles Savona-Ventura, *Outlines of Maltese Medical History* (Malta, 1997), is also extremely useful. C. Savona Ventura, *Knights Hospitaller Medicine in Malta* (Malta, 2004), was published after this article was written.

evolved to support both its charitable activities and military responsibilities. The Order's rules and statutes, beginning with the earliest Rule of Raymond du Puy (1120–60) called the recipients of Hospitaller charity "our Lords the Sick" and directed that the sick poor should be treated "as if he were a Lord."[2] The Chapter General of 1176 set aside the revenues of two casales (or estates) to provide the poor in the hospice with white bread, a luxury usually reserved for the wealthy.[3] By 1181, the Order had acquired European estates and organized itself by langues, or nations. While it considered its Jerusalem hospice inseparable from the main convent, it also encouraged the establishment of hospices at its European priories. Furthermore, the Order assigned each langue responsibility for supplying a particular need of the hospice, such as bedding, covers and lint. The Chapter General of 1181 defined the needs of the sick as large beds, each with its own coverlet and sheets; cradles for babies born in the hospice, and cloaks and boots for all the sick to travel to the latrine.[4] The four physicians who staffed the hospice provided syrups and administered the prescribed diet. In addition to the medical staff, all brethren of the Order served in the hospice.

The hospice was a considerable undertaking, requiring the Order to set aside as much as one third of its income. Contemporary travelers reported that the hospice could house 2,000 patients.[5] There is little evidence from this early period for treatments administered in the Jerusalem hospice. Some historians have argued that the Order was influenced by Arabic and Byzantine medical practices, particularly in the matter of diet.[6] Certainly the insistence in the statutes and the rules for the patients to enjoy a diet comparable to the members of the Order seems to support arguments for such influence. Other historians, however, think that the matter of diet reflected the Order's mission to treat the poor as "lords," aristocracy to be served by virtue of their debility. They argue that the hospice functioned as a destination for pilgrims who came to Jerusalem to die, citing the small medical staff and the prominence of last rites and burial practices in the rules.[7]

---

2   E.J. King, *The Rule Statutes and Customs of the Hospitallers, 1099–1310* (London, 1934), pp. 26–7.

3   Ibid., pp. 29–30.

4   Ibid., pp. 34–8.

5   See Benjamin Z. Kedar, "A Twelfth-Century Description of the Jerusalem Hospital," in *The Military Orders, Volume 2: Welfare and Warfare*, ed. Helen Nicholson (Aldershot, 1998) (hereafter cited as *Welfare and Warfare*), 3–26, for a discussion and a preliminary edition of Munich, CLM 4620, fols 132v–139v, which is the only surviving description of the Jerusalem hospice and its practices.

6   See Timothy S. Miller, "The Knights of Saint John and the Hospitals of the Latin West," *Speculum*, 53 (1978), 709–33. Christopher Toll, "Arabic Medicine and Hospitals in the Middle Ages: A Probable Model for the Military Orders," in *Welfare and Warfare*, pp. 35–41, infers Arabic influence, but does not make a direct comparison.

7   Susan Edgington, "Medical Care in the Hospital of St John in Jerusalem," in *Welfare and Warfare*, pp. 27–33.

Although the Order remained committed to its medical mission, its militarization and subsequent responsibility for the defense of the crusader kingdoms linked the Hospitallers with the fortunes of the Latin Christians in the East. After Saladin captured Jerusalem in 1187, the Order evacuated its main convent and established a hospital in the city of Acre.[8] The Order left Palestine when Acre fell in 1291. The Hospitallers stayed for two years on Cyprus before capturing the island of Rhodes, which they ruled as the Knights of Rhodes between 1310 and 1522. During this period of their history, western Europeans primarily viewed the Order as a crusading entity. Rhodes, located off the coast of Anatolia, was intended as the outpost of Christendom. The papacy ordered the Knights to assist any planned crusades in the eastern Mediterranean. Rhodes also became a major stopping point on the pilgrimage to the Holy Land. The Order fortified the city of Rhodes, constructing a separate walled quarter for itself within the city and a hospital for travelers, members of the order, and the Rhodians. Initially, the hospital was a small structure near the main gate, which was replaced by 1483 by a larger building within the Knights' quarter. The later hospital, which still stands, is organized around a central courtyard, with a large upstairs ward, niches between the beds, and smaller, separate wards. As with the earlier hospice in Jerusalem, the archives of this building are lost. The only written information is found in references in the statutes and rules of the Order.

After the Order surrendered Rhodes to Sultan Suleiman in 1522, Charles V gave it the island of Malta in 1530. The Order became known as the Knights of Malta, whose mission was to buttress Italy and the western Mediterranean against the advance of the Ottoman Empire. When the Knights first came to Malta, they had settled in the fortified fishing village of Birgu on the Great Harbor, where they built their first hospital on Malta in 1532–33.[9] The Knights gained renown for withstanding an Ottoman siege of the island in 1565. After the siege, the Knights constructed a new city, Valletta, on a peninsula jutting into the Great Harbor. After the Order began construction of the city of Valletta in 1565, they built there a new hospital, called the Sacra Infermeria, after 1574.[10] This massive structure combined many of the Order's charitable foundations, including a military hospital, a foundling hospital and a magdalene. It had separate wards for men and women, individual wards for the insane and sufferers from venereal disease, and segregated medical from surgical cases. The Sacra Infermeria had its own pharmacy. The Knights established a formal

---

8   Jonathan Riley-Smith, *The Knights of St John in Jerusalem and Cyprus 1050–1310* (London, 1967), p. 247. Ten Hospitallers remained to tend the sick for a year after Saladin captured the city. The Hospitallers returned after Frederick II reoccupied Jerusalem in the thirteenth century, but they kept their hospital in Acre.

9   This was not the first hospital on Malta, as the Santo Spirito Hospital in Rabat already existed in the fourteenth century. See Stanley Fiorini, *Santo Spirito Hospital at Rabat, Malta: The Early Years to 1575* (Malta, 1989).

10   The meeting of the Chapter General in 1574 ordered the construction of the Sacra Infermeria in Valletta, to replace the one in Birgu; Valletta, National Library, Archives of the Order of Malta (hereafter abbreviated AOM), 290, fol. 29. The Sacra Infermeria building still stands, although it suffered extensive bomb damage during the Second World War.

medical school for the Sacra Infermeria in 1675, and created a faculty for the study of medicine in the University of Malta in 1771. The library and archives of these institutions remained on the island when Napoleon expelled the Knights in 1798.

The Archives of the Sacra Infermeria

The archives of the Order's Hospital in Valletta in the National Library of Malta are contained in Section 11, the Hospital (see Appendix I). Section 11 comprises 46 volumes, dating from 1590 until 1798. Based on this description alone, the researcher might hope to find a treasure trove containing a wealth of information about the hospital's operations, early modern medical practices, diet and expenses. They would be disappointed. The Reverend J. Mizzi, who cataloged the archives of the *Ospedale*, wrote in his introduction:

> To the student of the history of the Hospitallers and of their main charitable institution this title [*Ospedale*] may appear very enticing. The scholar in search of unexplored sources is apt to imagine that the documents of this Section could enable him to probe deep into the early beginnings and later developments of the celebrated Hospice of Jerusalem. Or he may expect to unearth the secrets of the medical science and surgery of the Holy Infirmary erected in Valletta in 1574. If his aims are less ambitious, he may perhaps entertain the hope of discovering some interesting data relating to the care of the sick or the records dealing with the management of the Hospital. A cursory examination of the manuscripts of this Section, however, is likely to disappoint him utterly. ... The bulk of the volumes ... have handed down to us, though with many gaps, ... the last wills and testaments made in the Holy Infirmary of Valletta.[11]

Mizzi estimated that 6 volumes of the archive concerned the administration of the hospital, while 38 contained copies of wills made by Knights, Maltese and travelers admitted to the Sacra Infermeria between 1590 and 1798. It is apparent that only the archives of the Sacra Infermeria, and not those of the earlier hospitals, survived. A closer examination reveals that the surviving volumes were gathered up and deposited with the archives of the Master after 1798. These circumstances suggest that the Order's earlier hospitals in Jerusalem and Rhodes kept their own records, separate from the records maintained by the Master of the Order and his chancellor. These records would not necessarily have included details about patient care and medical practice.

According to the statutes of the Order, the head of the Sacra Infermeria was the Hospitaller, a high-ranking official of the Order who held a seat on the council of the Grand Master. The Infirmarian, the second in command, came from the French langue and was responsible for the well-being of the patients and other inmates. References to scribes and notaries in the Sacra Infermeria suggest that the Hospitaller or the Infirmarian kept the records of the institution. Each year the Grand Master and the

---

11 J. Mizzi, *Catalogue of the Records of the Order of St John of Jerusalem in the Royal Malta Library, Volume XI: Archives 1713–1758* (Malta, 1969), 1–2.

council chose two comptrollers, or *prud'hommes*. The comptrollers provisioned the Sacra Infermeria with food and equipment, took inventory and executed the wills of patients who died in the hospital. In addition to the statutory personnel, the knights in residence in the convent, including the Grand Master, took regular turns visiting the sick. Novices served in the Sacra Infermeria once a week. Members of the order served as physicians as well as spiritual caretakers.[12]

The Sacra Infermeria had its own printed Rule, a small 19-page book printed in Rome in 1725.[13] The Rule contains information about the staff of the Infermeria, its inventory of silver and tapestry, and its physical layout.[14] The archives also contain a contemporary handwritten copy of the published Rule, annotated and updated by its owner.[15] The handwritten copy has more detailed information than the printed volume. For example, the medical personnel listed in the printed Rule consisted of five physicians and five surgeons: two for Valletta, and one each for Birgu, Isola and Bormola, the coastal settlements around the Great Harbor. According to the handwritten copy, there were three principal physicians, who received a salary of 350 scudi a year, and three secondary physicians, who received 200 scudi a year.[16] In addition to the physicians, there were three principal surgeons who received 350 scudi a year, assisted by three secondary surgeons who received 175 scudi a year. Other volumes in the archives contain more detailed accounts about salaries, purchases and pensions in the Sacra Infermeria during the late eighteenth century.[17]

The archives also contain an eighteenth-century handwritten copy of a printed book.[18] The title and dedication pages of *Regole della Sac. Congregat. Sotto Titolo della Sstsa Trinita, Eretta nel Sac. Spe. Dale del Sacr' Ordine di S. Giovani Gerosolimitano* mimics the layout and format of a printed volume. The manuscript contains the Rule of the Congregation of the Holy Trinity, a separate confraternity

---

12 See H.J.A. Sire, *The Knights of Malta* (Yale, CT, 1994), pp. 217–20.

13 AOM 1713, *Notizia della Sacra Infermeria, e della Carica delli commissari, delle povere Inferme* (Rome, 1725); ed. and trans. W.K.R. Bedford, *The Regulation of the Old Hospital of the Knights of St. John at Valletta* (Edinburgh, 1882). Also trans. and corrected by Edgar Erskine Hume, *Medical Work of the Knights Hospitallers of Saint John of Jerusalem* (Baltimore, MD, 1940), pp. 136–48; ibid, "Regulations for the Sick Poor of Malta," pp. 159–65.

14 The patients of the Sacra Infermeria ate off silver plate because its value reinforced their status as "our Lords the Sick." It was also easy to keep clean, and more hygienic; Paul Cassar, *Medical History of Malta* (London, 1964), p. 52.

15 AOM 1714, *Regolamento per il governo spirituale, politico e economico del S. Ospedale dell'Ordine Gerosolimitano*, fols i–vii, 215.

16 AOM 1714, fol. 118.

17 AOM 1715, *Officciali del Sagro Ospedale che si passorono in Tesoro dal primo Settembre 1777* (28 fols), 14 cartas; AOM 1716, *Conto del S. Ospedale dal 1 Maggio 1795 fino a tutto Aprile 1796*, 31pp. AOM 1715, Carta 2, recorded that in 1777 the Chapter General ruled that all wages and salaries could only be paid in money, and not in kind.

18 AOM 1713A, *Regole della congregazione della Santissima Trinita*, 27 fols, dedication dated December 1704.

organized to provide charitable contributions to the Sacra Infermeria and to ensure their proper distribution. Upon entry into this brotherhood, the members paid one quarter of their income to the Congregation; subsequently, they paid annually one-eighth of their income. In return they received from the brotherhood a funeral mass upon their death and remembrance masses afterwards. The book contains handwritten notes of a visitation upon the sodality in 1736, which reformed rule number eight, which initially provided for one procurator selected from the chaplains, and changed it to two procurators selected from the fraters and the chaplains.

The scribes and notaries of the Sacra Infermia probably spent their time recording the patients' testaments. Thirty-eight volumes survive (see Appendix I, AOM 1720–58) containing the names and wills of those who died in the Sacra Infermeria. At the end of the eighteenth century, the Sacra Infermeria admitted almost four thousand patients a year, with a mortality rate of about 8 per cent.[19] The registers of testaments and mortality provide considerable information about the inhabitants of the Sacra Infermeria: name, gender, occupation, knightly status and origin of the deceased. The inhabitants of the hospital included members of the Order, Maltese men, women and children, and foreign visitors and sailors. The scribes meticulously recorded the distribution of the sacraments, but remained vague about the cause of death.[20] By the eighteenth century, the testament included information about the burial of the deceased and an inventory of his or her possessions.

The Library of the *Sacra Infermeria*

In addition to the archives, the National Library of Malta contains the residue of the Sacra Infermeria's library and medical books acquired from the estates of deceased knights. The collection reflects the growing interest in organized medical training on the island of Malta. In 1675, Grand Master Nicholas Cottoner established a chair of Anatomy and Surgery in the Sacra Infermeria.[21] The first holder of the chair, Frà Giuseppi Zammit, collected a large library to support the study of medicine, surgery, botany and anatomy.[22] He gave this library to the Sacra Infermeria in 1687. The library of the Sacra Infermeria was transferred to the Public Library (today the National Library) in 1797.[23] The Order created the Public Library fairly late in its history. Because each knight took a vow of poverty, upon his death his possessions, or "spoils," became the property of the Order. These spoils included some notable

---

19 Cassar, *Medical History of Malta*, p. 56.

20 For example, AOM 1720, fol. 20v, uses the phrase *retrouvant malade* to describe the cause of death.

21 The University of Malta established a Faculty of Medicine in 1771, which incorporated Cottoner's chair of Anatomy and Surgery; Cassar, *Medical History of Malta*, p. 445.

22 Nicola Zammit, "Il Dr. Giuseppe Zammit l'illustre Monaco maltese, il primo titolare della Cattedra di Medicina a Malta," *L'Arte* (Malta, 1865), 3/58: 2–4; Cassar, *Medical History of Malta*, p. 437.

23 Ibid., p. 438.

collections of books. They were not collected as a single library until 1766, when the collection of Frà Louis Guérin de Tencin formed the nucleus of the Order's Library. Prior to Napoleon Bonaparte's expulsion of the Knights from Malta in 1798, the library contained an estimated 80,000 volumes, but only 30,000 remained in 1812.[24] New books were added to the collection through the nineteenth and twentieth centuries. Today, the National Library of Malta contains notable medical books from the fifteenth through nineteenth centuries.

There is no published catalog identifying the books from the library of the Sacra Infermeria. The preliminary list (see Appendix II) is drawn from the catalog of the pre-1955 acquisitions of the National Library of Malta. The books in this catalog, which includes the remnants of the foundation collection, are classified by author and by Dewey Decimal subject number. Under the category 610 (medicine), the catalog contains 79 books published prior to 1798. A partial listing of the volumes shows that in addition to the classical authors, such as Celsus, Hippocrates and the medieval author Avicenna, the physicians of the Order read contemporary works by Paracelsus, Ettmüller and Boerhaave. The books are predominately in French, with some works in Italian, Latin and Spanish. English, German, Latin and Greek works appear in translated editions.

Of the 79 pre-1798 medical imprints, two notable volumes were gifts to the library in the nineteenth and twentieth centuries. These volumes do not bear any direct evidence of previous ownership by members of the Order.[25] Several books bear the names, or bookplates, of members of the Order. Two of the 79 volumes surveyed bear the name and bookplate of Frà Brossia, a seventeenth-century bibliophile who left a large collection of books to the Order.[26] One volume bears the name of Saintejay, a Knight who owned a French translation of Hippocrates bound

---

24 Albert E. Abela and William Zammit, *Guide to the National Library of Malta* (Malta, 2000), p. 9.

25 Professor S.L. Pisani presented Claudius Galen, *Galeni in Libros Hippograti & alior Commentarii* (Venice, 1562), in 1899. The annotations made by a sixteenth-century owner of this volume were trimmed when the volume was re-bound in the eighteenth century. In 1930, Carmello Micallef donated Jacopo Della Torre's *Medici Singularis expositio, et quaestiones in artem medicinalem Galen. Quae vulgo Techni appellatur quam emendatissime. Tabula etiam nuper accessit copiosissima a priori longe perfectiar* (Venice, 1547).

26 Louis Guyon and Lazare Meyssonnier, *Le cours de medecine en françois, contenant Le miroir de beauté et santé corporelle, par M. Louys Guyon Dolois, sieur de la Nauche ... et la Theorie avec un accomplissement de practique selon les principes tant dogmatiques, que chymiques ... par M. Lazare Meyssonnier...* 7th and final edn, and Michael Ettmüller, *Pratique generale de medecine de tout le corps humain*, new trans., 2nd revised and corrected edn (Lyons, 1699). Brosia's bookplate is an open crown, surmounting an eight-pointed cross, upon which is mounted a shield, white cross on perpendicular lines. Stars are in the upper quadrants of the shield; lower quadrants flowers. The eight-pointed cross is surrounded by a string of beads (rosary?) with eight-pointed cross pendant.

with a book about charitable medicine.[27] Other volumes carry earlier shelfmarks, indicating their inclusion in another collection, which could have been the library of the Sacra Infermeria.[28]

Readers' Concerns on Malta

Few of the books bear readers' marks, but those that do suggest a context for the practice of medicine on Malta. For example, a 1528 Aldine edition of Aulo Cornelio Celso's *Medicinae Libri VIII Quam emendatissimi, graecis etiam omnibus dictionibus restituti* contains marginal annotations and study notes in Latin.[29] Some of the text is underlined as well. The reader ticked the index entries for headaches, *signa percussi cerebri* and arthritis, *de articulorum doloribus in manibus, pedibusque*. The most heavily underlined and annotated portions are to be found in Book Three, "On Fevers," and in Book Four, Chapters 14 and 15, "On Dysentery."

Despite the absence of annotations in the books, an overview of the collection reveals the ethos of Hospitaller medical practice, one that remained consistent with their earlier approach towards patients and treatments. The scope of the collection and the variety of viewpoints represented suggests that the Order's physicians and surgeons took a practical approach to treatment, as opposed to a theoretical one. The study of medicine on Malta was both humanistic and practical. It was humanistic in the sense that the library of the Sacra Infermeria contained books that sought to reconcile classical medical treatises with practical observation.[30] It was practical because the library also contained such books as the works of Ambrose Paré (1510–90), a French physician and surgeon who learned by apprenticeship and who wrote in

27 Lazare Meyssonnier, *Le Medecin Charitable Abrégé, pour guerir toutes sortes de Maladies avec peu de Remedes*, 2nd edn (Lyons, 1668). This volume is bound together with Meyssonnier's *Les Aphorismes d'Hippocrate* (Lyons, 1668).

28 Pietro Andrea Mattioli, *Les commentaires de M. P. André Matthiolus, medecin senois sur les six livres de Pedacius Dioscoride Anazarbeen, de la matiere medecinale* (Lyons, 1620); Jean Prevost, *Medicina pauperum, mira serie continens remedia ad aegrotos cujuscunque generis persanandos aptissima* (Padua, 1719); François Quesnay, *Examen impartial des contestations des médecins & des chirurgiens* (n.p., 1748); Jean Riolan, *Universae medicinae compendium* (Paris, 1626).

29 The library also holds the latest (1722) edition of the same work: Aulo Cornelio Celso, *De medicina libri octo brevioribus Rob. Constantini Is Casauboni, aliorumque scholiis ac locis parallelis illustrate* ... (Padua, 1722).

30 See Hippocrates, *Opera quae extant graece et latine veterum codicum collatione restituta, novo ordine in quattuor classes digesta, interpretationis latinae emendatione & scholiis illustrata, à Hieron Mercuriali Torolisiens* (Venice, 1588); Aulus Cornelius Celsus, *De medicina libri octo* (Venice, 1528) and Celsus, *De medicina libri octo*, ed. Robert Constantin, Isaac Casaubon and Theodoor ab Almeloveen (Padua, 1722); see also Pietro Andrea Mattioli, *Les commentaires sur les six livres de Pedacius Dioscoride Anazarbeen* (Lyons, 1620).

the vernacular.[31] The collection reflects the Enlightenment's attitude toward illness, seeing it as caused by environment rather than the punishment of God.[32]

The Knights of Malta enthusiastically embraced the role of botany in medical therapy. The sixteenth and seventeenth centuries saw the importation of unknown plants from the New World. At the same time, scholars were identifying the Greek plants prescribed by Dioscorides.[33] These pharmaceuticals were expensive imports. In reaction, numerous books appeared on the subject of medicine and pharmacology of the poor, and these are well represented in the collection in Malta.[34] This genre addressed the substitution of cheaper pharmaceuticals for poor patients. These writers argued that human beings were made ill by environmental causes, and that local herbs and plants provided the best pharmacology. The Knights adopted this theory, especially after the discovery of Fungus Rock, located off the nearby island of Gozo. This rock is the habitat for *C. coccineum*, a rare mushroom also known as Maltese mushroom or tarthuth.[35] The Grand Master declared a monopoly on the mushroom, and limited access to it. The physicians of the Sacra Infermeria prescribed the fungus as a cure-all for dysentery, ulcers, hemorrhages, bandaged wounds, apoplexy, venereal disease, vomiting and irregular menstruation.

Conclusion

This chapter is a preliminary overview of the archives and library of the Sacra Infermeria. Even these brief notes, however, suggest that both offer more to the researcher than Mizzi thought possible. The names of thousands of patients survive, as do the eighteenth-century account books. The contents of the library provide further information about the medical practices of the Sacra Infermia. It appears that the physicians of the Order were well read, and consistently advocated a dietetic and botanical approach to medicine. While the Order never ignored the spiritual needs of its patients, it refused to consider illness a divine punishment. Further work needs to be done to determine whether this ethos was the result of outside influence or the continuation of an earlier medical tradition.

---

31 Andrew Wear, "Medicine in Early Modern Europe, 1500–1700," in *The Western Medical Tradition* (Cambridge, 1995), 294–5.

32 Ibid., 240–42.

33 Ibid., 298–99, 303–4.

34 See, for example, Nicolas Alesandre, *La medicine et la chiruigie des Pauvres, qui contiennent des remédes choisis, facilis a preparer & sans déspense, pour la ...* (Paris, 1758); Philippe Hecquel, *La Medicine, la chirugie et la pharmacie des pauvres par feu M. —*, new edn, revised and corrected version of the manuscript with a *catalogue raisonné* of his works (Paris, 1749), 4 vols; Joannes Praevotius, *Medicina Pauperum. Mira serie continens remedia ad aegrotos cujuscunque generis persanandos aptissima, facile parabilia, esctemporanea & nullius, vel perescigui sumptus* (Padua, 1719).

35 Robert W. Lebling, "The Treasure of Tarthuth," *Saudi Aramco World*, March/April 2003, 15–17.

Appendix I: Archives of the Knights of Malta, Section 11, The Hospital

AOM 1713 *Notizia della Sacra Infermeria, e della Carica delli commissari, delle povere Inferme* (Rome, 1725), 19 pp. Printed work.[36]

AOM 1713A *Regole della Sac. Congregat. Sotto Titolo della Sstsa Trinita, Eretta nel Sac. Spe. Dale del Sacr' Ordine di S. Giovani Gerosolimitano (December 1704)* 27 ff. Eighteenth-century handwritten copy of a printed book. The volume contains handwritten notes of a visitation upon the sodality in 1736, which changed rule number eight from the selection of one procurator from the chaplains, to two procurators selected from the fraters and the chaplains. The book concludes with an indulgence granted by Pope Clement XI to the sodality.

AOM 1714, *Regolamento per il Governo Spirituale, Politico, ed Economico del Sacro Ospedale del S. Ordine Gerosolimitano*, f. I + vii + 215. Eighteenth-century handwritten copy of AOM 1713. The text of the volume is written on the right-hand side of the page, leaving the left side of the page for notes and annotations. The owner of the volume used the space to note changes in the rules and in the procedures of the hospital. This section is followed by a copy of a 1699 magisterial bull of Raymond Perellos y Roccaful concerning physicians and surgeons.

AOM 1715, *Officciali del Sagro Ospedale che si passorono in Tesoro dal primo Settembre 1777* , 28 ff, is divided into 14 "cartas." With the exception of Cart 2, each carta contains information about salaries from 1777 until 1795. Carta 2 is a note, dated 1777, stating that the Chapter General had suppressed all the salaries, pensions, recompense and charity that had been paid in denaro and in kind from the Sacra Infermeria; and that it has been decided that the new wages would be paid only in money; that the coming salaries be paid according to the lists that will be submitted monthly to the Prodomo and to the Treasury.

AOM 1716 *Conto del S. Ospedale dal 1 Maggio 1795 fino a tutto Aprile 1796*, 31 pp. An account of the purchases of the hospital, which includes the amount of monthly salaries, pensions to retired physicians, and the purchase of food.

AOM 1720, *Registro dei Testamenti dall'Anno 1590 al 1634 e Registro dei Morti dall'Anno 1590 al 1634*, 217 ff. Registers the laity and Knights who died in the Sacra Infermeria; also, registers the wills of the laity and the disposition of goods made by the Knights.

---

36 AOM 1713; ed. and trans. W.K.R. Bedford, *The Regulation of the Old Hospital of the Knights of St John at Valletta* (Edinburgh, 1882). Also translated and corrected by Edgar Erskine Hume, *Medical Work of the Knights Hospitallers of Saint John of Jerusalem* (Baltimore, MD, 1940), pp. 136–48; ibid., "Regulations for the Sick Poor of Malta," pp. 159–65.

AOM 1721, *Registro dei Testamenti dall'Anno 1634 al 1650 e Registro dei Morti dal 1635 al 1676. Parte I: Registro dei Testamenti dall'anno 1635 al 1650. Parte II: Registro dei Testamenti dell'anno 1634 e 1635 e registro dei morti dall'anno 1633 al 1676.* 105 + 201 ff. Part one records the testaments and dispositions of goods made by those members of the Order and laity who died in the Sacra Infermeria between 1635 and 1650. Part Two lists the names of all the Knights and laity who died in the Sacra Infermeria between 1633 and 1676.

AOM 1722, *Registro dei Testamenti dall'Anno 1666 al 1693 e Dispropriamenti dei Signori dell'Abito dall'Anno 1661 al 1684. Parte I: [Titulo:] Les testaments ou derniers volontes des seculiers et autres personnes morts a la S. Infirmerie. Parte II: Depoullements des biens faits par les religieux freers de l'Ordre de St. Jean de Jerusalem et testaments des novices depuis l'annee 1666 jusqu' a 1684.* 342 pp + 1–18 + 26–42 pp. Part I contains the wills or last wishes of the lay (and other people) who died in the Sacra Infermeria; Part II contains the disposition of goods made by the members of the Order, including the wills of the novices, between 1666 and 1684.

AOM 1723, *Registre des Testaments Commencant au Mois D'Aout 1693* [–November 1742], 571 pp. Register of the wills made by the laity in the Sacra Infermeria.

AOM 1724, *Registro delli Testamenti che si Fanno nel Sacro Ospedale Principiato il 1 Gennaio 1743* [–14 December 1767], 650 pp. Register of the wills made by those who died in the Sacra Infermeria between 1741 and 1767.

AOM 1725, *Registro dei Testamenti: 1767–85*, 710 pp. Register of the wills made by those who died in the Sacra Infermeria between 4 December 1767 and 16 January 1785. Pages 669–703 contain an alphabetical index.

AOM 1726, *Registro dei Testamenti 1785* [–19 April 1798], 672 pp. Pages 633–67 contain an alphabetical index.

AOM 1727, *Libro dei Testamenti fatti nel S. Ospedale per mano dei Notari. 13 aprile 1773*, 282 pp. Pages 233–50 contain an index of the names.

AOM 1728 [*Raccolta di Testamenti Originali: 1666–79*], 146 ff. Title supplied.

AOM 1729 [*Raccolta di Testamenti Originali: 1680–89*], 271 ff. Title supplied.

AOM 1730 [volume missing].

AOM 1731 [*Testamenti Originali, 1700–1709*], 233 ff. Title supplied.

AOM 1732 [*Testamenti Originali 1710–19*], 431 ff. Title supplied.

AOM 1733 [*Testamenti Originali, 1720–29*], 388 ff. Title supplied.

AOM 1734 [*Testamenti Originali, 1730–39*], 357 ff. Title supplied.

AOM 1735 [*Testamenti Originali, 1740–44*], 204 ff. Title supplied.

AOM 1736 [*Testamenti Originali, 1750–52*], 180 ff. Title supplied.

AOM 1737 [*Testamenti Originali: 1753–56*], 197 ff. Title supplied.

AOM 1738 [*Testamenti Originali, 1757–59*], 272 ff. Title supplied.

AOM 1739 [*Testamenti Originali, 1760–63*], 288 ff. Title supplied.

AOM 1740 [*Testamenti Originali: 1764*], 84 ff. Title supplied.

AOM 1740a [*Testamenti Originali: 1764–66*], 170 ff. Title supplied.

AOM 1741 [*Testamenti Originali: 1766–69*], 247 ff. Title supplied.

AOM 1742 [*Testamenti Originali: 1770–74*], 300 ff. Title supplied.

AOM 1743 [*Testamenti Originali: 1776–79*], 219 ff. Title supplied.

AOM 1744 [T*estamenti Originali: 1780–84*], 262 ff. Title supplied.

AOM 1745 [*Testamenti Originali, 1786–89*], 282 ff. Title supplied.

AOM 1746 [*Testamenti Originali: 1790–95*], 276 ff. Title supplied.

AOM 1747 [*Testamenti Originali: 1795–98*], 197 ff. Title supplied.

AOM 1748 [*Testamenti, 1747*], 53 ff. Title supplied.

AOM 1749 [*Testamenti, 1775*], 76 ff. Title supplied.

AOM 1750 [*Testamenti Originali: 1776*], 67 ff. Title supplied.

AOM 1751 [volume missing].

AOM 1752 [*Testamenti Originali: 1745*], 48 ff. Title supplied.

AOM 1753 [T*estamenti Originali: 1746*], 29 ff. Title supplied.

AOM 1754 [Testamenti Originali: 1748], 47 ff. Title supplied.

AOM 1755 [Testamenti Originali: 1749], 48 ff. Title supplied.

AOM 1756 [Testamenti Originali: 1690–91], 214 ff. Title supplied.

AOM 1757 [Testamenti Originali: 1785], 132 ff. Title supplied.

AOM 1758 [Testamenti Originali], 101 ff. Title supplied. Folios. 2–19 are an alphabetical list of testators whose wills were recorded in a volume now lost; folios 99–100 contain a list of the names of the people buried in the cemetery of the Lazzaretto.

Appendix II: Preliminary Handlist of Pre-1798 Medical Books in the Collection of the National Library of Malta

Alexandre, Nicolas. *La medicine et la chiruigie des Pauvres, qui contiennent des remédes choisis, facilis à préparer & sans déspense, pour la plupart des maladies internes & externes qui attaquent le corps humain.* Paris, La Veuve Lecomte, 1758. Note: This work appeared in many editions between 1714 and 1782.

Azevedo, Manoel de. *Correccão de abusos introduzidos contra o verdadeiro methodo da medicina.* Lisboa, 1668. Note: 1 vol. Volume Two of this edition was published in 1680, with a slightly different title: *Correcçam de abusos. Introduzidos contra o verdadeiro methodo da medicina, & farol medicinal para medicos, cyrurgiones, & boticarios. II. parte em tres tratados ....* Second edition published Lisbon, 1690-1705.

Baccanelli, Giovanni. *De consensu medicorum in curandis morbis libri quatuor. Ejusdem praeterea accessit De consensu medicorum in cognoscendis simplicibus Liber unus.* Lugduni (Lyon), 1558. This work was reprinted many times: Lutetiae, 1554; Venice, 1553, 1556; Lyon, 1572,

Barker, John. *Essai sur la conformité de la medicine des anciens & des modernes, ou, Camparaison entre la pratique d'Hippocrate, Galien, Sydenhan & Boerhaave.* Amsterdam, Pierre Mortier, 1749. Notes: New French edition published in Paris in 1768. French translation by Ralph Schomberg of *An essay on the agreement betwixt ancient and modern physicians; or, A comparison between the practice of Hippocrates, Galen, Sydenham, and Boerhaave, in acute diseases.* London, 1748 [1747]. Also translated into Italian, 1779.

Barbeyrac, Charles de. *Traités nouveaux de medecine contenans les maladies de la poitrine, les maladies des femmes, & quelques autres maladies particulières selon les nouvelles opinions.* Nouvelle & dernière Edition. Lyon: Jacque Certe, 1732. 1 vol. Published anonymously in 1684. The National Library of Medicine attributes it to Barbeyrac, with the note that this attribution has been questioned.

Bernier, Jean. *Instructions de Medicine ou l'on voit tout ce qu'il fant suivre & eviter dans l'usage des alimens, & des remedes, pour conserver en sante, & pour se Guerir lors qui'on est Malade, par M. de Saint Hilaire, pseudonym of Jean Bernier.* Paris, Jean & Nicolas Conterot, 1694. 2 vols.

Boerhaave, Hermann. *Institutions de médicine de Mr. Herman Boerhaave traduites du Latin en François par M. De La Mettrie. Avec la vie de M. Hermann Boerhaave* (at the end of the second volume). Paris: Huart, Briasson, 1740. 2 vols. Note: Translation of *Institutiones medicae in usus annuae exercitationis domesticos.* A second edition in six volumes, with a commentary by Julien Offray de la Mettrie, appeared in 1742–47.

Boerhaave, Hermann. *Traité de la vertu des medicamens. Traduit du Latin de M. par M. de Vause.* Paris: J.B. Osmont Fils, 1729. Note: Translation of *Tractatus de viribus medicamentorum.* Reprinted in 1739 and 1747.

Brown, John. *Elementi di Medicina del Dottor Giovanni Brown con molte note di lucida gione e commendei dello stesso autore Tradotti dall'Inglese.* Naples, Illi Marotta 1796. 3 vols. Note: John Brown, also spelled John Browne, was the author of *Adenochoiradelogia; or, An anatomick-chirurgical treatise of glandules & strumaes, or Kings-Evil-swellings. Together with the royal gift of healing, or cure thereof by contact or imposition of hands, performed for above 640 years by our Kings of England, continued with their admirable effects, and miraculous events; and concluded with many wonderful examples of cures by their sacred touch ...* London. Printed by Tho. Newcomb for Sam. Lowndes, 1684. Manchester University Library holds numerous copies of his work, such as: *A compleat discourse of wounds both in general and particular ...* London, E. Flesher, 1678; *A compleat treatise of preternatural tumours ...* London, R. Clavel, 1678; *A compleat treatise of the muscles ...* London, Dorman Newman, 1683; *Myographia nova sive musculorum omnium ...* London, Joannes Redmayne, 1684; *Myographia nova: or, a graphical description of all the muscles in humane [sic] body, as they arise in dissection ...* London, Tho. Milbourn, 1697 and 1698.

[Brusaschus, Joannes Jacobus. *Encyclopaedia aphoristica.* Rome: Dom. aut Hercules, 1699. Note: unverified author and title.]

Buc'hoz, Pierre Joseph. *Manuel de médicine pratique, royale et bourgeoisie; ou, Pharmacopée tirée des trois regnes, appliquée aux maladies des habitans des villes.* Paris: J. P. Costard, 1771. 1 vol.

Catalan, Ignacio. *Medicina experimentada y remedies de desauciados, aprobados en consultas por los primeros medicas de esta corte.* Madrid: Oficina de Gabrièl Ramirez, 1745.

Celsus, Aulus Cornelius. *De medicina libri octo. Brevioribus Rob. Constantini, Is. Casauboni, aliorumque scholiis, ac locis parallelis illustrate. Cura et studio Th. J. ab Almeloveen.* Latest edition. Padua, J. Cominus, 1722. Note: An earlier edition in Italian, credited to Robert Constantin, Isaac Casaubon, and Theodoor ab Almeloveen, was published in Amsterdam in 1713.

Celsus, Aulus Cornelius. *Medicinae libri VIII. quam emendatissimi, graecis etiam omnibus dictionibus restitutis.* Venice: Aldus, 1528.

Chevalier, Claude. *Dissertation physico-médicale sur la causes de plusiers maladies dangereuse, & sur les proprietés d'une liqueur purgative & vulnéraire, qui est une pharmacofreí prisqu'universalle.* Paris: C. Herissant Fils, 1758.

Col de Vilars, Élie. *Dictionnaire françois-latin, des termes de medicine, et de chirugie, avec leur définition, leur division & leur etymologie.* Paris: Coignard Le Mercier J.B. Delesseme, 1741. Note: A later edition was published in 1759.

David, Henri. *Le timon et carte de navigation des jeunes chirugiens: pour leur apprendre à conduire en bon port les malades de leur bords.* Marseilles, Pierre Mesnier, 1675.

della Torre, Jacopo. [also Jacobi Foroliviensis]. *Expositio, et quaestiones in artem medicinalem Galen. Quae vulgo Techni appellatur quam emendatissime. Tabula etiam nuper accessit copiosissima a priori longe perfectiar.* Venice: I Giunti, 1547. Donation of Mr Carmello Micallef.

Devaux, Jean. *Le medecin de soi-même; ou L'art de se conserver la santé par l'instinct.* Leyden: Chez de Graef, pour l'autheur, 1682.

Dubé, Paul. *La médecine abbrégée en faveur des pauvres: fondée sur trois pastes purgatives, ou vomitives, données à propos, et sur plusieurs autres remèdes, faciles, et à peu de frais ...*, Paris, Edme Conterot, 1692. Note: Dubé's work, under the title *Le medecin des pauures: qui enseigne le moyen de guerir les maladies par des remedes faciles á trouuer dans le païs, & preparer á peu de frais par toutes personnes*, appeared in many editions through the late seventeenth and early eighteenth century.

Ettmüller, Michael. *Nouveaux instituts de medicine.* Lyon, Thomas Amaulry, 1693.

Ettmüller, Michael. *Pratique generale de medecine de tout le corps humain.* Traduction nouvelle, 2nd ed, revûë & corrigée. Lyon: Thomas Amaulry, 1699. Bears bookplate of Frà Brossia. Note: First edition appeared in 1691.

Ettmüller, Michael. *Quae actis eruditorum lipsiensibus anno MDCCXXI mense majo, pag. 229, De neapolitana operum Michaelis Ettmulleri editione publicata sunt animadversio.* Naples: 1732, 1 vol., 23 pp.

Fizes, Antoine. *Opera medica. De tumoribus suppuratione, cataracta, humani corporis partibus solidis, hominio liesse sano, ac secretione Bilis. His accessit de hominis generatione escercitatio digesta, concinnata latinitate donata a Nicolao Fizes, auctori Patre.* Montpellier: A. & P. Rigaud, 1742, 1 vol.

Gagnon, F.A.D. *La recherche de la verité dans la medecine, où paroît l'homme sur un noveau systeme qui fait voir comment il vit, le jeu de tous ses ressorts pour l'oeconomie naturelle de sa vie ....* Paris: Jean de Nuilly, 1698.

Galenus, Claudius. *Galeni Omnia, quae extant: singulari studio.* Venice: V. Valprisio, 1562. 10 vols in 7; each volume has special title page. This is Volume 8: *Galeni in libros Hippocrati & alior commentarii.* Gift of Professor S.L. Pisani, in 1899. Sixteenth-century marginalia trimmed when the volume was rebound in the eighteenth century.

Gatta, Constantino. *Il trionfo della medicina apologia contro Plinio.* Napoli: Dom. aut. Parrino. 1716. 1 vol.

Gorter, Johannes de. *Medicina Hippocratica: exponens aphorismos Hippocratis. Editio secunda italica.* Patavii: Typis Seminarii: Apud Joannen Manfrè, 1753.

Guyon, Louis, and Meyssonnier, Lazare. *Le cours de medecine en françois, contenant Le miroir de beauté et santé corporelle, par M. Louys Guyon Dolois, sieur de la Nauche ... et la Theorie avec un accomplissement de practique selon les principes tant dogmatiques, que chymiques ... par M. Lazare Meyssonnier. ...* 7th et derniere ed. "Et augmentée d'un discours des maladies veneneuses qui manquoient à la precedente, & d'une methode pour apprendre en bref la medecine par l'usage de la doctrine de l'auteur, mise à la fin." Lyon, Guillaume Barbier. Lyon, D. Gayet. 1678. Bears bookplate of Frà Brosia. Note: *Le miroir de la beauté* was first published in 1615. It was reprinted with Meyssonnier's additions through the seventeenth century.

Hecquet, Philippe. *La Medicine, la chirugie et la pharmacie des pauvres. Nouv. ed., rev. & corr. sur le manuscrit de l'auteur. On y a joint la vie de l'auteur, avec un catalogue raisonné de ses ouvrages.* Paris: David l'ainé et Durand, 1749. 4 vols. A three-volume edition appeared in 1740.

Hecquet, Philippe. *La medicine naturelle, vue dans la pathologie vivante; dans l'usage des calmants & différentes saignées: des veines & des artéres, ronges & blanches, spontanées ou artificielles: dans les substituées par les sang-sues, les scarifications, les ventouses.* Paris, Guillaume Cavelier, 1738. First edition. 2 vols.

Hippocrates. *Opera quae extant graece et latine veterum codicum collatione restituta, novo ordine in quattuor classes digesta, interpretationis latinae emendatione & scholiis illustrata, à Hieron Mercuriali Torolisiense. [Vita Auctoris ex Sorano].* Venetiis: Industria ac sumptibus juntarum, 1588. 1st edition. 2 vols.

Ibn Sina, Abu'Ali al Husayn b. Abd Allah (Avicenna). *Libri in remedica omnes qui hactenus ad nos pervenere. Id est Libri Canonis quinque De viribus cordis. De removendis nocumentis in regimine sanitatis. De sirupo acetose. Et Cantica. Omnia Novissime post aliorum omnium operam a Joanne Paulo Mongio Hydruntino Joanne Costaes Laudensi* ... Venetiis, apud Vincentium Valgrisium, 1564. 2 vols.

La Mettrie, Julien Offray de. *Observations de Medecine pratique par —*. Paris: Huart Briasson, Durand. Froncois Robistel. 1743. 1st edition.

Lémery, Nicolas. *Nouveau recueil des plus Beaux secrets de medecine pour la guérison de toutes sortes de maladies.* Nouvelle edition revue, corrigée & augmentée de plusieurs remedes qui n'etoient point dans les editions precedentes. 4 vols. Paris, Pierre de Bots, 1738. Note: The British Museum attributes an earlier edition (1737) to Antoine d'Emery.

Lieutaud, Joseph. *Précis de la médicine pratique, contenunt l'histoire des maladies, & la maniers de les traiter, avec des observations & remarques critiques sur les points les plus intéressans.* Paris: 1769: 3rd edition, 2 vols.

Linden, Johannes Antonides van der. *De scriptis medicis libri duo.* Editio Tertia & tertia auctior. Amstelredami, I. Blaeu, 1662. 1 volume. Note: Blaeu published earlier editions in 1637 and 1651.

Mattioli, Pietro Andrea. *Les commentaires de M. P. André Matthiolus, medecin senois sur les six livres de Pedacius Dioscoride Anazarbeen, de la matiere medecinale. Traduits de latin en françois par M. Antoine du Pinet, et illustrez de nouveau, d'un bon nombre de figures; & augmentez en plus de mille lieux à la dernière edition de l'auteur, tant de plusieurs remedes & diverses sortes de maladies; comme aussi des distillations, & de la cognoissance des simples* ...Lyon, Pierre Rigaud, 1620. 1 vol. Note: Reissue of 1619 edition. Antoine du Pinet's translation was first published in 1561.

Mayerne, Théodore Turquet de. *Oeuvres de Medecine.* N.p. 1692. 1 vol., 3 tomes.

Mead, Richard. *Opera medica. Figuris illustrata, ac variis mendis diligentissime esspurgata. Editio novissima ad Editionem Londinensem.* Neapoli: Benedetto Gessari...Expensis Dominici Terres. 1758. Latest edition. Note: Earlier Neapolitan editions appeared in 1748 and 1752. A later edition appeared in 1768.

Meyserey, Guillaume Mahieu de. *La medecine d'armée, contenant des moyens aisés.* Paris: Chez la Veuve. Cavalier & Fils, 1754. 1st edition. 3 vols.

Meyssonnier, Lazare. *Le Medecin Charitable Abrégé, pour guerir toutes sortes de Maladies avec peu de Remedes. Et l'Almanach perpetuel ou Regime Universel.* Lyon: Marcelin Gautherin, 1668. 2nd edition. 1 vol. 59 pp. One table (frontispiece, portrait of Meyssonier). Bears name of Frà Saintejay. Bound with *Les Aphorismes d'Hippocrate, traduits nouvellement en François suivant la verité du texte Grec; avec un messange de Paraphrases, d'Eclaircissement és lieux plus obsours, et A Clef de Cette Doctrine par le moyen de la Circulation du Sang, & d'autres Nouvelles décounertes de ce Siecle en Anatomie & Chymie.* Lyon: Pierre Compagnon, Marchand Libraire, 1668.

Meyssonnier, Lazare. *La Medecine Françoise.* Lyon, Pierre Anard, 1651. 1st edition. 1 vol., 7 tomes.

Monardi, Nicolai, and Clusius, Carolus. *Libri tres Magna medicinae secreta et varia experimenta continentes: et illi quidem hispanico sermone conscripti: nunc vero recens latio donati a Carolo Clusio.* N.p. [1605] 1 vol.

Morton, Richard, et al. *Opera medica : in qua praeter tractatus varios prioribus subjunctos, alii rursùs ad majorem illustrationem, & utilius augmentum adjiciuntur, quorum enumeratio, ac explicatio in subsequenti pagina continentur ....* Editio novissima. Venetiis: Apud Hyeroninum Savioni ..., 1733. Compilation of medical treatises by Morton, Walter Harris, William Cole, Martin Lister and Thomas Sydenham.

Nenter, Georg Philipp. *Fundamenta medicinae theoretico-practica, secundum celeberrimi D.D. Stahlii, potissimum, aliorumque celebriorum medicorum placita conscripta, & propria experientia confirmata, in forma tabularum exhibita.* Venezia: Sebastiano Coleti, 1753. 2nd edition, 1 vol.

Paracelsus. *Opera.* Durch Joannem Huserum Brisgoium in zehen unterscheiderch Theil in Truck gegeben. Strasburg: Lazari Zetzners, 1603. 1 vol.

Paré, Ambroise. *Les oeuvres d'Ambroise Paré conseiler et premier chirurgien du roy: corrigées et augmentées par luy-mesme, peu au paravant son decés.* Divisees en vingt-neuf livres. Avec les figures & portraicts, tant de l'anatomie que des instruments de chirurgie, & de plusieurs monstres. 7th ed. rev. & augm. en divers endroicts. Paris, 1614. 2 vols.

Pascoli, Alessandro. *De homine, sive de Corpore humano vitam habente ratione tum prosperae, tum afflicatae valetudinis libri tres. In quibus ad mentem tum veterum, tum recentiorum Theoria, ac praxis medica nova, clara, ac brevi methodo exponitur.* Romae: 1728. 3 vols.

Passera, Felice. *Pratica universale nella medicina, overo annotationi sopra tutte le infermità più particolare, che giornalmente fogliono avvenire ne corpi humani, convarie, et diverse belle osservagioni regole et avvertimenti pertinenti adesse. Divisa in quattro libri. Con una copiosa tavola di tutte le cose, che in essi si cotengono opera di Fra Felice Passera da Bergamo.* Milano, Carlo Antonio Malatesta, 1693. 1 vol.

Pechlin, Johann Nicolas. *Observationum physico-medicarum libri tres, quibus accessit, Ephemeris vulneris thoracici & in eam commentarius.* Hamburgi, Ex officina libraria Schultziana, 1691. 1st edition. Illustrated.

Piquer, Andrés. *Institutiones medicae ad usum scholae Valentinae.* Matriti: Viduam Joachimi Ibarra. 1790. 3rd edition. 1 vol. First published in Madrid, 1762.

Piquer, Andrés. *Praxis medica ad usum scholae Valentinae.* Matriti: 1786–89. 3rd edition. 2 vols. Originally published in Madrid, 1764–66.

Pitcarne, Archibald. *Elementa medicinae physico-mathematica libris duobus. Item ejusdem Opuscula medica, quibus postremo adjectus est ratiociniorum mechanicorum in medicina usus vindicatus per Christianum Strom.* Venetiis: 1740. 1st edition. 1 vol.

Prevost, Jean. *Medicina pauperum, mira serie continens remedia ad aegrotos cujuscunque generis persanandos aptissima, facilè parabilia, extemporanea & nullius, vel perexigui sumptus. Huic thesauro adjunguntur Jucundissimae pro delicatulis medicamenta non omisso ejusdem auctoris libello aureo De venenis.* Patavii: Jo. Bapt. Conzatti, 1719. 1 vol.

Polverino, Giovanni Girolamo. *De curandis, iuxta hodiernum usum singulis humani corporis morbis, opus; sive Praxi accurata brevi, dilucida & absoluta methodo explicata, ac tradita. Nunc quinta editio in lucem edita cum Indice Locupletissimo.* Neapoli: Lazarus Scoriggius, 1629. 5th edition. 1 vol.

Quesnay, François. *Examen impartial des contestations des médecins & des chirurgiens, considerées par rapport à l'intéret public par M. de B——.* N.p., no press. 1748. Clandestine (edition). 1 vol. 220 pp.

Riolan, Jean. *Universae medicinae compendium.* Parisiis: Simonem Perier, 1626. 1 vol.

Rivière, Lazare. *Les observations de medecine de Lazare Riviere ... qui contiennent quatre centuries de guerison trés-remarquables: auxquelles on a joint des Observations qui luy avoient été communiquées. Seconde Edition, reveue & corrigée sur le latin.* Lyon: Jean Certe, 1688. 2nd edition. 1 vol.

Rosetti, Josephus Thomas. *Systema novum mechanico Hippocraticum de morbis fluidorum, & solidorum, ac de singulis ipsorum curationibus Opus theorico-practicum Josephi Thomae Rosetti physicae & medicinae professoris.* Venetiis, 1734.

Serenus Sammonicus, Quintus. *De medicina praecepta saluberrima ex editione Lugdunensi A. 1566. Rob. Constantine, cum hujus notis variisque lectionibus. Quid praeterea in hac ultima praestitum sit, ex epistola ad lectorem, Celso praefixa, intelligi potest.* Patavii: Josephus Cominus, 1722, 1 vol.

Serenus Sammonicus, Quintus. *Liber de medicina et ipse castigatiss.* Accedit index … sine quam copiosus. Venice: Aldus & A Asulanus, 1528. 1 vol. Ff. 149–64.

[Santorio, Giov. Domenico. *De Structura & Motu Fibrae, De Nutritione Animale, De Haemorrhodibus & De Catameniis.* Vide: Baclivi, Giorgi, *Opera Omnia* pp. 560 to 635. n.d., n.p. pp. 560–635. Unverified].

Santorio, Santorio, *La medecine statique de Sanctorius ... ou, L'art de se conserver la santé par la transpiration traduite en françois.* Par feu M. Le Breton. Paris, 1722. 1 vol.

Santorio, Santorio, and Obizzi, Ippolito. *Ars Sanctorii Sanctorii ... De Statica Medicina Aphorismorum sectionibus septem comprehensa. Accessit Staticomastise sive Staticae Medicinae demolitio.* Leiden: Viduam: Cornelii Boutestein. 1713. New edition. 1 vol., 3 tomes.

Sarcone, Michele. *Il Caffé. Historia morbi a Sarconio scripta et clarissimi toncii testimonium.* Rome, 1775, 1 vol.

Secrets utiles et éprouvés dans la pratique de la médecine et de la chirurgie, pour conserver la santé, & prolonger la vie. Avec un appendix sur les maladies des chevaux. Nouvelle Edition, augmentée du *Traité du cassis* & du *Manuel des médecins & chirurgiens.* Paris, 1757. New edition. 1 vol.

Sennert, Daniel. *Epitome institutionum medicinae et Librorum de febribus.* Postremae huic editioni accessit index rerum. Padova, 1684. Latest edition. 1 vol.

Sydenham, Thomas. *Opera medica.* Editio novissima variis variorum praestantissimorum medicorum observantionibus, & plurium constitutionum epidemicarum recentiorum descriptione quam maxime illustrata: Imo + Mechanica tum morborum tum medicamentorum à Joanne-Baptista Mazino; necnon Caelestina Cocchii … Venezia, 1735. New edition. Folio size. 1 vol.

Tachenius, Otto. *Antiquissimae Hippocraticae medicinae clavis manuali experentia in naturae fontibus elaborata, qua per ignem & aquam inaudita methodo occulta naturae, & artis, compendiosa operandi ratione manifesta fiunt & dilucide aperiuntur.* Venice, 1669. 1 vol. 286 + Index.

Thierry, *Médecine expérimentale, ou résultat de nouvelles observations pratiques et anatomiques.* Paris, 1755. 1st edition. 1 vol.

Tissot, Simon André. *Avis au peuple sur sa santé, ou, Traité des maladies les plus fréquentes.* Seconde edition, augmentée sur la dernière de l'auteur, de la description & de la cure de plusieurs maladies & principalement de celles qui demandent de prompt secours. Paris, 1763. 2nd edition. 1 vol.

Tozzi, Luca. *Medicinae pars prior ΘΕΩΡΗΤΙΚΗ [theoretike]. Curiosa quaequae tum ex physiologicis, tum pathologicis deprompta; veterum, recentiorumque medendi methodum complectens.* Editio novissima multo auctior, & emendatior. Venezia: Nicolò Pezzana, 1728. Latest edition. 2 vols. Note: Earlier editions were published in London in 1681 and Naples in 1703.

[Villanova, Arnaldo de, and Milano, Giovanni (or Ferrario) da]. *Le regime de santé de l'Escole de Salerne. Traduit et commenté par maistre Michel le Long, avec l'Epistre de Diocle Carystien, touchant les presages des maladies à Antigon Roy d'Asie; et le Serment d'Hippocrate, mis de prose en vers françois par le mesme.* Paris: Nicolas & Jean de la Coste. 1643. 3rd edition. 1 vol.

Velez de Arciniega, Francisco. *Libro de los quadrupedes, y serpientes terrestres, recebidos en el uso de medicina, y de la manera de su preparacion.* Madrid: P. Madrigal, 1597. 1 vol.

Weinhart, Ferdinand Karl. *Medicus officiosus, praxi rationali methodico-aphoristica, cum selectis remediorum formulis, instructus.* Nunc autem magis limatus, correctus, ac typo & ordine meliori, denuò in lucem editus. Cum duplici, capitum & rerum indice. Venetiis, 1724. 1 vol.

Werloschnig, Johannes Baptist. *Curationis verno-autumnalis purgationi, venaesectioni, vomitioni etc. innitentis abusus sive Demonstratio physico-medica quod, sic dicta, cura verno-autumnal, inutilis sit & nociva.* Directa a Io. Baptista Werloschnig. Francofurti, 1713. 1 vol.

Zimmermann, Johann Georg. *Della esperienza nella medicina.* Traduzione dal Tedesco. Prima edizione veneta. Venezia, 1790–91. First Venetian edition. 3 vols.

Chapter 3

Historical Research Developments on Leprosy in France and Western Europe

Bruno Tabuteau

Introduction

It is a tragic fact of history that in 1321, people with leprosy ("the lepers") in the Kingdom of France were accused of poisoning wells and fountains at the instigation of "the Jews." The Jews themselves were said to have been incited to this terrible act by the Moorish King of Tunis or Granada, who hoped to harm the Christians by this act.[1] It is concerning this strange affair that the great romantic historian Jules Michelet evoked the misfortune of people with leprosy in that time. The medieval population would have associated "the lepers" with "the Jews" both in infamy and in that they lived on the margins of society. Separated from society by a lugubrious ritual, people with leprosy lived out their lives under many prohibitions, secluded in leprosaria that Michelet does not hesitate to describe as the "dirty residue of the Crusades!"[2]

This famous expression, like the somber picture it portrays, denotes a whole historiographic tradition for dealing with leprosy. This tradition was further elaborated during the Age of Enlightenment, and remained a standard until recently. Such a portrayal was sufficient to feed a legend that the Middle Ages were black and full of misery, with leprosy representing the pathological paradigm. In the minds of many people today, the Middle Ages are identified with leprosy – that is, the Middle Ages were leprosy ("Pour bien des esprits, *le Moyen Age c'est la lèpre*"), as described by one of the foremost specialists on the subject, François-Olivier Touati. He undertook to dismantle the classic historiographic process that has too often been

---

1   About this incident, see Malcolm Barber, "Lepers, Jews and Moslems: The plot to overthrow Christendom in 1321," *History*, 66 (1981), 1–17; Françoise Bériac, "La persécution des lépreux dans la France méridionale en 1321," *Le Moyen Age*, 93 (1987), 203–21, and Bériac, *Des lépreux aux cagots. Recherches sur les sociétés marginales en Aquitaine médiévale* (Bordeaux, 1990), pp. 119–38; Geneviève Pichon, "Quelques réflexions sur l'affaire des lépreux de 1321," *Sources. Travaux historiques* 13 (1988), 25–30; François-Olivier Touati, *Maladie et société au Moyen Age. La lèpre, les lépreux et les léproseries dans la province ecclésiastique de Sens jusqu'au milieu du XIVe siècle* (Paris, 1998), pp. 714–35.

2   "*L'institution des léproseries, ladreries, maladreries, ce sale résidu des croisades, était mal vue, mal voulue ...*"; Jules Michelet, *Histoire de France. Moyen Age*, (Paris, 1893–99), Vol. 3, 198–202.

used to assess the historical literature dealing with leprosy. In recent years, in the wake of *la nouvelle histoire* ("the new history") in France, research in Europe has not simply focused on criticizing and correcting these recurring stereotypes, but has also completely reopened the sinister file of medieval leprosy.

Renewal of Research in France

François-Olivier Touati's remarkable medieval history thesis on leprosy in the ecclesiastical province of Sens, located in the heart of the Paris Basin, begins with a historiographic analysis of the disease. This thesis, defended at the Sorbonne in 1992 was published in the 1990s.[3] Almost ten years earlier, in 1983, Françoise Bériac defended her own thesis on people with leprosy in the Aquitaine (published in 1990).[4] She continued this important research, extending it to cover all of France, publishing this work in 1988.[5] These two historians, by their vital research, have promoted renewed interest in the subject and research methods, thereby expanding what is known and indeed bringing about an indispensable reassessment of the field over the past two decades.

This research was based on what was called *la nouvelle histoire*, the daughter of the Annals school. It was a vitally important influence in determining the evolution of historical research in France in the second half of the twentieth century. In the 1960s and 1970s, supporters of new history techniques turned to ethnology, itself revolutionized by the success of Claude Lévi-Strauss's structural anthropology.[6] Having dominated the field, ethnology took over, giving new meaning to research in

---

3   Touati, *Maladie et société au Moyen Age. La lèpre, les lépreux et les léproseries dans la province ecclésiastique de Sens jusqu'au milieu du XIVᵉ siècle* (PhD Dissertation, University of Paris I Panthéon-Sorbonne, 1992); edition under the same title (see note 1 above). An inventory of sources, bibliography and atlas/index of leprosaria were published separately as *Archives de la lèpre, Atlas des léproseries entre Loire et Marne au Moyen Age* (Paris, 1996). A critical edition of two cartularies and one collection of charters of leprosaria are yet to be published.

4   Françoise Bériac, *Lèpre et société en Aquitaine, XIIIᵉ–XVIᵉ siècles* (PhD Dissertation, University of Paris IV Sorbonne, 1983); abridged edn, *Des lépreux aux cagots* (see note 1 above).

5   F. Bériac, *Histoire des lépreux au Moyen Age. Une société d'exclus* (Paris, 1988).

6   Structural anthropology attempts to identify in each socio-cultural system an unconscious structure underlying institutions and customs, so as to build a model of interpretation of all observable facts by comparing different systems. Lévi-Strauss's structuralism attempts to reach the universal from the singular: "il faut et il suffit d'atteindre la structure inconsciente, sous-jacente à chaque institution ou à chaque coutume, pour obtenir un principe d'interprétation valide pour d'autres institutions et d'autres coutumes"; Claude Lévi-Strauss, *Anthropologie structurale* (Paris, 1958), p. 28. As an example, Lévi-Strauss calls *structures élémentaires de la parenté* ("kinship elementary structures") kinship systems that vary from one society to another, but are in fact based on universal, underlying and unconscious rules such as the principle of reciprocity.

the field of anthropology as borrowed from English social and cultural anthropology. In France, the term "anthropology" had previously been applied only to physical anthropology.

From this fusion of history and ethnology was born "historical anthropology," in which the sphere of history was considerably expanded by the appropriation of new subjects of study and a diversified approach to the material. As a result, both the body and disease became the subjects of historical investigation that combined social and cultural anthropology with physical anthropology, thereby re-appropriating to the field of historical anthropology the concept of the *histoire des mentalités* into social history.[7] The anthropological dimension, including its structuralist component, was thoroughly adopted by Touati when he showed what language, mental representations and behaviors associated with disease reveal about the structures of a society at a given time.

It is also in Touati's work of that we find the aspiration of reaching total history (*l'histoire totale*) that is inherent in *la nouvelle histoire* and historical anthropology. Total history addresses a very old aspiration shared by Michelet and other pioneers: that is, to work toward creating an integral resurrection of the past through an examination of all its aspects.[8] Ethnology looks in the same way to create a global understanding of all peoples by integrating into research an essential concept of French sociologist and ethnologist Marcel Mauss. This is the concept of a *fait social total* ("total social fact"),[9] an individual fact which can refer to the whole of a system by revealing its deep structures.[10]

---

7   The historian Jacques Le Goff notes a difference between the French concept of *mentalité*, which is more affective as compared to the more cognitive and intellectual English meaning of the word 'mentality'; J. Le Goff, "Les mentalités. Une histoire ambiguë," in *Faire de l'histoire*, ed. Jacques Le Goff and Pierre Nora, Vol. 3 (Paris, 1974), 126, n. 13. In France, even before the Second World War, the *histoire des mentalités* was promoted by the Annals school. This new "anthropological" approach to the study of history broadly expanded the field of interest and approach by employing multiple research methods. Everything could be a source, and everything a subject: feelings, representations, knowledge, beliefs, systems of relationship and social values (love, marriage, violence, honor), stages of life, links between biological and social issues (attitudes toward life, body, disease, death) and so on – in short, everything that related to the *outillage mental* ("set of mental tools") of a civilization or an epoch, all the perceptions, conceptualizations, expressions, and categories of action that structure both individual and collective experience.

8   "Pour retrouver la vie historique, il faudrait patiemment la suivre en toutes ses voies, toutes ses formes, tous ses éléments ... rétablir l'action réciproque de ces forces diverses ... comme résurrection de la vie intégrale"; Michelet, *Histoire de France*, Vol. 1 (1869), Preface.

9   Marcel Mauss, "Essai sur le don," *Année sociologique*, 2nd series, 1 (1923–24), re-published in *Sociologie et anthropologie*, 4th edn (Paris, 1991), 273–9. See also Lévi-Strauss, "Introduction à l'oeuvre de Marcel Mauss," *Sociologie et anthropologie*, xxivff., and Touati, "Histoire des maladies, histoire totale? L'exemple de la lèpre et de la société au Moyen Age," *Sources. Travaux historiques*, 13 (1988), 4–5.

10   "Une autre voie de l'histoire globale s'est également définie en référence au fait social total selon Marcel Mauss, entendons par là un fait social particulier qui renvoie à l'ensemble

The work of Françoise Bériac and Touati can be placed in relation to the intellectual concept of *histoire-problèmes*, the themes of which clearly echo the concerns of our time about body and disease (such as AIDS) and unwanted members of our own society.[11]

The authors explore the full extent of leprosy as a phenomenon observed within various medieval social systems, and they measure the complexity of the relationship of these societies to their sufferers. One illustration of the technique they pioneered can be seen in a case study from Evreux in Normandy.[12] The research project involved re-evaluating the exclusion of people with leprosy and the segregative function of the leprosarium in the Middle Ages. In the twelfth and thirteenth centuries, people with leprosy were found to be living collectively in an open brotherhood, and not in a prison or sepulchral world. They lived a conventual existence, one that very probably arose from an original eremitic experience, and that was socially, religiously and economically integrated.[13] While certainly located outside the city at that time, the community was still to be found at the very junction of expanding rural and urban worlds, even located on a field made sacred by local processions that led around the city. Later, in the fourteenth to sixteenth centuries, the integration of the community continued, but by means of a different association. This fraternal community gradually gave way to an ecclesiastical benefice, and the leprosarium was incorporated into municipal institutions, largely to benefit the burghers (that is, the burghers controlled their local leper house, and they were often the only persons to keep the right to enter it). This change excluded people with leprosy from the house and marginalized those that retained the right to enter it. Their homeless and wandering peers were caught up in the rising pauperism, exciting fears and reaction to "the impure" and "the stranger." The result was that the exclusion of people with

---

d'un système et qui en révèle les structures profondes"; Guy Bourdé and Hervé Martin, *Les écoles historiques* (Paris, 1983), pp. 261–2.

11 The *histoire-problèmes* is not the investigation of historical problems! Those *problèmes* are the subject matter researched by the historian so as to understand past and present. On one hand they are problems of the epistemological nature of history itself, while on the other they are problems relating to subjects of history. One well-known example is the problem of different times of history, as pointed out by Fernand Braudel in his thesis, *La Méditerranée et le monde méditerranéen à l'époque de Philippe II* (Paris, 1966). Regarding our subject, another problem came first: are body and disease objects of history?

12 Bruno Tabuteau, *Une léproserie normande au Moyen Age. Le prieuré de Saint-Nicolas d'Evreux du XIIᵉ au XVIᵉ siècle. Histoire et corpus des sources* (PhD Dissertation, University of Rouen, 1996) (copies are available through Thèse à la carte, Presses Universitaires du Septentrion, BP 199, F-59654 Villeneuve d'Ascq cédex).

13 See also B. Tabuteau, "De l'expérience érémitique à la normalisation monastique: étude d'un processus de formation des léproseries aux XIIᵉ–XIIIᵉ siècles. Le cas d'Evreux," in *Fondations et oeuvres charitables au Moyen Age*, ed. Jean Dufour and Henri Platelle (Paris, 1999), 89–96 (published proceedings of the 121st National Congress of the Historical and Scientific Societies, Nice, 1996).

leprosy became indistinguishable from that of "the Jews," prostitutes, beggars and vagrants of all kinds.

A Total Heuristic Approach

The dynamic renewal of historical research into leprosy, people with leprosy and leprosaria was a main factor in a general progress in the study of hospital history and medieval welfare. This progress has continued, to create an anthropological and "globalized" update to the long tradition of charting the history of charitable institutions that started in the nineteenth century.[14] For instance, Daniel Le Blévec in his thesis research used the same approach when he undertook a study of leprosaria in the lower Rhone region in the Middle Ages.[15]

Marcel Mauss introduced the total social fact as an heuristic principle. Similarly, as expressed by Touati, to study the history of diseases requires a total heuristic approach. Such an approach, in the spirit of the new history, requires in turn a complete awareness of the corpus of relevant documents and knowledge of all historical sciences.[16]

And so, modern historians of leprosy continue to publish carefully researched editions of texts as they follow in the footsteps of learned archivists and scholars of the past two centuries. Two types of documents from leprosaria have held special attention: cartularies, and statutes and regulations. In his thesis, Touati edited the cartularies of the Popelin in Sens and Saint-Lazare in Meaux located in the Paris Basin.[17] For Normandy, there is an English edition of the cartulary of Saint-Gilles of Pont-Audemer published in 1978, and the cartulary of Saint-Nicolas of Evreux edited by the present author.[18] Damien Jeanne is currently preparing an edition of five other Norman cartularies: two from Caen, and one each from Bayeux Falaise

---

14 Touati, *Maladies, médecines et sociétés. Approches historiques pour le présent*, 2 vols (Paris, 1993), Vol. 1, 13 (published proceedings of the 6th Conference of the Association Histoire au Présent, Paris, 1990); Touati, "Un dossier à rouvrir: l'assistance au Moyen Age," in *Fondations et oeuvres charitables*, 23–5 (see note 13 above).

15 Daniel Le Blévec, *Recherches sur l'assistance dans les pays du Bas-Rhône du XIIe siècle au milieu du XVe siècle* (PhD dissertation, University of Paris IV Sorbonne, 1994); edition: *La part du pauvre. L'assistance dans les pays du Bas-Rhône du XIIe siècle au milieu du XVe siècle*, 2 vols (Rome, 2000); see "Les léproseries," 2: 822–46, esp. p. 823.

16 Mauss, "Essai sur le don," *Sociologie et anthropologie*, 274; Touati, "Histoire des maladies, histoire totale?", 5, 8; Jacques Le Goff, "L'histoire nouvelle," in *La Nouvelle Histoire* (Paris, 1988), 38–9.

17 See also Touati, "Cartulaires de léproserie dans la France du Nord (XIIIe–XVe siècle)," in *Les cartulaires*, ed. Olivier Guyotjeannin et al. (Paris, 1993), 467–501 (published proceedings of the Round Table of the Ecole nationale des Chartes and the GDR 121 CNRS, Paris, 1991); Simone Lefèvre, ed., *Recueil d'actes de Saint-Lazare de Paris 1124–1254* (Paris, 2005).

18 Simone C. Mesmin, *The Leper Hospital of Saint Gilles de Pont-Audemer: An Edition of its Cartulary and an Examination of the Problem of Leprosy in the Twelfth and Early*

and Bolleville. Outside France, there is an Italian edition of the cartulary of Santa Croce in Verona that was published in 1989.[19]

The need for published critical editions of statutes and regulations in corpuses has been voiced by historians gathered at Göttingen (1995) and Rouen (1998) led by Françoise Bériac.[20] Data processing (onomastic, thematic and lexical data) of suitable collections of edited texts would help to recognize families of statutes or regulations, thereby allowing for an examination of the structural aspects of leper houses. Even without using such a process, the Belgian historian and archivist Walter De Keyzer has already tried his hand at comparing clearly related statutes of the leprosaria of Hainaut which was the focus of his thesis.[21]

Twelfth-century statutes describe very conventual systems and attest to a preponderance of people with leprosy in these houses. However, in the thirteenth century, the number representing healthy staff increases along with their importance. For example, in the case of Cambrai, individual prebends were substituted for community goods, that is, instead of goods that are pooled within a religious community. Then later in the thirteenth and fourteenth centuries, episcopal supervision gave way to lay administration.[22] Looking at the great number of surviving documents by geographic region, the quantity of statutes and regulations seen in Flanders, Brabant and Hainaut appears to be connected with the strength of the communal movement in this region.

It was also at the 1995 Göttingen meeting that the goal of mapping the locations of all leprosaria was formulated. This work was already being undertaken in Germany by the Association of the Leprosy Museum of Munster.[23] Martin Uhrmacher at the University of Trier mapped Rhineland leprosaria.[24] In France, Nicolas Louis, a student of Michel Mollat, created an atlas of the hospitals and leper houses of the

---

Thirteen Century (PhD dissertation, University of Reading, 1978). Tabuteau, *Une léproserie normande au Moyen Age. Le prieuré de Saint-Nicolas d'Evreux du XIIᵉ au XVIᵉ siècle.*

19 Annamaria Rossi Saccomani, *Le carte dei lebbrosi di Verona tra XII e XIII secolo* (Padua, 1989).

20 Round Tables of the Group of Göttingen (see notes 22, 30, 44 and 47 below).

21 Walter De Keyzer, *La lèpre en Hainaut. Contribution à l'histoire des lépreux et des léproseries, du XIIᵉ au XVIᵉ siècle* (PhD dissertation, University of Brussels, 1992).

22 See also W. De Keyzer, "L'évolution interne des léproseries à la charnière des XIIᵉ et XIIIᵉ siècles: le cas de l'évêché de Cambrai," in *Lépreux et sociabilité du Moyen Age aux Temps modernes*, ed. Bruno Tabuteau (Rouen, 2000), 13–20 (published proceedings of the 2nd Round Table of the Group of Göttingen, Rouen, 1998); *Cahiers du GRHIS*, 11 (the Historical Research Group of Rouen University), and "Lépreux et léproseries dans le comté de Hainaut au Moyen Age," in *Recueil d'études d'histoire hainuyère offertes à M.-A. Arnould* (Mons, 1983), 521–44.

23 The association is Gesellschaft für Leprakunde, Münster. Its annual journal, *Die Klapper* ("The Clapper"), in existence since 1986, specializes in the history of leprosy. The museum is Lepra-Museum, Kinderhaus, Münster; URL: <www.uni-muenster.de/Rektorat/museum/d2muselm.htm>.

24 Martin Uhrmacher, *Leprosorien in Mittelalter und früher Neuzeit*, in *Geschichtlicher Atlas der Rheinlande*, VIII(5) (Cologne, 2000).

western part of the country in 1980.[25] In 1996, Touati produced a good atlas/inventory covering the Paris Basin.[26] A particular high point in the systematic, historical and archeological study of leper houses in the western part of Normandy is found in the work of Damien Jeanne, whose research even employed aerial photography.[27] Laurence Aubert, while a student at the University of Rouen, used a similar method in researching leper houses in the lower Seine valley.[28] Using the geographical distribution of the leprosaria helps us to understand population and organization of space at the time of their appearance around the twelfth century. This work reflects the religious, economic and social dynamics out of which they arose and in which they were involved. A case in point is the quite remarkable instance of a small rural leprosarium in the diocese of Bayeux. Situated at the center of a radiating plan of parcels of land, the role that the leprosarium played in the gradual clearing of the land for agriculture can be seen.[29]

The indispensable contribution made by archeology and physical anthropology to what is now known about leper houses and the epidemiology of the disease is widely acknowledged by historians of leprosy.[30] Some examples in France are: an excavation in the Chartres area (Gallardon, 1981 and 1984) that has been in progress since 1998 in Normandy of a complete leprosarium situated close to the estuary of the Seine,[31] and excavations especially in Bessin by Damien Jeanne and anthropologist Mark Guillon (1992 and 1996).[32] There were also excavations in Château-Thierry (1989) in Saint-Lazare of Angers (1991), of the cemetery of Saint-Lazare of Tours

25 Nicolas Louis, *Essai d'atlas historique des hôpitaux et léproseries dans l'Ouest de la France au Moyen Age* (MA Dissertation, University of Paris IV Sorbonne, 1980).

26 Touati, *Archives de la lèpre.*

27 Damien Jeanne, "Les lépreux et les léproseries en Normandie moyenne et occidentale au Moyen Age. Orientations de recherches," *Cahiers Léopold Delisle*, 46(1–2) (1997), 19–48, and "Les léproseries du diocèse de Bayeux du XIe à la fin du XIVe siècle: essai d'inventaire archéologique et architectural," in *Archéologie et architecture hospitalières de l'Antiquité tardive à l'aube des Temps modernes*, ed. François-Olivier Touati (Paris, 2004), 325–89 (proceedings of the conference at the University of Paris XII, Créteil, 1999).

28 Laurence Aubert, *Prospection topographique et archéologique sur des sites de léproseries dans les boucles de la vallée de la basse Seine.* (MA Dissertation, University of Rouen, 2003).

29 Jeanne, "Les lépreux et les léproseries en Normandie moyenne et occidentale au Moyen Age," 41–2; Jeanne, "Les léproseries du diocèse de Bayeux," 342–3.

30 See especially Tabuteau, "Histoire et archéologie de la lèpre et des lépreux en Europe et en Méditerranée du Moyen Age aux Temps modernes," *Annales de Normandie* 49 (1999), 567–600 (2nd Round Table of the Group of Göttingen, Rouen, 1998).

31 Marie-Cécile Truc et al., *Aizier (Eure), chapelle Saint-Thomas, fouille programmée d'une léproserie médiévale*, annual reports since 1998.

32 Jeanne, "Quelles problématiques pour la mort du lépreux? Sondages archéologiques du cimetière de Saint-Nicolas de la Chesnaie, Bayeux," *Annales de Normandie*, 47 (1997), 69–90; Mark Guillon, Vincent Grégoire, Damien Jeanne, "Histoire, archéologie et anthropologie d'une léproserie et de ses morts: Putot-en-Bessin," in *Archéologie et architecture hospitalières de l'Antiquité tardive à l'aube des Temps modernes*, 45–101. There were also some unpublished

(1992–93), at a site on the outskirts of Lyon (1994-95), and of the cemetery of Saint-Ladre of Reims (2000) and in Saint-Lazare of Beauvais (2003).[33] Outside France, Vilhelm Moeller-Christensen's early research in Naestved, Denmark in the 1950s and 1960s can be cited. Other important excavations were also carried out at Aachen (prior to 1991), and those led by John Magilton at Chichester (1986–87, 1993).[34] Also in England, numerous skeletons were recovered from a medieval churchyard at Norwich that showed evidence of leprosy, although there are no records of particular links with any of the leper houses or hospitals in or around the city![35]

---

archeological soundings in Eastern Normandy, in Sotteville-sur-Mer (1993) and Saint-Lazare of Gisors (1996).

33 Gallardon: M. Vie, "Fouilles de la maladrerie de Gallardon (Eure-et-Loire)", *15 années de recherches archéologiques en Eure-et-Loir* (Maintenon, 1991), 59–61; Château-Thierry, Angers: Collective, *Saint-Lazare: histoire d'une léproserie et d'un faubourg d'Angers, XIIe–XVIIe siècle* (Angers, 1997). François Blary and Denis Bougault, "Etude archéologique et paléopathologique de la maladrerie de Château-Thierry," in *Archéologie et architecture hospitalières*, 103–33. Tours: Christian Theureau, "Etude anthropologique, ossements humains et lèpre. Fouille de sauvetage de la chapelle Saint-Lazare (Tours, Indre-et-Loire)," *Mediarch*, February 1994. See also Theureau (no title), the chronicle of excavations in the review *Archéologie médiévale*, 23 (1993), 24 (1994). Beauvais: Jean-MArc Fémolant, "Un diagnostic archéologuque sur la maladrerie Saint-LAzare de Beauvais", *Hôpitaux et maladreries au Moyen Âge: espace et environnement* (amiens, 2004), 353–61; Lyon: Tommy Vicard, *La maladrerie de Balmont du Moyen Age à l'époque moderne: un espace de reclus (Lyon, 9e arr.). Document final de synthèse* (Lyon, 1995); Christine Dumont, *La maladrerie de Balmont. Rapport d'anthropologie* (Lyon, 1995). Reims (not yet published yet).

34 On Naestved, see Vilhelm Moeller-Christensen, *Bone Changes in Leprosy* (Copenhagen, 1961); Johannes G. Andersen, "Studies in the Mediaeval Diagnosis of Leprosy in Denmark : An Osteoarchaeological, Historical and Clinical Study," *Danish Medical Bulletin*, 16, Suppl. IX (1969), 1–124. On Aachen, see Egon Schmitz-Cliever, "Das mittelalterliche Leprosorium Melaten bei Aachen in der Diözese Lüttisch (1230–1550)," *Clio Medica*, 7 (1972), 13–34; Wilfried Maria Koch, "Das Leprosorium Aachen-Melaten. Vorbericht der Ausgrabungen 1988/89," *Zeitschrift des Aachener Geschichtsvereins*, 96 (1989), 409–36. On Chichester, see Frances Lee and John Magilton, "The Leper Hospital of St James and St Mary Magdalene, Chichester," in *Burial Archaeology: Current Research, Methods and Developments*, ed. Charlotte A. Roberts et al., BAR British Series, 211 (1989), 249–65, and "The Cemetery of the Hospital of St James and St Mary Magdalene, Chichester," *Chichester Excavations*, 11 (2001); J. Magilton, "Further Excavations at the Leper Hospital Cemetery, Swanfield Drive," in *The Archaeology of Chichester and District* (Chichester, 1993), pp. 11–12, and "The Hospital of St James and St Mary Magdalene, Chichester, and Other Leper Houses," in Tabuteau, *Lépreux et sociabilité*, 81–91; Isla Fay, *The Experience of Leprosy in the Middle Ages: The Cemetery of SS James and Mary Magdalene, Chichester* (MSc. Dissertation, University of Bradford, 2002).

35 The Castle Mall, Archaeological Project, Norwich, by the Norfolk Archaeological Unit, 1987–91 (to be published in the *East Anglian Archaeology* monograph series). See Sue Anderson, "Leprosy in a Medieval Churchyard in Norwich," in *Current and Recent Research in Osteoarchaeology*, ed. S. Anderson (Oxford, 1998) (published proceedings of the 3rd Meeting of the Osteoarchaeological Research Group, Leicester, 1995).

Interdisciplinary Study and International Collaboration

In 1978, the French medievalist Jacques Le Goff insisted on the importance of conducting interdisciplinary research as he called for a renewal in all fields of history, an aspiration of *la nouvelle histoire*.[36] The objective he proposed was: to create "a total history that progressed by assessing each problem and would be carried out through international collaboration."[37] In addition, he gladly admitted that the new history was not the sole prerogative of France.[38]

It is the same process for the study of leprosy as for the whole field of history; interdisciplinary cooperation must extend beyond the historical sciences. As was the case with ethnology, historians have a great deal to learn from anthropological surveys. Two such surveys are: one carried out by Paola Antolini on the permanence of *cagots*' marginality in a hamlet of the Spanish Basque Country; and the other is Anne Bargès's work on people with leprosy in Mali.[39] Even before the 1980s and 1990s, the move toward interdisciplinary research was increasing in medieval literature, especially in the field of mental and cultural representations. This is most notably to be seen in writings by Saul Nathaniel Brody and Geneviève Pichon-Berruyer's thesis.[40] Touati, joined the chorus of those historians of disease advocating the necessity of bringing history and medicine closer together.[41] An excellent example of this collaborative process at work is to be found in a proposed explanation for endemic leprosy's regression in the medieval period. Taken together, Mirko Grmek's concept of *pathocenosis* and Keith Manchester's work proposes that antagonistic

---

36 Le Goff, "L'histoire nouvelle," 35–37.

37 "L'objectif d'une histoire totale, progressant par problèmes et réalisée par la collaboration internationale reste l'objectif à atteindre"; ibid., 62.

38 Ibid., 52–4. For a general view of the changes in history in the world after the Second World War, see Geoffrey Barraclough, *Main Trends in History* (New York, 1978, expanded and updated by Michael Burns in 1991); in French: *Tendances actuelles de l'histoire* (Paris, 1980).

39 Paola Antolini, *Au-delà de la rivière. Les cagots: histoire d'une exclusion*, (Paris, 1991), p. 160; Anne Bargès, *La grande maladie. Le sens du trouble et de l'alliance entre institution occidentale, Afrique mandingue, lèpre et modernité* (PhD Dissertation, University of Aix-Marseille, 1997); A list of her publications can be found at: <http://perso.wanadoo.fr/anthropologique/ARTICLES/PUBLI.html>. On the reappearance of leprosy in contemporary Spain, see Josep Bernabeu Mestre and Teresa Ballester Artigues, "Le retour d'un péril: la lèpre dans l'Espagne contemporaine, 1878–1932. Aspects démographique et socio-sanitaire," *Annales de démographie historique* (1997), 115–34.

40 Saul N. Brody, *The Disease of the Soul. Leprosy in Medieval Literature* (London, 1974); Geneviève Pichon-Berruyer, *La représentation médiévale de la lèpre* (MA Dissertation, University of Paris III Sorbonne-Nouvelle, 1979); *La mutité, la surdité, la claudication, la cécité et la lèpre. Etude de représentations médiévales* (PhD Dissertation, University of Paris III, 1992).

41 Touati, "Histoire des maladies, histoire totale?", 4–5, and *Maladie et société au Moyen Age*, pp. 16–17; *Maladies, médecines et sociétés*, 1: 11–17. See also Bériac, *Histoire des lépreux au Moyen Age*, pp. 269–70.

immunological relationship between leprosy and tuberculosis form an explanation for this phenomenon. Such arguments have shown how historians must take the biological factor into account when researching the dynamics of past societies.[42]

The Third International Congress on the Evolution and Palaeoepidemiology of Infectious Diseases, held at Bradford England in 1999, was devoted to leprosy (clinical leprosy, skeletal diagnosis of leprosy, molecular diagnosis of leprosy in skeletal material, history and paleopathology of leprosy worldwide). It clearly illustrated the dialogue between the historians and those researching the history of leprosy using biomedical techniques.[43] Encouragement for the future of research can be found in the doctoral training programs in paleopathology based at such centers as the University of Bradford's Department of Archaeological Sciences and Copenhagen's Medical History Museum, which is run by the anthropologist Pia Bennike. Both universities hold large collections of skeletons, including those from the Naestved excavations, which give evidence of leprosy.

The congress of Bradford encouraged an interdisciplinary approach and an international collaboration for leprosy research. Although of lesser scale, the meetings held at Göttingen and Rouen, in 1995 and 1998, led the way in this area. These two were the first to hold round-table meetings of the Group of Göttingen. This international group of specialists in the history of leprosy was founded in October 1995, arising from the commitment shared by its German and French founders to make it possible to break out of the researchers' isolation and to go beyond linguistic barriers and historical and academic traditions.[44] This author has the privilege of coordinating the group at its beginnings at the University of Rouen, which allowed for a second round table to be organized.[45] Today, the Group of Göttingen includes several historians (mainly medievalists), archeologists, anthropologists, as well as physicians and paleopathologists, representing many European nationalities. Further, it has also attracted American researchers, for one Luke Demaitre from the

---

42 The concept of pathocenosis is based on the premise that whole pathological states are present within a population at a given time, and are to be considered in their relationship to symbiosis, indifference or antagonism; Mirko D. Grmek, *Les maladies à l'aube de la civilisation occidentale. Recherches sur la réalité pathologique dans le monde grec préhistorique, archaïque et classique* (Paris, 1983), 14–17, 297–300; Keith Manchester, "Tuberculosis and Leprosy in Antiquity: An Interpretation," *Museum of Applied Science Center for Archaeology*, 4 (1) (1986), 22–30.

43 *The Past and Present of Leprosy. Archaeological, historical, palaeopathological and clinical approaches*, ed. Charlotte A. Roberts, Mary E. Lewis and Keith Manchester (Oxford, 2002) (published proceedings of the 3rd International Congress on the Evolution and Palaeoepidemiology of the Infectious Diseases, Bradford, 1999).

44 Antje Schelberg, "Approches actuelles de l'histoire de la lèpre et des lépreux au Moyen Age," *Bulletin de la Mission Historique Française en Allemagne*, 30/31 (1995), 36–40 (published proceedings of the 1st Round Table of the Group of Göttingen, Göttingen, 1995).

45 "Histoire et archéologie de la lèpre et des lépreux en Europe et en Méditerranée du Moyen Age aux Temps modernes," report and proceedings, B. Tabuteau, ed., *Lépreux et sociabilité du Moyen Age aux Temps modernes*.

University of Virginia. At its third meeting at Trier, Germany in December 2000, the Group of Göttingen adopted the Latin name *Historia Leprosorum*. It is this Trier meeting that became the starting point for an European program to publish leprosaria statutes and regulations.[46]

Conclusion

This number of successive, groundbreaking, European academic meetings demonstrates the vitality of this area of historical research. This truly international research employs multiple approaches which focus on fully "totalizing" the study of leprosy.[47] For about twenty-five years, this vitality has likewise been expressed by a boom in academic research and solid scholarship. Some aspects of this research have already been mentioned, but others must not be overlooked.

More researchers and their work in the field should be recognized (see footnotes for bibliography). These are notably: Charlotte Roberts (the organizer of the Bradford conference), Stephen R. Ell, Carole Rawcliffe, Max Satchell, Gerard A. Lee, Giuseppina De Sandre Gasparini, Piera Borradori, Robert Jütte, Antje Schelberg.[48]

---

46 Kay P. Jankrift and M. Uhrmacher, eds, *Leprosorien und ihre Statuten. Normiertes Leben zwischen Ideal, Vorstellung und Abbild* (yet to be published) (proceedings of the 3rd Round Table of the Group of Göttingen, Trier, 2000).

47 There were many other such meetings that were at least partly devoted to leprosy. For example, the 2002 conference organized by Pascal Montaubin at the University of Picardy France: *Hôpitaux et maladreries au Moyen Age: espace et environnement*, about the location and the rural or urban environment of medieval hospitals and leprosaria (proceedings published at Amiens in 2004); a meeting organized by B. Tabuteau, in Normandy in 2005: "Archéologie et patrimoine des maladreries médiévales dans le nord de la France"; a session held at the annual International Medieval Congress at Leeds in 2001, concerned with the topic: "Leprosy, Exclusion, and Exile" (no published proceedings). There was also a conference at the University of Bielefeld Germany in 1986 on disease and society from the twelfth to the eighteenth centuries. The proceedings of this conference were published as: Neithard Bulst and Robert Delort, eds, *Maladies et société (XIIᵉ–XVIIIᵉ siècles)* (Paris, 1989).

48 See, among several articles, Stephen R. Ell, "Blood and Sexuality in Medieval Leprosy," *Janus* (Leiden), 71 (1984), 153–64; "Diet and Leprosy in the Medieval West: The Noble Leper," *Janus*, 72(1–3) (1985), 113–29; "Reconstructing the Epidemiology of Medieval Leprosy: Preliminary Efforts with Regards to Scandinavia", *Perspectives in Biology and Medicine*, 31(4) (1988), 496–506; Carole Rawcliffe, "Learning to Love the Leper: Aspects of Institutional Charity in Anglo Norman England," *Anglo Norman Studies*, 23 (2001), 233–52; Peter Richards, *The Medieval Leper and his Northern Heirs* (Cambridge, 1977; repr. in paperback, 2000); Max Satchell, *The Emergence of Leper Houses in Medieval England, 1100–1250* (PhD Dissertation, University of Oxford, 1998); Gerard A. Lee, *Leper Hospitals in Medieval Ireland, with a Short Account of the Military and Hospitaller Order of Saint Lazarus of Jerusalem* (Dublin, 1996); Gian Maria Varanini and Giuseppina De Sandre Gasparini, "Gli ospedali dei 'malsani' nella societa veneta del XII-XIII secolo," in *Citta e servizi sociali nell'Italia dei secoli XII–XV* (Pistoia, 1990), 141–200 (published proceedings of the 12th International Conference on Historical and Art Studies of Pistoia, 1987); Piera Borradori,

Kay Peter Jankrift, Rafaël Hyacinthe, David Marcombe and Piers Mitchell have been especially interested in the Order of St Lazarus of Jerusalem and leprosy in the Crusades.[49]

Certainly, many problems remain. Due largely to the cost of publication, too much work is still unpublished or of limited distribution (most notably editions of sources in unpublished theses and dissertations). There are significant expenses involved just in the preparation of translations alone. Further, there are an insufficient number of archeological excavations. This, taken together with the difficulty of preserving what vestiges of extant leper houses remain, has a profound influence on future research. A disinterest in leprosaria on the part of civil and scientific authorities is a further problem.

Modern research progresses nevertheless. By showing that the medieval sufferers of leprosy were fully involved in a multiform evolution of complex societies, and not the tragic and eternal pariah of an immutable world of coercion, the landscape of the history of leprosy has now been changed to be re-established on a better understanding of social constructs. This new perspective is: "Middle Ages in the mirror of leprosy." This "totalizing," multidisciplinary field of historical studies deserves a name. By analogy with historical anthropology, and in order to differentiate it from modern medical leprology, we suggest that it should be called "historical leprology."[50]

Mourir au Monde. Les lépreux dans le Pays de Vaud (XIIIᵉ–XVIIᵉ siècle) (Lausanne, 1992); Robert Jütte, "Lepra-Simulanten," *Medizin, Gesellschaft und Geschichte*, 6 (1995), 25–42; Antje Schelberg, *Die Leprosen in der Mittelalterlichen Gesellschaft* (PhD Dissertation, University of Göttingen, 2001); Walter De Keyzer et al., *La lèpre dans les Pays-Bas (XIIᵉ– XVIIIᵉ siècles)* (Brussels, 1989).

49 Kay P. Jankrift, *Leprose als Streiter Gottes. Institutionalisierung und Organisation des Ordens vom Heiligen Lazarus zu Jerusalem von seinen Anfängen bis zum Jahre 1350* (PhD Dissertation, University of Münster, 1995; edition: Münster, 1996); Rafaël Hyacinthe, *L'Ordre de Saint-Lazare de Jérusalem en Occident: histoire, iconographie, archéologie* (PhD Dissertation, University of Paris I Panthéon-Sorbonne, 2000), published as *L'Ordre de Saint-Lazare de Jérusalem au Moyen Age* (Millau, France, 2003); David Marcombe, *Leper Knights: The Order of St Lazarus of Jerusalem in England, 1150–1544* (Woodbridge, 2003); Piers D. Mitchell (among several papers), "An Evaluation of the Leprosy of King Baldwin IV of Jerusalem in the Context of the Mediaeval World," in *The Leper King and His Heirs: Baldwin IV and the Crusader Kingdom of Jerusalem*, ed. Bernard Hamilton (Cambridge, 2000), 245– 58, and "The Myth of the Spread of Leprosy with the Crusades," in *The Past and Present of Leprosy*, 171–7.

50 In 1997, members of the Group of Göttingen adopted the term "leprography" to designate the field of study devoted to historical and cultural understanding of leprosy and people with leprosy. While this designation mainly concerns human and social sciences (history, archaeology, ethnology, sociology), it also encompasses art, literature, physical anthropology and leprology. The German historian Antje Schelberg criticized this new concept for its formal lack of scientific rigor, as well as the leprography/leprology dualism; see "Unification des recherches sur la lèpre et les lépreux sous le nom de 'léprographie'? Une réponse," in *Lépreux et sociabilité*, 93–8). Might it be replaced by the notion of "social and cultural leprology," which would include historical leprology?

Bibliography

Andersen, Johannes G., "Studies in the Mediaeval Diagnosis of Leprosy in Denmark: An Osteoarchaeological, Historical and Clinical Study," *Danish Medical Bulletin*, 16, Suppl. 9 (1969), 1–124.

Anderson, Sue, ed., *Current and Recent Research in Osteoarchaeology* (Oxford, 1998).

Antolini, Paola, *Au-delà de la rivière. Les cagots: histoire d'une exclusion* (Paris, 1991).

Bériac, Françoise, *Histoire des lépreux au Moyen Age. Une société d'exclus* (Paris, 1988).

Bériac, Françoise, *Des lépreux aux cagots. Recherches sur les sociétés marginales en Aquitaine médiévale* (Bordeaux, 1990).

Bernabeu Mestre, Josep and Ballester Artigues, Teresa, "Le retour d'un péril: la lèpre dans l'Espagne contemporaine, 1878–1932. Aspects démographique et socio-sanitaire", *Annales de démographie historique* (1997), 115–34.

Borradori, Piera, *Mourir au Monde. Les lépreux dans le Pays de Vaud (XIIIe-XVIIe siècle)*, *Cahiers lausannois d'histoire médiévale*, Vol. 7 (Lausanne, 1992).

Bourdé, Guy and Martin, Hervé, *Les écoles historiques* (Paris, 1983).

Brody, Saul N., *The Disease of the Soul. Leprosy in Medieval Literature* (London, 1974).

De Keyzer, Walter, "Lépreux et léproseries dans le comté de Hainaut au Moyen Age," in *Recueil d'études d'histoire hainuyère offertes à M.-A. Arnould* (Belgium, 1983), 521–44.

De Keyzer, Walter et al., *La lèpre dans les Pays-Bas (XIIe–XVIIIe siècles)* (Brussels, 1989).

De Keyzer, Walter, "L'évolution interne des léproseries à la charnière des XIIe et XIIIe siècles: le cas de l'évêché de Cambrai," in *Lépreux et sociabilité du Moyen Age aux temps modernes*, *Cahiers du GRHIS*, 11 (Rouen, 2000) 13–20.

Ell, Stephen R., "Blood and Sexuality in Medieval Leprosy," *Janus*, 71 (1984), 153–164.

Ell, Stephen R., "Diet and Leprosy in the Medieval West: The Nobel Leper," *Janus*, 72 (1985), 113–29.

Ell, Stephen R., "Reconstructing the Epidemiology of Medieval Leprosy: Preliminary Efforts with Regards to Scandinavia," *Perspectives in Biology and Medicine*, 31(4) (1988), 496–506.

Grmek, Mirko D., *Les maladies à l'aube de la civilisation occidentale. Recherches sur la réalité pathologique dans le monde grec préhistorique, archaïque et classique* (Paris, 1983).

Jankrift, Kay P., *Leprose als Streiter Gottes. Institutionalisierung und Organisation des Ordens vom Heiligen Lazarus zu Jerusalem von seinen Anfängen bis zum Jahre 1350* (Münster, 1996).

Jeanne, Damien, "Les lépreux et les léproseries en Normandie moyenne et occidentale au Moyen Age. Orientations de recherches," *Cahiers Léopold Delisle*, 46(1–2) (1997), 19–48.

Jeanne, Damien, "Quelles problématiques pour la mort du lépreux? Sondages archéologiques du cimetière de Saint-Nicolas de la Chesnaie, Bayeux," *Annales de Normandie*, 1 (1997), 69–90.

Jütte, Robert, "Lepra-Simulanten", in *Medizin, Gesellschaft und Geschichte*, 6 (Stuttgart, 1995), 25–42.

Koch, Wilfried Maria, "Archäologischer Bericht 1988/89. Das Leprosorium Aachen-Melaten. Vorbericht der Ausgrabungen 1988/89," *Zeitschrift des Aachener Geschichtsvereins*, 96 (Aachen, 1989), 409–36.

Le Blévec, Daniel, *La part du pauvre. L'assistance dans les pays du Bas-Rhône du XIIe siècle au milieu du XVe siècle*, 2 vols (Rome, 2000).

Lee, Frances and Magilton, John, "The Leper Hospital of St James and St Mary Magdalene, Chichester," in *Burial Archaeology Current Research, Methods and Developments*, ed. Charlotte A. Roberts et al., BAR British Series, 211 (1989), 249–65.

Lee, Frances and Magilton, John, "The Cemetery of the Hospital of St James and St Mary Magdalene, Chichester," in *Chichester Excavations*, 11 (2001).

Lee, Gerard A., *Leper Hospitals in Medieval Ireland* (Dublin, 1996).

Lefèvre, Simone, ed., *Recueil d'actes de Saint-Lazare de Paris 1124–1254* (Paris, 2005).

Le Goff, Jacques, "L'histoire nouvelle," in *La Nouvelle Histoire*, new edn (Paris, 1988), 35–75.

Lévi-Strauss, Claude, "Introduction à l'oeuvre de Marcel Mauss," in *Sociologie et anthropologie*, 4th edn (Paris, 1991), ix–lii.

Magilton, John, "Further Excavations at the Leper Hospital Cemetery, Swanfield Drive," in *The Archaeology of Chichester and District* (Chichester District Council, 1993), 11–12.

Magilton, John, "The Hospital of St James and St Mary Magdalene, Chichester, and Other Leper Houses," in *Lépreux et sociabilité du Moyen Age aux temps modernes*, *Cahiers du GRHIS*, 11 (Rouen, 2000), 81–91.

Manchester, Keith, "Tuberculosis and Leprosy in Antiquity: An Interpretation," *Museum of Applied Science Center for Archaeology*, 4(1) (1986), 22–30.

Mauss, Marcel, "Essai sur le don," *Année sociologique* (1923–24), republished in *Sociologie et anthropologie*, 4th edn (Paris, 1991), 143–279.

Michelet, Jules, *Histoire de France. Moyen Age*, 16 vols (Paris, 1893–99).

Mitchell, Piers D., "An Evaluation of the Leprosy of King Baldwin IV of Jerusalem in the Context of the Mediaeval World," in B. Hamilton, ed., *The Leper King and His Heirs. Baldwin IV and the Crusader Kingdom of Jerusalem* (Cambridge, 2000), 245–58.

Moeller-Christensen, Vilhelm, *Bone Changes in Leprosy* (Copenhagen, 1961).

Montaubin, Pascal, ed., *Hôpitaux et maladreries au Moyen Age: espace et environnement* (Amiens, 2004).

Rawcliffe, Carole, "Learning to Love the Leper: Aspects of Institutional Charity in Anglo Norman England," *Anglo Norman Studies*, 23 (2001), 233–52.

Richards, Peter, *The Medieval Leper and His Northern Heirs* (Cambridge, 1977, repr. in paperback 2000).

Roberts, Charlotte A., Lewis, Mary E. and Manchester, Keith, eds, *The Past and Present of Leprosy* (Oxford, 2002).

Rossi Saccomani, Annamaria, ed. (Introduction by Giuseppina De Sandre Gasparini), *Le carte dei lebbrosi di Verona tra XII e XIII secolo* (Padua, 1989).

Schelberg, Antje, "Approches actuelles de l'histoire de la lèpre et des lépreux au Moyen Age," first round table of the Group of Göttingen, report in *Bulletin de la Mission Historique Française en Allemagne*, 30/31 (1995), 36–40.

Schelberg, Antje, "Unification des recherches sur la lèpre et les lépreux sous le nom de 'léprographie'? Une réponse," in *Lépreux et sociabilité du Moyen Age aux Temps modernes, Cahiers du GRHIS*, 11 (Rouen, 2000), 93–8.

Schmitz-Cliever, Egon, "Das mittelalterliche Leprosorium Melaten bei Aachen in der Diözese Lüttisch (1230–1550)," *Clio Medica*, 7 (1972), 13–34.

Tabuteau, Bruno, "De l'expérience érémitique à la normalisation monastique: étude d'un processus de formation des léproseries aux XIIe–XIIIe siècles. Le cas d'Evreux," in *Fondations et oeuvres charitables au Moyen Age* (Paris, 1999), 89–96.

Tabuteau, Bruno, "Histoire et archéologie de la lèpre et des lépreux en Europe et en Méditerranée du Moyen Age aux Temps modernes," 2nd round table of the Group of Göttingen, report in *Annales de Normandie*, 5 (1999), 567–600.

Tabuteau, Bruno, ed., *Lépreux et sociabilité du Moyen Age aux temps modernes, Cahiers du GRHIS*, 11 (Rouen, 2000).

Theureau, C., "Etude anthropologique, ossements humains et lèpre. Fouille de sauvetage de la chapelle Saint-Lazare (Tours, Indre-et-Loire)," in *Mediarch* (February 1994).

Touati, François-Olivier, "Histoire des maladies, histoire totale? L'exemple de la lèpre et de la société au Moyen Age," *Sources. Travaux historiques*, 13 (1988), 3–14.

Touati, François-Olivier, "Cartulaires de léproserie dans la France du Nord (XIIIe–XVe siècle)," in *Les cartulaires* (Paris, 1993), 467–501.

Touati, François-Olivier, *Maladies, médecines et sociétés. Approches historiques pour le présent*, 2 vols (Paris, 1993), Introduction, Vol. 1, 11–17.

Touati, François-Olivier, *Archives de la lèpre. Atlas des léproseries entre Loire et Marne au Moyen Age* (Paris, 1996).

Touati, François-Olivier, *Maladie et société au Moyen Age. La lèpre, les lépreux et les léproseries dans la province ecclésiastique de Sens jusqu'au milieu du XIVe siècle* (Paris, 1998).

Touati, François-Olivier, "Un dossier à rouvrir: l'assistance au Moyen Age," in *Fondations et oeuvres charitables au Moyen Age* (Paris, 1999), 23–38.

Touati, François-Olivier, ed., *Archéologie et architecture hospitalières de l'Antiquité tardive à l'aube des Temps modernes* (Paris, 2004).

Uhrmacher, Martin, *Leprosorien in Mittelalter und früher Neuzeit, in Geschichtlicher Atlas der Rheinlande*, ed. Franz Irsigler, VIII/5 (Cologne, 2000).

Varanini, G.M. and De Sandre Gasparini, Giuseppina, "Gli ospedali dei 'malsani' nella societa veneta del XII–XIII secolo," in *Citta e servizi sociali nell'Italia dei secoli XII–XV* (Pistoia, 1990), 141–200.

Section II
Physical Evidence: Archeology and Architecture Technology

Chapter 4

Excavations at St Mary Spital: Burial of the "Sick Poore" of Medieval London, the Evidence of Illness and Hospital Treatment

William White

Introduction

The recent redevelopment of the ancient fruit and vegetable traders' market in the Spitalfields district, to the east of the City of London, has provided a rare opportunity to study the design, layout and historic development of an English medieval hospital. A remarkable outcome of this episode in the urban archaeology of London was the excavation of a cemetery for the sick poor who were treated or cared for in the medieval Hospital of St Mary. More than 10 500 human skeletons were recovered, a record number for scientific excavation. These individuals, as opposed to those typically recovered from a conventional parochial cemetery, frequently showed signs of a disease process, possibly the ailment for which they were being treated at the Hospital. Here is an extremely important reference collection, which will provide research opportunities for the history of medicine for many years to come.

The detailed analysis of this enormous sample commenced in the summer of 2003. A team of four osteologists in the Museum of London Archaeology Service (MoLAS) have embarked upon the recording of the skeletons, and the results of this enormous project will not become fully available before the end of 2006. Important aspects of the work, such as the paleodemographic, paleopathological and epidemiology contingent in the analysis, await completion of the aforesaid recording phase. Meanwhile, interim comments made here are based on a visual scan of the skeletal remains that was performed to assess the post-excavation potential of the sample. Although quantitative statements are not possible at this stage of the investigation, the results to date do provide considerable information on the population that was served and housed by the hospital concerned.

History and Archeology of the Hospital

The Augustinian Priory and Hospital of the Blessed Virgin Mary without Bishopsgate, known colloquially by its contraction, "St Mary Spital," was founded in AD 1197 by a group of wealthy London merchants, who donated lands along the then ancient highway running north out of the City, modern Bishopsgate. The eminent founders included Walter Brunus, who was to become Sheriff of London in 1202–1203, his wife Roisia, Walter fitz Ailred, John Bloundie, William de Elie and Wymarke de Ebgate.[1] Although it was but one of several hundred hospitals founded in England during the twelfth century, St Mary Spital grew to be the largest hospital in medieval London. The Hospital was destroyed in the 1540s following the Dissolution of the Monasteries, but the site survives today as a Scheduled Ancient Monument, registered by English Heritage (GL162).

Major archeological excavations were performed by the Museum of London Department of Greater London Archaeology in the surrounding properties in Spital Square, Norton Folgate and Bishopsgate in the 1980s. These explored the foundation's original design, building construction and expansion phases. Subsequent work by MoLAS (1998–2003) within Spitalfields Market, bounded by Lamb Street and Brushfield Street, further explored these aspects. But it is the excavation of the Roman and medieval cemeteries on the site which provided the key interest.

From its inception, the establishment had a special responsibility for pregnant women (until the time of their delivery) and for destitute women and their children. The original foundation charter has been lost, but William Dugdale summarized this information in his *Monasticon Anglicanum* (1830). Burials of newborn children were encountered in the 1980s during excavations of the ruins of the Priory and Hospital buildings. One of the most important buildings so excavated was the Infirmary, which had provided 60 hospital beds at the time of the re-foundation in AD 1235, 30 for women and 30 for men. Expansion of the Infirmary buildings in the early fourteenth century raised the total to 90, with double occupation of beds allowing the capacity to rise to 180 inmates.

Reconstructions made chiefly as the result of archeological findings reveal that the Infirmary was a building with a T-shaped plan, therefore differing from other known hospital infirmaries such as those at St Dôl or Jerusalem.[2] Women were housed in one "ward," that is, in a wing of the building facing the ward for the men, and separated from it by the Chapel. The latter was a structure built perpendicular to the long axis of the Infirmary building. However, the area excavated most recently was chiefly the cemetery for the "sick poore" of medieval London, those who had died while resident or undergoing treatment in the Hospital.

Leprosaria tended to be sited outside the London city wall, but although St Mary Spital was in a similar situation to them, it was not an isolation hospital of

---

1   Christopher Thomas, Barney Sloane and Christopher Phillpotts, *Excavations at the Priory and Hospital of St Mary Spital, London* (London 1997), pp. 19–21.

2   Piers D. Mitchell, Chapter 14 in this volume.

this type. Nevertheless, the role of St Mary Spital as a hospital altered over time. At its foundation, St Mary's was intended to house the poor and the sick as the concomitant of benefiting the souls of the group of citizens who inaugurated this hospital. Subsequently, the institution extended its assistance to pilgrims, migrants, the elderly and the homeless by providing almshouses in addition to the infirmary function.

The archeological excavations have disclosed more than 10 500 burials. As was claimed earlier, this constitutes a world record for a scientifically excavated and documented group. The enormous sample has yet to be analyzed in detail, so in what follows there can only be a foretaste of what will be revealed given sufficient time.

Some of the burials were of persons of high status in the community, shown by their lavish interment in lead or stone-cut coffins. Several were definitely priests because they had been buried with a pewter chalice and patten, "dummy" liturgical items symbolic of their calling and office. However, the vast majority of the burials were simple, individual, shrouded interments made without coffins. However, it was found that a great many, accounting for over 3 000 of the total, were buried in mass graves: 20–42 people buried in (up to five) layers of bodies in pits, presumably the result of an epidemic or some other catastrophe. Not all were in the conventional east–west orientation, and some had been interred face down, rather than in the usual supine position. Owing to the fact that the date(s) for the use of the cemetery span the fourteenth century, there is the temptation to ascribe these hasty burials to victims of the "Black Death," brought out from the City for disposal. Unfortunately, the few radiocarbon dates available so far tend to cluster around the end of the thirteenth century. Are these people the victims of some earlier Plague epidemic, hitherto unrecorded, or of a different catastrophe entirely? More information is required, including carbon dating of further selected burials. The research will include also attempts to find traces of disease organism DNA in the bones of people buried in these mass graves.

Another medical emergency that was distressingly common was death during childbirth and there were many such examples at this site. Obstetric death, in which both mother and full-term fetus died, may have been an unfortunate but common failure of the institution's particular role in caring for pregnant women. Quite apart from this, the bodies of neonates and infants were encountered with great frequency.

Excavation and Post-excavation Techniques

During the excavation of neonate and infant burials, in order to retrieve all the tiny bones concerned, they were block-lifted with the associated soil then washed in running water over a 1 mm mesh sieve and laid out to dry. Larger skeletal elements such as the skull and limbs of adults were also washed over sieves, which tended to trap broken bone fragments, loose teeth and the small bones of the wrists and hands. These operations, the cleaning, washing and drying of excavated human bone are termed "processing," and the workers responsible for accomplishing these activities are known as "bone processors." When the bones were retrieved from graves dug into the local brick earth, the soil often could be removed readily; however, as the majority of the graves were cut into the London clay, the soil tended to adhere more persistently to bone and thus require greater attention. At the most intensive period of the cemetery excavation an astonishing fifty or so human skeletons were lifted per day. These in turn required the ministrations of 12 such processors. This represented a very large, perhaps unique, effort in British archeology. It also presented a remarkable sight, with all 12 processors involved in industrial-scale processing, drying and marking the bones with serial context numbers.

Two osteologists were based on the archeological site, and one of their duties was the assessment of the potential of the cumulative sample of medieval skeletons. They examined the condition of the bone, and determined the extent of each skeleton that was present. The sample was divided coarsely into adults and juveniles, and the sex was estimated if obvious on rapid inspection of pelvis and/or skull. Despite the rapidity with which the scanning of bone had to be performed, it was possible to observe gross pathological changes. A consequence of this procedure, however, was that as a great many pathological conditions were not immediately apparent, it was not possible to calculate prevalence for each condition. The cases noted at this stage accordingly represent the minimum number for the lesions observed, for further examples will be apparent during the more detailed analysis.

Interim Review of Pathological Changes

The bulk of those buried in the cemetery (more than 7 000 individuals) ostensibly were those who originally had arrived at the hospital for care or treatment. It is not known whether the minority interred in the mass graves were inmates of the hospital or had been brought out of the city for extra-mural burial. While only a minority of diseases and illnesses suffered by mankind leave any trace on bones, a relatively high proportion of those buried in the Hospital's cemetery showed skeletal evidence for disease or injury. Thus, about one-third of those interred showed some form of skeletal pathology, as compared to those from a traditional medieval parish church cemetery, where the figure perhaps would be only one in ten cases. A selection of the diseases exhibited will be surveyed by type of illness.

Many conditions were congenital in origin. Thus, there was a single instance of achondroplasia (a person of restricted growth of the most common type) but several examples of cleft palate, an ailment that could not be treated by the surgeons of the period. It appears that the staff of the Hospital had no means of dealing with dislocations of the large joints, such as the shoulder and hip, and several examples of each type of severe disability were encountered among the dead.

Joint disease, as usual, was rather common. Overwhelmingly this was expressed as osteoarthritis of the spine and of the joints, but a minority of cases were of the rheumatoid variant of the disease. Rheumatoid arthritis used to be considered to be a "modern" disease, but this is no longer thought to be the case, given the growing catalog of cases seen among earlier peoples. There were several conditions that led to fusion of the vertebrae in the spine evident at the site. These included ankylosing spondylitis, a condition that reduced spinal mobility, kyphosis and scoliosis (types of curvature of the spine). The latter caused major disability, especially so when it led to paralysis and atrophy of the lower legs; several such cases were encountered in the Hospital cemetery. Also at the site, osteoporosis of the spine was seen in some of the older women.

One unusual condition of the spine seen at the site was diffuse idiopathic skeletal hyperostosis (DISH). In its extreme expression, the backbone has a bizarre appearance, with many of the vertebrae fused together with extra bone overgrowth resembling "dripping wax." DISH today tends to occur in men over the age of 50 years, obese, living on a calorie-rich diet. For monastic sites, such as St Mary Spital, this immediately invokes the image of the "Fat Abbot" or "Prior." Indeed, recent research suggests that DISH was an occupational disease of the higher clergy, so frequently does it appear in male skeletons from excavated monastic sites.[3]

There were many examples of infections that had afflicted the bones, possibly following injury, and these included osteitis (non-specific infection of bone), osteomyelitis (infection of bone extending into the bone marrow) and, most frequently, periostitis (bone reaction to infection of the periosteum, the fibrous coating of the bone). Among specific infections suffered by the medieval dead, tuberculosis was the most common. Although tuberculosis is generally thought of as a disease that affects soft tissues, in up to 5 per cent of cases changes are caused to the spine or joints. Thus, the disease could be demonstrated in the hip joint with destruction of the head of the femur. In other cases there were tubercular thoracic lumbar vertebrae, showing destruction of the spinal column: classic Pott's disease, involving curvature of the spine. The lesions of tertiary syphilis were seen in several skeletons, interestingly of presumed pre-Columbian date. Radiocarbon dating will be performed in pursuit of this intriguing possibility. In at least one case, that of a child, the disease appears to have been congenitally acquired.

There was neither skeletal nor documentary evidence that any of the conditions mentioned above were directly treated in the Hospital. Certainly, though, it is clear that at St Mary Spital a great deal of care was dispensed. This is evident from the fact that many of the interred persons had very severe disabilities and would have required considerable care and support from the hospital well into adulthood.

Elsewhere on site, however, there was evidence for medical attention and surgical intervention. Most examples concerned some form of physical trauma. Thus, a well-healed fracture of a femur revealed evidence of great skill in setting the bone using traction to produce an accurately aligned result, without shortening of the limb. The London Augustinians thus appear to have been better experienced than, say, the Cistercians at Stratford Langthorne Abbey (an archeological site only a few

---

3   Juliet Rogers and Tony Waldron, "DISH and the monastic life," *International Journal of Osteoarchaeology*, 1 (2001), 357–65.

miles away to the east), who do not seem to have accumulated the necessary skills. This may be because the Cistercians literally interpreted papal edicts of the twelfth century which prohibited consulting surgeons, and directed that one should put up with pain and rely on the power of prayer alone for healing.

Other healed fractures encountered included frequent examples of multiple-fracture of ulna and radius, the classic "parry fracture," where an arm is held up to ward off a blow, leaving the bones of the lower arm exposed to injury as a consequence. There were at least 15 fractured skulls; one certainly a victim of assault and showing multiple wounds. Trepanation was a form of surgery practiced in at least two men for the treatment of their skull fractures. The cranial wounds healed without infection, and this is further evidence for care in the hospital environment. Deliberate treatment included also a single instance of below-the-knee amputation. Some other possible forms of treatment are dealt with in Geoff Egan's report (see Chapter 5 of this volume).

Epilogue

The author had the privilege of working as one of the on-site osteoarcheologists during the St Mary Spital excavation. He is pleased that the detailed osteological and pathological analysis of the vast sample of medieval human skeletal remains has commenced at last. The medical results discussed above are to be regarded as provisional, and any disease prevalences quoted are therefore to be regarded as arithmetical minima. The aforementioned detailed analysis will greatly increase the number of cases in all categories. These results are awaited with great interest.

Chapter 5

Material Culture of Care for the Sick: Some Excavated Evidence from English Medieval Hospitals and Other Sites

Geoff Egan

The compilation of this paper has proved to be a journey from presumption, through uncertainty, to a final destination somewhat different from the one originally envisaged. Initially, the expectation was that medieval medical equipment, well known from writings like the treatise on surgery by Albucasis, would be readily identifiable among the large assemblages of finds from the Middle Ages excavated in London and elsewhere, not the least at the sites of hospitals. As it emerged, no specifically medicinal tool has been definitively identified from medieval England at all. Instead, a small number of items found in graves in hospital cemeteries do seem to represent medical interventions, and there are also some other objects in similar contexts that probably catered for primarily spiritual rather than bodily well-being.

Among some half a dozen sites of religious houses in London which have been the subject of recent fieldwork is the hospital site of St Mary de Fonte or St Mary Spital. The series of excavations here has produced a sizeable finds assemblage, only part of which has so far been published.[1] More widely in England, there are published groups of material from the hospitals of Maison Dieu at Ospringe in Kent,[2] the infirmary of the Hospital of St John the Baptist at Oxford,[3] St Giles by Brompton Bridge in North Yorkshire,[4] and St Bartholemew's Hospital in Bristol.[5] Somewhere here should be at least a few examples of medieval medical equipment, even if they had not been identified when the reports were written. Contemporary illustrations

1   Christopher Thomas, Barney Sloane and Christopher Philpotts, eds, *Excavations at the Priory and Hospital of St Mary Spital, London.* Museum of London Archaeological Service Monograph 1 (London, 1997).

2   G.H. Smith, "The Excavation of the Hospital of St Mary of Ospringe, commonly called Maison Dieu," in *Archaeologia Cantiana*, 95 (1979), 81–184.

3   Brian Durham, "The Infirmary and Hall of the Medieval Hospital of St John the Baptist," in *Oxoniensia*, 56 (1992), 17–75.

4   Peter Cardwell, "Excavations at St Giles Hospital by Brompton Bridge, North Yorkshire," in *Archaeological Journal*, 152 (1995), 109–245.

5   Roger Price and Michael Ponsford, *St Bartholomew's Hospital, Bristol: The Excavation of a Medieval Hospital 1976–8*, Council for British Archaeology Research Report 110 (York, 1998).

should be particularly useful to help define such items. The eleventh-century Arabic text on surgery and the tools used for it by Albucasis[6] was written in Spain, translated into Latin at Toledo in the next century, and reproduced several times through the remainder of the medieval period, supplemented in some manuscript versions by large numbers of drawings of varied merit of medical instruments. The most notable illustrations are arguably those in the editions of 1271–72 and 1465–66, which are reproduced in the volume cited here. The text's fame spread in Europe, particularly after its first printing at Venice in 1471, but it was already well known in medical circles in France from the thirteenth century onwards. From these two strands of evidence, it was hoped, some progress would be made with what appeared to be a neglected subject in the study of the material culture of the Middle Ages. On the other hand, perhaps hospital finds would not feature strongly for surgery at least, as Pope Alexander III in 1163 had forbidden the clergy to take part in any practice that involved the shedding of blood,[7] and so, from the late twelfth century, surgery was strictly the province of the laity.

In the event, it quickly became clear that for some reason obvious items of medical equipment, which are fairly prominent in many Roman assemblages (not only from the occasional burial of pertinent equipment in some non-Christian surgeons' or doctors' tombs, but also from the common appearance of various probes and extracting tools for domestic use in many sizeable finds groups), were completely absent from finds reports for the later period.

Aside from personal grooming tools from the Middle Ages, like nail cleaners, toothpicks and tweezers,[8] a few of which might occasionally have seen more serious use outside the routine to deal with specific ailments, medieval medical equipment was not discussed. In short, not one medical tool from the later period seemed to have been identified. It appears that the Romans are thoroughly exceptional when set against most other cultures from a variety of periods in the prominence in their archeological record of relatively common, readily definable medical equipment.[9]

An emphasis on the clerkly/religious activities of writing and reading is striking in the assemblages excavated at religious-house sites of the medieval period.[10] Along with book mounts and styli for writing on wax tablets, there are some spectacle frame fragments. The latter, of course, represent medical provision of a kind, presumably mainly or entirely for the staff of the institution whose working lives emphasized reading to a degree rare outside the few universities at that time. About

---

6   M.S. Spink and G.L. Lewis, *Albucasis on Surgery and Instruments* (London, 1973).

7   Margaret Rule, *The Mary Rose: The Excavation and Raising of Henry VIII's Flagship* (London, 1982), p. 186.

8   Geoff Egan and Frances Pritchard, *Dress Accessories*, *Medieval Finds from Excavations in London*, Vol. 3 (London, 1991), 377–83.

9   Ralph Jackson, pers. comm. For a range of Roman doctors' instruments, see Ralph Jackson, "Roman doctors and their instruments: Recent research into ancient practice," in *Journal of Roman Archaeology*, 3 (1990), 6–27.

10   Geoff Egan, in Thomas et al., *Excavations at the Priory and Hospital of St Mary Spital, London*, 109, Table 14, detailing various recurrent categories of finds from such sites.

half of the known medieval spectacle frames from England are from the sites of religious institutions, but these ones were monasteries as opposed to hospitals.[11] By the same token, the health of those within religious houses in general appears from the archeological evidence overall to have been somewhat better provided for than that of the population at large, at least within the terms of the period, with everything from water pipes of lead, to ensure a good supply of water, to air vents in the sleeping quarters, and of course, an infirmary. Hospitals usually shared all these features, but the archeological evidence so far does not place any greater emphasis on these provisions at such sites when compared with those from well-endowed religious institutions of all kinds. Among the large number of knives and other tools around at hospital sites, some could have had medical, even surgical, uses but there is little prospect of taking this beyond speculation, even with finds from the area of an infirmary.[12]

In 1545, within ten years of the Reformation (by one definition, the end of the Middle Ages), the warship *Mary Rose* sank, taking with it to the bottom of Portsmouth Harbour a barber-surgeon's chest assemblage of some 64 objects, which in that particular context can be associated with medical care.[13] Here too should be strong clues to help identify at least some of the range of the equipment used by the latest medieval surgeons and medical doctors. A complete but provisional list of the chest's contents is on the Web, and even this is difficult to apply with a positive result to the present problem. The chest contained little definitive that in isolation would immediately be identifiable as medical beyond one of the two small metal syringes found in the same cabin, which were probably intended to treat urethral problems (these instruments are archeologically unknown so far from medieval contexts, despite documentary references). Tall turned-wood containers (known as "drug jars" in loose archeological parlance) include one still containing peppercorns, which in this specific context can readily be seen as a medicine, though if found elsewhere these would probably have been seen as expensive culinary ingredients, and another vessel contained frankincense, to which the same applies. There were nine wooden handles (all iron components had corroded away), eight smaller ones of the same size as those of seventeenth-century wound-cauterizing tools and one larger handle (possibly for an amputation knife or saw), a mallet, eight razors, a whetstone and also five common stoneware jars. The knives and the mallet are again medicinal because of their associations rather than any distinctive form – found in another context they would be simply household tools. These aside, the earliest

---

11 See Geoff Egan, *The Medieval Household, Medieval Finds from Excavations in London*, Vol. 6 (London, 1998), 277, fig. 213 below, for part of a particularly decorative frame from the site of Merton Priory; the spectacles are from secular sites London finds, see Judy Stevenson, "A new type of late medieval spectacles frame from the City of London," in *London Archaeologist*, 7(12) (1995), 321–7.

12 For example, see Durham, "The Infirmary and Hall of the Medieval Hospital of St John the Baptist," 54–7; Price and Ponsford, *St Bartholemew's Hospital, Bristol: The Excavation of a Medieval Hospital 1976–8*, figs 69–72.

13 Rule, *The Mary Rose*, pp. 186–93.

actual surviving post-Roman medical tool known to the writer is a *spatula mundani*, a fearsome-looking constipation de-clogging device, found in an early context at the colonial site of Jamestown in Virginia. It is not possible to parallel this object with any of the published medieval illustrations accompanying texts of Albucasis,[14] and it misses being medieval on several important criteria, having apparently been invented by John Woodall and published by him in *The Surgions Mate* in 1617.[15]

It is only too easy to annex a range of finds – both objects and plants – as doctors'/surgeons' working stock. An exception, perhaps (though even this is by no means certain), is one wooden vessel (Fig. 5.1) among a group of 18 discovered together at the site of St Mary Spital, which could provide a more specific hint.[16] This is a markedly heavy double bowl of ash, which can be turned over (presumably after a wipe, or following consuming dry food from the first side) and used again from the other. No parallel has been found. In the specific context of a hospital, it is possible that this unique English find, which is noticeably heavy, could be a design specifically for a second person to hold steady by the foot while an infirm patient was fed.

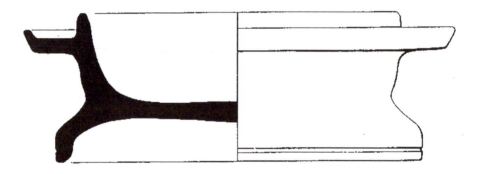

Figure 5.1   Reversible ash wood bowl of a design otherwise known only in
               Continental Europe, late thirteenth/early fourteenth century, found at
               the site of the hospital of St Mary de Fonte. The flange would have
               allowed a helper to support it while a frail patient ate or was fed (17 cm;
               from Egan, 1997, 60, Fig. 47, no. S68; drawing: Museum of London).

---

    14 Spink and Lewis, *Albucasis on Surgery and Instruments, passim*.

    15 Beverley Straube, "Medical equipment," in *Jamestown Rediscovery*, 3 (Richmond, 1997), 46–7, Figs 33–4; the illustration appears in the 2nd edn of Woodall.

    16 Geoff Egan, in *Excavations at the Priory and Hospital of St Mary Spital, London*. ed. Thomas et al. (London, 1997), Nos 60, 73 and 204, Fig. 47; Table 48, No. S68.

The transparency of glass was exploited in a specialized form of vessel, which is often found in groups in so-called "dissolution assemblages" thought to be from the clearance of religious houses at the Reformation. The urinal allowed a patient's state of health to be defined from the color of morning urine by the widely practiced pseudo-science of uroscopy.[17] Distilling equipment of glass or pottery is also a regular feature of later assemblages from religious houses, including apparent clearance groups. These vessels could have been for producing alcoholic beverages, which might include some medical preparations, or even for alchemical experimentation.[18]

Another unique vessel from London is a very rare object, which, although found in a dump at the Thames waterfront, some way from the nearest medieval hospital site, can be cited in the context of medical care, extended to include folk medicine. This is essentially a bowl of a normal early fifteenth-century form for treen, except that it made of the mineral jet (Fig. 5.2). This semi-precious stone occurs naturally at Whitby in Yorkshire, and was regularly used in the medieval period for jewelry and rosary beads, though it only exceptionally attains the dimensions required for an object like this bowl.[19]

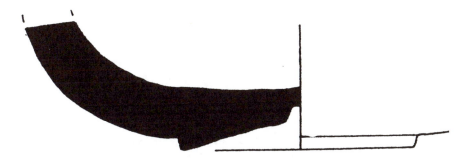

Figure 5.2   Turned bowl of jet, early fifteenth century. The form is essentially that of a routine table vessel, but the material suggests this was a magical object, which folk beliefs would have invested with special curative power (13.8 cm; Egan, 1998, 299, Fig. 227, no. 972; drawing: Museum of London).

---

17 Lynne Keys, "Glass Urinals," in Egan, *The Medieval Household*, 252–54; Danièle Foy and Geneviève Sennequier, *A Travers le Verre du Moyen Age au Renaissance*, Musées et Monuments Départementaux de la Seine Maritime (Paris, 1989), Fig. 374.

18 Stephen Moorhouse, "Pottery and Glass in the Medieval Monastery," in *Advances in Monastic Archaeology*, ed. Roberta Gilchrist and Harold Mytum, *British Archaeological Report* 227 (1993), 127–48.

19 Ibid.

An enduring magical tradition from the Roman period onwards associated jet with women, and from contemporary medieval lapidaries (manuals on the supposed properties of different stones to protect against ills and to heal), among a range of these virtues, jet put into water for three days gave it the power to ease the mother's labor pangs at a birth; how much more powerful a potion, then, if the water were put in a vessel that was itself of this remarkable material? There are a few instances from medieval graveyards in London where young women's bodies were buried with a full-term fetus still in the womb because some skeletal abnormality of the pelvis prevented delivery, for example at the cemetery of St Nicholas Shambles[20] – vivid demonstrations of the reality of the mortal danger that could attend childbirth in the medieval period, and which expensive "medical" equipment like the jet bowl probably sought to prevent. Magic and medicine, not so far apart in the Middle Ages, are equally difficult to pinpoint in the archeological record, and there is likely always to be an element of doubt for each instance suggested.

A group of seven of the gold coins issued under Henry VIII, known as "angels" from their designs with the archangel St Michael spearing the devil, is another of the notable finds from the hospital of St Mary Spital.[21] This small hoard was discarded just before the Reformation. These particular coins came to have a reputation as a powerful protection against evil because of the main image, together with a Latin legend meaning "Through your cross, save us, Christ, Redeemer" on the other side. This notion was underlined by the regular practice of donations by the monarch at special ceremonies, of angel coins that had been pierced for suspension so that they could be worn around the neck, to selected sufferers from the serious skin disease scrofula, otherwise known as the King's Evil.[22] This was in an attempt to alleviate or cure a condition on which contemporary medicine had little effect. Finds of gold coins are most unusual. The hoard would have been worth just under £3 in monetary terms at the time it was lost – a considerable sum. Although the precise circumstances of loss will never be known for the Spital group, it is perhaps more than coincidence that of all issues it should be the angel that figures in a find at a hospital; these seven coins may have been part of the institution's spiritual armory against disease as much as a substantial sum of worldly collateral.

More directly convincing still as remedial treatment are three sheet-metal plates found at the knees of burials during the latest (currently unpublished) fieldwork on the cemetery of St Mary Spital: two of made copper alloy have holes around the perimeter for attachment in some way (SRP98 acc. no. 2678 is oval and acc. no. 2973 is sub-round), and a possible cruder version of lead (acc. no. 1312) is just bent around a leg. The first two have clear traces of textile on the inner surface

---

20 William White, *Skeletal Remains from the Cemetery of St Nicholas Shambles, City of London,* London and Middlesex Archaeological Society Special Paper 9, 72, Fig. 58.

21 Geoff Egan, "Gold Angels: Cure or Commerce?", in *Archaeology Matters*, 8 (2002), unpaginated (Museum of London).

22 Helen Farquhar, "Royal Charities, Part 1: Angels as Healing Pieces for the King's Evil," in *British Numismatic Journal*, 12 (1915), 39–135.

– that is, the one towards the flesh. It seems probable that these are the remains of some kind of long-term, possibly replaceable protectors for bandaging (that is, the textile), which probably held some kind of medicinal preparation against an area of serious trauma or disease. Similar objects have been reported on other burials, like one at Merton Priory in Surrey near London (MPY86 site acc. no. 123, found at the knee of an individual with *osteochronditis desiccans*, from Stratford Langthorne Abbey (Cistercian), to the east of London, are another two candidates – HWLT94 site acc. no. 1,204, a 72 mm diameter roundel with perforations and traces of (?) linen, found at the right elbow of a burial, and acc. no. 1,255, 68 mm in diameter, both assigned to the late thirteenth/early fourteenth century), and there is another at the Gilbertine Priory of St Andrew at Fishergate in York.[23] The latter was at the knee on a skeleton with identifiable trauma. Not included in the published discussions cited of this phenomenon is a further instance excavated some time ago on a burial at Reading Abbey of a somewhat more elaborate two-part box-like arrangement of copper-alloy sheeting, each component having a larger concavity than those already noted, that would have accommodated a much more substantial amount of medicinal preparation[24] (an early description suggests that an ivy leaf was identified, but the whole ensemble needs an up-to-date reassessment). It is perhaps salutary to warn against drawing conclusions too readily at such an early stage of studying a limited number of instances. One commentator has suggested, because this phenomenon was first reported at a Cistercian site, that the practice was associated specifically with that order. Both of the London area sites at which examples have been noted are in fact Augustinian foundations, so it was not confined to one order only. The instance at York has been claimed possibly to be an adaptation of a remedy for a dislocated knee given in Hippocrates, which specified leather to hold a plate of copper – a metal with recognized curative properties – in a form of padded splint.[25]

The 11,000 burials being examined from St Mary Spital include cases of amputation and two rare instances of medieval trepanation (one with evidence of at

23 Gillian Stroud and Richard L Kemp, *Cemeteries of the Church and Priory of St Andrew, Fishergate, The Archaeology of York, The Medieval Cemeteries*, 12 (York, Council for British Archaeology) (1993), 217; Christopher J Knüsel, "Evidence for Remedial Medical Treatment of a Severe Knee Injury from the Fishergate Gilbertine Monastery in the City of York," in *Journal of Archaeological Science*, 22 (1995), 369–84; The best publication (in that it has a good photograph and interpreted drawing of what is left of the metal) of the York "medication sheet" is now: Patrick Ottaway and Nicola Rogers 2002, "Copper alloy medical plates," in *Craft, Industry and Everyday Life: Finds from Medieval York, The Archaeology of York*, 17/15 (York, Council for British Archaeology, 2002), 2 931–2, No. 15 226, Figs 1499–1500. Christopher Daniell, *Death and Burial in Medieval England 1066–1550* (London, 1997), pp. 139–40.

24 Charlotte Roberts and Keith Manchester, *The Archaeology of Disease*, 2nd edn. (Ithaca, NY, 1995), 97, Fig. 5.21.

25 Stroud and Kemp, *Cemeteries of the Church and Priory of St Andrew, Fishergate*, p. 381.

least six months' healing)[26] – the latter a serious operation probably carried out with a particular readily recognizable form of circular saw, but again, no such implement has yet been noted anywhere.

A handful of instances of these sheet-metal plates, apparently to hold medicinal preparations to the sites of disease or trauma, are now known or suggested on burials at medieval hospitals in England. The initial difficulties (particularly when dealing with soil conditions where preservation of metals is not good) in recognizing the potential significance of these unspectacular items means that many others may have been missed during fieldwork.

Also at Merton Priory was a burial with a series of strap accessories including a buckle in the pelvic area, along with a mass of corroded iron thought to be the remains of a surgical truss, perhaps for a scrotal disorder.[27] This was a priory, not a hospital, so the excavated items noted here from the burials at the site underline a broader point already made – medieval religious institutions in general had a better standard of medical provision than that available to the population at large. With a wider appreciation now of the existence of a variety of medicinal appliances that may be anticipated, it is almost certain that many more will be reported in the course of cemetery excavations.

Also excavated along with human burials at St Mary Spital are five papal lead seals (bullae) assignable to the fourteenth century, which were originally attached to documents.[28] The circumstances of these particular finds leave little doubt as to the nature of the perished documents they were intended to authenticate. These were indulgences, purchased from the Church and buried with an individual, who would in this way have to hand documentary evidence that his sins were already pardoned to show whatever authority confronted him at the resurrection of the dead.[29] The practice of selling indulgences seems to have been particularly prevalent during the Avignon papacies (1305–78); it certainly gave grounds for bitter accusations of corruption. The people who bought these five indulgences are now unknown, but another was found in the tomb of Sir Walter Manny, a prominent military leader who was laid to rest in his own religious foundation, the Charterhouse, located just to the north of the City of London.[30] Manny's bull has the name of Clement VI, who was in office 1342–52. In 1351 he is recorded as having given Manny the right to

---

26 Brian Connell, pers. comm. This work is still in progress. See William White, Chapter 4 in this volume, for a preliminary report.

27 Helen Ganiaris, report on surgical truss found on a burial, in Alison Steele, ed., report on excavations at Merton Priory (forthcoming).

28 Geoff Egan, in *Excavations at the Priory and Hospital of St Mary Spital, London*, ed. Thomas et al. (London, 1997), 69, Fig. 54, and 201, No. S2 with the name of Urban VI (1378–89). This was a burial in a chapel. See also SPT98 site acc. nos 599, 1 426, 2 028 and 2 268, all with that of Clement VI (1342–52).

29 With regard to seals in burials as amuletic, which is only one aspect of the story, see Daniell, *Death and Burial in Medieval England 1066–1550*, pp. 168–9.

30 D. Knowles and William F. Grimes, *The London Charterhouse* (London, 1954), pp. 49, 89–90 and Plate 3B.

select a confessor for deathbed absolution. The knight did not die until 1372, so if the document buried alongside him relates to this grant in 1351, he had made early provision for the time he would come to be laid to rest.

Other categories of finds occasionally accompany burials. The most common are pewter ware sets consisting of a chalice and a paten. There are five sets from St Mary Spital (SRP98 acc. nos. 1 394–5 from layer 7 652, nos. 1 657–8 from 8 942, nos. 2 779–80 from 12 565), and apparently unaccompanied chalices (no. 2 139 from 11 387 and no. 2 806 from 12 652). There are many others from a variety of other religious institutions.[31] These items were placed, as cheap substitutes for precious-metal plate that was too expensive to give up even for this solemn purpose, in the graves of priests so that they too would be prepared at the resurrection – in their case, to administer the sacraments to others newly risen. A remarkable wax chalice served the same purpose in a burial excavated at the site of Hulton Abbey in the Midlands.[32] With these grave goods the intention was clearly to administer to spiritual needs rather than the worldly concerns with ill health. An analogy may nevertheless be made between these respective concerns, the well-being of the soul and of the body, and the provision made for each.

Unknown in London so far are grave goods in the form of the lead/tin souvenir badges of pilgrims who had visited shrines as acts of devotion. Two of these trinkets accompanied a male burial with circulatory problems (*osteochondritis dissicans*) in the cemetery of St Giles by Brompton Bridge in North Yorkshire, one from the shrine of the Patriarchs Peter and Paul at Rome and the other from that of the Rood known as the *Volto Santo* ("holy face") at Lucca in northern Italy on the way to Rome.[33] In this instance, the intention of taking these treasured mementoes to the grave was to demonstrate the effort taken by a pious individual to travel to distant lands for his faith.

Although none is so far associated with a burial, finds of badges for St Anthony may have a special significance in the present context (his hospital on Threadneedle Street, within the walls of London, has not been excavated; several hospitals elsewhere in Europe belonged to this international order). *Tau*-form crosses that were the symbol of St Anthony are among the most frequently encountered of pilgrim souvenirs in England, and they are also known in Continental Europe.[34] The English

---

31 Daniell, *Death and Burial in Medieval England 1066–1550*, pp. 169–171, gives a listing of examples. Eight out of nine thirteenth-century burials at Lincoln Cathedral had these burial goods; see Rupert L. Bruce Mitford, "Chapter House Vestibule Graves and the Body of St Hugh of Avalon," in *Tribute to an Antiquary: Essays Presented to Marc Fitch*, ed. F. Emmison and R. Stephens (London, 1976), 127–40.

32 Brian Spencer and Frances Pritchard, "Pilgrim Souvenirs," in Peter Cardwell, *Excavations at St Giles Hospital by Brompton Bridge, North Yorkshire*, 201–2, Fig. 43, Nos 6 and 5; for the pathology, see 218, No. 1 659.

33 For example, see Brian Spencer, *Pilgrim Badges and Secular Souvenirs: Medieval Finds from Excavations in London*, 7 (London, 1998), pp. 177–18.

34 Brian Spencer on the pilgrim badges, in G.H. Smith, "The Excavation of the Hospital of St Mary of Ospringe, commonly called Maison Dieu," 145–47, Fig. 29, No. 179.

finds may well include ones from the London institution. The only other souvenir actually found at a hospital site (not in this instance from a human burial) is one for St John the Baptist from Amiens in northern France, unearthed at the site of Maison Dieu in Kent. Another potentially pertinent discovery from this site is a copper-alloy mount, perhaps from a late medieval purse frame, bearing a prominent *tau* cross.[35]

The saints represented by finds in graves and at hospitals may have had no obvious specific connection with health beyond a general power to channel healing. St Roche, who was a pilgrim afflicted with plague sores and so was thought to have had a particular sympathy with fellow sufferers, is so far not among them, nor are others the manner of whose martyrdom gave them power over parts of the body, like St Lucy for the eyes. The remarkable discovery at Canterbury of more than 230 pilgrims' badges in the River Stour at the Eastbridge presumably reflects some kind of cumulative mass votive thanks for successful journeys to this important pilgrim destination.[36] The range of shrines represented among the group is wide, both within England and on the Continent. About half are for the obvious local cult of Thomas Becket. Eighty-six of these are representations of the Head Reliquary, most of them being from different molds.[37] The significance of this assemblage for the present discussion is that the Eastgate Hospital, founded in *c.* 1175, right at the beginning of the Becket cult, was located on the south side of the river here.[38] It is likely that at least a proportion of this concentration of souvenirs was left behind by pilgrims who had received comfort, if not a cure for sickness, at Becket's shrine and the adjacent hospital. Some at least of the discarded trinkets could be votive offerings from pilgrims still living, as opposed to the exclusively dead hospital inmates on whom this chapter has largely concentrated.

One variety of holy water container (*ampulla*) from Canterbury, which was found on the Thames waterfront in London and is assigned to the mid-thirteenth century (Fig. 5.3) has a legend which succinctly sums up the idea of saintly power to cure sickness. Along with an image of the archbishop, it is inscribed *optimvs egrorvm medicvs fit Toma bonorvm* ("Thomas [Becket] is the best doctor for the pious sick") – in this case, through the miraculous power of water once held in the vessel.[38] What this object catered for was bodily sickness, but only for those who were spiritually sound.

---

35 Brian Spencer, "Medieval Pilgrim Badges Found at Canterbury, England," in *Lost and Found: Essays on Medieval Archaeology for HJE van Beuningen*, ed. Dory Kickcn, Jos Koldeweij and Johan ter Molen, *Rotterdam Papers*, 11 (Rotterdam, 2000), 316–26.

36 Ibid., p. 324, Fig. 20.

37 Ibid., p. 316.

38 See Spencer, *Pilgrim Badges and Secular Souvenirs*, pp. 52–53, No. 9.

5.3   Holy water container souvenir from Canterbury, mid-fourteenth century, found in London. The Latin legend around the figure of Thomas Becket means "Thomas is the best doctor of the pious sick" (6.7 cm; Spencer, 1998, 52–3, Fig. 9; photograph: Museum of London).

Archaeological evidence for medical care is generally elusive, particularly when it comes to trying to identify the tools of the doctor's and surgeon's trades. There is slightly firmer ground for identifying a limited range of medical interventions from burials at the sites of various medieval religious institutions – not just hospitals. What is arguably the most convincing evidence so far recognized in England is a series of clumsy metal devices, the full incidence of which is only beginning to be recognized. It is highly likely that more instances are likely to come under scrutiny. It is worth noting that even the most prolific occurrence of the sheet patches, the three at St Mary Spital, constitutes less than one sixth of 1 per cent of the approximately 11 000 burials excavated in the cemetery. Perhaps more surprising at first is the extent of survival of a variety of evidence for spiritual aid – a conclusion that corresponds well with Carole Rawcliffe's view of provision at medieval hospitals catering primarily for that realm rather than for temporal illnesses.[39] To give this, too, some perspective, the five indulgences found in graves and five chalices/patens from priestly burials at that same institution were together recovered from less than 1 per cent of the thousands of burials examined there. To put it another way, medieval medical provision is, so far, most readily evident in burials at religious institutions rather than more generally at hospital sites. Even at the former, it has at best been noted only in about 1 in every 200 excavated burials in an urban hospital cemetery (which is about the same as the statistic for the presence in the same series of graves of obvious religious goods). It may not be much, but at least it does show up, once one knows specifically what to look for. The incidence recognized of such provision can only increase as enhanced background knowledge accumulates to inform the excavator in the field. More widely, the prospects of definitively identifying medical tools from the Middle Ages for the moment does not look anything like as promising.

---

39 Carole Rawcliffe, "A Word from Our Sponsor: Patronage in the Medieval Hospital" (paper presented at the 36th International Congress on Medieval Studies, Kalamazoo, MI, May 2001).

Chapter 6

The Hospital of Notre Dame des Fontenilles at Tonnerre: Medicine as *Misericordia*

Lynn T. Courtenay

Introduction

The late thirteenth-century hospital of Notre Dame des Fontenilles at Tonnerre, whose infirmary, chapel and grounds survive (Fig. 6.1), attests vividly to an elite form of medical patronage that fused religious and secular institutions.[1] While this hospital, or *maison-Dieu*, remains far less known than the exceptionally well maintained fifteenth-century hospice at Beaune, the hospital at Tonnerre, whose splendid open ward was imitated at Beaune,[2] is a far more remarkable building for its time. In a wider context, Notre Dame des Fontenilles belongs to a period of notable increase in hospital foundations by secular patrons, specifically by lay women in France and the Low Countries. In general, as Jean Imbert and others have noted, the number of hospitals increased rapidly from about 1130 until the 1260s; in ducal Burgundy, this

---

1 This chapter represents a portion of a larger project on aristocratic patronage and medieval halls roofed in timber. My research has been facilitated by the generous help of the directors of the Municipal Hospital in Tonnerre, Madame Senellant-Paccot and Monsieur Jacques Maurel, and the staff member, Mademoiselle Lucie JoVale.

2 The Hospital of Notre Dame des Fontenilles forms part of the Muncipal Hospital of Tonnerre (Yonne) and has been restored as the Musée Hospitalier, open to the public. It contains notable sculpture, documents and artifacts, including a timber model (1988) of the great ward. The site became an historical monument in 1842, prior to the construction of the modern hospital (begun 1848). The major monograph on the hospital remains the museum booklet by Noël Quénée (hereafter cited as Quénée), *L'Hôpital Notre Dame des Fontenilles à Tonnerre*, 2nd edn (Tonnerre, 1979).

   The *hôtel-Dieu* at Beaune was founded in 1443 by Nicholas Rolin, chancellor of Philip the Good, Duke of Burgundy, and his wife, Guigogne de Salins. Like Tonnerre, the open ward has a paneled wooden vault. For more detail, see Anne Leflaive, *L'Hôtel-Dieu de Beaune et les hospitalières* (Paris, 1959); R. de Narbonne, *Hospices de Beaune: Hôtel-Dieu (Paris, 1988)*. Cf. hospital plans in Ulrich Craemer, *Das Hospital als Bautyp des Mittelalters* (Cologne, 1963); John D. Thompson and Grace Goldin, *The Hospital: A Social and Architectural History* (New Haven, CT, 1975).

Figure 6.1   Tonnerre: Notre Dame des Fontenilles. Infirmary exterior from the north-east (photograph: author).

expansion reached its zenith *c.* 1300.[3] Thus the establishment of the *maison-Dieu* at Tonnerre in 1293 in the northern part of the Duchy (diocese of Langres) belongs to this vital period in the development of a network of public assistance in France.

Like traditional canonical or monastic infirmaries, leprosaria and hospices, lay hospitals emerged adjacent to towns and along primary routes of travel as "houses" to receive and shelter pilgrims, to care for the sick and the poor, and to maintain and segregate communities of lepers. In exchange for fiscal endowment, these private charities offered considerable soteriological benefits to their founders and provided an important institutional outlet for personal piety, familial commemoration and architectural patronage. From a patron's personal perspective, the gains were both tangible and psychological, enhanced by an institution created to sustain the body, ease the mind and redeem the soul.

Typically, the organization of such lay hospitals was similar to but legally distinct from the infirmaries and leprosaria attached to canonical houses that generally provided urban welfare in the form of the *hôtels-Dieu*. Like private or corporate chantries, hospitals had consecrated altars, and most supported some kind of religious community to perform the necessary sacraments, masses and liturgical services. In northern Europe, the fundamental guidelines for management and conduct within hospitals like Tonnerre were based on the Rule of St Augustine, as noted by Jacques de Vitry (*c.* 1170–1240).[4] Given this Augustinian derivation, it is not surprising that statutes for medieval hospitals often have a general similarity. Thus the special provisions included by patrons form a critical variant and are an important source for individual agendas, the economic resources of the institution, and the nature of medical care

Hospital statutes of the period are characteristically more concerned with the internal organization and conduct of the religious community than with medical practice. The emphasis is on regimen, prayer and the sacraments that eased the life and death of the afflicted. Typically the lay brothers and sisters took vows of chastity, obedience, stability (permanence of residence) and the renunciation of personal property. Along with the poor for whom they cared, the brothers, sisters, novices

---

3   Jean Imbert, *Les Hôpitaux en France*, 4th edn (Paris, 1981), esp. pp. 36–63; Michel Mollat, *Les Pauvres au Moyen Âge* (Paris, 1978), trans. A. Goldhammer (New Haven, CT, 1986), pp. 146–57, and specifically, Alain Saint-Denis, "L'Assistance en Bourgogne ducale (XIᵉ–XVᵉ siècles)," in *Hôpitaux et Maladreries au Moyen Âge: Espace et Environment, Actes du colloque international d'Amiens-Beauvais 22, 23 et 24 novembre 2002*, ed. Pascal Montaubin, *Histoire Médiévale et Archéologie*, 17 (Compiègne, 2004), pp. 255–69.

4   "Vivunt autem secundum sancti Augustini regulam absque proprio et in communi sub unius maioris obedientia ..."; Jacques de Vitry, *Historia occidentalis*, 29, ed. John Frederick Hinnebusch (Freiburg, 1972). For French hospital statutes, the pioneering work is Lèon Le Grand, *Statuts d'Hôtels-Dieu et de léprosaria* (Paris, 1901); on the council of Paris in 1212 concerning hospital regulations, see Dorothy-Louise MacKay, *Les Hôpitaux et la charité à Paris* (Paris, 1923), pp. 43–5, and for a recent typological overview of hospital sources and rules, see Annie Saunier, "La trame hospitalière médiévale: hiérarchies ou réseaux?", in *Hôpitaux et Maladreries*, pp. 201–19.

and priests formed a legal corporate body that possessed an inalienable endowment held in perpetuity. In this system of incorporated charities, the poor and the sick, as perpetual owners, were a critical part of the economic and spiritual equation. Depending on the wealth and prestige of the foundation, communal "property" might well include rights to ecclesiastical revenues from tithes, altars and Church property that belonged in theory to the bishop's fiscal patrimony (*temporalia*). Thus hospitals came under the authority of canon law and were sufficiently important economically to require monitoring by the diocesan authorities from whom patrons often sought exemption, as stipulated at Notre Dame des Fontenilles. In addition to the hospital's exclusion from Episcopal jurisdiction (see below), the foundation charter at Tonnerre containing the statutes forms the basis for understanding the internal organization of the *maison-Dieu*, its architecture, the medical environment, and especially, the piety and aspirations of its founder, Marguerite of Burgundy and Nevers (1249–1308), Queen of Sicily and Jerusalem, and hereditary Countess of Tonnerre.

Marguerite of Burgundy and Nevers

While recent studies of aristocratic households and female influence and largesse have brought to light a number of independently minded women who were not saints, the foundations of Marguerite of Burgundy have received little notice apart from Meredith Lillich's monograph on the stained glass at Tonnerre and the church of Mussy-sur-Seine.[5] Thus Marguerite and her *maison-Dieu* at Tonnerre offer an important addition to the literature on the activity, religious piety and patronage of aristocratic women as well as to the history of medieval hospitals in France. As with other noble women with money and property, Marguerite's position as a royal widow with dower property and a countess in full control of her patrimony allowed her considerable choice as to how she would live after her husband's death.[6] Her decision to remain single and to lead a life of pious activity is manifest in her founding the splendid hospital complex at Tonnerre where she chose to retire.

Born in 1248 or 1249, Marguerite was the second of three surviving daughters of Matilde (Mahaut) de Bourbon (d. 1257) and Eudes of Burgundy and Nevers (d. 1266), son and heir of Hugues IV, Duke of Burgundy (1213–72). She was educated

---

5   Meredith P. Lillich, *The Hospital of Tonnerre and the Queen of Sicily, The American Philosophical Society* (Philadelphia, PA, 1998), 88: 3. It is surprising that Marguerite is not mentioned in Le Goff's discussions of Louis IX and Charles of Anjou in Jacques LeGoff, *Saint Louis* (Paris, 1996), and so briefly by Jean Dunbabin, "The Household and Entourage of Charles I d'Anjou, king of the Regno, 1266–85," *Historical Research* (2004), 77: 197, 313–36.

6   For comparative material, see Katheleen Nolan, ed., *Capetian Women* (New York, 2003); Loveday Lewes Gee, *Women, Art and Patronage from Henry III to Edward III: 1216–1377* (Bury St Edmunds, 2002); Shulamith Shahar, *The Fourth Estate*, revised edn (London and New York, 2003), and Theodore Evergates, ed., *Aristocratic Women in Medieval France* (Philidelphia, PA, 1999).

at the Abbey of Fontevrault, and then returned to the ducal court in Dijon.[7] In 1268, when she was 19 years old, Marguerite married the widower Charles of Anjou, the youngest brother of King Louis IX of France (St Louis, d. 1270). As Charles's queen at the lavish court in Naples, Marguerite, Queen of Sicily and Jerusalem, supervised her own extensive household, undertook the care of Charles's children, and presided over magnificent ceremonial occasions at the Regno court.[8]

In 1285, after Charles's death in Naples, Marguerite returned to France via the holy places of Rome, and brought back her husband's heart, which was buried in the Jacobin church in Paris.[9] Although Marguerite had the choice of several places to reside within her country, such as Ligny-le-Chatel, Montmirail or the fortified chateau of Argenteuil-sur-Armançon, she settled at the old chateau of Montbeillant at Tonnerre, where she possessed extensive domains and seigniorial rights, including that of titular defender of the Cistercian Abbey of Pontigny.[10] She was accompanied

---

7   The Abbey of Fontevrault (also Fontevraud, Maine-et-Loire) was founded by Robert of Abrissel *c.* 1099; it was a double monastery under the rule of the abbess. The convent was patronized by the French and English nobility, but it is mainly known for the tombs of the early Plantagenet kings of England, those of Eleanor of Aquitaine, Isabella of Angoulême, wife of King John of England, and the recently discovered burial of Count Raymond VII of Toulouse. Of general interest is Lindy Grant, "Aspects of the architectural patronage of the family of the counts of Anjou in the twelfth century," in *Anjou: Medieval Art, Architecture and Archaeology*, ed. John McNeill and Daniel Prigent (Leeds, 2003), pp. 96–110.

8   The primary sources for her life are: Robert Luyt, *La Princesse charitable et aulmoniere ou l'Histoire de la Reine Marguerite de Bourgogne, Comtesse de Tonnerre, Fondatrice du Grand Hôpital N. D. des Fontenilles en la ville de Tonnerre* (Troyes, 1653; repr. Tonnerre, 1979), p. 73 (hereafter cited as Luyt); Louis Le Maistre, "Marguerite de Bourgogne, reine de Naples, de Sicile, et de Jerusalem, comtesse de Tonnerre," *Annuaire historique du department de l'Yonne* (1867), 43–109, and Jean Fromageot "Marguerite de Bourgogne, Comtesse de Tonnerre," in *VIIe Centenaire de la Fondation de l'Hôtel-Dieu de Tonnerre, 1292–1992* (Tonnerre, 1992), pp. 3–7. The separate households of Marguerite and Charles are discussed in Dunbabin, "The Household and Entourage," 323–25, and also in Jean Dunbabin, *Charles I of Anjou of Anjou: Power, Kingship and State Making in Thirteenth-century Europe* (London and New York, 1998). Lillich's discussion of Marguerite's patronage includes sites other than the *maison-Dieu* and is most helpful; Lillich, *The Hospital of Tonnerre and the Queen of Sicily*.

9   Luyt, p. 42. It should be noted in connection with her extensive family ties that Marguerite's grandfather, Hugues IV, acted as regent in Naples during Charles's Tunisian campaign; Dunbabin, *Charles I of Anjou*, p. 86. Charles's architectural patronage in Naples is discussed extensively in: Caroline Bruzelius, "'ad modum franciae' Charles of Anjou and Gothic Architecture in the Kingdom of Sicily," *Journal of the Society of Architectural Historians* (1991), 50(4), 402–20, and more recently in *L'Europe des Anjou, Exhibition Catalogue*, 15 June–6 September 2001 (Fontevraud, 2001), pp. 52–56. See also Annick Beau, "Un grand prince capétien, époux de Marguerite de Bourgogne, Charles of Anjou," in *VIIe Centenaire de la Fondation* (Tonnerre, 1992), pp. 8–15.

10 For the connections between Marguerite and the Cistercians, see Lillich, *The Hospital of Tonnerre and the Queen of Sicily*, p. 71. The old chateau situated on the Montagne de Vieux-Château was built on the ruins of the Roman *castrum* high above the river valley; it

by members of her household, which included her personal confessor, Jean d'Icy, a small domestic staff, and Robert of Luzarches, her chief adviser and possible author of and adviser to the plan of Notre Dame des Fontenilles.[11] Later, Marguerite was joined at Tonnerre by two noble companions, Charles's orphaned granddaughter, Catherine de Courtenay, who was there briefly and intermittently, and the widow Marguerite de Beaumont, Princess of Antioch and Countess of Tripoli, who remained at Tonnerre for the rest of her life and was a co-executrix of the queen's estate.[12]

Between 1285 and 1293, Marguerite took vigorous steps to consolidate her inheritance and income, and to select her heir, William of Chalons.[13] In 1293, she undertook her greatest endeavor: the foundation of the perpetual charity of the *maison-Dieu* of Notre Dame des Fontenilles on her property just outside the city walls.[14] The hospital (or at least a substantial portion of it) was apparently constructed

---

was destroyed in 1414; Maximillian Quantin, *Répertoire archéologique du Département de L'Yonne* (Paris, 1868), p. 273.

11 Jean Fromageot, *Tonnerre et son comté des origines à la Révolution de 1789*, *Association bourguignonne des sociétés savantes*, 24 (Dijon, 1973). pp. 93–6. Robert of Luzarches (a town north of Paris) was presumably the son of Adam of Luzarches (d. 1277), Charles of Anjou's seneschal in Provence; Robert (d. 1309) probably came to Naples with other officials from northern France; he is mentioned in the foundation charter as the queen's "faithful cleric and member of her household and who also desired the establishment of the hospital" of which he was appointed its first master. He died at Tonnerre, and was buried in the chapel near Marguerite; F. Salet, "L'Hôpital Notre Dame des Fontenilles à Tonnerre," in *Congrès archéologique de France*, 116 (1958), 226; A. Challe (hereafter cited as Challe), *Histoire du comté de Tonnerre* (Auxerre, 1875), p. 94, and Dunbabin, *Charles I of Anjou,* p. 51.

12 Catherine de Courtenay (1274–1307) was the daughter of Phillipe de Courtenay (d. 1283) and Beatrice of Naples (m. 1273; d. 1275), Charles of Anjou's youngest daughter by his first wife, Beatrice of Provence (d. 1266). Catherine was an important heiress and the only granddaughter of Boudouin II, Emperor of Constantinople. In *c.* 1299–1300 (?) Catherine left Tonnerre and married the widowed Charles of Valois (1270–1325), the brother of King Philip IV, the Fair (1268–1314). One of the two beautiful polychrome statues remaining at the hospital is putatively the crowned figure of Catherine, but there is no agreement as to which females are represented. Catherine is consistently described as Marguerite's *nièce*, which in archaic French can mean a cousin, granddaughter or female relative. Luyt, p. 48, Fromageot, *Tonnerre et son comté*, p. 98. See also Ernest Petit, "Archives de l'hôpital de Tonnerre, le cartulaire, l'obituaire," in *Bulletin historique et philologique*, 1 (1906), 14–15, 30. Marguerite de Beaumont, like her companion, had no living children. She was the widow of Bohemond VII, Prince of Antioch and Count of Tripoli. Fromageot, *Tonnerre et son comté*, pp. 98–9.

13 Marguerite's heir, to whom she entrusted the jurisdiction of Tonnerre, was her nephew (the son of her sister, Alix, Countess of Auxerre), who became count of Tonnerre, although Marguerite retained the title of countess until her death. Fromageot, *Tonnerre et son comté*, pp. 93–100. On earlier property disputes among the heirs of Hugues IV involving Marguerite, see Jean Richard, *Les Ducs de Bourgogne et la formation du duché* (Paris, 1954), pp. 322–9, and Dunbabin, *Charles I of Anjou*, p. 36.

14 It is interesting to note that Tonnerre already possessed several hospitals or hospices, notably the leprosaria of St Blaise and the Hospital of the Order of the Holy Spirit, founded

in a remarkably short time; for, just two years later, on 16 March 1295, the foundation was blessed by Simon of Beaulieu (d. 1297), Cardinal-bishop of Palestrina and papal legate to France, in the presence of Marguerite, prelates of the region, clergy and people of Tonnerre. The hospital was placed under the direct authority of the Pope with the special protection of the King of France, thus exempting the community and its properties from any intervention or visitation by local ecclesiastical and lay authorities unless sanctioned by the master of the hospital, the countess or the future counts of Tonnerre. In a broader political sphere, this privileged charity represented a continuation of the Papal-Capetian alliance that had made Charles of Anjou King of Sicily. The exempt status is confirmed by subsequent papal intervention supporting the hospital in litigation *vis-à-vis* the Bishop of Langres.[15]

Since the hospital and Marguerite's new chateau shared the same site, it should be kept in mind that the combination of a religious institution with a secular, aristocratic household was bound to have implications for the overall plan (see Fig. 6.3). In this respect, the hospital of Notre Dame des Fontenilles provides a valuable example of the architecture of a planned residence and hospital in late thirteenth-century Burgundy. The archeology of the domestic architecture and its context remains a subject for future study.

Even from a modern perspective, Marguerite's decisions seem wise. Widowed at about age 35, she was clearly near the end of her childbearing years but could well expect to remain economically independent and active.[16] She could avoid a second political marriage, potentially dangerous pregnancies, and more importantly, atone for her past sins and those of her late husband. As patron of a self-perpetuating community for whom she provided, she could expect care in her own later years. She thus created for herself a comparatively austere but comfortable quasi-religious retirement within the social hierarchy of Capetian Burgundy. With the martial support of her nephew, the countess continued to exercise her property rights and remained physically present as the hospital's protector and servant, accomplishing the duties of both lordship and piety. Significantly, Marguerite never became a nun, but remained a lay countess within her modest but privileged household until her death in September 1308.

---

c. 1200 by Duke Hugues III (b. 1148) of Burgundy, Marguerite's great-great-grandfather; Fromageot, *Tonnerre et son comté*, pp. 34–8.

15 Henri Chaput, "Un hôpital d'autrefois: Notre-Dame-des-Fontenilles de Tonnerre," *Bulletin de la société française d'histoire de la médecine*, 1 (1902), 129.

16 An important recent study of aristocratic widows, although prior to the thirteenth century, offers useful paradigms for the context in which to place Marguerite; see Emmanuelle Santinelli, *Des Femmes Éplorées? Les veuves dans la sociétée aristocratique du haut Moyen Âge* (Villeneuve-d'Ascq, 2003). Privileged widows as patrons are discussed by Margaret W. Labarge, "Three Medieval Widows and a Second Career," in *Ageing and the Aged in Medieval Europe,* ed. Michael M. Sheehan (Toronto, 1990), pp. 159–72.

The Foundation

The foundation Charter of Notre-Dame des Fontenilles incorporates the rules for the community and offers considerable information on the internal and external organization of the *maison-Dieu*, its rights and economic assets.[17] It also provides a clear understanding of the motivations of the foundress, her provisions relating to medical care, and stipulations regarding the necessary buildings.

The Charter begins with a formal decree stating the reasons for this pious donation made at Tonnerre in 1293, "the Thursday after the Octave of Easter" (9 April):

> We, Marguerite, by the grace of God, Queen of Jerusalem and of Sicily, countess of Tonnerre make it known … that we, considering the word of the Gospel where one reads: 'Be merciful always, as your Father is merciful!' And considering the mercy of our Father … who gave us creation, redemption, and the bounty of earthly possessions, in order not to be judged ungrateful or displeasing to God, having compassion for the poor of Jesus Christ, and wishing to obey the Gospel … not only because we ought but also because it is within our means and desire to extend corporeal mercy … with the aspiration of receiving the recompense promised in the Gospel to all those who are merciful [that is] to receive eternal life, and to avoid the pain of those who are punished and who were not merciful, namely, the eternal fire, found a hospital or "*maison-Dieu*", and we establish it at Tonnerre in the street of the said place called Fontenilles.[18]

Although the opening is predictably formulaic and includes the persistent desire for salvation that accompanies pious donations throughout the medieval period, there is no reason to doubt its sincerity. Marguerite's motivations are as clear as they are traditional, so too her conviction that by offering temporal charity in this world, she would receive the promised spiritual rewards of the next. She draws a parallel between serving the "poor of Christ" and receiving the rewards of piety associated with the popular *imitatio Christi* and *vita activa* exemplified by the mendicants and outstanding female role models, such as St Clare of Assisi (1194–1253), her sister-in-law, Isabelle of France (1223–69), and St Elisabeth of Thuringia, to whom an altar in the chapel was dedicated (see below).[19]

---

17 The original manuscript of the foundation charter is on display in the *Musée Hospitalier*. The text is in Latin and has been translated into French by Challe and appended to his *Histoire du comté*, pp. 203–20; Chaput cites the charter frequently in French, and in places his translation differs slightly from Challe: Chaput, "Un hôpital d'autrefois," *passim*.

18 My English translation is from the French text published by Challe, *Histoire du comté*, pp. 203–4.

19 A well-published role model was Clare de Favorone, foundress of the female Franciscan order, the "Poor Clares," noted for her apostolic poverty and care for the sick; she was canonized shortly after her death (by Innocent IV in 1255); F.L. Cross, ed., *The Oxford Dictionary of the Christian Church* (London, 1957), pp. 446, 294. Isabelle of France was the sister of Charles of Anjou, and founded the Franciscan convent at Longchamp near Paris in 1259; she was known in her lifetime for her piety and charity. The foundation was richly endowed by Louis IX; however, Charles of Anjou, seems to have been especially interested

The Charter records explicit boundaries and visual landmarks for the hospital precinct, and then lists the buildings and their function. In addition to the infirmary, the hospital was to have: a chapel, or oratory, with four altars, the major one dedicated to the Virgin and the others to John the Baptist, Mary Magdalene and Elisabeth of Thuringia. The hospital also required a cemetery, lodgings for the staff, namely separate houses (*maisons*) for the master, the brothers, the matron, and the sisters, as well as various service buildings such as a wash house, cellars, kitchens and so on. All of these were to be entirely within the enclosure. Finally, the hospital should constitute and should remain hereafter, by hereditary right, a *seigneurie* with all its rights of justice.[20]

The delineation of the physical domain[21] is followed by a description of the legal realm, clauses of exceptions, jurisdiction and punishments for the infractions of rules or crimes committed within the hospital precinct. Exemptions for the hospital and its community are enumerated; the protection of the future counts of Tonnerre is enlisted to safeguard these rights, since any alienation of the endowment would jeopardize the security of a perpetual charity of this kind. The fiscal concerns and the protection of privilege seen here are, of course, far removed from the renunciation of all property and status exemplified in the extraordinary lives of SS Clare and Elisabeth; thus the foundation of the hospital at Tonnerre demonstrates how radical

---

in promoting Isabelle's potential canonization as well as that of his brother. See S. Fíeld, ed., *The Writings of Agnes of Harcourt, the Life of Isabelle of France and the Letter on Louis IX and Longchamp* (Notre Dame, IN, 2003) (hereafter cited as Field).

Elisabeth of Thuringia (1207–31) also known as St Elisabeth of Hungary, a contemporary admirer of St Francis, was an appropriate saint for Marguerite to emulate, since she was also of the high nobility and in widowhood became actively involved in her hospital. Elisabeth's asceticism and her radical rejection of wealth and power clearly made a profound impact on her generation, since procedures for her canonization began in 1235, shortly after her death. On female spirituality and the foundation of hospitals as a means to channel and institutionalize non-conformist and non-cloistered women, see Jo Ann McNamara, "The Need to Give: Suffering and Female Sanctity in the Middle Ages," in *Images of Sainthood in Medieval Europe*, ed. Renate Blumenfed-Kosinski and Timea Szell, (Ithaca, NY and London, 1991), pp. 199–221.

20 "… voulons qu'ils appartiennent dès maintennant comme à toujours audit hôpital par forme de droit successif, ensemble en domaine (seigneurie) et toutes sortes de justice esdits lieux"; Challe, *Histoire du comté*, p. 205. In this period, the term *seigneurie* describes an exclusive jurisdictional domain that pertains to a title or office and the associated feudal benefices and properties. Seigneural lordship, backed up by military force, involved extensive privileges, as well as the obligations traditionally assigned to rulers and peacekeepers.

21 Fromageot has calculated that the holdings of the hospital extended about 50 km north-east and 40 km in all other directions, with an estimated total property, excluding woodland, of 1,153 hectares, 55 ares, and 69 centiares, or about 2,850 acres; the woods were determined to be about 1,376 acres; Jean Fromageot, "Persistence d'une Fondation du XIIIᵉ Siècle à travers les âges, L'Hôpital-Hospice de Tonnerre," *Memoires de la Société pour l'histoire du droit et des anciens pays bourguignons, comtois et romands*, 26 (1965), 249–252.

ideals of one generation may become institutionalized into the traditional hierarchy in a later period.

Medicine as *Misericordia*

The religious ideals and liturgical life of the community provide more insight into the concepts that shaped the nature of the care given to the poor and infirm. The "medicine" was based on the Seven Acts of Mercy, derived from the Gospel of Matthew: "at which hospital we wish it known that the Seven [corporeal] Acts of Mercy are performed."[22] The charter makes it clear that Christ is identified with the poor and suffering, as in the Gospel, when Christ speaks: "… whatever you did for the least of these, you did for me" (Matt. 25:40), a phrase that is found in the prologue of similar charters, significantly, the redaction of the statutes (1265–70) for the hospital at Vernon, richly endowed by Marguerite's brother-in-law, St Louis.[23]

While altruistic compassion for the sick poor and esteem of the *vita activa* may have stimulated the foundation of numerous individual or collective charitable hospitals, fear of the Last Judgment and eternal punishment constituted powerful motives for the performance of the Seven Acts of Mercy: "Depart from me, you who are cursed into the eternal fire prepared for the devil and his angels. For I was hungry and you did not feed me …" and so on (Matt. 25:41–3). It is this dread of the eternal fire and of a neglect of charity that also appear to be important psychological factors for Marguerite (and one may conjecture that her fears might be related to the violent acts of her late husband and her former luxurious life at the Neapolitan court). Given the pervasive concern for salvation in medieval society and the didactic imagery that was commonplace by the mid-thirteenth century in sculptural programs across France, it is not surprising that a sculpted representation of the Last Judgment formed

---

22 The Seven Corporeal Works of Mercy are mainly derived from the Gospel of Matthew (25:34–40). They consist of: feeding those who hunger, giving drink to those who thirst, receiving and sheltering strangers and pilgrims, clothing the naked, visiting and tending the sick, consoling prisoners and burying the dead. Other charters of similar date relate the Acts of Mercy to hospital care, and equate Christ with the poor, the stranger and the sick. These include the hospitals of Tournai (1238), Lille (1245) and Château-Thierry (1304). Annie Saunier, *Le pauvre malade dans le cadre hospitalier médiéval: France du Nord, vers 1300–1500* (Paris, 1993), pp. 23–5. For the relevant section of the Tonnerre charter, see Challe, *Histoire du comté*, p. 206. Significantly for the late thirteenth century, there is no mention of Purgatory in the statutes.

23 According to Le Grand, the rule for the *hôtel-Dieu* at Vernon (Paris, Bibliothèque nationale de France, MS Fr. nouv. acq. 4 171), resembles in many respects the statutes for the hospitals at Troyes, Pontoise, Saint-Pol, and in part that of the *hôtel-Dieu* in Paris (with the exception of pregnant women). Le Grand, *Statuts d'Hôtels-Dieu et de léprosaria*, p. 17; for the text, see p. 152. On royal foundations of St Louis such as the *Quinze-Vingts*, the *maisons-Dieu* at Bernay, Pontoise and Vernon, see Imbert, *Les Hôpitaux en France*, pp. 61–2, and also Louis Carolus-Barré, *Le Procès de Canonisation de Saint Louis (1272–1297)*, Collection de L'École Française de Rome, 195 (Rome, 1994), pp. 253–61.

part of the hospital's iconography. On the exterior, however, a near life-size figure of a blessing Christ welcomed pilgrims and the poor seeking hospitality and care.[24]

When the psychological elements of Marguerite's charter are placed in the context of other hospitals, charities, and spirituality of the thirteenth century, it becomes clear that the language of the document corresponds with the ideology described in Annie Saunier's study of late medieval attitudes towards the *pauvre malade,* the sick poor, as a living manifestation of Christ and his Passion.[25] While concern for personal salvation remained a constant component in pious donations, the real sufferings of the poor, the popularity of the mendicants, the *imitatio Christi* of the Gospels, and influential saints like Francis of Assisi and Elisabeth of Thuringia all contributed to the subsequent outpouring of charity that appeared in the urban environment of the late twelfth century. Moreover, charities that also included private chantries seem to have had a long-lived appeal among members of the French nobility. By allowing unrestricted admission to the poor and pilgrims alike, hospitals such as Tonnerre either implicitly or explicitly recognized the importance of the poor in the soteriological system of elite society. What is difficult to discern at Tonnerre, however, is exactly who these poor and infirm were: local or vagrant? And did the charities that emerged in the thirteenth century make any impact on medical practice? Were the diseases and afflictions to be treated in Marguerite's hospital seen as a blessing, or as a punishment for sin? Unfortunately, the charter, as with similar texts, does not elaborate on the perceived causes or reasons for medical conditions. In short, such judgments are not formalized. Those who came to Notre Dame des Fontenilles in need of food, rest or medical attention were, from a documentary standpoint, simply the "poor of Christ," who were considered blessed individuals who merited care without discrimination. They received hospitality in the fullest sense of the Acts of Mercy, which provided the medical and psychological benefits of confession, absolution, rest, warmth, cleanliness, food, drink and continual liturgical prayer, all for seven days.

Scholars such as Michel Mollat and Annie Saunier have investigated changes in the often ambivalent attitudes towards poor and afflicted persons at various periods in the Middle Ages. During the first half of the thirteenth century, Mollat has discerned a rise (at least theologically) in the socio-psychological status, or "value", of the poor in the great scheme of creation and redemption. This view holds true for Marguerite of Burgundy at the end of the thirteenth century, nearly half a century after Mollat's

---

24 The Last Judgment stood inside the two-bay vaulted narthex porch. The Christ stood above the large entrance portal. This ensemble was destroyed when the front block was drastically altered in 1764. Immediately to the left of the entrance was a room for hospital supplies (possibly a reception room), and to the right, the chapel of Notre-Dame-des-Vertus, founded at the beginning of the fourteenth century; Camille Dormois, "Description des bâtiments de l'hôpital de Tonnerre," *Bulletin de la société des sciences historiques et naturelles de l'Yonne,* 6 (1852), 178 (hereafter cited as Dormois).

25 Saunier, *Les pauvres maladies,* includes a number of pre-1300 sources, despite her focus on the later Middle Ages. For example, see Saunier's discussion of Vincent of Beauvais (d. 1264), *De visitatione infirmorum,* p. 22.

high point of hospital foundations by the laity.[26] Precisely when and where (possibly at Fontevrault) Marguerite encountered these theological teachings that formed her desire to take up the *vita activa* cannot be known from the sources available. Luyt, for example, claims that her spiritual education was influenced by her great-great-great-grandmother, Mahaut de Courtenay, whom he mistakenly believed like many noble widows had become a nun at Fontevrault after the death of her second husband.[27] However, the piety exhibited at the Parisian court of Louis IX was certainly well known and would have been a natural and highly influential part of the culture of both Charles of Anjou and Marguerite.[28] Similarly, there were clearly numerous possibilities for influences to account for hospital patronage emanating from role models like St Elisabeth, as well as Cistercian spirituality and Franciscan piety; however, it seems more logical to look within the immediate family.[29] Charitable foundations for the poor and the sick were ubiquitous among the French nobility, including the Dukes of Burgundy (Marguerite's relatives), her husband, Charles of Anjou, his brother, Louis IX, and their sister, Isabelle of France.

Internal Organization of the Hospital

The statutes prescribe the hospital staff to be maintained by the endowment: an "educated" clerical master (originally Robert of Luzarches), eight chaplains, four clerics and four young choirboys, to perform two daily masses and the canonical hours. The choirboys were to be instructed in grammar and music, and were to assist in the services; thus, in a limited way, the hospital functioned as an educational institution. Interestingly, the Charter specifies that the chaplains and boys must chant

---

26 Mollat, *Les Pauvres au Moyen Âge*, pp. 87–157.

27 Luyt, p. 8. The "education" Marguerite received from her great-great-great-grandmother who died when she was just 8 or 9 years old remains highly speculative; however, it is significant that Robert of Aubrissel referred to his community as the "poor of Christ." On the development of the piety of the *imitatio Christi* and the *vita activa*, see Giles Constable, *Three Studies in Medieval Religious and Social Thought* (New York, 1995), pp. 218–48. Mahaut II (Matilda) de Courtenay (1188–1257) was the daughter of Pierre II de Courtenay and Agnes of Nevers, and was countess of Auxerre, Nevers and Tonnerre; Fromageot, *Tonnerre et son comté*, pp. 74–5; 86–90.

28 Dunbabin describes the Neapolitan household as essentially French and very much modeled on that of Charles's brother, Louis IX; Dunbabin, "The Household and Entourage," 319.

29 For example, Charles of Anjou endowed a strict community of Franciscans at San Lorenzo Maggiore in Naples and, interestingly in our context, provided wood and stone from the woods and quarries of the Tonnerrois that were Marguerite's inherited property; Bruzelius, *L'Europe des Anjou*, p. 53. The patronage of religious orders by Louis IX (St Louis) is well known, as is that of Isabelle of France and her convent at Longchamp. William Chester Jordan, "Isabelle of France and Religious Devotion at the Court of Louis IX," in *Capetian Women*, pp. 209–23. See also the depositions described for the canonization of Louis IX in Carolus-Barré, *Le Procès de Canonisation de Saint Louis*, pp. 59–139

in a loud voice so that they can be heard by those in the infirmary: "... *diront la messe et les heures canoniales, chantants à haute voix en sorte qu'il puissant être entendus par les malades.*"[30] We can assume, therefore, that in a holistic approach to the care of soul and body, liturgical music was thought to play a significant role in the patients' well-being, just as prayers, relics of saints, and the divine office were deemed efficacious in cure.[31] Given the importance of daily masses and maintenance of the cult, it is not surprising that the chapel and infirmary architecture reflects a desire to enhance acoustical properties (see below).

The non-liturgical community consisted of a mistress (under the authority of the clerical master) and 12 sisters, who were to wear the prescribed habit, and who, like the master and chaplains, were bound by the customary canonical vows (see above, p. 79).[32] The sisters, in addition to Marguerite, thus tended the sick, dressed wounds, and fed, bathed and clothed the poor. The mistress took charge of daily physical care and was to report the hospital's weekly needs to the master. Upon admission to the hospital, the poor received the attention of the master or a chaplain, who heard their confessions lest they die in a state of mortal sin. The master and chaplains, as required, administered the sacraments of Confession and Absolution, the Eucharist, Baptism and Extreme Unction.

The staff of hospital communities varied according to their endowment and how many persons could be reasonably supported. At Notre Dame des Fontenilles, the serving community was comparatively large and consisted of 8 chaplains for the male community and up to 20 lay sisters for the females. With an initial 12 sisters and a mistress, the entire original community numbered about 22 persons, excluding Marguerite, the manual laborers and servants on the estates of the hospital, and the countess's private household. The larger proportion of female care givers in relation to the clerical staff was common, but may also relate to the fact that Marguerite extended charity to pregnant women, who would be assisted by *matrones* (probably midwives). If the women died in childbirth, they were to be honorably buried in the hospital cemetery.[33]

It is likely, in view of comparative evidence, that the hospital offered foster care to the surviving infants and foundlings until they could be placed in a home. Infant care is not stipulated in any detail at Tonnerre, but that is not to say that this did not

---

30 Challe, *Histoire du comté*, p. 207.

31 The importance of patients hearing the services is a fundamental aspect of care in medieval hospitals; it is mentioned in Jacques de Vitry's description of contemporary hospitals and their customs, *Historia occidentalis*, p. 147.

32 Challe, *Histoire du comté*, p. 209.

33 "... les femmes qui accoucheront seront gardées et relevées; Et arrivant leur décès dans ledit maison, le maître ou quelqu'ns des susdits chapelains les fera honorablement ensépulturer dans ledit cimietière"; Challe, *Histoire du comté*, p. 207. The concern for pregnant women may relate to the fact that from her probable two pregnancies, Marguerite had no surviving children. She was apparently a loving stepmother to Charles's children and grandchildren living in the largely female, queen's household in Naples; Dunbabin, *Charles of Anjou*, pp. 182–4, and more recently, Dunbabin, "Household and Entourage," 323.

exist. The hospital's fourteenth-century cartulary refers to a medieval equivalent of baby bottles: terra cotta vessels (*biberons*) with a lip or a spout. The care of infants up to the age of four years old seems to have been practiced by the fourteenth century, since babies whose mothers died in childbirth must have remained for some time in the care of the hospital.[34] Statutes of similar institutions like Vernon are specific in stipulating a three-week period for childbirth, including baptism and purification of the mother as well as provisions for infant care if the mother should die and there was no father. [35]

The Charter for Tonnerre also specified, perhaps optimistically, that those who recovered should remain at the hospital in good health for a week, lest they fall ill again. It can therefore be inferred that seven days was perhaps a minimal stay in this institution. Upon their departure, the needy were given shoes and clothing, "so that they would not return naked into the world."[36]

In the hospital of Fontenilles, a veritable palace for the poor of Christ, the infirm were to be nourished spiritually and physically, but not by doctors. Patients were well fed with whatever the mistress deemed necessary, including bread, salted pork and wine.[37] Physicians or surgeons do not occur regularly in the accounts until the sixteenth century, although it is conceivable that Marguerite and her social equals may have consulted a personal physician.[38]

Although not mentioned in the statutes, one of the hospital's potential sources of healing (as widely believed) could have been the presence of sacred relics. We

---

34 The reference to baby "bottles" occurs in a donation made in 1334, and is quoted by Céline Pin, "*L'Hôtel-Dieu de Tonnerre*" (Thèse maîtresse, University of Dijon, 1997), p. 99. I am grateful to Mlle JoVale for bringing this work to my attention.

35 For example, at Pontoise (article 11) and at Vernon specifically: "Les femes qui seront recues en la Meson Dieu por gesir de enfent en gesine seront procurées et soutenues des biens de la Meson Dieu par III semaines après le enfentemnet, se elles vollent tant demorer en la Meson Dieu. Quan que'il couvendra despendre a baptizer le enfent et a la purification de sa mère leur serra aministré des biens de la Meson Dieu, et tout cen que l'en donra à l'enfent au bataisme l'en rendra a la mere quant elle se despartira de le ostel. Se la mère muert en la Meson Dieu, ses enfes sera norri des biens de la Meson Dieu, meesmement s'il n' point de père;" Le Grand, p. 162.

36 Challe, *Histoire du comté*, pp. 208–9.

37 Ibid., p. 208.

38 The lack of doctors of medicine is puzzling since physicians were such an important component of Charles of Anjou's personal household (for example, Thomas of Florence and Jean de Nesle); also, Charles actively "encouraged medical studies"; Dunbabin, "The Household and Entourage," 16–17. Marguerite's view of medical doctors cannot be known from the sources available. The first mention of a potential medical practitioner is a fee paid to a barber in 1333. In 1334, a certain Nicholas, physician, was summoned and his fee was paid by Symon de Laignes, presumably one of the chaplains who was ill. In the next year, the master of the hospital was also seen by Nicholas, and was paid the same. It is not until 1507 that one finds the barber-surgeon Droyn Bardot attending the sick in the infirmary. In the sixteenth century, surgeons and barber-surgeons appear regularly; Chaput, "Un hôpital d'autrefois," 132–3.

know that important relics were bequeathed to Marguerite's executors for the benefit of the hospital, along with other chapel ornaments (a chalice, basins and clothing). Moreover, Luyt had certainly seen the relics placed on the altar in the seventeenth century. These consisted of a silver and bejeweled reliquary cross containing a fragment of the True Cross, and the head of St Sigerne, one of the 11,000 virgins of St Ursula.[39] Given the larger picture one gains of thirteenth- century piety, when articles of clothing of highly religious persons and potential saints were eagerly collected, as in the case of Isabelle of Longchamp, the importance of the belief in the power of relics to effect miraculous cures cannot be overstressed.[40] I suggest, therefore, that it is quite possible that Marguerite's personal relics were placed in the hospital chapel at least for special liturgical occasions during her life, and that they were deposited there after her death, near the place she had designated for her tomb. In sum, it was the hospital's devotional environment that physically, emotionally, psychologically and spiritually provided the primary "medicine" at Tonnerre, and it is here that the architecture played a critical role.

The Building Ensemble

For an elite institution envisioned on a grand scale, the practice of the corporeal Acts of Mercy translates into considerable physical needs that included: an ample water supply, an infirmary with sufficient beds and good air circulation, kitchens, gardens, a place of reception, bathing and washing facilities, a sanctuary or chapel, and a cemetery, as well as storage facilities for enormous amounts of food, utensils, bed linen, shrouds, and clothing for the poor as well as the serving community.

Since the hospital staff included both male clerics and a community of sisters, the architectural plan had to accommodate segregated eating, sleeping and hygiene

---

39 Luyt, p. 67. No reference to this cross occurs in the foundation charter; however, it survived until the Revolution, and its post-medieval history is recounted by Quénée. During the Hundred Years War, the hospital's valuable objects were taken for safety to Marguerite's fortified chateau at Argenteuil-sur- Armançon; Quénée, pp. 79–80.

40 While the cult of saints' relics has long been associated with miracles, pilgrimage, healing and salvation, the psychological power of these beliefs in the thirteenth century can be demonstrated by the assignation of special properties to artifacts merely associated with the relics of a saintly person. This devotional mentality is especially captured in Agnes of Harcourt's *Life of Isabelle of France*, where she relates how the community of Longchamp took Isabelle's body from her tomb to place her in "another coffin more suitable." Agnes (then abbess) continues: "we removed the robe that she had had on for nine days in the ground, which was so pretty and so clean that it did not seem that it had ever been worn. Since we wanted to have this robe as a relic, we dressed her again ...." The event was witnessed by Marguerite, Countess of Flanders, and Marie, her daughter, a nun and many others. During the process of re-entombment, the nuns opened the window of the monastery and lifted the tomb chest with the body to the view of spectators, who "strove as best they could to dangle their caps, their rings, their broaches, their hats, their belts, their purses to touch the holy body through great devotion, and what had touched it they kept as relics"; Field, p. 75.

facilities convenient to water conduits. Patients were also segregated by sex, but it is not stipulated precisely how the genders were to be arranged in the 40 beds in the cubicles that lined the north and south infirmary walls. In addition to the ward, chapel and houses for the serving communities, Marguerite's personal household required additional accommodation, all of which had to be coordinated within the site comprising the adjacent wetlands, springs, the river and pre-existing roadway.

The choice of site was determined no doubt by the location of land owned by the countess, by its easy access to water supplied by the river Armançon, the streams and springs of Fontenilles, the location along an important public thoroughfare, and possibly by a need for a hospital just outside the town. In fact, a portion of the city walls (evidently controlled by the countess) was used to build the hospital, a concession that would have provided quarried stone on site for immediate use in the foundations.[41] Situated on a broad plain parallel to the pre-existing Rue des Fontenilles and the natural springs, this hospice would have been an impressive refuge attractive to pilgrims, since Tonnerre lay on the major north-west to south-east thoroughfare between Sens and Dijon via Alesia.[42]

Archeological evidence, early plans and drawings indicate that the hospital precinct had crenellated walls, towers and was moated. Externally it would have appeared in the landscape like a citadel with its impressive massing of stone buildings and steep roofs covered with brilliant glazed tiles. By the early fourteenth century, an elegant, painted and gilded timber *flèche* rose above the continuous roof of the ward and chapel (Fig. 6.2).[43] Writing in the mid-nineteenth century, Dormois also records traces of the original iron cresting that embellished the roof's ridge and which would have enhanced the external refinement of the building.

---

41 "Pour la bâtisse duquel hôpital, ou maison-Dieu, nous donnons et concédons nos murs de la ville de Tonnerre assis es lieux susdits et par nous concédés hors d'icelle bâtisse et fondation pour bâtir ledit ..."; Challe, *Histoire du comté*, p. 211.

42 Major routes used in Burgundy in the thirteenth century are described in Richard, *Les Ducs*, Fig. 1; see also Victor Petit, *Descriptions des villes et compagnes du Département du L'Yonne*, 2 vols (Auxerre, 1870; repr. Paris, 1999). Many of the chapter papers included in the Amiens conference volume use a geographical approach and map the density and distribution of hospitals; see Montaubin, *Hôpitaux et Maladreries au Moyen Âge*.

43 One might look to the brightly-colored roofs at Beaune or to medieval manuscripts to obtain some idea of the color and splendor of this huge complex in the late thirteenth century. The hospital's original spire, seen as a symbol of the feudal aristocracy, was dismantled in the French Revolution; Dormois, 182.

Figure 6.2   Tonnerre: Notre Dame des Fontenilles, site prior to major alterations of the nineteenth century. Anonymous engraving of the seventeenth century, illustrating the walled precinct and Marguerite's former residence in the foreground.

The Plan

The plan of 1760 in the hospital archives shows how the entire site was bounded by the branches of the river that enclosed the property on two sides and filled the fortification ditches on the east and north sides. From this and the evidence of subsequent plans, a fairly complete picture of the medieval site emerges (Fig. 6.3).[44]

---

44 Figure 6.3 is a digitized plan drawn by N.W. Alcock and based on the 1760 plan published by Fromageot. See Fromageot, *Tonnerre et son comté*, pp. 100–106. Fromageot's identification of the features has been augmented by the texts of Luyt, Dormois and Salet, as well as a plan published by Salet, 226; additional information can also be gleaned from Viollet-le-Duc's plan of the *Hôtel-Dieu*: E.E. Viollet-le-Duc, *Dictionnaire raisonné de l'architecture française du xi au xvi siècle*, 10 vols (Paris, 1859–68), 6 (1863), p. 106. A general plan with the modern additions is printed in Quénée, pp. 26–7. All references are to my Figure 6.3.

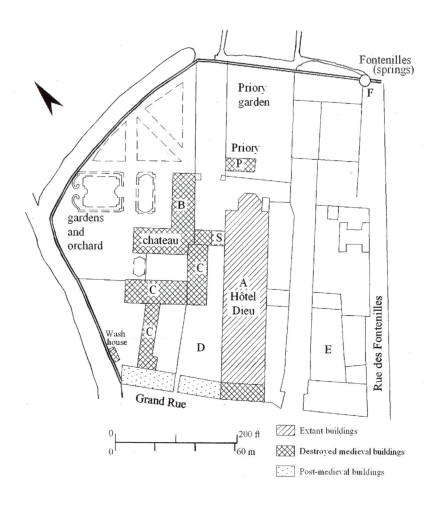

Figure 6.3   Tonnerre: Notre Dame des Fontenilles: digitized plan of the medieval
               precinct c. 1760 (drawn by N.W. Alcock, based on plans of 1840 by
               Viard-Vallier published by Salet, 1965, and Fromageot's 1973 plan).

Key: A Hôtel-Dieu (maison-Dieu); B Chateau; C Communal and service
               buildings; D Cemetery of the Hospital; E. Municipal Cemetery; F Les
               Fontenilles (springs); P Priory; S Stair tower

The infirmary (A) is a ground-level hall with an essentially east–west orientation, so that the porch and west entrance gate fronted on the public street, the Rue de Tonnellerie (afterwards Grand Rue de l'Hôpital); the chapel, conventionally, was at the east end in axial alignment. The great cemetery (D) lay adjacent to the hospital on the north side, and a second, municipal, cemetery (E) was added to the far southeast corner of the enclosure when the ward and chapel served as a parish church in the Early Modern period.[45] Significantly, Marguerite's chateau (B) terminated in an external stair tower (S) that communicated via a corridor with the hospital and chapel as well as with one of the staff ranges (C) situated opposite an open court further to the west. Extensive gardens (the design shown dates to the eighteenth century), orchards and arbors lay further to the north and east, extending as far as the enclosing wall and ditches originally fed by natural springs of les Fontenilles (F), located at the east end of the Rue des Fontenilles. Since a source of fresh water was essential to the hygiene of any hospital, it is not surprising that, as Luyt records, the stream issuing from the springs was used by Marguerite's builders to create two subterranean channels on either side of the infirmary that flushed the drains of the hospital and service buildings and carried waste to the river.[46] The relieving arch of what appears to be a drain is still visible in the south wall of the infirmary.

The plans show long ranges and a semi-cloistral layout with open courts for the chateau, staff accommodations and service ranges. The position of the river, the natural springs and an easy access to the site via a public thoroughfare were critical factors, as well as the desire to create a walled semi-fortified enclosure. Unfortunately, there is no specific indication of a medicinal garden, but there was ample space for one to have been included, along with the extensive gardens and orchards within the enclosure.

Given the size of the community serving the hospital, it is likely that the original communal buildings were two-storied ranges with separate apartments for the priests, choirboys and lay sisters. The disposition of these chambers and various ancillary buildings needs further investigation. From a general knowledge of contemporary monastic and domestic buildings, it can be inferred that the kitchens, larder, dairy, wine cellars and storage areas were probably incorporated into the residential buildings at ground level with living and eating quarters on the first (upper) floor. If, however, the communal *maisons* were based on a traditional monastic plan, the refectories for the clerics and sisters would have been ground-level halls. Presumably they slept in upper-floor dormitories rather than private rooms?

One of the most interesting and original features of this hospital is the physical connection between the infirmary and the residence of the countess. For example,

---

45 Luyt, p. 76, informs us that in 1649, the infirm were transported from the "nave of the church" to new apartments. These chambers are in the west range of buildings that appear as post-medieval construction in Figure 6.3.

46 Luyt, p. 75; noted also in Viollet-le-Duc: "*Deux canaux souterrains passant des deux côtés de la grande salle entraînaient dans la rivière les vidanges de l'établissement*"; Viollet-le-Duc, *Dictionnaire*, 6 (1863), pp. 109–10.

documentary evidence as well as a drawing of the elevation of Marguerite's chateau (preserved in the Musée Hospitalier) indicate that her chateau was a two-story residence connected to the north side of the ward via an enclosed corridor and stair tower. All sources agree that there was easy access between Marguerite's private residence and the former timber gallery in the infirmary, visible on the exterior in the engraving of *c.* 1600 (Fig. 6.2). Thus Marguerite had privileged upper-floor access to the north gallery adjacent to the chapel (the end bay is now blocked) where she could have listened to and possibly observed the liturgical services.[47]

The Interior

Looking at the interior of the hospital from west to east (Fig. 6.4), the single-nave plan of the ward terminates in the elegant polygonal apse of the chapel. Because there are no transepts or internal supports, the focal point of this dramatically elongated and spacious interior is the flood of light from the windows of the chapel, framed by the chancel arch rising to the full height of the timber vault. Many have noted the enormous scale of these eastern windows (12 meters tall!), whose proportions dominate the chapel in a manner not dissimilar to the more elaborate windows of the chapel at St. Germain-en-Laye (1238) outside Paris.[48]

As an architectural ensemble, the tall chancel arch, enormous timber barrel vault of the hall and intense light from the chapel windows enhance the grandeur and austerity of this carefully conceived space. The east end is vaulted entirely in stone and comprises a wide central chapel, designed to contain the high altar and Marguerite's tomb; the central polygonal chapel is flanked by lower lateral chapels with a later addition on the south side. The choir is set apart structurally from the infirmary by the tripartite ensemble of the central arch and much lower flanking arches opening onto the lateral chapels. The openings of this "triumphal arch," however, are so large that they hardly conceal the chapels, a design that may well have been devised for both visual and acoustical effect.

---

47 Dormois describes the placement of earlier openings in the last (east) bay of the north wall leading to the stairs, 183. See also Viollet-le-Duc's reconstruction, my Figure 6.5.

48 For St. Germain-en-Laye, see Jean Bony, *French Gothic Architecture of the 12th and 13th Centuries* (Berkeley, CA, 1983), pp. 378–9, and Daniel H. Weiss, *Art and Crusade in the Age of Saint Louis* (Cambridge, 1998), pp. 26–32. For comparative material on the architecture of sainte-chapelles in France, see Claudine Billot, 'Les Saintes-chapelles du XIIIe au XVIe Siècles', in *L'Eglise et le chateau Xᵉ–XVIIIᵉ siècle*, ed. André Chastel (Bordeaux, 1988), pp. 95–114.

Figure 6.4   Notre Dame des Fontenilles: interior of the great ward looking east (photo used by permission of the administration of the Municipal Hospital of Tonnerre).

Unfortunately, the chapel area was drastically altered in 1621 and a classical-style altar installed; therefore, exactly what type of additional screening or internal partitioning may have existed when the ward and chapel were built remains speculative. Both current opinion and antiquarian material support the presence of a low screen, or *jubé*, separating the ward from the chapel, although this could conceivably belong to the post-medieval phase when the chapel served as a parish church.[49]

Fenestration

As in all medieval hospitals, the organization of windows and wall space for beds was crucial; thus the windows at Notre Dame des Fontenilles were placed as high as possible along the north and south walls to admit the maximum amount of light and to allow for rows of alcoves and beds at ground level and a timber walkway at window level, as shown in the transverse section reconstructed by Viollet-le-Duc (Fig. 6.5). A deliberate contrast in fenestration differentiates the chapel from the infirmary. On the exterior, the elegant traceried windows of the chapel immediately express the hierarchical division of the building. Like the infirmary, the chapel windows are also placed high on the walls, but they are strikingly different in proportion from those of the ward. While both ward and chapel have a double lancet form, the chapel windows have refined bar tracery composed of elongated lancets and quatrefoils in contrast to the wider and simpler round-headed windows of the infirmary (Figs 6.1 and 6.6). The windows and the immense light they admit visually dominate the mural surfaces of both ward and chapel, and there can be little doubt that they and their placement were key features planned by the designer.

Using surviving fragments and comparative material from the church at Mussy-sur-Seine, Meredith Lillich has recently reconstructed the glazing program at Tonnerre. Her findings affirm that *grisaille* (monochromatic patterned glass typical of Cistercian glazing) and colored glass were combined in the windows of both the infirmary and chapel, as noted earlier by Dormois.[50] The principal colors were deep red, royal blue, green, white and yellow gold in addition to the *grisaille*.[51] In the chapel, the quatrefoil lobes of the eastern windows were filled with colored glass, but the main part of the windows were *grisaille*, with a colored border and insets containing heraldic devices and crowned portrait busts of Charles of Anjou and Marguerite wearing a white veil and golden crown. Likewise, the infirmary windows combined monochromatic and colored glass with three rows of *grisaille* panels, again containing the colored portraits of Marguerite and her husband as well as heraldic inserts.[52]

---

49 Alterations to the original building are noted by Luyt, pp. 76–8; Quénée, (1979) *passim*; Chaput, 128, and most importantly, Dormois, 177–89.

50 Lillich, pp. 92–4. This research corrects some earlier assertions that the chapel contained only colored glass, and the ward only *grisaille*.

51 Dormois, 179–80.

52 Lillich, (citing Luyt), p. 78.

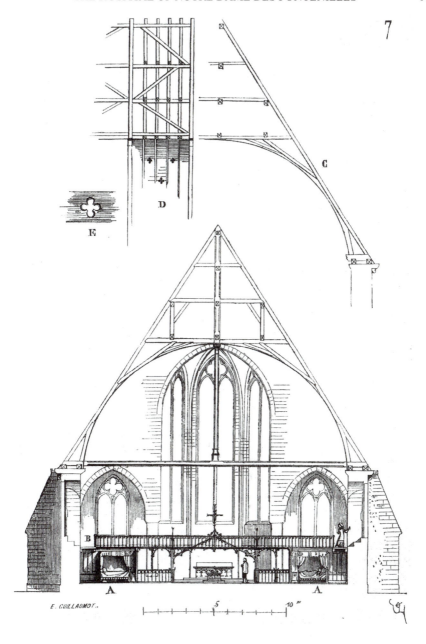

Figure 6.5   Notre Dame des Fontenilles: transverse section and reconstruction of
the fittings of the medieval infirmary showing the choir screen, patient
alcoves, gallery and window access (E.E. Viollet-le-Duc, 1862).

Respective heraldic devices of Marguerite and Charles also appear in the frieze at the top of the long walls of the infirmary (Fig. 6.6). The mural painting is much damaged, although the deep blue of the ground and fragments of red, ochre and white are still discernable. Ichnographically, the combined portraits and heraldry indicate they are the primary patrons, and thus, by familial extension, Charles of Anjou becomes a posthumous founder. Marguerite also stipulated that prayers be said for her soul and that of her husband.

Figure 6.6   Notre Dame des Fontenilles: infirmary, north wall showing the partially preserved heraldic frieze at the top of the windows and the squared beam sockets for the former gallery support (photograph: author).

From Lillich's research, several very interesting observations emerge that relate to Marguerite's hospital-cum-residence, which combines a religious charity and a feudal *seigneurie*. First, what is perhaps most astonishing is that there was not a single religious image in the glazing program! This contrasts dramatically with the liturgical and spiritual care emphasized at the hospital and the iconography of the façade and porch sculpture. Yet, if one takes a high-status domestic hall as an alternative model for the open ward, the architecture can be equally "read" as a seigniorial *grande salle*, with an attached private chapel. Moreover, the secular milieu of the infirmary is reinforced by the heraldic frieze (Fig. 6.6), and re-states the same concepts of lineage and status as did the original glazing.[53]

Because the same pictorial imagery appeared in the infirmary and chapel, the architecture *per se* – the great chancel arch; the difference between stone ribbed vaults in the chapel versus the rounded timber vault of the hospital, and the contrasting window designs – functions as the primary means of formally differentiating the sacred from the secular space. (One must, of course, mentally supply the furnishings, altars, candles and so on that would have adorned the chapel and the vestments worn by those taking part in the liturgical ceremony to achieve the full visual effect.)

Scale and Space

The infirmary is roughly 88 meters long, and the chapel 10.9 meters, thus giving an overall length of nearly 100 meters. The walls of the infirmary were originally 9.15 meters high, but the floor level was raised in 1619 by about 50 centimeters.[54] From the original floor to the ridge of the roof measures close to 27 meters, of which the masonry walls comprise a third of the elevation and the timber vault and the hidden roof framing each another third. The full height of the hospital, its great triangular profile and the vast sweep of the roof, which covers a surface area of 4,500 square meters, can only be appreciated from the exterior.

Apart from the scale and proportions, what gives the *maison-Dieu* its sense of grandeur is the enormous timber vault above an unaisled interior. While the carpentry of the great ward has been described elsewhere,[55] several aspects of the construction pertain to the hospital, its architectural prototypes and the patron's goals. In France and Belgium, the paneled timber vault was a popular design in elite domestic halls and churches from the thirteenth to the seventeenth century; thus Marguerite and her builders would certainly have known it.[56] At Tonnerre, however, the single span

53 The frieze has been partially salvaged, and is discussed in Quénée, p. 14.

54 Salet, 230.

55 Lynn T. Courtenay, "Medieval Roof Carpentry: *charpente lambrissée*," in *Journal of the Timber Framers Guild*, 72 (June 2004), 8–15.

56 A good example is the synodal hall in former episcopal palace at Auxerre, not far from Tonnerre, and recently dated by dendrochronology to 1248–49. Patrick Hoffsummer et al., *Les charpentes du xie au xixe siècle, Typologie et évolution en France du Nord et en Belgique* (Paris, 2002), pp. 142–44. The grand' salle of the Palais de la Cité in Paris, built by King

is exceptional (a width of 18.5 meters internally and nearly 22 meters externally). This surpasses anything known to have been built at that date, including the similar ground-floor infirmary of the Cistercian convent at Byloke, Ghent (*c.* 1255).[57] Since Notre Dame des Fontenilles was built on an unencumbered and carefully selected site, the large scale of the infirmary as well as the single-nave plan must have been desired for specific reasons and communicated to the builders. To what extent this magnificent architecture contributed to the health of the poor and reflected the medicinal concepts of the foundress is, of course, a more difficult question. What can be said, however, is that the building provided an environment in which profuse light, exchange of air, and good acoustical space for liturgical prayer were created to facilitate the spiritual and physical care provided by the hospital staff. The scientific evidence for how or whether the environment within medieval hospitals produced a sense of well-being and the extent to which this factor mediated illness remains a topic for further exploration.

To accommodate the infirm (male and female separately), the space of the open ward, as in most hospitals, was organized longitudinally with a wide central aisle and partitioned alcoves for the patients' beds along the sides. At Tonnerre, and, to my knowledge, not found elsewhere, timber galleries above the beds ran the full length of the infirmary on both sides. Although these disappeared in the seventeenth century when the hospital became a parish church, the prominent beam sockets and traces on the walls give a good idea of their placement and size, if not their precise design (Fig. 6.6). Accounts for their repair in 1556 indicate that the galleries were about 2 meters wide, presumably the same dimensions as originally, and that the stairs leading to them were covered.[58]

The galleries were clearly inserted for practical reasons: primarily to access the windows to adjust their openings as well as the shutters (fittings for which remain in situ), and secondarily to provide an observation platform from which the attending sisters could check on the patients in their cubicles. Dormois has suggested that the galleries may also have provided space to hang the bed linen.[59] There is no known

---

Philip the Fair *c.* 1306–31, was a double-aisled hall (destr.) with similar paneled vaults; it is known from an engraving by Cerceau: Paris, Bibliothèque Nationale, Etampes, Vx 15.

57 The internal span of the Byloke infirmary is just under 16 meters; on the dating, see Patrick Hoffsummer, "La Charpente de la Salle des Malades de l'Hôpital de La Biloque à Gand," in *Actes du 51e Congrès de la Federation des Cercles d'archéologie et d'histoire de Belgique*, 1 (1992), 94–5, and also Lynn T. Courtenay, "Scale and Scantling: Technological Issues in Large-scale Timberwork of the High Middle Ages," in *Technology and Resource Use in Medieval Europe, Cathedrals, the Mills, and Mines*, ed. Elizabeth B. Smith and M. Wolfe (Aldershot, 1997), pp. 42–75.

58 The carpenter, Jehan Desmains, received 91 *livres*, 10 *sous* in 1556, being paid for rebuilding or repairing galleries 20 *toise* long and 2 *toise* wide (39 meters x nearly 4 meters, rather smaller if the Roman rather than Parisian foot was used in Tonnerre at this period); Viollet-le-Duc, *Dictionnaire*, 6, p. 109, citing accounts recorded by Dormois, 183–4, who also gives the wages of the mason, the smith and the transport costs.

59 Dormois, 183.

prototype for a long internal gallery in other French hospitals surviving from this period; thus one has to look to other potential models in domestic architecture, including episcopal palaces and chateaux. [60]

The infirmary had a total of 40 partitioned alcoves, each containing a bed (20 along each side, each about 3.3 meters wide). Thus, allowing two patients per bed as was customary at that time, there would have been ample space for 80 patients. The spacious compartments had no ceilings, but would have been partially covered by the projection of the galleries. No doubt, as at Beaune and as depicted in manuscript illuminations of the period, the cubicles were furnished with curtains or partitions for insulation and privacy and were well equipped with bed linen and woolen covers. Since there was no hearth or fireplace in the infirmary, the only heating available was supplied by portable braziers.

Communication and convenience must have been important concerns in the architectural design. Originally there were stairs to the gallery at both the north-west and north-east ends of the infirmary, the latter mainly for Marguerite, but the west end was perhaps more convenient for the staff. Viollet-le-Duc's transverse section (Fig. 6.5) reconstructs the arrangement for regulating light, temperature and fresh air in the ward, which must have become permeated with incense, fumes from the braziers, and bodily odors. Unfortunately, the specific provisions for sanitation within the ward are obscure, but water flow was carefully managed in such institutions.

The decision to create an undivided space of enormous breadth and also allow large openings in the upper walls in the infirmary made a timber vault a structural necessity.[61] However, other factors may have contributed to the decision to use timber, namely: the expediency of construction and reduced weight of such a vault; the easy provision for ventilation created by the quatrefoil openings in the wooden panels (see Fig. 6.5), and the acoustical properties of a wooden shell with an extensive loft area above. When combined with a stone vaulted choir for resonance, a timber vault would be an excellent solution to meet Marguerite's desires for good acoustics and magnificent scale.

---

60 Historians of French domestic architecture attest to the presence of galleries, meaning covered corridors or passageways either at or above ground level, although it is difficult to find any existing thirteenth-century prototype. The rare examples of timber *galleries* or horizontal means of communication between ranges in domestic buildings that survive are later in date, and the galleries are often partially external and associated with a rectangular, courtyard plan. For example, a reconstructed plan and an inventory dating to 1395 illustrate the courtyard house in Dijon of Regnaud Chevalier, tailor to the Duke of Burgundy; it had galleries connecting the service and domestic ranges of the house. It also had a private chapel with chambers on either side; Yves Esquieu and Jean-Marie Pesez, *Cent maisons médiévales en France* (Paris, 1998), pp. 324–6.

61 The technically simpler alternative would have been an aisled plan with stone vaults, as in the large-scale infirmary of the hospital of St. Jean at Angers, where the vault loads are concentrated on intermediate piers, thus allowing large openings in the upper walls as was done in numerous aisled halls and refectories.

As has already been noted, the Charter refers directly to the need for sufficient loudness in chanting the liturgy and to the musical education of the choirboys, from which one can infer the importance ascribed to the healing benefits of liturgical chant. Indeed, is not music still a source of well-being and comfort? While architectural historians often emphasize visual features and mathematical proportions as conveyors of meaning, I maintain that the practical and acoustical properties of stone and wood should be considered equally, keeping in mind that the visual and aural attributes must have certainly enhanced one another.

Conclusion and Summary

It is evident that hospitals such as Notre Dame des Fontenilles, while revealing aspects of medieval medical practice, illuminate aristocratic piety in Capetian France as well as wider social and religious concerns for welfare distribution, poor relief and the desire for a family memorial augmented by perpetual prayer for salvation. In the thirteenth century, these issues transcended the medical science of curing disease. As demonstrated by the example of the *maison-Dieu* at Tonnerre, hospitals founded by the nobility are best seen in a socio-religious rather than a scientific context. As vividly described in the foundation Charter, the teachings of the Gospels and incentives to practice the Seven Acts of Mercy that inspired Marguerite's active charity had become by the second half of the thirteenth century, if Mollat is correct, a pan-European phenomenon. The new sensibility and regard for the poor that emerged *c.* 1100 flourished in the developing towns, universities and courts, and penetrated society on many levels. In particular, the *vita activa* found expression in the mendicant orders, lay movements like the Poor Clares and the Beguines, canonical reforms, the foundation of communal and individual charities, but far closer socially to Marguerite's personal experiences, in the intense devotions and benevolence practiced by the Capetian royal family, especially Louis IX and Isabelle of Longchamp.[62]

Mollat has argued that twelfth-century society experienced a need for spiritual cleansing among the rich and powerful, especially the avaricious aristocracy and urban patriciate, who benefited materially from the labors of the lower classes. From contextual evidence, he suggests that the rich began to voice a psychological insecurity regarding salvation, and an urgency to gain God's blessing from God's poor. Following the Gospels and the spirit of the *imitatio Christi*, the true follower of Christ was morally obliged not only to give alms, but also actively to serve the poor. Given this mentality, the rich became (demonstratively, as in the public piety of St Louis) the servants of the poor. Menial tasks done with love and tenderness toward the afflicted and infirm (such as feeding, cleansing, dressing wounds, washing feet,

---

62 Representations of the active piety of St Louis continued after his death, for example in prayer books such as the *Hours of Jeanne D'Evreux* (*c.* 1325) in the Metropolitan Museum in New York. Vivid descriptions of Isabelle's acts of piety are found in her *vita* written by Agnes of Harcourt *c.* 1280–85; Field, p. 10.

and so on) became valuable currency in the "economy of salvation" and part of the ritual of piety associated with hospitals. Because Marguerite, a countess and former queen, participated (as had Elisabeth of Hungary and Isabelle of France) in the physical care of the poor of Christ along with the sisters, she has become regarded locally as a quasi-saintly figure, and the anniversary of her death is still celebrated at her hospital. Though overtly biased towards the Countess, Robert Luyt, her biographer, eloquently praises Marguerite's humility and reminds his reader that the "almsgiving princess" gave not just her wealth, but thirteen years of her life to the Corporeal Acts of Mercy.[63]

As a monumental testimony to the wealth, will and piety of the patron, the hospital of Notre Dame des Fontenilles was designed and embellished to function simultaneously as a charitable institution and seigniorial domain whose concerns were mainly fiscal and legal. It is precisely this amalgam of a religious and a feudal institution that most accurately characterizes the *maison-Dieu* at Tonnerre and its architecture. While the components of Marguerite's fortified hospital are familiar within the architectural milieu of thirteenth-century France, this simultaneously conceived and built ensemble of chateau and hospital appears to be unique in Burgundy at this time. It is probable that Marguerite's planned retirement at Tonnerre and her continued presence at the hospital account for the individuality of the architectural assembly. Or perhaps her decision was influenced by a similar disposition of Isabelle of France's convent at Longchamp, where the Capetian princess maintained a separate residence within the nun's enclosure? Since there is no documentation to establish the potential influence of the "blessed" Isabelle on Marguerite's patronage, apart from the family connection, this inference must remain a tempting conjecture.[64] What is certain, however, is that the *maison-Dieu* of Fontenilles displays a synthesis of secular and sacred architectural features and decoration that communicate an elite, seigniorial concept of temporal assistance.

Finally, it should be remembered that in this age of pilgrimage, crusade and lay piety, the belief in the miraculous powers of the saints and their relics to heal body,

---

63 Luyt, pp. 78–9: "… cette princesse … s'estoit occupee elle mesme treize ans Durant au service de l'Hospital … levant & couchant les pauvres maladies, cousant & refaisant leurs habits, lavant leurs linges, nettoyant leurs ordures, preparant leur viands & faisans tous les services les plus abjets de cette grande Maison."

64 For the site, plan; and history of Longchamp Abbey (destr.) in the Bois de Boulogne, Paris, see Gaston Duchesne, *Histoire de L'Abbaye Royale de Longchamp (1255 à 1789)*, (Paris, 1906).

The most prevalent models for thirteenth-century France that combine high-status domestic and religious architecture are episcopal and canonical residences, or chateaux to which private chapels and parish churches were attached. See, for example, Thierry Crepin-Leblond, *Recherche sur les palais épiscopaux en France au Moyen Âge, XIIe et XIIIe siècles* (thèse de l'École nationale des chartes, Paris, 1986), and "Le palais épiscopal de Senlis au Moyen Âge: étude historique et monumentale," in *Memoires de la Société d'histoire et d'archéologique de Senlis* (1995), 197–218; Jean Mesqui, "Le Palais du comtes de Champagne à Provins (XIIe–XIIIe siècles," *Bulletin Monumental*, 151(2) (1993), 221–355.

mind and soul were part of the psychological fabric or rich and poor alike. All sought relief from pain and anguish, but foremost they wanted assurance of salvation. The exceptional relics that Marguerite possessed were surely known to the serving community at Tonnerre, and very likely increased her status as a medicinal care giver. Her queenly "servitude" was also a significant manifestation of her sincerity and humility. Thus Marguerite shared her spiritual and personal property, no doubt in the confidence that the chaplains, the poor and the sick, whom she tended lovingly with her own hands, would pray in perpetuity for the salvation of her soul and of her husband, just as she, with all the temporal means of this world, sought to achieve reconciliation with her Creator.

Chapter 7

Function and Epidemiology in Filarete's Ospedale Maggiore[1]

Renzo Baldasso

Less than two hundred yards away from the Duomo of Milan stands the Ospedale Maggiore, one of the largest buildings and the largest hospital ever built during the Renaissance.[2] While one may argue from a formal perspective for its place among the seminal buildings of fifteenth-century Italian architecture, this chapter considers the technical innovations that made this hospital famous as "a building without equal throughout Europe" in the expert eyes of the artist, architect and art writer Giorgio Vasari.[3] Such high praise was well deserved, but not on account of its remarkable size, perfectly symmetrical layout or innovative architectural style. Rather, the object of Vasari's marvel and admiration was its sewer system, the *destri*.

---

1   This research developed from a Master's Thesis defended at the University of Oklahoma (2000). I would like to thank Peter Barker, Susan Caldwell, David Freedberg, Alison Palmer and Phoebe Segal for their suggestions and encouragement.

2   The two monographs on this hospital are by Liliana Grassi, *Lo 'spedale di poveri' del Filarete* (Milan, 1972) and *La Ca' Granda. Cinque secoli di storia e d'arte dell'Ospedale Maggiore di Milano* (Milan, 1981). Grassi was the architect in charge of the reconstruction of the building after it suffered extensive damage in 1943. The best introduction in English by Evelyn Welch, "The Architecture of Charity," in *Art and Authority in Renaissance Milan* (New Haven, CT, 1995), pp. 145–66.

3   See Giorgio Vasari, *Vite de' più eccellenti pittori, scultori e architectti scritte da Giorgio Vasari pittore aretino con nuove annotazioni e commenti di Gaetano Milanesi*, 9 vols (Florence, 1906), 2:456: "fu condotto Antonio a Milano dal duca Francesco Sforza, gonfallonier allora di Santa Chiesa, per egli aver vedute l'opere sue in Roma, per fare, come fece, col suo disegno, l'albergo de' poveri di Dio, che è uno spedale che serve per uomini e donne infermi e per i putti innocenti, nati non legitimamente. ... E per dirlo brevemente, è questo luogo tanto ben fatto et ordinato, che per simile non credo che ne sia un altro in tutta l'Europa." Gaston Du C. De Vere in his *The Lives of the Artists* (London 1912) translates: "Antonio was summoned to Milan by Duke Francesco Sforza, the Gonfalonier of the Holy Church (who had seen his works in Rome), to that end that there might be made with his design, as it afterwards was, the Albergo de' poveri di Dio, which is a hospital that serves for sick men and women and for the innocent children born out of wedlock. ... In a word, this place is so well built and design, that I do not believe that there is its like in Europe." It is interesting to note that, despite the low opinion of the work and writings of Filarete, Vasari based his description and measurements of the Ospedale Maggiore on information he read in *Filarete's Trattato di Architettura (Treatise on Architecture)*.

Undoubtedly, from the perspective of historians, the Ospedale Maggiore is a building without equal because its architect, Antonio Averlino, better known as Filarete ("lover of virtue"), left us a detailed discussion of the rationale behind the innovative design of this hospital. Written in the early 1460s, Filarete's *Trattato di Architettura* (*Treatise on Architecture*) allows us to understand how he combined into his plan ideals of functionality with epidemiological notions. He envisioned the Ospedale Maggiore as a structure capable of offering an environment both effective in preventing the spread of infectious diseases among the patients and also proactive toward their recovery.[4] In endowing the space with these qualities, Filarete created a new type of hospital that was vastly superior to medieval precedents. The achievement of his plan consists in the successful integration of late medieval medical theories with classical architectural principles.

Filarete was a Florentine artist who flourished in Italy during the second third of the fifteenth century.[5] Little is known about his life and work. After achieving fame by casting the bronze doors of Saint Peter's in Rome (1433–45) and several small bronze sculptures after antique models, he dedicated himself to architecture and engineering. When Francesco Sforza conquered Milan displacing the Ambrosian Republic, he invited Filarete to his court to introduce the *maniera antica* made famous by Brunelleschi and theorized by Leon Battista Alberti.[6] However, because of the artist's stylistic inclinations and the intense political tensions between the duke and Milanese patricians who preferred the late medieval *maniera moderna*, Filarete was not accepted by local builders. In the end, this prevented him from bringing any of his buildings to completion, and perhaps become the next Brunelleschi or Michelozzo.[7] Despite the several commissions he received and his prestigious appointment to the post of head architect of the *fabbrica* (building site) of the Duomo, the only "architectural" masterpiece Filarete ever completed was his *Trattato di Architettura*,

---

4   The standard edition is edited by Anna Maria Finoli and Liliana Grassi: *Antonio Averlino detto il Filarete, Trattato di architettura*, 2 vols (Milan, 1972), hereafter cited as *Trattato*. The hospital is described in Book 11, 1:297–322. The *Trattato* has been translated into English by John R. Spenser, *Treatise on architecture; being the treatise by Antonio di Piero Averlino, known as Filarete*, 2 vols (New Haven, CT, 1965), hereafter cited as Spenser. The passages on the hospital are: 1:137–46.

5   There is no recent monograph on Filarete. A dated but still valuable text is by Michele Lazzaroni and Antonio Muñoz, *Filarete, scultore e architetto del secolo XV* (Rome, 1908). A useful collection of essays appeared as Volume 18 of the journal *Arte Lombarda* (1973).

6   See Piero Pierotti, Prima di Machiavelli: *Filarete e Francesco di Giorgio consiglieri del principe* (Ospedaletto, 1995). According to Pierotti, Sforza called Filarete to court for his abilities as architect and as military engineer; specifically, the artist had claimed to be able to build a defensive wall for a city in the record time of two weeks.

7   During his stay at the Sforza court, Filarete worked on the Duomo, the Castello, the Palazzo del Banco Mediceo and the Cathedral of Bergamo.

a long treatise on architecture and urban planning, the riches of which art historians have seldom exploited.[8]

Written in the early 1460s as a fictitious dialog between an artist and a prince, Filarete's treatise describes an urban utopia, "Sforzinda." Its hospital closely mirrors the Ospedale Maggiore, a fact that Filarete himself stresses in stating that: "When [the Prince] told me to make a drawing of the hospital, I said, 'My lord, I will make one like the one I did in Milan. If it please you, I will tell you how it was.'"[9] In the long and detailed description that follows this quotation, Sforzinda's hospital is quickly erected under the artist's careful supervision. Unlike the utopian hospital, the Ospedale Maggiore developed as a true civic enterprise, a faithful reflection of Renaissance Milanese culture and political compromise. Exasperated by the difficulties created by those who opposed the duke, Filarete himself left the building project in 1465 when only one arm of the men's *crociera* (cross) was completed.[10]

The 1791 plan (Fig. 7.1) is helpful in understanding Filarete's plan as well as the various building campaigns. The men's *crociera* (the right cross) was completed by 1476. The women's *crociera* (the left cross) was built in the seventeenth century, with construction beginning in 1624. It is important to note that there are some differences between the utopian hospital described in the *Trattato* and the real Ospedale Maggiore. In fact, the Ospedale's elevated floors do not resemble the *Trattato*'s drawings of the facade, because there are no towers, no multiple entablatures and no lavish decorations. Moreover, in the building's layout, the central component is square rather than rectangular. Despite these differences, the essence of the building is found below ground level in the foundations – a fact that Vasari already understood well before anyone could appreciate the building as it later stood finished at the end of the seventeenth century. Fortunately, these foundations and the canal system running through them were built according to Filarete's original plan (Fig. 7.2).[11]

---

8 Although it was not printed, the *Trattato* circulated widely during the fifteenth century; it was even translated into Latin. See the recent edition by Maria Beltramini, *Antonio Bonfini, La latinizzazione del Trattato d'architettura di Filarete (1488–89)* (Pisa, 2000). While praising the Ospedale, after briefly describing the *Trattato*'s contents, Vasari consigned the *Trattato* to oblivion by concluding: "e comecchè alcuna cosa buona in essa [opera] si ritruovi, è non-dimeno per lo più ridicola, e tanto sciocca, che per avventura è nulla più." DeVere translates: "But although there is something of the good to the found in it, it is nevertheless mostly ridiculous, and perhaps the most stupid book that was ever written" (*Lives*, p. 5). Vasari then sealed this treatise's fate by remarking that Filarete "ha durato fatica, come si dice, per impoverire, e per esser tenuto di poco giudizio, in mettersi a far quello che non sapeva" (see Vasari, *Vite*, p. 457). DeVere translates: "he has toiled only to beggar himself, as the saying goes, and to be thought a man of little judgement for meddling with something that he did not understand" (*Lives*, p. 6).

9 *Trattato*, p. 298; Spenser, p. 137.

10 The important sources and documents pertaining to this history have been collected by Pio Pecchiai, *L'Ospedale Maggiore di Milano nella storia e nell'arte* (Milan, 1927). The most detailed account of the hospital's early history is offered by Franca Leverotti, "Ricerche sulle origini dell'Ospedale Maggiore di Milano," *Archivio Lombardo* 107 (1984), 77–114.

11 For a recent discussion of the drawings appended to the manuscript, see Maria Beltramini, "Le illustrazioni del Trattato d'architettura di Filarete: storia, analisi e fortuna,"

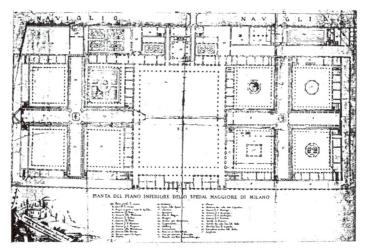

Figure 7.1   Plan of the Ospedale Maggiore (Archivio dell'Ospedale Maggiore, 1791; used by permission of Ospedale Maggiore di Milano).

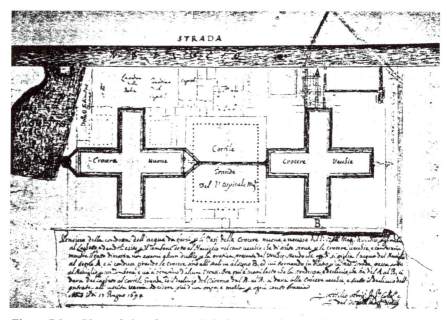

Figure 7.2   Plan of the *destri* and their connection to the Navigio (Archivio dell'Ospedale Maggiore, 1694; used by permission of Ospedale Maggiore di Milano; photograph edited by B.S. Bowers).

Annali di architettura rivista del centro internazionale di studi di architettura Andrea Palladio, 13 (2001), 25–52.

Construction of the Ospedale Maggiore began in the midst of an *urbis renovatio* (city-wide rebuilding campaign). Mid-century Milan had no fewer than forty construction sites, the most important one being the fabbrica odel Duomo.[12] While this building euphoria had been financed by the wealth and political power that Milan had enjoyed since the fourteenth century, the late 1440s proved to be a period of political instability and social strife. In 1447, after ruling for thirty years, Filippo Maria Visconti died without having produced a male heir, thus leaving the city with an uncertain political future. Out of this unstable political situation emerged the Ambrosian Republic, an enlightened oligarchy that fell victim to an unfortunate combination of events: the famine in 1448 while drained the Republic's financial resources, and a virulent outbreak of plague in 1449 brought the Republic it to its knees, threatening the very survival of the Milanese. As a result, in 1450 the decimated city was conquered without difficulty by Francesco Sforza, the successful *condottiere* (mercenary captain) who had served the Visconti and had married Bianca Maria, Filippo Maria's only heir.

Despite their military weakness, the Milanese were reluctant subjects. To win them over Sforza who understood that his popularity depended upon his success in controlling the plague, directly addressed the epidemic in his first legislative acts. Instead of acting as a despotic ruler, he hoped to govern through established institutions. Within two weeks of his entry into the city, he held new elections to replace the 24 members of the health and hygiene board an important political body, because rather than being simply advisory, this board was in charge of managing civic resources to fight the epidemic. Entrusted with producing, enacting and enforcing its own decrees.[13] In such an unstable political environment, Sforza decided not to interfere with the elections. As a result, the newly elected board members constituted a stronghold of Visconti loyalists and Republican advocates whose political inclinations coupled with their power posed a considerable internal threat to the duke's government. To remedy this dangerous situation, some time in early 1451 Sforza conceived the idea of founding a magnificent hospital as a way of gaining control of the health and hygiene board while also winning the people's favor. Moreover in his view, this building was to serve as the administrative headquarters of Milan's hospital reform, therefore tangibly demonstrating the duke's commitment to the Milanese. Perhaps more importantly still, the Ospedale offered the opportunity to the Milanese to bond and commit to their new ruler. In fact, beyond functioning as a counterbalance to the equally grand expansion project for his castle, this grand new building was intended by the duke to attract the Milanese's charitable donations, diverting them away from

---

12 For an overview of fifteenth-century architecture in Milan, see Luciano Patetta, *L'architettura del Quattrocento a Milano* (Milan, 1987), esp. pp. 275–291.

13 For a brief introduction to this topic, see Carlo Cipolla, "The Health Boards in Italy and Epidemiological Concepts," in *Miasmas and Disease: Public Health and the Environment in the Preindustrial Age* (New Haven, CT, 1992), 1–9.

the *fabbrica* of the Duomo, the Visconti symbol *par excellence*.[14] In the end, the duke's plan was successful. By becoming the patron of the building and by donating considerable funds toward the start of the project, Sforza was eventually allowed to nominate 36 candidates from whom the archbishop would select the health and hygiene board members.[15]

There were many implications to conceiving the Ospedale Maggiore as the pivotal structure in Milan's hospital reform.[16] The aim of this reform was the creation of an integrated civic hospital system that would consolidate and rationalize the care that was then being offered by private and religious charitable institutions scattered throughout the city. Integrated into a new health care network available to all citizens, these institutions would be staffed with doctors and surgeons at the city's expense; each one would specialize in a particular medical or sanitary task. The Ospedale Maggiore, beyond housing some patients, was to serve as an admission center where the infirm would be diagnosed and redirected to the institution in the network that offered the most appropriate care for his or her case. The also provided office space for the administrative personal charged with overseeing the financial aspects of the new integrated system. In the eyes of the citizens, this meant that the Ospedale Maggiore protected their interests by taking the control of these institutions out of the hands of ecclesiastical authorities, who in the past they had mismanaged these institutions and created many scandals by selling the administrative posts. In short, by setting in motion the hospital reform and becoming the patron of a grand new hospital, Sforza proved to the Milanese people that he was their paladin, and not simply a ruthless *condottiere*. Because Milan's hospital reform had been planned for almost a century, but had never materialized by bringing about the reform of Milan's hospitals, he succeeded where the Visconti and the Republic had repeatedly failed. Despite his good intentions, Sforza prevailed only after overcoming the fierce opposition mounted by the religious leaders who derived their livelihood from these institutions. While the papal bull necessary to suppress the existing institutions and create a new church in the centre of the Ospedale Maggiore came only come after the Visconti archbishop was succeeded by Sforza's brother. This latter change demanded a political compromise, truly quid pro quo of international dimension, for which the duke had to pledge his military support for the crusade against the advancing Turks that Pope Pius II proposed at the Diet of Mantua in 1459.[17]

---

14 On this latter topic, see Giuliana Albini, "Continuità e innovazione: la carità a Milano fra tensioni private e strategie pubbliche," in *La carità Milano nei secoli XII–XV*, ed. M.P. Alberzoni and O. Grassi (Milan, 1989), pp. 137–51.

15 For a detailed account of these events, see Leverotti, "Ricerche sulle origini"; for the documentary evidence, see Pecchiai, *L'Ospedale Maggiore*.

16 See Giuliana Albini, "La gestione dell'Ospedale Maggiore di Milano nel Quattrocento: un esempio di concentrazione ospedaliera," in *Ospedali e città: l'Italia del Centro-Nord, XIII–XV secolo*, ed. Allen Grieco and Lucia Sandri (Florence, 1997), pp. 157–78.

17 Pius II signed the Bull on December 9, 1459. Among other provisions, it specified that the administrators of the suppressed institutions were to receive a lifetime pension and that the administrative board of the Ospedale Maggiore was to be reduced in number to 18 from

Upon deciding to build a new hospital in 1451, Sforza proceeded with hiring an architect, and invited Filarete to Milan. Unfortunately, the project could not immediately get under way for several reasons: the plague drained the city and the duke's finances, while religious leaders mounted a skilful resistance. By 1456 the site had been officially chosen. The symbolic first stone was laid in April, and demolition of existing structures on the site was begun in June of that year. Several documents suggest that until that time, no definite plan for the hospital had been approved. In fact, surviving diplomatic correspondence between Sforza and the Medici indicates that during the summer of 1456 Filarete, *inzegnero* (engineer), and Johanne de Sancto Ambrogio, *maestro da muro* (master stonemason) visited Florence to inspect and copy the plans of its famous hospitals. While the results of this expedition are not known, passages in the *Trattato* make it clear that the duke was not satisfied with the plans of existing structures, and doubted that their design could even be re-worked.[18] His reservations – implicitly representing Filarete's opinion – applied to the two famous Tuscan institutions, and likely to the Lombard hospitals either then under construction or recently built: Cremona, Brescia, Pavia and Mantua had built new hospitals following their own hospital reform. [19]

As seen in the *Trattato*'s drawings and in the 1791 site plan (Fig. 7.1), the layout of the Ospedale Maggiore integrates the cruciform with the longitudinal plan. That is, from the outside the building is a longitudinal structure. But the interior of the rectangular area it occupies is divided into three spaces: two Greek crosses inscribed within squares that are separated by a rectangular area. In the scholarly literature, from Philip Foster's early study to Adriano Peroni's recent article, historians have argued that Filarete's plan represents a rejection of the Tuscan model and an

---

the 24 original members; 12 were to be chosen by the Duke, and 6 were to be elected. See Pecchiai, *L'Ospedale Maggiore*, pp. 170–73. Pius II had also instituted an indulgence for the Ospedale Maggiore. Half of the profits were to fund the crusade against the Turks; the other half was to be divided between the *fabbrica* of the Duomo and the Ospedale Maggiore. See *La Ca' Granda*, p. 82.

18 This is clearified by Filarete in the following passage: "E lui, impostomi questo, ch'io dovessi fare uno disegno, in prima mi domandó's'io avevo veduto quello di Firenze o di Siena, e se mi ricordavo come stavano. Dissi di sí. Volle vedere uno certo congetto del fondamento, e io cosí lineato come meglio mi ricordavo gliene disegnai uno come quello di Firenze. Pur parendo a lui non essere sí idonio come lui avrebbe voluto e ancora per vantaggiare gli altri, stava pure sospeso. ... Dissi che ne farei uno come a me pareva fusse conveniente al bisogno di quello edificio per che si faceva." And after Filarete describes in detail his plan for the hospital, the Duke says "Piacemi assai infino a qui," later concluding: "Io ti commendo che tu abbi fatto meglio a farlo in questa forma. ... A me piace più in questa forma che nell'altra per ogni aspetto"; *Trattato*, pp. 299–300 and 306–7.

19 Brescia's hospital was completed in the late 1440s, while the hospital that Sforza himself had been the patron of in Pavia was completed in 1449. On hospital reform in northern Italy, see Guiliana Albini, *Città e ospedali nella Lombardia medievale* (Bologna, 1993), and *Guerra, fame, peste. Crisi di mortalità e sistema sanitario nella Lombardia tardomedievale* (Bologna, 1982).

adoption of the cruciform plan.[20] It has also been noted that the Greek cross model was not Filarete's own innovation, but one already adopted in Lombard hospitals in the 1440s, while this design type might actually have its roots in Cairo's Qalaum hospital begun in 1286.[21] However, a close reading of Filarete's own description of the Ospedale Maggiore's plan and the sequence of events that led to its design suggests that the geometrical layout of the building was neither innovative nor a crucial consideration for either the architect or his patron. First and foremost, Sforza and his advisers were concerned with the quality of the air circulating in the building. To address this design priority, Filarete created a brilliant plan that integrated an effective sewer system to ensure that the air circulating in the building would not be a vehicle causing disease to spread.[22]

This concern for air quality and the avoidance of noxious odors was well established within medieval medical and public health knowledge. At the time it was believed that, rather than microbes and vectors, infectious diseases were caused by a corruption of the air. Inhaling miasmatic atoms from noxious fumes would poison the lungs and create a humoral imbalance; the body would try to correct this imbalance by ridding itself of the poison through buboes. Furthermore, the idea that clean air is not only beneficial but a sine qua non for the recovery of the sick had been defended by Leon Battista Alberti in his *De re aedificatoria* only a few years before Filarete developed his plan.[23] In this work, Alberti specifies that it is essential for any building in which sick are to be cared for to keep the air pure and the water clean.[24] Furthermore, it is also noteworthy that Alberti does not recommend any specific type of hospital plan. He does mention that Tuscan institutions were famous, but when he presents model hospitals, he takes as his primary example the ancient temples of Apollo. He recognized that the sick recovered not through divine intervention, but because of the temple's chosen location and the sanitary conditions of the building – that is, fresh air and the availability of clean water.

---

20 See Philip Foster, "Per il disegno dell'Ospedale di Milano," *Arte Lombarda* 18 (1973), 1–22; and Adriano Peroni, "Il modello dell'ospedale cruciforme: il problema del rapporto tra l'Ospedale di Santa Maria Nuova di Firenze e gli ospedali lombardi," in *Florence and Milan: Comparisons and Relations*, ed. S. Bertelli, N. Rubinstein and C. Hugh Smyth, 2 vols (Florence, 1989), 2:53–66.

21 See Ralph Quadflieg, *Filaretes Ospedale Maggiore in Mailand: Zur Rezeption islamischen Hospitalwesens in der italienischen Frührenaissance* (PhD Dissertation, University of Cologne, 1981).

22 Art and architectural historians have indeed overlooked the importance of this functional aspect of building. Epitomizing this attitude is a passing remark by Welch: "[Reguardati's] theories written in *De conservatione sanitatis* were straight forward and could easily be transformed into architectural practice"; *Art and Authority in Renaissance Milan*, p. 163.

23 See the recent study by Ida Mastrorosa, "Leon Battista Alberti 'epidemiologo': esiti umanistici di dottrine classiche," *Albertiana*, 4 (2001), 21–44.

24 Ibid.

While Alberti's recommendations undoubtedly influenced Sforza and Filarete, it is most likely that the duke's personal physician, Benedetto Reguardati, was the person who stressed and clarified the importance of the quality of the air circulating in the new hospital. Beyond being highly regarded within the medical profession and having often served Sforza as a political administrator, Reguardati was the ducal adviser on matters concerning the plague when the *condottiere* entered Milan.[25] Reguardati's writings explicitly linked the cause of the epidemic to the air present in the immediate environment. Rather than being revolutionary, his epidemiological notions precisely reflect the traditional views held by his predecessors. These are epitomized in the writings of three Lombard doctors who had dedicated their treatises on the plague to the Visconti.[26] Specifically, the explanation of the plague in terms of corruption of the air and the idea that contagion results from exposure to putrefying fumes were clearly presented by Cardono de' Spanzoti in his 1360 treatise *De preservatione a pestilentia*. Pietro Curialti and Antonio Guaniero presented that same beliefs and conclusions in their own writings, respectively of 1398 and the 1440s. It is precisely a concern with the quality of the air and avoidance of the formation of putrifying fumes that is repeated in Filarete's description of the Ospedale Maggiore.[27]

Among the *Trattato*'s first remarks on the subject, Filarete emphasizes that the site chosen by the duke "was beautiful and really suitable for such a building."[28] The beauty and appropriateness of the site was based on the fact that on the southern, long side of the rectangular area there was a canal (which was covered in the late nineteenth century). The advantages this canal offered are then explained in the text as the description continues. Filarete makes the character of the prince ask his architect how he ensured that the hospital would "be beautiful and capable of fulfilling the needs of infirm men and women."[29]

---

25 For his biography and diplomatic career, see Gonario Deffenu, *Benedetto Reguardati medico e diplomatico di Francesco Sforza* (Milan, 1955), and Juliana Hill Cotton, "Benedetto Reguardati of Nursia (1398–1469)," *Medical History*, 13 (1969), 175–89. Highlights of his medical theories are presented by Cotton, "Benedetto Reguardati, author of Ugo Benzi's Tractato de la conservatione de la sanitade," *Medical History*, 12 (1968), 76–83.

26 Although focussed on the 1468 plague, a fundamental study is by Ann G. Carmichael, "Contagion Theory and Contagion Practice in Fifteenth-century Milan," *Renaissance Quarterly*, 44 (1991), 213–56.

27 An apt summary of the ancient and medieval views about the importance of the salubrity of the air that survive in the Renaissance is found in Chapter XLIX of Guilielmo Copo's summary of Paul of Aegina's *Praecepta Salubria* (Paris, 1511) (or Book I of his larger *Epitome medicae libri septem*, a fundamental encyclopedia of the ancient medical knowledge written in the sixth century and well known through the Renaissance): "Aere exacte puro, utpote qui neque stagnorum negne paludumum, neque barathri cuiuspiam pestilentem auram eructantis, vaporis inficitur, haud non alius melior est. Contra malus est, quem cloaca aliqua magna urbem purgans, perturbat et nebulosus, item qui in valle undique aeditis montibus contentus, nullam suscipit auram. Igitur qui sic infectus est aer, omnem aetatem, omnemque temperaturam similiter laedit, optimus vero omnibus prodest. At in qualitate, ut calore, frigore, ariditate, humiditate, aer mutatus, haudquaque similiter omnes afficit. Quippe temperato corpori, temperatus, distenperatis vero qui contrariam habuerit temperaturam aer utilis est."

28 *Trattato*, p. 299; Spenser, p. 137.

29 Ibid.

Next, Filarete presents a detailed account of the hospital's conception, beginning with the prince's rejection of the model plans of the famous hospitals of Florence and Siena. The prince had requested the artist to draw these plans because, beyond measuring the artist's credentials and knowledge on the matter, he wanted to analyze – and Filarete's wanted to explain – the rationale of the design of their foundations. And it is the properties of the design of the foundations, *uno certo congetto del fondamento*, that provide the real basis for comparison among plans.[30] Upon seeing the plans of these Tuscan hospitals, the prince rejects them, finding them inappropriate and unfit for amelioration. Then the architect proposes his own plan, remarking that "because [the prince] was really keen on the functionality and the cleaning of the sewers, and the site so appropriate, I thought that the very same water [of the canal] could be used to wash and clean the sewers."[31] Underscoring the importance of this subject, and unlike the discussion of any other aspect of the hospital, Filarete devotes the next folio to a detailed description of how the *destri* function.

As can be seen from the sixteenth-century bird's-eye view of Milan published by Georg Bruin (Fig. 7.3), Filarete diverted some of the water from a nearby canal, channeling it into the building. Flowing through the vaulted conduits built into the foundations, the water then exited at the opposite end of the Ospedale Maggiore into a small lake, the *laghetto*, which emptied into the canal, thereby offering "great benefits for those having fields downstream."[32]

As clearly depicted in a later plan (Fig. 7.2), the underground system of canals was completed and fully operative at an early stage of building's life. Certainly, the portion of the *destri* serving the men's *crociera* was completed when this section was erected in the fifteenth century, while the *destri* serving the women's *crociera* were finished in the early seventeenth century, but very likely operated already earlier.[33] Equally certain is the fact the *destri* were conceived of as an integral structure during Filarete's tenure in Milan. This is implied by the carefully planned system of dams and the conduits' degree of inclination which produced the driving power for the vigorous water flow necessary to keep the sewer system clean, and thereby avoid the formation of stagnant, putrid waters and their noxious vapors. Following Filarete's description of the *destri* system, Liliana

---

30 *Trattato*, p. 300; Spenser, p. 137.

31 Ibid.

32 *Trattato*, p. 303; Spenser, p. 138. It is interesting to note that, according to Michele Lazzaroni and Antonio Muñoz, the Pope had praised the idea of building a hospital near the *laghetto* in the early stages of planning; see *Filarete, scultore e architetto del secolo XV* (Rome, 1908), p. 185. This remark by Nicodemo da Pantremoli, Sforza's envoy to Rome, is found in a 4 May 1451 account of the Pope's reply to the Duke's request for permission to consolidate Milan's hospitals into an integrated system (unfortunately, no further reference is given on the location of these documents).

33 This is suggested by Pietro Canetta in his short study entitled *Cenni storici sugli acquedotti sotterranei dell'Ospedale Maggiore di Milano servienti a smaltire le materie fecali* (Milan: 1884), p. 8.

Grassi was able to find the channels and the various conduits he mentions during the post-war reconstruction of the building (Fig. 7.4).[34]

Figure 7.3   Detail from the view of Mediolanum (where the "Ospital gr[ande]" and the "laghetto" are clearly labelled) (from Georg Buin, *Civitates Orbis Terrarum*, 1572; used by permission of Ospedale Maggiore di Milano; photograph edited by B.S. Bowers).

After describing the engineering and architectural solutions embodied by the *destri*, Filarete has the character of the prince continue the discussion to explain why this system is so important and useful for his hospital: "I think that I have clearly understood this [discussion] of the cleaning and the water that you say goes around [this arm of] the cross. So far it pleases me. Now, explain to me briefly how these [*destri*] are made useful for the sick, and how do they not give off a bad odor."[35] Despite the less than regal subject matter, the architect goes on to describe how small pipes connect the main *destri* to each of the hospital beds, and how large terracotta pipes, passing inside some of the structural piers of the building, rise from the canals to the roof, exhausting any fumes that may have formed underground, and how they also function as gutters for rainwater to flush the channels clean. Furthermore, the

---

34 The relevant photographs, reproduced as Figs 211–13, are discussed in Grassi, *Lo 'spedale*, p. 135.Spenser, p. 138. The original passage reads: "E mi pare assai bene avere inteso questa acqua e questo lavamento che tu di' che va intorno a questa crociera. ... Infino a qui mi piace, dami un poco a' intendere questi destri come stanno, che siano comodi a l'infermi e che non faccino cattivo odore"; *Trattato*, pp. 303–4.

35 Spenser, p. 138. The original passage reads: "E mi pare assai bene avere inteso questa acqua e questo lavamento che tu di' che va intorno a questa crociera. ... Infino a qui mi piace, dami un poco a' intendere questi destri come stanno, che siano comodi a l'infermi e che non faccino cattivo odore"; *Trattato*, pp. 303–4.

pull-down seats facing the wall openings by the beds are designed so well that all the waste falls down into the canal, where running water will carry everything away. "No bad odor whatsoever can be caused, because they are so well arranged that they are always covered and always washed and cleaned by flowing water."[36]

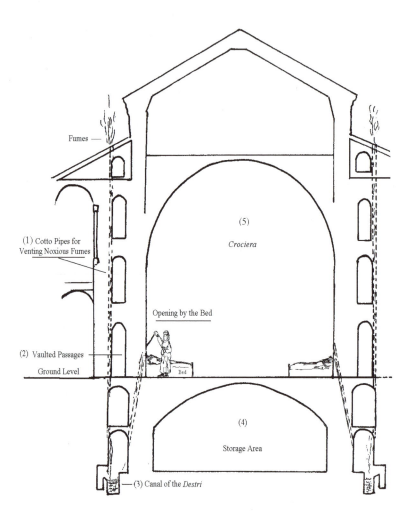

Figure 7.4   Cross-section of a *crociera* with the conduits of the destri (after the illustration by Liliana Grassi, Fig. 29 in Grassi, Lo "*spedale di poveri*" del Filarete, Milan, 1972; drawn by the author; additional editing/drawing by B.S. Bowers).

36 Ibid., p. 305; Spenser, p. 138.

The recurrent point of the functionality of the *destri* clarifies that they, rather than the building's layout, are the essence of the building. Above all, the *destri* are the innovation Filarete introduces into the hospital's plan since they have no known precedents, as no other early Renaissance hospital had such a complex and efficient sewer system.[37]

Although several medieval monasteries had developed extended water systems and some cities had a canal-based sewer system, Filarete likely found inspiration through his antiquarian studies and pursuits.[38] It is not known for certain that he inspected the still famous Roman sewer system at Pavia. However, both Sforza and Reguardati would have been familiar with it. Sforza had conquered Pavia in 1448, and was the patron of the new hospital of San Matteo. Reguardati had studied and taught, and served as city administrator in Pavia, where a city-wide sewer system built in Roman imperial times remained in working condition.[39] It is interesting to observe that this system operated according to the same engineering principles Filarete employed more than a thousand years later: it was constructed using wide, vaulted underground canals through which water diverted from a river flowed, regulated by dams and a variable declining slope. While circumstantial, this evidence supports the hypothesis that Pavia's Roman sewers were the inspiration for the *destri* devised by Filarete.[40] Although it is likely that Alberti's and Reguardati's writings made Filarete

---

37 See Roberta Magnusson, *Water Technology in the Middle Ages: Cities, Monasteries and Waterworks after the Roman Empire* (Baltimore, MD, 2001), and especially the chapter on "Users," pp. 133–62; Magnusson and Paolo Squatriti, "The Technologies of Water in Medieval Italy," in *Working with Water in Medieval Europe: Technology and Resource-use*, ed. Paolo Squatriti (Boston, MA, 2000), 217–66, especially the section on "Waste Water." Filarete's antiquarian interests are demonstrated both the sculptural style of Saint Peter's doors, which reflect a careful observation of late Roman examples, and also in the *Trattato*'s many references to classical monuments and Latin literature.

38 It is very likely that Filarete's (and Alberti's) interests in the waterworks originated with Poggio Bracciolini's recovery of a manuscript of Frontinus' *De Acquaeductu Urbis Romae* – he found it in 1429 and "published" it in 1448. Written at the end of the first century and unknown in the Middle Ages, *De Aquaeductu* celebrates Rome's aqueducts, sewer system and fountains, describing these waterworks in minute technical details. Moreover, Frontinus praises Emperor Nerva for his contributions to Rome's waterworks for his successful effort to eliminate the noxious exhalations, liberating the city of its long-standing ill repute of having poor air quality; see Bk II, 88.

39 See Carlamaria Tomaselli, *Il sistema di fognature romane di Pavia* (Pavia, 1978). Described by many medieval writers, the grid system ran under the streets, using water diverted from the Ticino river. A steady current flow was maintained by a gentle downhill slope, through a system of dams. Built mostly of brick, the passages are vaulted. The main ones, like those of the Ospedale Maggiore, have two levels, a lower one to carry flowing waters and an upper one to allow a person access to inspect and clean the canals whenever necessary.

40 Unfortunately, information on the condition or design principles of the *cloaca* of Milan is unavailable. From a remark in a medieval manuscript, it seems that two canals were designated to receive dirty and polluted water from sewers and commercial operations; see

aware of the hygiene challenges that a new grand and functional hospital posed, it is important to note that Filarete's *destri*, the solution to such challenges, reflected both his attention to function and his own architectural theories presented in the opening of the *Trattato*.[41] For Filarete, a building was like a living person, a human body that needs to breathe and to expel bodily fluids. The Ospedale Maggiore does this through its complex system of *destri*.

In conclusion, the Ospedale Maggiore emerges as the best example of the Renaissance hospital. It epitomizes perfectly the combination of elements that during the late Trecento and early Quattrocento created a new concept of hospital. In many cities in central and northern Italy during the fifteenth century, the hospital became a civic and a medical institution. Thanks to the various programs of hospital reform, new and often grand hospitals were built; these functioned both as places of healing and as administrative headquarters for integrated health care systems. The Ospedale Maggiore further excelled because it integrated medical and epidemiological notions through its innovative design, making its space an environment that worked positively toward the patients' recovery.

Angelo La Cava, *Igiene e sanità negli statuti di Milano del sec. XIV* (Milan, 1946), especially, pp. 43–4. Also insightful are the sections on "Acque" and "Cloache e pozzi neri" in the fourteenth-century *Codex Statutorum Veterum Mediolanensis* conserved in the archive of the Ospedale Maggiore. These sections, transcribed by La Cava (*Igiene*, p. 64, Chapter 12, 171 v.) read as follows:

De cloacis et magolijs removendis

Cum cloacae et magolcia in civitate pestilentem reddant aerem, statuitur, quod aque, que de plateis decurrunt in domibus privatorum, et ibi faciunt cloacas, vel magolcia redducantur ad fossatum, vel Neronum, vel Sevisium, per viam illam, per quam melius et facilius decurrere possint. Et quod potestas et eius iudices, et iudex stratarum et domini sex, et quilibet eorum, sub poena librarum decem tertiolorum qualibet vice, si requisiti fuerint, teneantur hoc exequi. Et possint hoc facere illi, in quorum domibus sunt cloace vel magolcia. Hoc tamen fiat expensis illorum in quorum domibus sint ipse cloace vel magolcia hoc fieri petentium, et cum minori lesione aliorum quam fieri potest.

41 See Spenser, pp. 12–13: "I have shown you by means of a simile that a building is derived from man, that is, from form, members and measure. Vitruvius also says that the building is derived from the human form. Now, as I told you above, I will show you how the building is given form and substance by analogy with the members and form of man. ... I will then show you that the building is truly a living man. You will see what it must eat in order to live, exactly as it is with man. It sickens and dies or sometimes is cured of its sickness by a good doctor. Sometimes, like a man, it becomes ill again because it neglects its health. Many times, through [the care] of a good doctor, it returns to health and lives a long while and finally dies in its own time."

Section III
New Approaches to Written Sources

Chapter 8

Religion and Discipline in the Hospitals of Thirteenth-century France

James W. Brodman

Hospitals in medieval and late medieval Europe were sacred places; they were not, in the modern sense, secular institutions. Hospital statutes from throughout medieval Europe always give priority to the spiritual over the secular well-being of sick inmates, to sacramental care over medical treatment. A commemorative Mass and proper burial for patients were as much a concern as a fit diet or medicinal regimen. Indeed, many if not most hospitals were as much a place to die as a locus of cure. Thus, whatever their mode of governance or place within the civil or ecclesiastical hierarchy, hospitals were served by chaplains or parish priests who carried out the *cura pauperum* (care of the poor) in much the same fashion as the parochial clergy held the *cura animarum* (care of the soul).[1] Yet there is considerable variation in the internal governance of medieval houses of charity: some were served by members of an extended religious order like the Trinitarians, the Antonines or the brethren of the Holy Spirit; others, such as those in the medieval Crown of Aragon, had a mixed staff of salaried servants and administrators assisted by various kinds of *volunteers*. Those to be examined here, the *hôtels-Dieu* and *maisons-Dieu* of thirteenth-century France, were staffed by essentially local communities of religious men and/or women.[2]

This type of hospital is characterized by its local character, namely the absence of any affiliation with a larger organization or with other hospitals, and the existence within it of an independent community of religious women and/or men who serve the poor while under religious vows. Those of the second variety were also local in character, but were served by individuals not subject to systematic religious discipline. Those of the first type, being affiliated with religious orders, naturally followed the Rule of the larger organization. The questions this study asks are: why

---

1 For a general discussion of the religious character of the medieval hospital, and the historiographical debate that it has engendered, see James W. Brodman, *Charity and Welfare: Hospitals and the Poor in Medieval Catalonia* (Philadelphia, PA, 1998), pp. 125–44; Joseph Avril, "Le statut des maisons-dieu dans l'organisation ecclésiastique médiévale," in *110ᵉ Congrès national des Societés savantes, Montpellier, 1985* (Paris, 1987), 1:289. The term "hospitaller" refers to hospitals and to those who served in them; "Hospitaller," on the other hand, designates the military order of St John of the Hospital, or Knights Hospitaller. See also Chapters 2, 13 and 14 in this volume.

2 Brodman, *Charity and Welfare*, pp. 54–7.

does this third variety develop, and why did the discipline that one associates with monks or friars come to be imposed upon those who served the poor in municipal hospitals? Because these institutions had a variety of patrons (bishops, cathedral chapters as well as prosperous lay people), the answers to these questions are not immediately evident.

The most obvious factor in the development of religious observance within local hospitals is that of size. In France, as in the neighboring Crown of Aragon or elsewhere in Europe, most institutions were small hospitals of the second type. Catalan and Valencian hospitals, for example, rarely served more than a score of the poor and had staffs that numbered fewer than half a dozen chaplains and attendants. A document of 1307, for example, shows that the almost defunct Hospital of Bernat Marcús in Barcelona had a staff that numbered only three. On the other hand, in northern Castile, where hospitals built along the pilgrimage routes were larger than their Catalan counterparts, hospitallers were organized under a religious Rule. For example, there is the case of the Hospital del Rey in Burgos, established by King Alfonso VIII in 1209 and served by a community of 13 brothers who lived according to the Cistercian Rule.[3] Likewise in France, a significant number of hospitals achieved a size that made feasible the practice of a regular religious observance among those who served there. Furthermore, in France a strong tradition of episcopal and royal leadership existed which came to promote an imposition of such a discipline upon larger local hospitals.[4]

The question of the reform of hospitals and the imposition of religious discipline upon their staffs was first addressed at a number of regional ecclesiastical councils held in France between 1213 and 1215 in preparation for the upcoming Fourth Lateran Council. These were summoned by Robert de Courçon, a recently appointed Cardinal and Papal Legate. Robert, moreover, was also a member of a group of reformist clerics, along with Jacques de Vitry and Foulques de Neuilly, who belonged to the circle of the Parisian master Peter the Chanter. Not coincidentally, both Peter and Robert had an interest in the fate of the poor and argued that those in power, especially ecclesiastics, had an obligation to assist the needy in times of distress. John Baldwin believes that Robert deliberately introduced the reformist ideals of Peter's followers at these six Gallican councils as a rehearsal for their introduction at the forthcoming

---

3   Ibid., pp. 56–57 and 62–3; Luis Martínez García, *El Hospital del Rey de Burgos: Un señorío medieval en la expansión y en la crisis (siglos XIII y XIV)* (Burgos, 1986), pp. 58–73.

4   In Catalonia, on the other hand, there was scant episcopal interest in hospitaller reform. Peter Linehan sketches a portrait of an episcopacy in disarray. In the thirteenth century, the only reformist archbishop was Pedro de Albalat of Tarragona, who fought against the ill-discipline of the clergy, such as concubinage, apostasy, pluralism and so on. Even this basic agenda, evidently, was frustrated by entrenched corruption; see Peter Linehan, *The Spanish Church and the Papacy in the Thirteenth Century* (Cambridge, 1971), pp. 54, 61 and 85. One assumes that the monarchy was consumed by its military and colonial activities in the Balearic Islands and Valencia, and by its political machinations in Occitania. But there is simply no good study of the interaction of king and Church in the thirteenth or fourteenth centuries.

ecumenical assemblage in Rome.[5] As a consequence, the councils held at Paris in 1213 and at Rouen in 1214 affirmed the Church's responsibility over all hospitals, particularly to ensure the honesty and propriety of their administration. At the first of these, Robert de Courçon, recommended the introduction of a regular discipline into hospitaller institutions in order to deal with instances of fraud and abuse, a problem also noted by the near-contemporary French chronicler and bishop, Jacques de Vitry. The latter describes instances of abuse in his *Historia Occidentalis*:[6]

> For under the pretext of hospitality and the guise of piety, they become alms-collectors, improperly extorting monies by lies and deception and by every means at their disposal, feasting on the poor, not caring for them except with they, by giving a little to the poor and infirm, are able to demand alms from the faithful. This pestilential corruption and hateful hypocrisy does not affect all hospitals. For some are regular congregations and principal convents or hospitaller chapters in which the fervor of charity, the unction of piety, the decor of honesty or the severity of discipline have not departed.

The bishops at Paris in 1213 also worried that funds were being diverted from care of the poor, either through fraud or misappropriation, for example, for the support of religious communities whose size exceeded the numbers of the poor being assisted. The remedy offered at Paris was to subject men, women and married couples who served in such hospitals to the discipline of the religious life:

> Concerning houses of lepers and hospitals of the sick and pilgrims with wise advice we establish that, if the resources of the place are sufficient for those who reside there to live a common life, a suitable rule be enacted for them, whose substance is to be contained particularly in three articles, namely, that they renounce personal property, take the vow of continence, and promise faithful and devoted obedience to their prelate, and wear religious, not secular, garb. … Therefore, we decree that they live religiously in the habit of religion or be ejected from [their] houses.

Three years later, however, Lateran IV was less ambitious than the French reformers in its regulation of hospitals. In 1215, the assembled bishops did reiterate this concern with misappropriation of funds. Canon 62, a decree on relics, also exhorted the faithful to give alms to hospitals since resources were inadequate for support of the staff and the needy who flock to them; on the other hand, agents who collect any alms were to be licensed by the pope or a local bishop. Canon 22 touched tangentially upon hospitals by warning physicians who treat the seriously ill that they have the responsibility to summon a priest even before they commenced any medical ministrations. Unlike the French bishops, however, those assembled in

---

5 The six councils were (chronologically) at: Paris, Rouen, Bordeaux, Clermont, Montpellier and Bourges. The *acta* of Paris, Rouen and Montpellier are almost identical; John W. Baldwin, *Masters, Princes and Merchants: The Social Views of Peter the Changer and His Circle* (Princeton, NJ, 1970), 1:19–21 and 236–7.

6 Jacques de Vitry, *The Historia occidentalis of Jacques de Vitry*, ed. J.F. Hinnebusch (Freiburg, 1972), pp. 148–9, cap. 29.

Rome made no effort to impose the religious life upon all those who ministered to the poor in hospitals.[7] The issue of probity of hospital administration, however, remained a concern that would be taken up later by French moralists like the one-time Dominican master-general, Humbert de Romans. His sermons, written in the early 1270s, accused hospital staff of the sins of envy and avarice when they withheld benefits from the poor in whose interest their institution was endowed.[8]

This interest in hospital reform therefore appears to have begun in France and to have had its greatest impact there. Among its effects was the implementation of the religious life upon the hospitaller communities of many *hôtels-Dieu* or local, community-based hospitals. The evidence for the religious regimen that developed in France is found in a series of texts from the thirteenth century. Some of these were published in 1901 by Léon Le Grand, whose collection contains the statutes of 12 municipal hospitals and another 13 leprosaria.[9] The earliest and simplest cited text is that of the Pyrenean Hospital of Aubrac that dates from 1162. A subsequent 11 statutes date from *c.* 1200 to 1270; of these, nine were issued by the local bishop or his cathedral chapter, one by a local count and another by the king. Collectively, these customs were influential in that they were widely imitated and adopted throughout northern France in the thirteenth century.

Legislation prescribing a regular observance applied for the most part to establishments whose communities were large enough to sustain meaningful corporate worship.[10] The exact contours of the communities in Le Grand's collection are, of course, unknown, but these statutes often state a maximum size for the professed community. Of those that do, ideal congregations ranged from a high of 63 for the *hôtel-Dieu* of Paris to as few as 12 at St. Pol, with the rest being no higher than 30.

Penelope Johnson estimates that the typical community of nuns that served in hospitals and almshouses in thirteenth-century France had 10–14 members.[11] These hospitaller communities were divided into three groups: clerics (including priests), lay brothers, and lay sisters. Priests and other clerics were normally the smallest in

---

7   *Decrees of the Ecumenical Councils*, ed. Norman P. Tanner (Washington, DC, 1990), 1: 245–6, no. 22.

8   Alexander Murray, "Religion among the Poor in Thirteenth-century France: The Testimony of Humbert de Romans," *Traditio*, 30 (1974), 289, 308.

9   Léon Le Grand, ed., *Statuts d'Hôtels-Dieu et de Léprosaries: Recueil de texts du XIIIe au XIVe siècle* (Paris, 1901) (hereafter cited as Le Grand).

10   Penelope D. Johnson raises the interesting point that observance in some instances held priority over vocation. She cites the example of an almshouse at the bridge of Couilly, which some years after its foundation accepted the Cistercian Rule for whatever reason, only to become a cloistered convent in 1239 when Hugh, Count of Saint Pol, moved the community into larger quarters that later became the Abbey of Pont-aux-Dames. See her *Equal in Monastic Profession: Religious Women in Medieval France* (Chicago, IL, 1991), p. 39.

11   This seems to be about half the size of other types of female communities; Johnson, *Equal in Monastic Profession*, p. 173.

number, but their role was essential. Not only would they serve as chaplains to inmates of the hospital, but they also typically said daily Mass for the lay brethren, were at times required to say a full office of the hours, and could also serve as administrators of the hospital. The majority of the community consisted of lay brothers and lay sisters. While the proportion among the lay brethren usually favored the sisters, this was not always the case. For example, at Angers laymen outnumbered laywomen by 12 to 8, and at Paris by 30 to 25, but women outnumbered lay brothers at Amiens 8 to 4, at St. Pol by 6 to 2, and at Pontoise by 13 to 2.

The statutes, while making exceptions for ailing brethren and for those in attendance upon the sick, usually required both private and community devotion from the entire congregation. At Aubrac, whose usages date from the 1160s, the lay brethren were merely advised to pray in church and say the *paternoster* 30 times in lieu of the canonical hours; interestingly, women are specifically barred from praying the office.[12]

In the thirteenth century, regulations become more elaborate. Typically, all members of the community were now required to attend matins and Mass in the morning, and sometimes vespers in the evening.[13] In addition, some statutes required that a series of both *paternosters* and *ave marias* be said at other times of the day in lieu of the psalms of the divine office.

Discipline, however, overshadows devotion in these hospitaller statutes.[14] This is understandable for two reasons. First of all, these were small, almost intimate communities, in which religious of both genders lived in close proximity both to each other and to the surrounding urban society. Second, one imagines that hospitaller staff were recruited locally, and thus would have had strong familial ties to the community, with relatives who lived in the neighborhood. Thus the sort of stipulations against sexual transgressions that one finds in the constitutions of single-gender communities are obviously going to require major amplification in this context, and great care will also be taken to maintain some sense of separateness between the religious community and its urban milieu. While the prohibition issued at Angers against the reception of beautiful girls and women, either as sisters or as servants,[15] is not repeated elsewhere, the strict segregation of men and women within the hospital for all activities other than work and prayer, the prohibitions against unauthorized or unaccompanied travel outside the house, and the limitations placed

---

12 Le Grand, pp. 18–19.

13 For example, this is the regimen at Paris, Lille, St. Pol, Pointoise, Vernon and so on.

14 Le Grand argues that the inspiration for the disciplinary regulations came from varied sources. Those that touch upon diet, community life, travel and morality he sees as Augustinian in inspiration; Cistercian influence is seen in those that require weekly chapters and secrecy; Dominican influence can be found in the statutes at Lille (perhaps reflected in the requirement of mandatory bleedings); Le Grand, pp. xvii and xx. Sisters who received episcopal confirmation for their almshouse in Bar-sur-Aube in 1239 followed the Rule of Saint-Victor of Paris; Johnson, *Equal in Monastic Profession*, p. 50; Hinnebusch, *A History of the Dominican Order*, 1:134.

15 See cap. 38 in Le Grand, p. 29.

upon contact with secular society are fairly standard everywhere. Similarly, the increasingly prescriptive dress requirements and periodic bleedings seem designed to assist hospitallers in keeping their vow of chastity.[16] In short, there is much to these statutes that has more in common with any house of religious observance than with hospitals *per se*. Are there points at which religious discipline and hospitaller administration intersect, however?

In the earlier statutes, there is only a vaguely expressed concern that the serving brethren be fit to do the work of the house. At Amiens and Montdidier, the prospective sisters are to be strong; at Paris, they are to be suitable. At Angers, they are to be merely of good reputation and be received into the community without the payment of any sort of gift or dowry of money or property.[17] The subtext here is a concern about corrodians, that is, elderly or sick individuals who in their declining years sought care and shelter from all sorts of ecclesiastical corporations in return for a gift of money and/or property. In this sense, monasteries and the houses of canons, friars and even the military orders served as the nursing homes of the Middle Ages. Hospitals, precisely because they were set up to provide care and shelter, became logical habitats for the medieval elderly, both willingly and unwillingly. For example, in the hospitals of northern England studied by Patricia Cullum, this became a well-established institution, while in mid-thirteenth-century Valencia, hospitals like that of Sant Guillem were forced to care for a quota of royal pensioners.[18] Because this type of extended care, if unaccompanied by a compensating endowment, would be a serious financial drain upon institutional resources, reformers in France generally sought to exclude such individuals.[19] The Council of Paris in 1212 worried "that it is unfitting that the number of the healthy living there exceed those of the sick and

---

16 In the matter of religious dress or habit, for example, the Statutes of Aubrac (1162) merely admonish against the wearing of costly garments and prescribe clothing made of white, brown or black wool; those of Troyes (1263), on the other hand, provide a detailed description of what clerics, lay brothers and nuns are each to wear. At Lille and Pontoise, both brothers and sisters were to be bled bi-monthly. This also was the case for the sisters of the female community of Vernon. Le Grand, pp. 17, no. 3, 106–7, nos 7–15, 73, no. 8, 137, no. 10 and 171, no. 16. Bloodletting was thought to draw off corrupt matter from the body: Nancy Siraisi, *Medieval and Early Renaissance Medicine: An Introduction to Knowledge and Practice* (Chicago, IL, 1990), p. 139. See also Mary K.K. Yearl, Chapter 11 in this volume.

17 Le Grand, pp. 26, no. 18, 35, no. 4 and 44, no. 4.

18 Patricia Cullum, *Cremets and Corrodies: Care of the Poor and Sick at St. Leonard's Hospital, York, in the Middle Ages* (York, 1991), pp. 21 and 26–7; Robert Ignatius Burns SJ, *The Crusader Kingdom of Valencia: Reconstruction on a Thirteenth-century Frontier* (Cambridge, MA, 1967), 1:285–9.

19 This is expressed explicitly in the statutes at Saint-Pol (1265), where entrance is forbidden to any above the number provided for by the hospital's endowment, "… unless someone confer additional endowment on the hospital so they can live there and so not diminish the portion of the poor, and this only with our [that is, the Count of Saint-Pol's] consent"; Le Grand, p. 121, no. 12.

of pilgrims."[20] By the mid-thirteenth century, this concern is seen articulated in the statutes.

At Lille, for example, because care was meant to be of short duration, there is a prohibition against the reception of the handicapped and the chronically ill. There is also an age restriction that is evidently intended to exclude pensioners (corrodians). Here, no brother or sister could be received before the age of 20, nor, if a sister, after 50, or if a brother, after 60. At Pontoise, the ages for admission were 20–40 for a brother, and 18–50 for a sister. At Vernon, an entirely female community, the ages were 20–60.[21] Twenty is somewhat older than minima seen in monastic or mendicant observance, and could suggest that recruits came from those unable to marry; certainly, at this age the candidate might be expected to have developed a mature work ethic. Saint-Pol argued that hospital work requires physical strength, for example the ability to lift patients into and out of bed, and so required that sisters be both strong and skilled in the treatment of sickness.[22]

The relatively advanced maximum ages are clarified by the statutes of Troyes (1263) that tell us recruits came not only from among the never married, but also from the ranks of widows and widowers. Entry charters from Angers indicate that women still married also were admitted.[23] Presumably these older novices were still fit, however, because the statutes sternly warn that "no one is owed perpetual care in the House of God," and that no bread is to be given to anyone who does not merit a place in the house. Indeed, any sort of payment for admission to the community, which would be expected of corrodians, is here labeled as simony. The Almoner of Troyes, the author of these statutes, however, was not without compassion, for he also recognized that even able workers would grow too sick or weak to continue their functions, and acknowledged the house's responsibility to support them until death. Lepers, however, were a different case. Brothers so afflicted were to be provided with a shelter on the fringes of town, and not housed within the hospital, which itself forbade the admission of lepers and others who would require long-term care.[24]

The purity of these intentions, however, must have proven to be impossible to maintain. The contemporary statutes of Le Puy (1249), for example, acknowledge that room and board in the local hospital was a privilege held by some of the canons

---

20 Mansi, *Collectio conciliorum sacrorum*, 11.1:73, no. 9.

21 Le Grand, pp. 81–2, no. 2, 140, no. 11 and 154, no. 5.

22 Ibid., p. 120, nos 5 and 9. Penelope D. Johnson argues that medical training was a natural part of the education of nuns; *Equal in Monastic Profession*, pp. 51–54. By way of illustration, she cites the medical writings of Hildegard of Bingen, the example of nuns caring for the sick, French King Louis IX, and the fact that the care of patients within the medieval hospital normally fell to women.

23 Johnson, *Equal in Monastic Profession*, p. 32. The statutes of the Council of Paris seem to accept the admission of married couples to hospitaller service, even though individual hospitals forbade the practice. In 1212, the concern was that some laics sought refuge in hospitaller communities as a way to evade the bonds of serfdom, or other forms of seigniorial jurisdiction, Mansi, *Collectio conciliorum sacrorum*, 11.1:73, no. 9.

24 Le Grand, pp. 102, 105, no. 6, 115, no. 90 and 118, no. 116.

of the cathedral and perhaps by other favored townsfolk as well. Indeed, a distinction is made in this legislation between brothers and *donati*, which is one of the terms used in the sources to describe corrodians. In fact, interesting loopholes afforded by these statutes suggest the existence of a privileged contingent among the brethren. In one, the master is allowed to guarantee a specific ration of food and particular conditions of care to individuals, and in another, he can give permission for some brothers to hold property, to make wills and bequeath legacies, something that those bound by the vow of poverty would not ordinarily be able to do. Another provision prohibits any of the sisters from wearing gold or silk in their hair, the sort of transgression that one would associate more with a woman of wealth than with a serving sister.[25]

At Angers, the line demarcating sisters from corrodians blurred. Here in 1259, for example, Audeardis Lespeingnole replaced her recently deceased sister as a professed member of the community, moving into the same room once occupied by her sibling and gaining from the hospital a guarantee of an ample diet and an annual cash income of £4. When the widow Mathea entered the same community six years later, she was permitted to draw up a will in which she reserved funds for her own burial and for a number of charitable causes that included the mendicant friars, other convents, and former servants and friends.[26]

Even at Troyes, which saw itself as a place of strict discipline, where, unlike in other houses, "people do not just come and go," there is some ambiguity since the master was explicitly permitted to waive the prohibition against the reception of married couples into the community. And at Pontoise, the prioress could dispense with the age requirement, "for the profit of the house." While for many thirteenth-century communities, such as the Dominicans, these dispensations would be in favor of the young, it may be suspected that here the opposite is true.[27]

Another important quality for professed religious in these French hospitals was patience and good humor, since the old and sick could often be slow and unresponsive. The statement of religious profession at St-Pol (1265) obliges the brethren "… to live in observance and under the Rule of St Augustine as servants and servers of the poor … which is difficult to do if God does not aid and comfort you."[28] The Statutes of Troyes say much the same thing in assigning a penance of bread and water for three days to any who complained about the sick or in any way showed anger toward them.[29]

An allied issue to the qualities and character of hospitaller personnel is their degree of separation from the world. Secular ties in this case would not only undermine the quality of religious observance, but would also serve to demarcate those who truly served the poor from those who merely sought food and lodging within the hospital.

---

25 Ibid., pp. 97–8.

26 Johnson, *Equal in Monastic Profession*, pp. 248, 250 and 258.

27 Le Grand, pp. 103, 105, no. 2 and 140, no. 11. For the Dominicans, see Hinnebusch, *A History of the Dominican Order*, 1:283.

28 Le Grand, p. 149.

29 Ibid., p. 115, no. 85.

The statutes thus speak of those who are permitted to enter the house from the community as guests and visitors, and of the conditions under which the brethren are permitted to venture back into familiar secular surroundings. Turning to the former, it appears that visitation became an issue during the thirteenth century, perhaps as patrons sought to secure rights of hospitality or as families attempted to maintain links to professed relatives. In any case, the extended statutes that were redacted after 1250 address this issue. Some, like Troyes, permit the reception of guests, some of whom are described as *noble* and *friendly*, likely references to institutional patrons. Generally, such visitations required the prior's approval, but it seems that the brethren could entertain, both at meals and overnight, guests of the same gender. Sisters, evidently with permission, could dine even with male guests. Prohibitions against parallel hospitality for birds and dogs give further evidence of an exalted status for these outsiders. Pointoise (1265) also permitted such visitations, but St-Pol (1265), on the other hand, attempted to ban them absolutely.[30]

More restrictive were provisions that governed excursions of the brethren out into town. Among the legitimate reasons for leaving the cloister was the management of external properties; the *hôtel-Dieu* of Paris, for example, held a number of granges and acknowledged that both brothers and sisters might be absent on business. Lille excuses from the Office those who are abroad.[31] Others stipulate that at least one of the brethren serve as a business agent.[32] A *business* that was particular to hospitals is addressed by the statutes of Angers, which require that two agents or *nuntii* be sent out into town each week, on Wednesdays and Fridays, to seek out the sick, although here it is unclear whether these *nuntii* were religious drawn from the community. In a similar vein, at Le Puy all brothers and sisters were required to accompany the bodies of the dead in procession to the cemetery, unless specifically excused by the master.[33] Other legitimate excursions might involve visits to ecclesiastical patrons, since several statutes, like those of Vernon, permit the brethren to dine at the bishop's table.[34] There is also the suggestion that the brethren engaged in work from which they received an income. Enactments at Troyes at least require that such personal earnings be turned over to the prior for the benefit of the poor.[35]

The hospitals that have been the subject of this discussion are clearly religious institutions as measured by the character of their staff and their institutional mission. But are they more religious than other hospitals operated by a secular staff? For example, at the Hospital of Santa Creu, a large hospital established in early fifteenth-century Barcelona which was served by a salaried staff, the same provisions

---

30 Ibid., pp. 112–13, nos 54, 57, 59, 60, 65, 121, no. 20 and 139, no. 11.

31 Ibid., pp. 44, 46, nos 6, 20 and 65, no. 2.

32 For example, at Troyes the prior is to appoint a brother to receive legacies and to tend to the secular business of the house; ibid., p. 116, no. 97.

33 While imitative of the Statutes of the Order of the Holy Spirit which required that this be done once a week, the brethren at Angers were seemingly more active; ibid., pp. 23, no. 5 and 99, no. 11. For the Holy Spirit, see PL 217:1147, no. 11.

34 Le Grand, p. 169, no. 15.

35 Ibid., p. 116, no. 96.

mandating confession and the reception of the sacraments for those admitted to the hospital are found as existed in the *hôtels-Dieu* of thirteenth-century France.[36] Indeed, such practice was mandated for all hospitals by Church councils, such as Lateran IV. Thus, if the religious regimes that characterize the municipal hospitals of thirteenth-century France had a particular purpose, the objective appears to have had more to do with the imposition of discipline over the staff than the enhancement of care (religious or palliative) for the poor. In fact, much of the legislation reviewed here focusses upon questions of discipline, and not upon the care of the poor. The reform councils of Paris and Rouen in the early thirteenth century saw the imposition of the religious life upon hospitallers as a cure for problems of fraud and malfeasance that beset contemporary institutions. The increasingly prescriptive hospitaller legislation of the thirteenth century demonstrates that both ecclesiastical as well as lay patrons continued to share this view.[37] Consequently, the imposition of a Rule and religious discipline upon communities that served the *hôtels-Dieu* of medieval France did not create their religious character, but rather constituted a strategy to ensure that this spiritual function was in fact properly discharged.

---

36 The model for the religious care of patients come from the Rule of the Hospitallers of St John written by Raymond of Le Puy; see *The Rule, Statutes and Customs of the Hospitallers, 1099–1310*, ed. E.J. King (London, 1934), pp. 26–7, no. 16. The earliest appearance of this formula in French statutes is in those of Mondidier (1207)/Amiens (1233). It is repeated at Paris (1220), Troyes (1263) and Saint-Pol (1265), Le Grand, pp. 39, no. 34, 46, no. 21, 113, no. 73 and 127, no. 26. For Barcelona's practice, see *Ordinacions del Hospital General de la Santa Creu de Barcelona (any MCCCCXVII): Copiades textualment del manuscrit original y prologodes*, ed. Joseph María Roca (Barcelona, 1920), pp. x–xii, xvi and xxxii–iii.

37 For example: the later statutes of Lille (1250) were granted by Countess Jeanne; Troyes (1263) by the almoner of the cathedral; Saint-Pol (1265) by the local count; Pointoise (1265) by the Bishop of Rouen, and Vernon (1265–70) by King Louis IX. Consequently, as far as the rigor of observance was concerned, it seems to have been a matter of no importance whether the status of the patron was either lay or clerical.

Chapter 9

A Non-natural Environment: Medicine without Doctors and the Medieval European Hospital

Peregrine Horden

Introduction

Norman Cousins' *Anatomy of an Illness*[1] ought to be required reading for historians of pre-modern medicine. Cousins was diagnosed with a collagen illness, a disease of the connective tissue. He had, especially, ankylosing spondylitis, a disease of the spine which would bring about its disintegration. The prognosis was grave – literally so, and soon. Cousins discharged himself from hospital and moved into a hotel. There, he embarked on a prolonged, and eventually successful, therapy of his own devising. He arranged to be drip-fed massive doses of Vitamin C to build up his resistance. He also watched Marx Brothers videos. "Ten minutes of genuine belly laughter ...," he writes, "would give me at least two hours of pain-free sleep."

His experience is an excellent introduction to the topic of this chapter, not so much because he provides a shining example of the power of positive thinking, but more for two other reasons (which are, ultimately, related). First, because his auto-therapy is a clear instance of what can reasonably be called "medicine without doctors." Second, less obviously, because the psychological element in that auto-therapy is so medieval. Norman Cousins would be thoroughly at home with medieval medical theory, particularly that part of it which insists that the right emotions – in essence, good cheer – are essential to the preservation or restoration of health. This theory is as well known to medical historians as it was to medieval physicians. Yet the historians have not always appreciated its implications; and the possible consequences of its vernacular understanding, beyond the medical profession, have been very little explored. What happens if, in a deliberately simplistic way, both the notion of medicine without doctors and the medical theory of the emotions are pushed to their limits? What might taking them both seriously do for an understanding of the medieval hospital? The answer suggested below is that, in the medieval hospital,

---

1 Norman Cousins, *Anatomy of an Illness* (New York, 1979), p. 39. Many Websites are now devoted to laughter as "the best medicine." See also Esther M. Sternberg, *The Balance Within: The Science Connecting Health and the Emotions* (New York, 2000), for the controversial field of psycho-neuro-immunology.

medicine without doctors can achieve its fullest expression. It does so under the influence of a vulgarized form of medical theory. Hence the two exemplary aspects of Norman Cousins' case intersect. The hospital as a non-natural environment is the extreme instance of medicine without doctors.[2]

Passions of the Soul

The origins of the relevant medical theory lie in various passages of Galen,[3] but the theory was first systematically elaborated by Islamic writers.[4] The briefest exposition of the underlying ideas can be found in the work later known to Western medicine as the *Isagoge*, or "Introduction," of Johannitius (Hunayn ibn Ishaq, died *c.* 877). This Arabic synopsis was so convenient that, in a partial Latin translation, it was widely diffused across medieval Europe. Available by the beginning of the twelfth century, it served as an introduction to Galen's *Ars medica* (*Tegni*) and became the first book in the corpus of treatises known as the *Articella*, in effect the basic university medical textbook.[5] Vernacular translations followed during the later Middle Ages.[6]

Hunayn distinguishes between *res naturales*, the *naturals* (chiefly the four elements, qualities such as hot or moist, and the four humors) which are the constituents or faculties of a healthy organism, *res contra naturam*, the *contra-naturals* (disease, its causes and sequelae) which upset that healthy state, and *res non naturales*, the *non-naturals*. The last are the pertinent ones here. Generally six in number (though Johannitius in fact enlarged them through his inclusion of coitus and bathing), they are the determinants of health. In standard medieval form, they include ambient air, food and drink, exercise and rest, sleeping and waking, evacuation and

---

2   This chapter attempts to clarify and develop some of the ideas presented at greater length, but in more tangled form, in "Religion as Medicine: Music in Medieval Hospitals," in *Religion and Medicine in the Middle Ages*, ed. Peter Biller and Joseph Ziegler (Woodbridge, NY, 2001), 135–53. It owes much to John Henderson and Carole Rawcliffe, and to the publications of Faye Getz and Glending Olson. I am also grateful to Caroline Barron, Jonathan Hughes, Jennifer Neville and Sethina Watson for advice on specific matters. The usual exculpation of scholarly creditors is more than usually necessary.

3   Luis García-Ballester, "On the Origin of the 'Six Non-Natural Things' in Galen," in *Galen und das Hellenistische Erbe*, ed. Jutta Kollesch and Diethard Nickel (Stuttgart, 1993), 105–15.

4   Glending Olson, *Literature as Recreation in the Later Middle Ages* (hereafter cited as Olson), (Ithaca, NY, 1982), pp. 40–44; for earlier bibliography, see esp. 41 n. 3; Heikki Mikkeli, *Hygiene in the Early Modern Medical Tradition* (Helsinki, 1999), pp. 9–10; for bibliography, see esp. 10 n. 4, pp. 14–23.

5   See Jon Arrizabalaga, "The Death of a Medieval Text: The *Articella* and the Early Press," in *Medicine from the Black Death to the French Disease*, ed. Roger French et al. (Aldershot, 1998), 185–6, for summary and full bibliography.

6   See Linda Ehrsam Voigts and Patricia Deery Kurtz, *Scientific and Medical Writings in Old and Middle English: An Electronic Reference*, CD-ROM (Ann Arbor, MI, 2000).

repletion, and the *passions of the soul*, or *accidents of the soul* (*accidentia animae*) as physicians tended to call them. Hunayn writes of these accidents:

> Sundry affections of the mind produce an effect within the body, such as those which bring the natural heat from the interior of the body to the outer parts or the surface of the skin. Sometimes this happens suddenly, as with anger; sometimes gently and slowly, as with delight and joy ... some affections disturb the natural energy both internal and external, as, for instance, with grief.[7]

So emotions are as important for health as is the state of the body or the condition of the environment, which means that emotions fall within the sphere of medicine. Negative emotions can generate somatic illness; positive ones can counteract it, or keep illness at bay. For Hunayn and his followers, practical medicine divides into three parts, and the regulation of the non-naturals is one of them, alongside surgery and the administration of drugs. The salutary importance of moderating emotions such as joy and sadness was made familiar to the whole medieval audience of medical learning through its inclusion in many medical treatises, theoretical and practical, even surgical ones.[8] It appeared in numerous regimens of health (especially the hundred or so manuscript versions of the *Regimen sanitatis salernitanum*), and was mentioned in even more numerous letters of advice from physicians to better-off patients (*consilia*).[9]

What matters here is neither the learned vocabulary nor the physiological details,[10] but the simple underlying psychosomatic anthropology. That emotions can determine health was appreciated well beyond the circles of university physicians and their patients. But historians have devoted little attention to the matter, and the evidence remains to be collected. All that can be offered are some examples of the sort of material we might look for.

"Because of my worries I got dry pimples and my skin peeled off my bones."[11] So wrote a Jewish inhabitant of medieval Old Cairo, echoing, perhaps unconsciously, Proverbs 17:22, "a cheerful heart is a good medicine, but a downcast spirit dries up

---

7   Edward Grant, trans., *Sourcebook of Medieval Science* (Cambridge, MA, 1974), pp. 708–9.

8   Carole Rawcliffe, "Hospital Nurses and their Work," in *Daily Life in the Middle Ages*, ed. Richard Britnell (Stroud, 1998), 43–64; see esp. 62; Olson, 46.

9   Mikkeli, *Hygiene*, pp. 19–23; Jole Agrimi and Chiara Crisciani, *Les "consilia" médicaux*, *Typologie des sources du moyen âge*, 69 (Turnhout, 1994); Peter Murray Jones, "Music Therapy in the Later Middle Ages: The Case of Hugo van der Goes," in *Music as Medicine: The History of Music Therapy since Antiquity*, ed. Peregrine Horden (Aldershot, 2000), 134–40.

10 See Pedro Gil-Sotres, "Modelo teórico y observación clínica: las pasiones del alma en la psicología medica medieval," in *Comprendre et maîtriser la nature au Moyen Age: mélanges d'histoire des sciences offerts à Guy Beaujouan* (Geneva, 1994), 181–204.

11 S.D. Goitein, *A Mediterranean Society, Volume 5: The Individual* (Berkeley, CA, 1988), 56.

the bones,"[12] and reminding us thereby of the endorsement that these medical notions must have gained from a range of non-medical sources, and indeed from common sense and observation.[13] Several of the twelfth-century biographies of Thomas Becket describe how the archbishop's pain in his side was caused or aggravated by the anxieties of his trial at Northampton in October 1164.[14] Exchanges about regimen between Francesco di Marco Datini, the fourteenth-century "Merchant of Prato" made famous by Iris Origo, and his physician Lorenzo Sassoli can be followed closely through the abundant surviving correspondence.[15] At one point Maestro Lorenzo writes: "I think the chill you have taken is your own fault, for I am certain that it came to you only because you take your troubles and anxieties as if you were a man of thirty, and this you must not do." And later: "pray tell me how you feel, and that you now take the vexations of your trade more easily. For if you do not, ailments and bodily anguish will be your first profits." Again, in a long letter that was tantamount to a personal regimen, Lorenzo referred specifically to the accidents of the spirit:

> as to [which] … let me tell you the things of which you must most beware. To get angry and shout at times pleases me, for this will keep up your natural heat; but what displeases me is your being vexed and taking everything so much to heart. For it is this, as the whole of physic teaches, which destroys our body, more than any other cause.

This is the physician speaking, not the patient; and the patient does not seem to be following the repeated advice. Still, one could hardly claim that Francesco remained ignorant of the principles of psychosomatic medicine.

Francesco's near contemporary, Geoffrey Chaucer, is another famous figure who can be called upon here, a medical "layman" who clearly knew his non-naturals. Recall both the author and the knight who are suffering physically from melancholy in *The Book of the Duchess*,[16] or the lovesick Troilus in *Troilus and Criseyde*, and Arcite in the *Knight's Tale* whose "loveres maladye of hereos" is overlaid with more serious mania.[17] But the clearest instance of Chaucer's awareness of the non-naturals

---

12 Revised Standard Version. For the confluence of medicine and theology in the medieval interpretation of such passages, see Beryl Smalley, *The Study of the Bible in the Middle Ages*, 3rd edn (Oxford, 1983), pp. 314–16.

13 And, in the West, from medieval traditions of Stoicism. See Faye Getz, *Medicine in the English Middle Ages* (Princeton, NJ, 1998), p. 85.

14 David Knowles, *The Episcopal Colleagues of Archbishop Thomas Becket* (Cambridge, 1951), App. V; see also Stephen Wilson, *The Magical Universe* (London and New York, 2000), p. 311, wrongly, I believe, aligning such material under "magical influences"; and for another Archbishop of Canterbury prone to stress-related illness, see Eadmer, *Life of St. Anselm*, ed. Richard W. Southern (London, 1962), p. 80.

15 For what follows, see Iris Origo, *The Merchant of Prato* (Harmondsworth, 1963), pp. 306–8.

16 See esp. lines 487–501; Olson, pp. 44, 85–9.

17 Lines 1,373–4. On the physical symptoms, see Mary Frances Wack, *Lovesickness in the Middle Ages: The "Viaticum" and its Commentaries* (Philadelphia, PA, 1990), pp. 63–6,

is the poor but virtuous woman farmer in the *Nun's Priest's Tale* (lines 2,837–9): "Repleccioun ne made hire nevere sik; / Attempree diete was al hir phisik, / And exercise, and hertes suffisaunce"[18] – that is, moderation in the accidents of the soul. Medical theory is used to assert the effectiveness of medicine without doctors.

How representative is Chaucer of educated attitudes in later medieval England? The nature and scale of his contemporary audience is, of course, controversial. The majority of scholars seem, however, to conceive of it as far broader than a coterie or an elite.[19] Moreover, similar echoes of medical psychology emerge in non-fictional material. In the 1430s, for example, Stephen Scrope, member of a cadet branch of a baronial family, wrote to his stepfather Sir John Fastolf accusing him of bringing on Scrope's chronic and disfiguring skin condition by sending him away to school *c.* 1411.[20]

The idea that attention to the emotions could prevent or mitigate illness gained perhaps its widest diffusion from the numerous plague treatises of the post-Black Death period. Like regimens, these were often partly organized according to the non-naturals. Hence many had some advice about the accidents of the soul. As the masters of the Paris medical faculty put it in 1348, in the most influential of these treatises (soon translated into the vernacular), the *Compendium de epidimia*:

> Since bodily infirmity is sometimes related to the accidents of the soul, one should avoid anger, excessive sadness, and anxiety. Be of good hope and resolute mind; make peace with God, for death will be less fearsome as a result. Live in joy and gladness as much as possible, for although joy may sometimes moisten the body, it nevertheless comforts both spirit and heart.[21]

In times of epidemic, given this pathogenicity of the emotions, the fear of disease could easily become the disease of fear – a disease as lethal as plague.[22]

135–9; for context, see Linda Phyllis Austern, "Musical Treatments for Lovesickness: The Early Modern Heritage," in *Music as Medicine*, ed. Peregrine Horden, 213–45

18 Neville Coghill, trans.: "Repletion never left her in disquiet / And all her physic was a temperate diet, / Hard work for exercise and heart's content."

19 John Burrow, *Medieval Writers and Their Work* (Oxford, 1982), Ch. 2; Paul Strohm, *Social Chaucer* (Cambridge, MA and London, 1989), Ch. 3.

20 Jonathan Hughes, "Stephen Scrope and the Circle of Sir John Fastolf: Moral and Intellectual Outlooks," in *Medieval Knighthood IV: Papers from the Fifth Strawberry Hill Conference*, ed. Christopher Harper-Bill and Ruth Harvey (Woodbridge, 1990), 109–46.

21 Olson, trans., p. 169; for context, see 164–74; see also Jon Arrizabalaga, "Facing the Black Death: Perceptions and Reactions of Medical Practitioners," in *Practical Medicine from Salerno to the Black Death*, ed. Luis García-Ballester et al. (Cambridge, 1994), 279–80.

22 David Gentilcore, "The Fear of Disease and the Disease of Fear," in *Fear in Early Modern Society*, ed. William G. Naphy and Penny Roberts (Manchester and New York, 1997), 190–96; Andrew Wear, "Fear, Anxiety and the Plague in Early Modern England," in *Religion, Health and Suffering*, ed. John R. Hinnells and Roy Porter (London and New York, 1999), 339–63: see esp. 51–2 for Van Helmont's argument that the worst cases of plague were *entirely* the product of fear.

Five Steps to the Hospital

Now consider the theme of medicine without doctors from a different angle, one which has less to do with theory and its vernacular transformations and more to do with modern historiography's perceptions. Begin with what is probably a fundamental image of the physician, the image of the *doctor doctoring*, that is, actively intervening in an attempt to restore health through medication or surgery. We can then move away from that image in a sequence of steps so as to prepare the way for another image, that of the medieval hospital as a non-natural environment.

The first step is to recognize that, in treating the sick, medieval healers of all kinds – physicians, apothecaries, empirics, magicians, living holy men, even surgeons – probably said much more than they did. (Dead saints working healing miracles may be the exception.) The interaction between healer and patient might well be imagined, in its verbosity, its domination by question and answer, as more akin to a modern session with a psychotherapist than to an encounter with a practitioner of biomedicine. The analogy is not intended as a full endorsement of David Harley's recent analysis of the "construction" of *all* healing through rhetoric; his strong thesis seems to me to raise more philosophical problems than it offers historical solutions.[23] Undoubtedly, though, the significance of the clinical talking of pre-modern healers has been underestimated by medical historians, partly because it is little documented, partly because our historical imagination is still, on the whole, "infected" by the technological, interventionist, bias of modern biomedicine.

Step two: talk is not necessarily a prelude to action. It is expected that medical rhetoric will focus on diagnosis, and that diagnosis will lead to treatment. But pre-modern healing focussed at least as much on prognosis, on saying what would happen with, or just as likely, without medication. The role of prognosis is easily downplayed. Faye Getz is unusual in opening her recent synopsis of *Medicine in the English Middle Ages* with an account, derived from the chronicler Ralph of Coggeshall, of the last illness of Archbishop Hubert Walter in the summer of 1205.[24] The learned physician in the archbishop's entourage, Gilbertus Anglicus, is portrayed as doing nothing but prognosticate, instructing his patient in the *ars moriendi*. He neither inspects urine nor administers any drug. Instead he advises *medicina sacramentalis*: first confession, then the last rites. "Physical remedies" are taken only when this prescient advice is ignored, and at the behest of another attendant physician. That the archbishop's was an extreme case, a terminal one, should not lead us to think that it was in every other respect exceptional.

Step three: much more of medical doctoring than is now generally acknowledged concerned prevention rather than cure (diet in the pre-modern sense, regimen). But

---

23 David Harley, "Rhetoric and the Social Construction of Illness and Healing," *Social History of Medicine*, 12 (1999), 407–35, with debate in Vol. 13 (2000), 147–51, 535–46.

24 Getz, *Medicine in the English Middle Ages*, pp. 3–4, with Ralph of Coggeshall, *Radulphi de Coggeshall Chronicon Anglicanum*, ed. Joseph Stevenson, Rolls Series 66 (London, 1875), pp. 156–9. See now also Luke Demaitre, "The Art and Science of Prognostication in Early University Medicine," *Bulletin of the History of Medicine*, 77 (2003), 765–88.

preventative medicine is the poor relation of medical historiography, just as it is the poor relation of modern therapeutics. Few synopses say much about it. Only one recent scholarly overview of medieval medicine devotes a chapter to the topic.[25] Yet the sheer bulk of the writings about regimen from the Hippocratic corpus to the voluminous dietetic writings of the later Middle Ages bears witness to its importance.[26]

The fourth step is marked by *non*-doctors doctoring. It brings the non-naturals back into the picture. To review: in the first three steps, they were only a background presence. First, the reassuring rhetoric could itself be regarded as therapeutic, whether in modern psychosomatic terms or in pre-modern terms of the effects of emotion on health. Second, even a bleak prognosis can relieve suffering through the clarity and certainty it brings, and with that the chance to prepare properly for death (seizing which chance may make all the difference to one's prospects in eternity). Third, regimen in its medieval form is often structured around the non-naturals: they determine the form the preventative medicinal advice takes.

The right emotions are even more important to the preservation of health than they are to its recovery. The fourth step, however, involves the non-naturals on a broader front, not just the psychological one. If motion and rest, evacuation and repletion, good cheer, sex and other such basics belong to medicine, then the recipients of regimens or medical *consilia* who try (*à la* Norman Cousins) to change their own non-naturals are dealing in medical matters. As the *Salernitan Regimen* put it, in a passage that Chaucer might well have known: *Si tibi deficiant medici, medici tibi fiant / Hec tria: mens leta, requies, moderata dieta* ("If you should lack doctors, these three shall be doctors to you: a joyful mind, rest and a moderate diet").[27]

Those who promote balance of the non-naturals in others are all, in a sense, medical practitioners. Nurses provide the most obvious and the most neglected of examples. This should be stressed, against the weight of received opinion of the medieval medical elite, and even against that of some modern historians attempting sympathetically to recover women's obscured medical activities.[28] It hardly needs stating that many medieval doctors took a dim view of nurses' capabilities, in part so as to enhance patients' perception of their own. They did not apply the theory of the non-naturals impartially. Other countervailing voices therefore deserve amplification. In the Hospital of St Nicholas de Bruille in Tournai, for example, care of the sick was provided by six Augustinian sisters and some novices. The fifteenth-

25 Pedro Gil Sotres, "The Regimens of Health," in *Western Medical Thought from Antiquity to the Middle Ages*, ed. Mirko D. Grmek (Cambridge, MA and London, 1998), 291–318.

26 See now G.J. Hardingham, "The Regimen in Late Medieval England" (PhD Thesis, University of Cambridge, 2005).

27 Jones, "Music Therapy," 136.

28 See note 8 above. Contrast the stark separation between nursing and medicine enjoined by Monica H. Green, "Documenting Medieval Women's Medical Practice," in *Practical Medicine from Salerno to the Black Death*, 341.

century Rule of the house gave full weight to the connection between nursing and health. It stipulated that:

> before the sisters take their food, the said sick patients shall be fed in accordance with their infirmities and their wishes, so far as can be arranged and so long as nothing is harmful to their health. As funds allow, they will be diligently supplied with their needs until they regain their health.[29]

Several other rules specified that nurses were to be patient, friendly and cheerful, so as not to depress their patients.[30]

Fifth and final step: under the banner of the non-naturals, the scope of medicine broadens so that it extends beyond the efforts of people (doctors, nurses, auto-therapists) to the effects of things. Within the body there lies, of course, the healing power of nature, *vis medicatrix naturae*.[31] But the aspect of medicine without doctors to be emphasized here is environmental. And, like the topic of nursing, this too brings us to the hospital.

Hospital Healing

Much of the attention of medieval hospital historians used to be absorbed by the question of whether or not hospitals had doctors on their staffs. Florence took the prize for precocity; England trailed in last, with the Savoy Hospital. Contrast, for instance, the hospital of Santa Maria Nuova in Florence with that of St Giles, Norwich (the "Great Hospital," as it became known after the Reformation). Santa Maria Nuova had its retained corps of physicians who admitted only patients with acute but not life-threatening conditions and discharged them rapidly.[32] St Giles helped the chronically sick and elderly to live out their days in minimum pain. It had no doctors until after the Reformation.[33] The contrast could hardly be starker. The future of hospitals seems to lie on one side, in Tuscany. Their past lies on the other, in East Anglia. Medicalization of this kind – medicalization in the literal sense of the arrival of *medici* – is easily seen as the one development that really mattered. It

---

29 Cited from Rawcliffe, "Hospital Nurses," 57.

30 Ibid., 62.

31 Mikkele, *Hygiene*, p. 17.

32 Katherine Park and John Henderson, "'The First Hospital among Christians': The Ospedale di Santa Maria Nuova in Early Sixteenth-century Florence," *Medical History*, 35 (1991), 164–88; Henderson, "Splendide case di cura: spedali, medicina ed assistenza a Firenze nel trecento", in *Ospedali e città: L'Italia del Centro-Nord, XIII–XVI*, ed. A.J. Grieco and L. Sandri (Florence, 1997), pp. 15–50; Henderson, "'Antechambers of Death'? Poverty and Sickness in the Hospitals of Renaissance Florence," in *Forme di povertà e innovazioni istituzionali in Italia dal Medioevo ad oggi*, ed. V. Zamagna (Bologna, 2000), 111–29.

33 Carole Rawcliffe, *Medicine for the Soul: The Life, Death and Resurrection of an English Medieval Hospital* (Stroud, 1999).

becomes the *Leitmotif* of an implicit teleological narrative, from caring to curing, from the medieval to the modern.

The work of Carole Rawcliffe and John Henderson (among others), on English and Florentine hospitals respectively, undermines this contrast and subverts this teleology. Later medieval hospitals in both cities, as they have shown, were above all quasi-monastic religious institutions, with liturgy at their heart. Patients in both Norwich and Florence lay within sight of the sacrament, either because the ward opened out into a chapel or because there was an altar within the ward. In both places, daily life was punctuated by the monastic hours more than by the ward round.[34] The cure of the soul, through the medicine of the sacraments, was more important than the relief of bodily infirmity, not least because, as the fathers of the Fourth Lateran Council had reminded the faithful (Canon 22), the soul's health was an essential precondition for the recovery of the body. Exposure to the host, even without reception; regular confession, without which one sin might remain to contaminate the whole hospital; the proximity of relics in the hospital chapel; contemplation of devotional imagery – all these are likely features of the overriding purpose of hospital life. They erode the stark contrast between England and Italy, rendering the presence or absence of physicians less decisive for our estimation of the hospital's therapeutic capacity.[35]

Against those who maintain that doctors make all the difference, it could be said that the true medicine of hospitals is religion. Hospitals, in their ideal form, exemplified that subordination of the care of the body to the care of the soul, and of the earthly physician to *Christus medicus*, which the Church attempted to diffuse through society at large. Yet the analysis need not stop there. *Medicina sacramentalis*, the medicine of the soul, is acknowledged by its latest historians as potentially affecting the body as well: exposure to the host was supposed, for example, to alleviate bodily infirmities.[36] In his *Instructions for Parish Priests* (c. 1400), John Myrc claimed that anyone who saw a priest bearing the host would be safe for the rest of the day from death and blindness.[37] It was, presumably, on the basis of similar beliefs that, *c.* 1500, a local priest left money for masses to be sung every week in the hospital of

---

34 John Henderson, "Healing the Body and Saving the Soul: Hospitals in Renaissance Florence," *Renaissance Studies* 15 (2001), 188–216.

35 Carole Rawcliffe, "Medicine for the Soul: The Medieval English Hospital and the Quest for Spiritual Health," in *Religion, Health and Suffering*, ed. John R. Hinnells and Roy Porter (London, 1999), 316–38.

36 Rawcliffe, *Medicine for the Soul*, p. 103. Compare Oliver Sacks, *The Man who Mistook his Wife for a Hat* (London, 1985), p. 36, for the relief from the effects of extreme amnesia (Korsakov's syndrome) brought to a patient by taking communion.

37 Edward Peacock, ed., Early English Text Society (London, 1868), p. 10. On such "virtues" of the Mass, see further Adolph Franz, *Die Messe im deutschen Mittelalter: Beiträge zur Geschichte der Liturgie und des religiösen Volkslebens* (Freiburg im Breisgau, 1902, repr. Darmstadt, 1963), pp. 36–72.

the Holy Cross, Orléans, "for the sustenance of the *bodies* and souls of the poor."[38] Still, despite such examples, secularist historians may be tempted, first, to conceive of soul medicine as really only a spiritual remedy, and second, *a fortiori*, to conceive of that same medicine as medicine only by analogy – as not quite the real thing.

These misconceptions obscure medieval understanding of the phenomena in question, an understanding predicated upon the non-naturals. The contrary argument can be put in dialectical form. Thesis: hospitals are medical only if they have attendant doctors. Antithesis: the primary medicine of all hospitals is religion. Synthesis: the religion of hospitals is a type of medicine. Spiritual medicine is genuinely medicinal, not just in theological but also in medical terms. It is another kind of medicine without doctors. Anything that promotes medicine for the soul – sacraments, devotional images and the like – can be seen as altering the accidents of the soul. Medieval doctors knew this. In a *consilium*, Bartholomaeus da Montagnana urges the study of moral or theological narratives, along with the singing of psalms, as among the exercises "that bring delight" and therefore health.[39] In the sixteenth century, Alvise Luisini claimed that physicians could detect physical improvements in patients who had confessed one day previously. The ensuing freedom from anxiety led directly to better health, including the remission of fever.[40]

This is not only a "professional" medical insight. To the examples of public understanding of the non-naturals adduced above (Chaucer, Scrope et al.) can now be added that of the fathers of the Fourth Lateran Council. In what might seem to be their most emphatically theological mode, they also, in Canon 22, embrace basic medical psychosomatics. That is, they recognize the disease of fear:

> This among other things has occasioned this decree [that "physicians of the body" must persuade their patients to summon "physicians of the soul" before they treat them], namely that some people on their sickbed, when they are advised by physicians to arrange for the health of their souls, *fall into despair and so the more readily incur the danger of death.*[41]

If summoning a physician of the soul to the bedside became routine at the outset of treatment, instead of a later sign that the case was considered terminal, then fewer patients would succumb to the disease of fear and make their physical conditions more perilous.[42]

---

38 Annie Saunier, *"Le pauvre malade" dans le cadre hospitalier médiéval: France du Nord vers 1300–1500* (Paris, 1993), p. 104; italics added.

39 Olson, pp. 61–2.

40 Richard Palmer, "The Church, Leprosy and Plague in Medieval and Early Modern Europe," *Studies in Church History*, 19 (1982), 86, citing [Alvise] Luisini, *Tractatus de confessione a die decubitus instituenda* (Venice, 1563), 74–5.

41 Norman Tanner, ed. and trans., *Decrees of the Ecumenical Councils*, 2 vols (London and Washington, DC, 1990), 1:245–6; italics added.

42 For the resistance of some physicians to any summoning of priests, see Michael McVaugh, "Bedside Manners in the Middle Ages," *Bulletin of the History of Medicine*, 71 (1997), 217.

For illustration of the psychosomatic potential of the sacraments, even in a terminal case, we can return for a moment to the last, measured, hours of Hubert Walter as represented by Ralph of Coggeshall. Gilbert the physician advised his patient to confess. "On doing so, the fire of the archbishop's remorse and charity rose up and caused the moisture in his brain to dissolve, bringing forth from him a torrent of tears and great relief."[43] After receiving the last rites Hubert was again much relieved.[44]

Hospital Inmates

Of course, this evidence does not relate specifically to hospitals. But there is no reason why hospital patients should have responded any differently to the sacraments. According to the statutes of one thirteenth-century English hospital, for example, the steward of the sick was the "distributor" of relics, presumably because he paraded them around the ward to "irradiate" the patients.[45] The surrounding religious images that, along with the administration of the sacraments, constituted the hospital as a religious house could also have encouraged a salutary cheerfulness. Consider the most medicalized of Renaissance hospitals, Santa Maria Nuova. From about 1420 onward, a half-length statue of Christ showing his wounds stood in the lunette above the doorway to the hospital cemetery, and a terra cotta Coronation of the Virgin adorned the tympanum of the entrance to the church of S. Egidio, the hospital chapel. Both were images of healing and redemption, potential promoters of a salutary optimism. The Virgin, present not only here but, later on, inside the chapel in the famous Portinari altarpiece and in a fresco cycle, was, in her compassion, a role model of the hospital nurse, and her coronation signified triumph over death. Christ, meanwhile, "came as a doctor not just to visit us but to cure us."[46] His corporeal sufferings, so emphasized in the statue, were a "bitter medicine" which he took on our behalf to heal us of the "sickness of sin." Such is the Augustinian interpretation of *Christus medicus* provided by the early fifteenth-century Dominican friar Domenico Cavalca. It comes in a treatise sometimes entitled *Medicina del cuore*, as in a manuscript of 1410 that originated in a convent contiguous with Santa Maria Nuova. The title nicely captures the interpenetration of medicine and theology in the statue's message.[47]

It is obviously not only the religious aspects of the hospital that can be conceived in this medical fashion. Anything that promoted optimism among the patients is susceptible of the same kind of interpretation. The contributions of diet, rest, and

---

43   The paraphrase of Getz's *Medicine in the English Middle Ages*, p. 3.

44   Ralph of Coggeshall, *Chronicon Anglicanum*, p. 158.

45   Sethina Watson, "*Fundatio, ordinatio* and *statuta*: The Statutes and Constitutional Documents of English Hospitals to 1300" (DPhil. Thesis, University of Oxford, 2003), p. 258.

46   Henderson, "Healing the Body," 196–9, with n. 21.

47   Ibid.

good nursing have already been mentioned. A royal visit might work equally well. When, in 1405, Christine de Pisan urged the merits of charitable work and extolled the benefits of such a visit, she too was a "non-naturalist." The good princess, she wrote, should tour the hospital in all her grandeur and with a magnificent retinue because this honoring of the poor inmates would raise their spirits.[48] Sound medical theory chimed with common sense. In the non-natural scheme of things, the most therapeutic emotion was a moderate cheerfulness.

The dialectical synthesis extends, therefore, beyond religion, and embraces any aspect of the hospital, whether involving persons or things; whether working directly on the body, or indirectly on it through the accidents of the soul. That is why the hospital is, at least potentially, a *total non-natural environment*. It is vital to stress the "potentially" in that formulation. This is an ideal type, perhaps a Platonic hospital. It scarcely needs stating that not every real hospital functioned in this way. Not all potentially therapeutic aspects of any one establishment were equally efficacious.[49]

Nor can it be argued that the creation of such an environment inevitably formed part of a hospital founder's plan, unless that founder was an educated physician. Some benefactors may have had a lay awareness of the non-naturals; others will have cared little for them. This paper offers a conjecture, less about the *origins* of hospitals than about their *evolution* during the later Middle Ages, when, as Michael McVaugh has proposed, there was considerable popular appetite for medical theory.[50]

Just occasionally, some association of the non-naturals with a hospital can even be documented. John Mirfeld (d. 1407) lived for forty years in rooms near St Bartholomew's Hospital, London. While there, he composed a *Breviarium* of excerpts from medical texts for those without a suitable library.[51] It includes a discussion of the non-naturals as indispensable to basic hospital know-how. Toward the end of his life, Mirfeld prepared a comparable anthology of religious texts, the *Florarium*. In that later work, he reproduced the passages on regimen from the *Breviarium*.[52] As a model of self-discipline, regimen belonged first to medicine and then to religion. According to an inventory of 1448, another London hospital, St Mary Elsyng, Cripplegate (dedicated to the care of sick clergy), had a copy of the *Florarium* in its library.[53] This is unusual evidence. Mostly, the non-naturalness of the hospital

---

48 Christine de Pisan, *The Treasure of the City of Ladies*, trans. Sarah Lawson (London, 1985), p. 53.

49 It seems unlikely that, quite generally, medieval "hospitals, clinics, and health spas sounded with rhythm and melody," treating the soul with music therapy: Madeleine Pelner Cosman, "Machaut's Medical Musical World," *Annals of the New York Academy of Sciences* 314 (1978), 1–36, quotation from p. 1. This confuses ideal type with typical reality.

50 Michael McVaugh, *Medicine before the Plague: Practitioners and their Patients in the Crown of Aragon, 1285–1345* (Cambridge, 1993).

51 Getz, *Medicine in the English Middle Ages*, pp. 49–50.

52 Percival Horton-Smith Hartley and Harold R. Aldridge, *Johannes de Mirfeld of St Bartholomew's, Smithfield: His Life and Works* (Cambridge, 1936), p. 154.

53 J.P. Malcolm, ed., *Londinium Redivivum*, 4 vols (London, 1803–7), 1:29, cited by Carole Rawcliffe, "The Eighth Comfortable Work: Education and the Medieval English

can only be inferred. But if there is any general validity in what is here suggested, then many more medieval hospital patients were getting their medicine than might have been thought. Their non-naturals were being regulated, both spiritually and somatically. It was just that they were not necessarily getting that regulation, that medicine, through doctors. Even in Santa Maria Nuova, with its medical personnel, the medicine *without* doctors that was provided by religion and by the rest of the environment may have been as significant as the medicine *from* doctors.

Conclusion

There are many ways in which those propositions could be further illustrated. Carole Rawcliffe has, for example, emphasized the role of hospital gardens not just as sources of food and medicinal herbs, but as vehicles of aromatherapy and objects of aesthetic, and thus non-naturally beneficial, delight.[54] She has also proposed the later medieval English monastic infirmary, together with its "seyney house" in which monks were prophylactically bled, as one likely setting for the fullest realization of a regimen based on the non-naturals. Sick or elderly monks, or simply those for whom the liturgical round was proving oppressive, were granted a holiday from their duties, a nourishing diet, and ready access to the gladdening beauties of nature.[55] Elsewhere I have explored medical conceptions of the non-natural impact of the liturgy in hospital chapels.[56]

Slowly, the different aspects of this non-natural environment are being colored in. And doctors are scarcely to be seen.

Hospital," in *The Church and Learning in Late Medieval Society: Studies in Honour of Professor R. B. Dobson*, ed. Caroline Barron and Jenny Stratford (Donington, 2002), 390.

54 Rawcliffe, *Medicine for the Soul*, pp. 51–3; Rawcliffe, "Hospital Nurses," 58–9. See also William C. Cosgrove, "Medicine in the *Twelve Books on Rural Practices* of Petrus de Crescentiis," in *Manuscript Sources of Medieval Medicine*, ed. Margaret R. Schleissner (London, 1995), pp. 86–7.

55 Rawcliffe, "'On the Threshold of Eternity': Care of the Sick in East Anglian Monasteries," in *East Anglia's History: Studies in Honour of Norman Scarfe*, ed. Christopher Harper-Bill, Carole Rawcliffe and Richard G. Wilson (Woodbridge, 2002), 71–2; see further Mary Yearl, Chapter 11 in this volume.

56 Horden, "Religion as Medicine" (see note 2 above).

Chapter 10

Byzantine Hospital Manuals (*Iatrosophia*) as a Source for the Study of Therapeutics

Alain Touwaide

> L'étude de la médecine des xénons selon les divers siècles mérite un examen plus minutieux, quoique la tâche ainsi imposée est assez grande, vu l'immensité des textes ...
>
> (The study of medicine in [Byzantine] xenons [*sic*] century by century deserves a more careful analysis, even though the task that this poses is rather large, given the enormity of textual sources ...)[1]

Introduction

Although the Byzantine hospital has been increasingly studied in recent times, rarely has it been approached from a mere medical viewpoint. Indeed, analysis has often focussed on such general topics as the origin of the hospital, some individual foundations, and the hospital's charitable role in Byzantine society. Its medical organization, the epidemiology of its patients, and the treatment of diseases have been explored only very little. To remedy this gap in knowledge, this chapter will focus on therapeutics, a "branch of medicine concerned with the remedial treatment of disease."[2]

The scarcity of studies on this matter certainly results from the difficulty of the topic, as Vivian Nutton rightly pointed out twenty years ago:

> To the historian of medicine, there are few topics more central, or more daunting, than the history of therapeutics ... the principles of healing ... can vary wildly from society to society and from century to century. Furthermore, evaluating the effectiveness of these

---

1   Aristoteles Kousis, "Contribution à l'étude de la médecine des zénons pendant le XVe siècle," *Byzantinische-Neugriechische Jahrbücher*, 6 (1927–28), 77.

2   Guenter B. Risse, "The history of therapeutics," in *Essays in the History of Therapeutic*, eds W.F. Bynum and V. Nutton (Amsterdam, 1991), 3–11. For the definition of therapeutics, see 5–6.

principles, especially those that appear no longer to be in use, is fraught with enormous difficulties, conceptual as well as practical, for there is an unconscious tendency to believe that the therapeutics favored by one's own society must be the most authoritative, and hence that little can be gained from the therapeutics of others … [3]

For the Byzantine world, one could add other specific problems to the list. For one, relevant sources have been insufficiently identified. For another, these sources have been poorly inventoried. And, compounding these source problems, is the fact that a specific method for their study is grossly absent.

One documentary source seldom taken into consideration is the *iatrosophion* (plural: *iatrosophia*). Although it is usually defined as a notebook and therapeutic compendium compiled by a single physician for use in his own private practice, it can also be the collaborative work of a community of physicians in a hospital setting.[4] Previous research literature has often viewed the *iatrosophion* as a simple handy manual, devoid of any medical theory. As such, *iatrosophia* are considered to be simply a debasement of the great founding medical texts of classical antiquity.

A better understanding of *iatrosophia* is possible in that such notebooks do indeed constitute a primary source particularly relevant in reconstructing therapeutics (including such matters as *materia medica* and pharmacy) and epidemiology, both fundamental aspects of Byzantine hospitals.

Within the field of ancient medical literature, the *iatrosophion* constitutes a genre of its own, arising from the re-organization of medicine and medical literature following the diffusion of Christianity and the Christianization of knowledge. Set within this frame, *iatrosophia* have a specific function both in medical literature and practice (the remedial treatment of diseases).

Provided that *iatrosophia* can be dated and located as to place of origin with sufficient precision, their study reveals that they demonstrate a constant adaptation to variations in the epidemiology of patients. As a consequence, *iatrosophia* closely reflected the health conditions of the places, times and institutions of their origin.

Methodologically, such an approach entails analyzing a large amount of information. It is necessary not only to process systematically an exhaustive inventory of preserved *iatrosophia*, but also to extract many kinds of information that they contain. Computer analysis is essential so as to be able to record, retrieve and analyze data according to different and changing parameters. In first instance, data arranged in this way must be interpreted philologically, to guarantee a proper understanding of the texts. In order to understand all textual elements in their contemporary context, associations from a broad spectrum of disciplines (such as

---

3   Vivian Nutton, "Introduction," in *History of Therapy: Proceedings of the 10th International Symposium on the Comparative History of Medicine – East and West. September 8–September 15, 1985*, ed. Y. Kawakita, S. Sakai and Y. Ostuka (Tokyo, 1990), ix–xviii (see ix for the quotation here).

4   See, for example, Agamemnôn Tselikas, "Ta ellônika giatrosophia," in *Iatrika byzantina cheirographa*, ed. Thanasês Diamantopoulos (Athens, 1995), 57–69.

history, pathology, knowledge of the natural substances used in medicine, pharmacy, ethno-botany and ethno-pharmacology) are brought to bear.

The *Iatrosophion* Defined

Etymologically, the term *iatrosophion* means *medical wisdom*. It refers to books and medical works in the Greek language. Traditionally, the term has designated both the books and their text(s). Here it will be mainly used for the text(s) contained in books.

The books themselves are essentially handwritten volumes dating back to the mid- and late Byzantine periods (from the tenth century AD to the fall of the Byzantine Empire, 1453) and the Ottoman period (from 1453 to Greek independence in 1832), and even somewhat later.

The texts usually contain a description of a number of medicines grouped by ailments. Such groups are ordered according to the organs affected, from head to toe, *a capite ad calcem*. For each medicine, the text is structured according to a pattern that, when complete, includes the following information:

a   name of the medicine or of the ailment for which the medicine was prescribed;
b   author of the medicine;[5]
c   the *materia medica*, that is, the ingredients for the medicines, and their preparation;
d   how to administer the medicine: dosage, frequency, time of day, duration of treatment;
e   the expected therapeutic effect of the medicine.

Iatrosophia thus can be best approached when considered as therapeutic compendia. As medical literature, they are compilations of extracts from earlier, classical or early Byzantine sources, and often reproduce other previous compilations. These earlier collections especially reflect adaptations to the specific needs and the resources of the time and place where they were made.

In many cases, particularly for later *iatrosophia*, the compilers signed their work, mentioning not only the date, but also the place where they were writing. For unsigned *iatrosophia*, textual and codicological analyses can reveal geographic location and date. Textual analysis focuses on material content. Codicological analysis, also called "archeology of books," considers the following: medium (parchment or paper), watermarks, ink, handwriting, marks of ownership, annotations, when appropriate, and additions that include elements of place and date (for example, references to meteorological or astronomical phenomena such as floods or eclipses). In the best cases, textual and codicological analysis can lead to an approximate date and location for when and where the books were made. However, since *iatrosophia* can often reproduce earlier compilations, analysis requires caution.

---

5   In many cases, medicines are attributed to Hippocrates, Dioscorides, Galen or some other famous ancient or Early Byzantine physician such as Oreibasios or Aetios.

The Current State of Research

Iatrosophia ceased to be used in daily medical practice in Greek-speaking communities at the end of the nineteenth century. Apart from some sporadic studies, these medical compendia were left largely unstudied until the 1920s. Pioneering research was carried out by Edouard Jeanselme, Lysimachos Oeconomos, Aristoteles Kouzis and Kônstantinos Amantos.

After an initial 1921 study of the diet of recovering hospital patients, the French physician Jeanselme in collaboration with the Byzantinist Oeconomos, analyzed a miniature representing a medical dispensary in a medical manuscript dated AD 1339 (Bibliothèque nationale de France, *graecus* 2,243).[6] In the image, a physician examines a urine flask to diagnose a patient's disease. An assistant is seen accompanying two other patients. A druggist (identified as a *spetsialos* in Greek) holds a medicine box in his left hand, while his assistant, seated below a shelf filled with bottles and drug jars, pulverizes drugs in a mortar.[7] Around the same time as this publication, Kouzis, a Greek physician and professor of the history of medicine at the University of Athens, published extracts from two *iatrosophia*.[8] One is contained in the manuscript *Baroccianus* 150 (Bodleian Library, Oxford), and the other is in the *Codex medicus graecus* 48 (National Library of Austria). His analysis stressed both an interest in, as well as problems associated with, these texts. In 1930, Jeanselme translated a similar Byzantine work contained in a thirteenth-century manuscript into French (Bibliothèque Nationale de France, *supplementum graecum* 764).[9] His method of analysis for this *iatrosophion* aimed at identifying the author, or at least the sources. He compared Byzantine iatrosophic texts with lists of medicines present in the 1930s in the consultation rooms of French hospitals, highlighting in this way the genesis of *iatrosophia*. Such lists mentioned, indeed, the most commonly used medicines in each hospital. They were collective works made by all the doctors of the hospital, the result of the notes physicians took in their daily practice. At a certain moment, such lists were assembled and checked over by a commission within the hospital, and so constituted a coherent and homogeneous in-house reference work. In

---

6   Edouard Jeanselme, "Calcul de la ration alimentaire des malades de l'hôpital et de l'asile des vieillards annexé au monatère du Pantocrator à Byzance," in *2e Congrès d'Histoire de la Médecine. Actes du Congrès* (Paris, 1921), 411–20.

7   Edouard Jeanselme and L Oeconomos, "Un Dispensaire Médical à Byzance au temps des Paléologues D'après une Peinture du MS GREC PARIS Paris 2243," *Aesculape*, Février (1924), n.p.

8   Aristoteles Kouzis, "Contribution à l'étude de la médecine des zénons pendant le XVème siècle," *Byzantinische-Neugriechische Jahrbücher* : 6 (1927–28), 77–90.

9   Edouard Jeanselme, "Sur un aide-mémoire de thérapeutique byzantin contenu dans un manuscrit de la Bibliothèque Nationale de Paris (Supplément Grec 764). Traduction, notes et commentaires," in *Etudes sur l'histoire et sur l'art de Byzance*, ed. Charles Diehl, 2 vols (Paris, 1930), 1:147–70.

1931, K. Amantos published the chapter titles from a fifteenth-century *iatrosophion* and from a sixteenth-century manuscript that he had bought in Chios.[10]

Interest in Byzantine hospital therapeutics decreased dramatically after these publications appeared, and remained low until very recently. An explanation for such disinterest may have to do with the conclusions reached by Jeanselme and Kouzis. According to Jeanselme, indeed:

> ... As all Byzantine therapeutic manuals (formularies), the one translated here got its inspiration from the ancient Greek pharmacopoeia. It reproduces the same classical formulas. . . . But the majority of its formulas, without being original, are not textually reproduced in other therapeutics manuals ...[11]

And:

> ... Here is the interest of this small work. It is certainly not original since the authors of its formulas have taken their elements from ancient Greek medicine; however, it neither literally borrows [its formulas] from the writings of Hippocrates, Galen and the Arabs ...[12]

Yet such therapeutic compendia were to be found in hospital library collections, where they were used by both practitioners and teachers:

> ... Byzantine hospitals kept therapeutic formulas in their archives ... such works summarized all medical and surgical knowledge [of the hospital] and could be consulted not only by the physicians of the hospital, but also by those who were in charge of instructing students in the school adjacent to the hospital ...[13]

In spite of the above, however, Jeanselme concluded that such therapeutic notebooks did not contain any original contributions by Byzantine physicians, and were just servile reproductions of ancient texts:

---

10 K. Amantos, "Iatrosophikos kôdix," *Athêna*, 43 (1931), 148–70.

11 Edouard Jeanselme, "Sur un aide-mémoire," p. 163: "Comme tous les formulaires byzantins, celui dont on vient de lire la traduction s'inspire de l'ancienne pharmacopée grecque. Il reproduit même des formules classiques. ... Mais la plupart des recettes qu'il contient, sans être originales, ne son pas copiées textuellement dans d'autres manuels thérapeutiques ..." (author's translation).

12 Ibid., p. 170: "En cela réside l'intérêt de cet opuscule. Sans doute, il n'est pas original en ce sens que les auteurs de ces recettes en ont puisé les éléments dans la médecine grecque ancienne, mais il n'est pas non plus un emprunt littéral aux écrits d'Hippocrate, de Galien et des Arabes ..." (author's translation).

13 Ibid., pp. 168–9: "... les hôpitaux byzantins conservaient dans leurs archives des formules thérapeutiques ... Ces ouvrages qui résumaient toutes les connaissances médicales et chirurgicales pouvaient être consultés non seulement par les médecins de l'hôpital, mais aussi par ceux qui étaient chargés d'instruire les étudiants dans l'école annexée à l'établissement ..." (author's translation).

... Byzantine works on the healing art are so poor ... In this long sequence of centuries from the foundation of Constantinople [that is, AD 324] until its fall, one would unsuccessfully search for a real effort by physicians to free themselves from tradition, a willingness for independence and of autonomy. The art of healing in Byzantium was so static that, three or four centuries after its writing, the summary [of classical knowledge] redacted by Nonnus [in fact Theophanes Chrysobalantes, tenth century] was still copied and used later on. If one wished to take into account only the original works, there would not be anything to record and the page devoted to this period – more than one millennium – would be white. How may times did scholars in search for a novelty believe to discover it in some passage of a manuscript! How many times were their hopes disappointed, because they found very soon the ancient source where the supposedly original fragment was copied from, word by word ...[14]

Kouzis had a more positive approach, and suggested a specific method to analyze Byzantine therapeutic collections:

... one needs to take into consideration not only the anonymous and unpublished therapeutic manuals to be found in libraries – manuals that were used as *aide-mémoires* for both the physicians of the hospitals and the students of medicine -, but also the works by the physicians of these institutions in which one can trace the spirit and conditions of their writing, the conclusions principally drawn [by physicians] from their experience in the xenon [that is, the hospitals], as well as the most common medical conditions or, rather, the medical conditions most commonly diagnosed in those times and their cure ...[15]

He then exposed the elements that led him to these conclusions by reconstructing the use of medical books and texts in Byzantine hospitals. In so doing, Kouzis approached text history in a dynamic way, suggesting that the way books and texts

---

14 Ibid., p. 170: "... Les travaux byzantins relatifs à l'art de guérir sont d'une telle indigence ... Vainement on chercherait dans cette longue suite de siècles qui se succèdent depuis la fondation de Constantinople jusqu'à sa chute un réel effort du médecin pour se dégager de la tradition, une velléité d'indépendance et de libre examen. L'art de guérir à Byzance était à ce point stationnaire que, trois ou quatres siècles aprè sa rédaction, l'épitomé de Nonnus [10th century] était encore copié et par suite en usage. Si l'on voulait ne tenir compte que des ouvrages originaux, il n'y aurait rien à enregistrer et la page consacrée à cette période plus que millénaire resterait blanche. Combien de fois le chercheur en quête d'un fait nouveau a-t-il cru le découvrir enfin dans quelque passage d'un manuscrit! Combien de fois son espoir a-t-il été déçu, car il n'a pas tardé à retrouver la source ancienne où le prétendu fragment original avait été copié presque mot pour mot! ..." (author's translation).

15 Aristoteles Kouzis, "Contribution à l'étude," p. 77: "... il faut prendre en considération non seulement les manuels thérapeutiques anonymes, encore inédits, qui se trouvent dans les bibliothèques, manuels qui servaient d'aide-mémoires aux médecins de xénons et aux étudiants de la médecine, mais aussi les écrits de médecins de ces établissements, dans lesquels on peut suivre l'esprit et les conditions de leur rédaction, les conclusions puisées surtout de leur expérience dans les xénons, ainsi que les maladies fréquentes ou plutôt diagnostiquées dans ces temps et leur traitement" (author's translation).

were used in practice changed over centuries. In a first period, earlier works were copied by Byzantine physicians and incorporated into new medical treatises:

> ... It is evident that there were medical libraries in the xenons [*sic*; that is, the hospitals]. They contained copies of works by such ancient Greek physicians as Hippocrates, Dioscorides, Galen, etc, and also, according to the epoch, the major works by Byzantine physicians ... Such works were the main source where all the monks and physicians of the hospitals who subsequently wrote on medicine took their information from ...[16]

Then, the use of earlier works changed over time, as did also the way therapeutic compendia were written:

> ... gradually, the copies of ancient physicians' works were made only of the fragments or chapters from each of these works that were mostly used; such copies thus formed mere collections from different authors ... These collections ... formed mere guides/manuals for the use of physicians during their visits [to the patients] in the hospitals ... During the last centuries, writings of this kind mainly took the form of iatrosophic medicine, which was born in the same way ...[17]

Both Jeanselme and Kousis thus agreed that Byzantine therapeutic manuals were composed by a process of accumulating prescriptions, repeated over time. But while Jeanselme considered that no new elements were introduced from one generation to another (if not from one century to another), Kousis affirmed that texts composed in that way also included new and original data coming from contemporary practice:

> ... it is necessary to take into consideration not only the anonymous manuals of therapeutics ... but also the works written by the physicians in these institutions [that is, the hospitals] in which one can find the spirit and context of their writing, the conclusions principally drawn [by physicians] from their experience in the *xenon*s [*sic*] [that is, the hospitals], as well as the common medical conditions or, rather, the medical conditions most commonly diagnosed in those times and their cure ...[18]

---

16 Ibid., pp. 77–8: "Il est évident que dans les xénons existaient des bibliothèques médicales. Elles étaient composées des copies d'oeuvres des anciens médecins grecs, d'Hippocrate, de Dioscoride, de Galien etc., et, selon les temps, des principaux livres des médecins byzantins [p. 78]. ... Ces oeuvres furent la principale source, où puisèrent tous les moines et les médecins des xénons, qui écrivirent dans la suite ..." (author's translation).

17 Ibid., p. 78: "... Peu à peu ces copies des oeuvres d'anciens médecins ne furent composées que des fragments ou des chapitres les plus en usage dans chacune de ces oeuvres, formant une véritable collection de divers auteurs ... Ces collections ... ont formé de vrais guides-manuels à l'usage des médecins lors de la visite des xénons ... Pendant les derniers siècles ces écrits ont pris principalement la forme de l'iatrosophie, qui est née d'une manière tout-à-fait identique ..." (author's translation).

18 Ibid., p. 77: "... il faut prendre en considération non seulement les manuels thérapeutiques anonymes ... mais aussi les écrits de médecins de ces établissements, dans lesquels on peut suivre l'esprit et les conditions de leur rédaction, les conclusions puisées

Both authors thought it worthwhile to examine as many manuscripts with medical contents as possible (that is, the *iatrosophia* as books) and to read a large number of texts (that is, the *iatrosophia* as texts), however similar they might be. Their aim was to identify original data concerning the new developments of therapeutics by Byzantine physicians. While Jeanselme considered that instances of such data were very few, Kousis implicitly believed them to occur more frequently. He thus thought that by making a comprehensive compilation of iatrosophic books it would be possible to reconstitute the history of Byzantine therapeutics.

Since then, no specific study has been devoted to Byzantine *iatrosophia* apart two inventories (mentioned below). In current literature, the common opinion is that such books are infinitely repetitive and have very little of new or interesting information to offer, as the following quotation shows:

> ... Nobody will accept to devote months of work to read poorly written manuscripts in order to eventually have in his hands one more collection of formulas extracted from the jungle [*sic*] of the *iatrosophia* ...[19]

Such a statement, though made in a widely respected manual by one of the twentieth century's most authoritative Byzantinist, does not differ much from the one made eighty years before by Karal Krumbacher, for the time an equally influential Byzantinist:

> ... the so-called iatrosophia, the collections of formulas etc. The most part here is a diluted and darkened decoction [*sic*] of the ancient teaching, mixed with all kinds of superstitious ingredients, sympathetic [therapeutic] means, and exorcism formulas ...[20]

Nevertheless, some works proposed a more equilibrated evaluation:

> ... If, on one hand, Byzantine scholars assimilated the lessons of Hellenic philosophy ... on the other hand they added to this teaching new knowledge resulting from their own experience by creating a truly intellectual activity in their several cultural institutions ...[21]

---

surtout de leur expérience dans les xénons, ainsi que les maladies fréquentes ou plutôt diagnostiquées dans ces temps et leur traitemen ..." (author's translation).

19 Herbert Hunger, *Die hochsprachliche profane Literatur der Byzantiner*, vol. 2, *Philologie, Profandichtung, Musik, Mathematik and astronomie, Naturwissenschaften, Medizin, Kriegswissenschaft, Rechtsliteratur* (Munich, 1978), 2:304: "... Niemand wird monatelange Arbeit auf das Lesen elend geschriebener Codices aufwenden wollen, um zuletzt eine Rezeptsammlung mehr aus dem Dschungelbereich der Iatrosophia in Händen zu haben ..." (author's translation).

20 K. Krumbacher, *Geschichte der byzantinischen Litteratur von Justinian bis zum Ende des oströmischn Reiches (527–1453)* (Munich, 1897), p. 616: "... die sogenannten Iatrosophien (iatrosophia), Rezeptensammlungen u.s.w. Meist is hier ein verdünnter und getrübter Aufguss alter Lehren mit allerlei abergläubischen Ingredienzien, Sympathiemitteln, Beschwörungsformeln u.s.w. untermischt ..." (author's translation).

21 P.G. Kritikos and S.N. Papadaki, "Contribution à l'histoire de la Pharmacie chez les Byzantins," in *Die Vorträge der Hauptversammlung der Internationalen Gesellschaft für*

Inventorying *Iatrosophia*

As all authors who tackled the topic recognized, the creation of an inventory of *iatrosophia* is a key issue whatever the approach. This is particularly true if the research aim is to reconstruct phenomena that occur over the so-called *longue durée*. Further, the research cannot be limited to a small set of cases, but rather, needs to rely on as great a sample size as possible to reach significant conclusions.

Although Greek medical manuscripts have been repeatedly inventoried, *iatrosophia* have been seldom taken into consideration. At the beginning of the nineteenth century, the German philologist Friedrich Reinhold Dietz (1804–36) did pioneering work, traveling all across Europe to personally analyze codices in libraries where they were preserved. He died before he published the material he gathered. The French scholar Charles Daremberg (1817–72) took over this research. He traveled to England in 1847 and 1849, and published a report, frequently citing references to manuscripts in Parisian libraries (principally the then *Bibliothèque Impériale*).[22] At the very end of the nineteenth century, the Greek philologist Geôrgios Costomiris, relying on a wider compilation of data, published a partial inventory of manuscripts by ancient medical authors in five issues of the French *Revue des Etudes Grecques*.[23] In a sort of Franco-German scientific competition, a large team of scholars directed by Hermann Diels (1848–1922), a philologist and historian of ancient philosophy, published a supposedly exhaustive inventory of Greek medical manuscripts by authors and texts in 1905–1906.[24] As authoritative as it was (and still is), this work has a strong classical bias: non-classical and Byzantine works were not included in the inventory. Given this research history, it is no wonder that *iatrosophia* had not been taken into consideration, particularly after the historian of Byzantine literature Karl Krumbacher had disparaged their usefulness as source material (see above). Robert E. Sinkewicz has recently compiled inventories of the texts contained in all Greek manuscripts currently known, listed by authors from classical antiquity

---

Geschichte der Pharmazie e. V. Während des Internationalen Pharmaziegeschichtlichen Kongresses in Athen von 8. bis 14. April 1967, ed., G.E. Dann (Stuttgart, 1969), 73: "... Si les savants de l'époque byzantine assimilèrent les enseignements de la philosophie hellénique ... ils ajoutèrent à ces enseignements des conaissances [*sic*] dues à leur expérience propre instituant dans leurs divers centres culturels une discipline intellectuelle propre ..." (author's translation).

22 Charles Daremberg, *Notices et extraits des manuscrits médicaux grecs, latins et français, des principales bibliothèques d'Europe* (Paris, 1853).

23 Georges A. Costomiris, "Etudes sur les écrits inédits des anciens médecins (et ceux dont le texte original est perdu, mais qui existent en latin ou en arabe)," *Revue des Etudes Grecques*, 2 (1889), 343–83; 3 (1890), 145–79; 4 (1891), 97–110; 5 (1892), 61–72; 10 (1897), 405–45.

24 The work was first published in the proceedings of the Berlin Academy of Sciences (1905 and 1906), and republished in 1906 under a separate title (this version is quoted here): Hermann Diels, *Die Handschriften der antiken Ärzte. Griechische Abteilung* (Berlin, 1906).

to the late Byzantine period.[25] Though not specifically limited to medical authors, these are included in the lists along with anonymous treatises such as *iatrosophia*. Most recently, the Greek historian of science G. Karas has published an inventory of Greek scientific manuscripts and printed books of the Ottoman period. One volume in this work is devoted to medicine, and includes some earlier, Byzantine items.[26]

The main problem of such inventories is that they all rely on printed catalogs of manuscripts. Yet *iatrosophia* are not necessarily well identified! A good example is provided by A. Kousis's article quoted above: while the title (in French) refers to "zénons" (with no clearly understandable meaning), the text discusses the "xénons", that is, hospitals. As Jeanselme pointed out, this difference resulted from an incorrect reading in the title of the *iatrosophion* with a confusion between the Greek letters *xi* (*xenôn*) and *zêta* (*zenôn*). While *xenôn* is one of the Byzantine terms for an hospital, *Zenôn* is a personal name that seems in the manuscripts to indicate the author of the texts that follows. The origin of this mistake is to be found in the Oxford catalog of Greek manuscripts compiled in 1853 by Henry O. Coxe (1811–81).[27] As a consequence, the text in this manuscript (Oxford, Bodleian Library, *Baroccianus* 150) has been attributed to no less than the Byzantine Emperor Zeno (AD 474–91) or to a physician known as Zenon of Cyprus, the famous teacher of Oreibasios, the fourth-century Byzantine physician. In fact, the manuscript came from an hospital (*xenôn*), and is one among the many *iatrosophia* important to the study of Byzantine therapeutics.

In the past decade a major research program has been launched to correct past problems in documenting texts. The fruit of this endeavor is the *Corpus of Greek Medical Manuscripts*. The aim of this research program is, on a first-hand basis, to:

a   inventory and examine all manuscripts currently known in library collections;
b   produce, preferably by a first-hand analysis of manuscripts and their the texts, a written description (codicological, textual and historical) of the inventoried items.[28]

The resulting data are being recorded electronically to create a computerized database. Text references can then be retrieved according to various search descriptors, for

---

25 All works were published in the *Greek Index Project Series* by the Pontifical Institute of Mediaeval Studies: Robert E. Sinkewicz and Walter M. Hayes, "Manuscript listings for the authored works of the Paleaeologan period," in *Greek Index Project Series* (Toronto, 1989); Robert E. Sinkewicz, "Manuscript listings for the authors of classical and late antiquity, " in *Greek Index Project Series* (Toronto, 1990), and "Manuscript listings for the authors of the patristic and Byzantine periods, " in *Greek Index Project Series* (Toronto, 1992).

26 Giannis Karas, *Oi epistêmes stên tourkokratia. Cheirographa kai entupa*. Tomos 3: *Oi epistêmes tês zôês* (Athens, 1994).

27 Henry O. Coxe, *Catalogi codicum manuscriptorum Bibliothecae Bodleianae pars prima recensionem codicum graecorum continens* (Oxford, 1853), p. 263.

28 Alain Touwaide, "The Corpus of Greek Medical Manuscripts: A Computerized Inventory and Catalogue," in *Bibliographic Access to Medieval and Renaissance Manuscripts: A Survey of Computerized Data Bases and Information Services*, ed., W.M. Stevens (New York, 1992), 75–92; Alain Touwaide, "Pour un Corpus des manuscrits médicaux grecs, " in

example: textual types (hospital notebooks), origins (hospital libraries) and intended readership (including hospital doctors).

The major problem of such a cataloging enterprise is the correct identification of texts. This is especially critical in the case of *iatrosophia*, where the texts are extremely repetitive and vary only in small but important details. Careful scrutiny (even in the case of a small group of texts) is required, as shown in the exemplary research conducted by David Bennett on hospital *iatrosophia*.[29] His philological study principally aimed at the following, critical research goals:

a to verify by means of textual analysis, attribution of some iatrosophia to hospitals;
b to ascertain that apparently differing texts were variant forms of the same core text;
c to selectively edit a number of texts.

The Scientific Context of *Iatrosophia*

Iatrosophia (as texts) can be seen as a part of Byzantine discourse on therapeutics. They are made of passages from the *Corpus Hippocraticum*, Dioscorides' *De materia medica*, Galen's works on therapeutics (see below) and additional reference material on simple and compound drugs.

A content analysis is very revealing. While none of the 62 treatises which form the *Corpus Hippocraticum* are explicitly devoted to therapeutics, several report clinical cases, including a description of therapies administered to patients. These are as follow: *Diseases II* and *III*, *Diseases of Women I* and *II*, *Sterile Women*, *Epidemics I* and *III*, the *Appendix* to the *Regimen in acute diseases*, *Internal affections*, *Diseases IV*, *Epidemics II*, *IV* and *V*, *Affections* and *Diseases I*, *Epidemics V* and *VII* and *Remedies*.[30] In addition, two treatises on dietetics are also usually included: *Regimen in acute diseases* and *Regimen*.

Dioscorides' work, *De materia medica*, is an encyclopedia of natural products of all kinds (plant, mineral or animal) used for therapeutic treatment at that time. Almost all of the work's 1,003 chapters are assembled using the following pattern: name and description of the natural substance used in preparing the medicines; therapeutic properties of the substance, and indications of the medicines, which also

---

Tradizione e ecdotica dei testi medici tardo-antichi e bizantini. Atti del Convegno internazionale, Anacapri, 29–31 ottobre 1990, ed. A. Garzya (Naples, 1992), 356–666.

29 David Bennett, "Three Xenon Texts," in *Byzantine Medicine*, 2 vols, eds L.R. Angeletti and A. Touwaide (Rome, 1999), 2:507–19; David Bennett, "Medical Practice and Manuscripts in Byzantium," *Social History of Medicine* 13 (2000), 279–91; David Bennett, "Xenonika" (unpublished PhD Thesis, University of London, 2003).

30 On the Hippocratic literature, see Jacques Jouanna, *Hippocrate* (Paris, 1992), English trans. *Hippocrates* (Baltimore, MD, 1999). For the Greek text of the Hippocratic treatises, together with an English translation, see the several volumes of the Loeb Classical Library currently published by Harvard University Press.

included recommended dose, expected result, side-effects, and adulterations, along with tests to detect them.

Galen's works related to therapeutics can be classified into four groups according to their use as follows:

a   the principles to be followed to properly conduct a therapeutic strategy: *Therapeutic method* and *On the therapeutic method dedicated to Glaukôn*;
b   the *materia medica* to be used for the preparation of medicines: *On the mixtures and properties of simple medicines*;
c   the medicines to be prescribed for the treatment of specific diseases: *On compound medicines*, *On antidotes*, *On medicines according to the [affected] places of the body*;
d   the pharmaceutical techniques for the preparation of medicines: *On medicines according to their types*.

All these works constituted a coherent reference set covering the whole topic of therapeutics, the theoretical principles governing the strategy for therapeutic use of medicines, *materia medica*, composition and preparation of the medicines. The general principles also included (explicit or implicit) theories on the nature and origin of the therapeutic properties of medicines.[31]

In the *Corpus Hippocraticum* and in the anonymous *Problems* redacted by the colleagues and successors of Aristotle (384–22 BC), the causes of disease and effects of therapy are related to the four humors which constitute the body (black bile, yellow bile, phlegm and blood). In Dioscorides' *De materia medica*, no theory of disease is explicitly presented. However, a holistic system can be detected underpinning the work. Health is a state of equilibrium in the body. Disease is a disequilibrium caused by an alteration in the quantity or the quality of the physiological components of the body, the four humors. To counteract diseases, a substance is brought into the body to oppose the action of the process causing the disease. Galen, possibly following earlier medical theories, wrote suggesting that the action of medicines should be analyzed according to a material system, which can be summarized as follows: since the substance of the medicines is made of particles that interact with the particles of the body, such substances can compensate for a lack of some physiological component, or they can restore an altered physiological constituent to a pristine state.

---

31 Alain Touwaide, "Le strategie terapeutiche: i farmaci," in *Storia del pensiero medico occidentale*, vol. 1, *Antichità e Medio-Evo*, ed. M.D. Grmek (Rome, 1993), 1:353–73, English trans. "Therapeutic Strategies: Drugs," in *Western Medical Thought form Antiquity to the Middle Ages*, ed. M.D. Grmek (Cambridge, MA, 1999), 259–72, 390–94; Alain Touwaide, "The Aristotelian school and the birth of theoretical pharmacology in Ancient Greece," in *The Pharmacy. Windows on History* (Basle, 1996), 11–22; Alain Touwaide, "La thérapeutique médicamenteuse de Dioscoride à Galien: du pharmaco-centrisme au médico-centrisme," in *Galen on Pharmacology. Philosophy, History and Medicine: Proceedings of the 5th International Galen Colloquium, Lille, 16–18 March 1995*, ed. A. Debru (Leiden, 1997), 255–82.

Early Byzantine physicians such as Oribasius (fourth century AD), Aetius (sixth century) and Paul of Egina (seventh century) sought to combine Dioscorides' and Galen's works in different ways. Their work had a unique objective: to bring together Dioscorides' descriptive inventory and description of the natural substances of medicines with Galen's theory on the action of medicines.

The Genesis of the *Iatrosophion*

The genesis of the *iatrosophion* (as a genre in medical literature) is best understood within the context of the Christianization of late antique and early Byzantine society in general, and of medicine in particular. With the Christianization of medicine from the fourth to the sixth centuries AD, the theories on pathogenesis and therapeutic properties of medicines were re-cast.[32] Evidence is particularly clear in looking at the legends of Kosmas and Damian, the so-called *Anargyroi* (that is, "The Unpaid [physicians]"). Historically, these twin brothers were born around AD 250 and martyred some time between 285 and 287. They did not attend any medical school, but received their medical knowledge directly from God. They successfully treated sick patients without asking nor even accepting any financial compensation. As the story goes, during a period of persecution of Christians they were summoned to the court of the Roman governor, who attempted to coerce them to venerate the Roman emperor's statue, which they refused to do, and so were martyred. Stories of miraculous healings followed their deaths, and they began to be venerated. By the time the Byzantine Emperor Justinian (born *c*. 482; emp. 527; d. 565) restored their church in Constantinople, imploring their intercession to heal his own illness, the cult of *The Two Holy Healers* was already ancient.

According to legends, the cases treated by Kosmas and Damian present similar features: the illnesses were not necessarily due to physiological causes, but often resulted from morally deviant behaviors or a refusal to venerate God. Similarly, the medicines administered by *The Holy Healers* did not owe their therapeutic action to any intrinsic property, but to the grace of God, working through Kosmas and Damian as mediators. This demonstrates the change that Christianization brought to medicine. Both theories of pathology and therapeutic healing had to be radically modified. Pathogenesis and therapeutic action of drugs were no longer material processes subject to scientific analysis. They became a province of theology, for both disease and health were dependent on God's will. As a consequence, science and

---

32 On this point, see mainly, and in chronological order, Owsei Temkin, *Hippocrates in a World of Pagans and Christians* (Baltimore, MD, 1991); Darrel W. Amundsen and Garry B. Ferngren, "The early Christian tradition," in *Caring and Curing: Health and Medicine in the Western Religious Traditions*, ed. Ronald L. Numbers and Darrel W. Amundsen (Baltimore, MD, 1998); Hector Avalos, *Health Care and the Rise of Christianity* (Peabody, 1999), and the several essays contained in the following two volumes edited by Gary B. Ferngren: *The History of Science and Religion in the Western Tradition: An Encyclopedia* (New York, 2000), and *Science and Religion: A Historical Introduction* (Baltimore, MD, 2002).

scientific literature were re-organized. The older material approach to pathology and therapeutics was no longer favored, and was replaced by theology. Christianization in effect eliminated theory in favor of ascribing all things to God's will. This change may explain the different fortunes that Galen's and Dioscorides' works had in Byzantium. Galen's treatises seem not to have been widely diffused, probably because of their material approach to therapeutics, which was incompatible with theologically based, Christian explanations. Dioscorides' *De materia medica* was easily adapted to the new Christianized medicine thanks to its descriptive approach. The effect of the Christianization of medical literature was paradoxical. From a theoretical point of view, speculation about the way medicines acted no longer became necessary; all effects and properties resulted from the action of God's will. This had an impact on such texts as *iatrosophia*: they were liberated from the domination of theoretical orthodoxy, and were thereby opened up to study by empirical observation.

Recent studies of classical medical texts show that, at the same point in time, texts were faithfully transmitted, reproduced and studied in Byzantium. There were indeed different attitudes toward texts, which co-existed simultaneously. Classical texts were used for study, and such other texts as the *iatrosophia* were used in the practice of medicine. Each kind of text represented a different genre within the field of medical literature, and was ruled by different principles. Classical texts had to be transmitted as correctly as possible, even though they were annotated. Manuals for the practice of medicine, *iatrosophia*, although rooted in the classical tradition, were not dominated by the pressure of conservatism to preserve textual integrity and/or theoretical orthodoxy. Medical manuals reflect a free use of the body of classical medical knowledge as a reference to be validated by experience and further developed according to its usefulness in daily therapeutic practice.

The Function of *Iatrosophia* in Byzantine Hospitals and in the Practice of Therapeutics

The collections of formulas for medicines extracted from classical medical literature that compose *iatrosophia* were constantly reproduced by physicians, either by individuals working in their own practice or by groups of physicians working in a hospital. In their tradition, *iatrosophia* demonstrate a specific dynamic, different from textual erosion and entropy that is normally the case in the transmission of literary texts. When the texts of these manuals were reproduced, they were also constantly transformed. This is particularly because they were often, if not always, linked with health centers, as Kouzis has already suggested. This association of text and location can be shown by codicological analysis of manuscripts, and historical study of texts. This explains the double characteristic of *iatrosophia*: globally they are similar, but with varying texts.

When *iatrosophia* are considered as a group, textual changes that are introduced in fact mark practical adaptations to changing circumstances. Changes in the text reveal differences in many areas: in the medical conditions to be treated, therapeutic strategies, *materia medica*, techniques to be used to transform primary substances into medicine, forms of the medicines, and their administration.

Twentieth- or twenty-first-century traditional medical practice confirms the validity of such an approach. While a strong case could be made using the traditional medical practice of any contemporary cultural group in the world, it is especially meaningful to look at contemporary Greek populations or other groups whose medical practice is rooted in the Greek tradition.

Patricia Clark studied a therapeutic handbook that recorded the modern practice of Kônstantinos Theodorakis, a Cretan healer (1866–1916).[33] The book, dated 1930, was written by Kônstantinos' son, Nikolaos. Like his father he was a traditional healer, not a doctor with a formal medical education. In her work, Clark provides a detailed analysis of the handbook. She writes her conclusions as follows:

> ... the note book of early twentieth century Cretan village healer, Nikolaos Theodorakis, ... [shows] continuities in the healing tradition and, equally, ... [a] capacity to evolve: mutating, adapting, accreting over time ... These characteristics ... are the key to its resilience: a respect for the authority of tradition, an ability to experiment and innovate, and an intimate knowledge of the resources of the local landscape ...[34]

And:

> ... indigenous knowledge of the healing properties of plants, is best viewed as a living system, one that has functioned over the centuries with healers engaged in a long process of learning about, remembering, forgetting, and adjusting to their cultural heritage and their physical "therapeutic landscape" ...[35]

Two large-scale studies by two independent research groups on contemporary Turkish ethnobotanical and ethnopharmacological practices reached similar conclusions. One, published over the period 1996–2001, dealt with four regions of Turkey.[36] The other, also published as a series of reports between 1991 and 2001, was more general and covered almost all of Turkey region by region.[37] Both proceeded using the

---

33 Patricia A. Clark, "Landscape, Memories, and Medicine: Traditional Healing in Amari, Crete," *Journal of Modern Greek Studies*, 20 (2002), 339–65.

34 Ibid., 339.

35 Ibid., 358.

36 A. Yazicioğlu and Ertan Tuzlaci, "Turkish folk medicinal plants of Trabzon (Turkey)," *Fitoterapia*, 67 (1996), 308–18; Ertan Tuzlaci and M.K. Erol, "Turkish folk medicinal plants II," *Fitoterapia*, 70 (1999), 593–610; Ertan Tuzlaci and E. Tolon, "Turkish folk medicinal plants IIII," *Fitoterapia*, 71 (2000), 673–85; Ertan Tuzlaci and Pinar Eryaşar Aymaz, "Turkish folk medicinal plants IV," *Fitoterapia*, 72 (2001), 323–43.

37 Ekrem Sezik, Mamoru Tabata, Erdem Yeşilada, Gisho Honda, Katsumi Goto and Yasumasa Ikeshiro, "Traditional medicine in Turkey I: Folk medicine in Northeast Anatolia," *Journal of Ethnopharmacology*, 35 (1991), 191–6; Ekrem Sezik, Zor M., Erdem Yeşilada, "Traditional medicine in Turkey II: Folk medicine in Kastamonu," *International Journal of Pharmacognosy*, 30 (1992), 233–9; Mamoru Tabata, Ekrem Sezik, Gisho Honda, Erdem Yeşilada, Hiroshi Fukui, Katsumi Goto and Yasumasa Ikeshiro, "Traditional medicine

same method: researchers interviewed local informants, who were older villagers, peasants, shepherds, and also a number of medical practitioners. The informants being interviewed were asked to bring the medicines or the plants (fresh or dried) they used, or if this was not possible, to indicate the places where they collected these plants. On the basis of these interviews, a collection of samples was assembled, and each item was analyzed and correctly identified. The publications that resulted from this study, produced a wealth of detailed information: plant names (scientific and vernacular), locations where plants were collected, parts of the plants used, the way medicines were made and administered, and the medical conditions for which they were prescribed. The general conclusions reached in these two important research studies were identical: contemporary practice results from a tradition that was constantly adapted to actual needs and resources.[38]

When the constitutive elements of single iatrosophic texts are studied and such approach is also applied to a large corpus of such texts, a wholly new picture emerges of therapeutic practice in a Byzantine hospital. This approach is clearly seen in the extensive research of the *Corpus of Greek Medical Manuscripts*. In the following sections, three main elements of the *iatrosophia* will be considered: diseases, *materia medica* and pharmaceutical techniques.

---

in Turkey III: Folk medicine in East Anatolia, Van and Bitlis Provinces," *International Journal of Pharmacognosy*, 32 (1994), 3–12; Erdem Yeşilada, Gisho Honda, Ekrem Sezik, Mamoru Tabata, Katsumi Goto and Yasumasa Ikeshiro, "Traditional medicine in Turkey IV: Folk medicine in the Mediterranean subdivision," *Journal of Ethnopharmacology*, 39 (1993), 31–8; Erdem Yeşilada, Gisho Honda, Ekrem Sezik, Mamoru Tabata, Tetsuro Fujita, Toshihiro Tanaka, Yoshio Takeda and Yoshihisa Takaishi, "Traditional medicine in Turkey V: Folk medicine in the inner Taurus Mountain," *Journal of Ethnopharmacology*, 46 (1995), 133–52; Gisho Honda, Erdem Yeşilada, Mamoru Tabata, Ekrem Sezik, Tetsuro Fujita, Yoshio Takeda, Yoshihisa Takaishi and Toshihiro Tanaka, "Traditional medicine in Turkey VI: Folk medicine in West Anatolia: Afyon, Kütahya, Denizli, Muğla, Aydin provinces," *Journal of Ethnopharmacology*, 53 (1996), 75–87; Tetsuro Fujita, Ekrem Sezik, Mamoru Tabata, Erdem Yeşilada, Gisho Honda, Yoshio Takeda, Toshihiro Tanaka and Yoshihisa Takaishi, "Traditional medicine in Turkey VII: Folk medicine in Middle and West Black Sea Regions," *Economic Botany*, 49 (1995), 406–22; Ekrem Sezik, Erdem Yeşilada, Mamoru Tabata, Gisho Honda, Yoshihisa Takaishi, Tetsuro Fujita, Toshihiro Tanaka and Yoshio Takeda, "Traditional medicine in Turkey VIII: Folk medicine in East Anatolia: Erzurum, Erzincan, Ağri, Kars, Iğdir provinces," *Economic Botany*, 51 (1997), 195–211; Erdem Yeşilada, Ekrem Sezik, Gisho Honda, Yoshihisa Takaishi, Yoshio Takeda and Toshihiro Tanaka, "Traditional medicine in Turkey IX: Folk medicine in north-west Anatolia," *Journal of Ethnopharmacology*, 64 (1999), 195–210; Ekrem Sezik, Erdem Yeşilada, Gisho Honda, Yoshihisa Takaishi, Yoshio Takeda and Toshihiro Tanaka, "Traditional medicine in Turkey X: Folk medicine in Central Anatolia," *Journal of Ethnopharmacology*, 75 (2001), 95–115.

38 Two recent studies done in different fields on the contemporary use of traditional dying plants in Turkey reached identical conclusions; see Fevzi Özgökçe and Ibrahim Yilmaz, "Dye plants of East Anatolia region (Turkey)," *Economic Botany*, 57 (2003), 454–60, and Yunus Doğan, Süleyman Başlar, Hasan Hüseyin Mert and Güngör Ay, "Plants used as natural dye sources in Turkey," *Economic Botany*, 57 (2003), 442–53.

Diseases

When formulas taken from *iatrosophia* are compared with those from classical sources, differences appear in the diseases the formulas treated. Such differences can be explained in two ways. They indicate either an expansion in the use of the medicines (that is, applications to other diseases) or differences in the pathologies the physicians were treating. In the first case, these changes reflect an attempt by physicians, possibly through empirical observation, to expand the range of applications for the medicines at their disposal. In other words: this reflects an attempt to optimize the use of available medicines so as to have an impact on the population's health. In the second case (differences in diseases treated), modifications may indicate that physicians were seeking therapeutic treatments for new or previously unidentified medical conditions. This may suggest that physicians followed an epidemiological approach to pathology in the populations they were treating.

On this basis, two different images of Byzantine medical activity emerge. The first case may suggest an expansion of the range of diseases treated with the medicines available. Physicians created new applications, from the necessities of practice. The second case suggests that they followed the health conditions of their patients by responding and reacting to changes. In both cases, physicians would have followed a process of transferring treatment applications for a medicine from one pathology to another. This process could have resulted by means of two different (and probably complementary) approaches to therapeutics: a theoretical one and an empirical one. Theoretically, physicians could have reasoned that different pathologies resulted from identical or similar causes and processes. In this case, they would have logically deduced by inference that medicines for one illness could be effective to treat another. Byzantine physicians could also have proceeded in a more empirical way. On the basis of clinical observation, they could have grouped diseases according to identical or similar symptoms. The next step would have been to transfer the medicines used in treating known cases to new ones. If so, it may be a reasonable conclusion that Byzantine physicians had a certain degree of clinical training and experience of pathological analysis. Both ways of proceeding, *a priori* reasoning and clinical observation, while not exclusive, could have been associated over time in a complementary and adaptive way.

Materia medica

Materia medica can be submitted to an analysis similar to the one just used for diseases. Though an enormous task, given the considerable number of texts to be screened, research using this method has already produced significant results.[39] For example,

---

39 Alain Touwaide, "Arabic medicine in Greek translation: A preliminary report," *Journal of the International Society for the History of Islamic Medicine*, 1 (2002), 45–53; Alain Touwaide, "Arabic Materia Medica in Byzantium during the 11th century A.D. and the problems of transfer of knowledge in Medieval science," in *Science and Technology in*

it has been possible to fix a precise time for the introduction (or perhaps better, the re-introduction) of oriental drugs into Byzantine *materia medica*. After the recovery of Constantinople in 1261 and until *c.* 1340, the Byzantine therapeutic practice was markedly "Arabized." Not only does an analysis of *iatrosophia* demonstrate a peak in the frequency of Eastern drugs and Arabic plant names mentioned, but also these are not even translated, but simply transliterated into Greek. Further, manuscripts of this and subsequent periods in time contain many bilingual Greco-Arabic and Arabo-Greek lexica.[40] Paleographical examination of some original manuscript lexica significantly shows drugs listed in two columns, with one column written in a well-formed Greek script, and the other column containing the equivalent of such terms in Arabic transliterated in Greek alphabet and written by a hand manifestly unaccustomed to writing the Greek alphabet. It thus seems clear that each column is by a different writer. This could well indicate that these manuscripts were written by a native Greek writer and a non-native Greek writer; or perhaps by an Arabic speaker transliterating and writing Arabic plant names into the Greek alphabet. Such conclusions suggest that Arabic physicians were present in Byzantium.[41] A possible explanation is that Arabic physicians came to Byzantium following the Mongol conquest of Baghdad in 1258 (especially after 1261 with the recovery of Constantinople). If so, they well could have assisted their Byzantine colleagues in reconstructing hospitals and related health care institutions.

Pharmaceutical Techniques

Similar results can be obtained using this method to investigate changes in pharmaceutical techniques. In classical texts, medicines for internal use are produced mainly by two methods: infusion and decoction. This may be by using different kinds of liquids, and possibly with different additives. Following the transfer of Arabic medical knowledge to Byzantium, new forms of drugs appear in Byzantine *iatrosophia*. These changes result mostly from the use of sugar for making syrups, and from distillation.

Future Research

The method of analysis demonstrated here depends on the crucial aspect of collecting texts in such a quantity as to indicate the historical processes from which they result and which they reflect.

---

the Islamic World, ed. R. Ansari (Turnhout, 2002), 223–46. See especially references to the previous literature in both.

40 Alain Touwaide, "Lexica medico-botanica byzantina. Prolégomènes à une étude," in *Tês filiês tade dôra: Miscelánea léxica en memoria de Conchita Serrano* (Madrid, 2000), 211–28.

41 The manuscripts we are dealing with come mainly from Constantinople.

Future analysis of *iatrosophia* will open up new perspectives on research, not only in response to the history of Byzantine hospitals, but also into other aspects of Byzantine society (for example, epidemiology, and pharmaceutics). Such investigations will be all the more significant if they can be set within the context of a larger study to cover other periods and places. Research could take as a foundation the analysis of texts from classical antiquity (particularly the *materia medica* of the *Corpus Hippocraticum* or illnesses mentioned in Dioscorides' *De materia medica*). From such sources, data would form the cornerstone upon which comparable Byzantine texts could be analyzed so as to identify and study longitudinally processes of change, adaptation and innovation.

Taking as a test case the *materia medica* in the *Corpus Hippocraticum*, there are 380 different plant names that correspond to approximately 340 modern species. These plants were used in a total of 3,100 formulas. Significantly, almost half of these formulas (1,500) used only 44 plants. Among the other 1,500 formulas, 1,100 used 80 different plants. The remaining 500 were made of 255 plants. Table 10.1 refers to the 44 plants most frequently used, classified according to their number of uses (rank ordered from highest to lowest). It provides the following information: total number of uses, Greek name, English common name, and gynecological uses (these have been especially noted because they constitute the vast majority of uses in the *Corpus*), and other uses with some of them.[42]

---

42 Identification of plants and diseases relies on current bibliography. Both topics require fresh research.

Table 10.1   The 44 most frequently used plants in the *materia medica* of the *Corpus Hippocraticum*.

No. of occurrences	Greek name	English name	Indications (gynecological and others)
87	*smurna*	myrrh	69 + 18 (ophthalmology [5], wounds [2], ...)
72	*kuminon*	cumin	51 + 21 (stomach [3], fever [3], ...)
63	*helleboros*	hellebore	16 + 47 (phthisis [7], purge [4], dropsy [3], arthritis [2], ...)
49	*skorodon*	garlic	34 + 15 (leucophlegmasy [2], rectum [affections] [2], respiratory system [2], fever, ophthalmology ...)
47	*linozôstis*	mercury	39 + 8 (fever [3], ...)
46	*selinon*	celery	29 + 17 (jaundice [4], cold [2], brain [2], ...)
46	*prason*	leek	38 + 8 (*cholera* [2], diarrhea, jaundice, ...)
45	*linon*	linen	38 + 7 (wounds. pleurisy, rectum, cough [children], *tumors*, stomach, wounds)
45	*libanôtos*	frankincense	36 + 9 (wounds [4], burns, dyspnea [children], pneumonia, head ulcers)
45	*silfion*	silphium	25 + 20 (fever [3], bile [2], dropsy [2], typhus [2], ...)
43	*annéson*	anise	39 + 4 (diaphragm, jaundice, respiration [children])
43	*teutlon*	beet	8 + 35 (cold [2], leucophlegmasy [2], phthisis [2], ...)
41	*krambê*	cabbage	38 + 3 (brain, *cholera*, phthisis)
40	*origanon*	origanum	15 + 25 (cold [3], phthisis[3], lungs [3], pneumonia [2], *tumors* [2], ...)
37	*roé + sidion*	pomegranate	25 + 12 (*cholera* [2], wounds [2], diarrhea, dysentery, fever, ophthalmology, ...)
35	*akté*	elder tree	30 + 5 (brain, *cholera*, diarrhea, dyscrasia, pituite)
35	*murrinê*	myrtle	24 + 1 (rectum)
33	*elatêrion*	squirting cucumber	24 + 9 (bile [2], nyctalopia [1], *opisthotonos* [1], ...)
31	*elelisfakon*	sage	26 + 5 (*pulmonary apoplexy, cholera*, diarrhea, pneumonia, lungs)
31	*kuparittos*	cypress	30 + 1 (head ulcers)
30	*krithê*	barley	23 + 6 (coxalgia, pain, fever, acute diseases, pleurisy rectum)
30	*péganon*	rue	20 + 10 (phthisis [2], cold, opisthotonos, pneumonia, rate, *tumors*, ...)
29	*dafnê*	laurel	29 + –
29	*sukon*	figs	18 + 11 (aliment:ary excess [2], cold, bile, *cholera*, diarrhea, hemostatic, *tumors*, wounds, ...)

26	*elaia*	olive	22 + 4 (cholera, diarrhea, inflammation, *tumors*)
26	*glukusidé*	peony	25 + 1 (*typhus*)
26	*marathon*	fennel	24 + 2 (jaundice, respiratory system)
26	*puros*	wheat	19 + 7 (neck [2], feces [2], contusions [noose], dropsy, ...)
25	*fakos*	lentils	11 + 14 (*cholera* [2], wounds [2], ...)
25	*knidios kokkos*	Cnidian berry	6 + 19 (coxalgia [2], dropsy [2], leucophlegmasy [2], phthisis [2], rate [2], *typhus* [2], ...)
25	*lôtos*	lotus	19 + 6 (wounds [3], ...)
25	*sikua*	bottle-gourd	20 + 5 (bile [2], coxalgia, liver, stranguria)
24	*gléchon*	pennyroyal	19 + 5 (*cholera*, diarrhea, dyscrasia, fever, purge)
23	*kuklaminos*	cyclamen	20 + 3 (bile [2], pneumonia)
22	*kupeiros*	galingale	22 + –
21	*melanthion*	black cumin	21 + –
19	*astafis*	stavesacre	18 + 1 (chute du rectum)
19	*batos*	bramble	17 + 2 (*cholera*, diarrhea)
19	*kegchros*	millet	– + 19 (fièvre [3], pleurisy [3], brain [2], ...)
19	*skammónia*	scammony	11 + 8 (reins [2], coxalgia, fever, hepatitis, lungs, arthritis, *typhus*)
18	*agnos*	chaste-tree	11 + 7 (*cholera* [2], ...)
18	*sésamon*	sesame	7 + 11 (bronchitis, hemoptysy, jaundice, *opisthotonos*, arthritis, cough [children], ...)
17	*krommuon*	onions	10 + 7 (purge [2], bile, brain, *cholera*, jaundice, leucophlegmasy)
14	*koriannon*	coriander	7 + 7 (jaundice [2], phthisis [2], *cholera* [1], ...)

Note: Identification of plants and diseases relies on current bibliography. Both topics require fresh research.

The inventory of the diseases mentioned in Dioscorides' *De materia medica* is summarized in Table 10.2. It is organized by: category of diseases listed by frequency of occurrence (descending order from most frequent mentioned to least); total number of occurrences; and listing frequency expressed as a percentage of the total number.

Table 10.2   Inventory of the diseases mentioned in Dioscorides' *De materia medica*.

Category	Occurrences	Percentage
Skin, nails, mucous	626	11.64
Gastro-intestinal system	596	11.08
Toxicology	481	8.94
Gynecology, obstetrics	377	7.01
Urinary tract	348	6.47
Respiratory system	327	6.08
Eye and sight	316	5.87
Bones, joins, fractures	231	4.29
Wounds and ulcers	223	4.14
Humors	140	2.60
Inflammations	138	2.56
Mouth, gums, throat, voice	130	2.42
Ears and hearing	120	2.23
Iatrogenic diseases	120	2.23
Nervous system, spasms, shivering	110	2.04
Blood and veins	107	1.99
Swellings, dropsy	96	1.78
Hepatic system	92	1.71
Totals	**5,375**	**98.98**

Making an application of this approach to one rearrangement of Dioscorides' *De materia medica* is revealing. The chapters of this work, each one devoted to a single substance, were supposedly listed according to their therapeutic properties. A reduced number of chapters form what is traditionally called Dioscorides' *Alphabetical Herbal*. Such rearranged texts are a particularly rich source of new data. In one respect, their size may suggest that a manual with a thousand chapters (the size of Dioscorides' full text) would be impractically large for use in a physician's daily practice. The number of chapters was reduced to around 300, a quantity that reflects the approximate number of items that a traditional system of medicine is able to manage. The selection of plants that the chapters record indicate only species common to the Mediterranean, those found in the natural environment (growing wild) or those cultivated. Rare and expensive drugs, mostly from the Near and Far East, have been eliminated from the chapter lists. A third body of information reflected in these manuals indicates the medical conditions that the plants were used to treat. Tables 10.2 and 10.3 present a quantitative view of frequency of medical conditions listed in Dioscorides' full text (Table 10.2) and in the *Alphabetical Herbal* (Table 10.3) respectively.

Table 10.3   Inventory of the diseases mentioned in the *Alphabetical Herbal*.

Medical condition	Occurrences	Percentage
Skin, nails, mucous	256	11.46
Gastro-intestinal system	252	11.20
Gynecology, obstetrics	184	8.24
Toxicology	182	8.33
Urinary tract	162	7.25
Respiratory systems	132	5.91
Bones, joins, fractures	128	5.73
Eye and sight	102	4.56
Wounds and ulcers	90	4.03
Inflammations	67	3.00
Hepatic system	6	2.50
Swellings, dropsy	54	2.41
Mouth, gum, throat, voice	50	2.23
Humors	46	2.06
Spleen	46	2.06
Nervous system, spasms, shivering	45	2.01
Ears and hearing	39	1.74
Diet, digestion	35	1.61
Totals	**2333**	**99.16**

It is particularly significant that, when the results of Table 10.3 and 10.2 are compared, the percentage of each category is very similar. Total number of occurrences is sharply reduced when the complete text is compared to the *Alphabetical Herbal*, because of a reduction in the number of chapters in the *Herbal*.

Table 10.4 illustrates the correspondence in the order of importance of the several categories of medical conditions in *De materia medica* (the original text) and the *Alphabetical Herbal*.

Table 10.4   Comparison between *De materia medica* (original text) and the *Alphabetical Herbal*.

Medical condition	De materia medica		Alphabetical Herbal	
	No.	%	No.	%
Skin, nails, mucous	626	11.64	256	11.46
Gastro-intestinal system	596	11.08	252	11.20
Toxicology	481	8.94	182	8.33
Gynecology, obstetrics	377	7.01	184	8.24
Urinary tract	348	6.47	162	7.25
Respiratory systems	327	6.08	132	5.91
Eye and sight	316	5.87	102	4.56
Bones, joins, fractures	231	4.29	128	5.73
Wounds and ulcers	223	4.14	90	4.03
Humors	140	2.60	46	2.06
Inflammations	138	2.56	67	3.00
Mouth, gums, throat, voice	130	2.42	50	2.23
Ears and hearing	120	2.23	39	1.74
Iatrogenic diseases	120	2.23	3	1.03
Nervous system, spasms	110	2.04	45	2.01
Blood and veins	107	1.99	32	1.43
Swellings, dropsy	96	1.78	54	2.41
Hepatic system	92	1.71	56	2.50

There are some changes, however: gynecological pathologies and obstetrics (sharply reduced from the *Corpus Hippocraticum* to *De materia medica*) are here increased from 7.01 to 8.24 per cent, as are the pathologies of the urinary tract (6.47 and 7.25 per cent); bones, joints and fractures (4.29 and 5.73 per cent); swellings and dropsy (1.78 and 2.41 per cent); and hepatic system (1.71 and 2.50 per cent). For some categories, instead, the numbers decrease: eye and sight (5.87 and 4.56 per cent) and iatrogenic diseases (2.23 and 1.03 per cent).

No immediate conclusion should be made as to whether comparing *De materia medica* with the *Alphabetical Herbal* reflects changes in their associated, population's epidemiology. Changes in the numbers above can indicate a shift in the physician's focus, as an analysis of the listing of toxicological pathologies might suggest (see Table 10.5).

Table 10.5   Comparison of occurrences of toxicological diseases in *De materia medica* and the *Alphabetical Herbal*.

Toxic agents	De materia medica	Alphabetical Herbal
General		
antidotos – antidotes	23	9
dêlêtêria – poison, venom	1	0
fthartika farmaka – toxic substance	1	0
Venomous animals		
dêgmata – (venomous) bites	2	1
erpeta – reptiles, snakes	49	17
iobola – venomous animals	15	3
thêria – venomous animals	75	8
Venomous snakes		
aimorrois – species of viper	1	0
aspis – cobra	4	1
echis – viper	25	1
prêstêr – species of viper	2	1
sêps – species of viper	3	1
Spiders		
arachnê – spider	1	0
falagx – spider	24	14
Venomous fishes		
drakôn thalassias – venomous fish	6	2
trugôn - sting ray	1	1
Insects		
melissai – bees	4	3
sfêkes – wasp	4	2
skolopendra – scolopendre	3	0
skorpion – scorpion	40	17
tenthrêdôn – wasp	1	0
Others		
anthrôpodêktos – human bite	1	0
krokodêlodêktos – crocodile bite	1	0
lussa – rabies	34	9
mugalê – field-mouse	5	3

There was an increased interest in venoms and poisons in Dioscorides' time, because such substances were studied in order to understand the action of substances introduced into the human body, and to build explanatory theories that would have been further transferred to the actions of medicines.

Similarly, Table 10.6 shows that diseases which might have been spectacular or interesting from a theoretical viewpoint for a time were not necessarily considered so over time, and were thus left out of the rearrangement of *De materia medica* by eliminating the substances that treated them. Some occurrences are sharply reduced, and others in a softer but none the less significant way.

Table 10.6   Differences in frequency of pathologies, comparing *De materia medica* and the *Alphabetical Herbal.*

Pathology	De materia medica	Alphabetical Herbal
Those showing a sharp reduction in frequency of occurrence		
nuktalopia	3	0
small spots on the pupil	28	3
opisthotonos	9	1
iatrogenic pathologies	120	23
hysteric suffocation	27	8
kidney problems	50	17
dusenteria	74	28
Those showing a less strong reduction in frequency of occurrence		
leichen	33	13
diarrhoea	70	27
stomach pain	70	27
gout	48	21
belly pain	97	45
sciatica	67	39
wounds	109	49
amenorrhoea	136	79
traumatic wounds	56	32

If this method of extracting data were to be applied to a significantly large corpus of iatrosophic texts, it is highly probable that such an analysis could bring to light a variety of different phenomena not evident in other sources, such as: possible epidemiological changes in the populations the *iatrosophia* are associated with, and also to reflect changes in what physicians or others were interested in.

Comparing the data extracted from *iatrosophia* to those in these tables, significant differences may appear as reflecting changes in *materia medica* and also a changing epidemiology. In the case of changing epidemiology in a population, textual data would need further analysis from a medico-pathological point of view. This would be not only to identify potential new disease occurrences (toward composing a global picture), but also to ascertain the interactions between different components of the epidemiology, and the possible dynamic evolution of their interactions. Such research would require data analysis to be conducted in a complex inter- and trans-disciplinary way.

Conclusion

Kouzis's conclusions and expectations prove to be more true than ever. *Iatrosophia* result from the experience gained by physicians in the daily practice of clinical medicine. Jeanselme's skepticism on the interest and originality of *iatrosophia*, instead, might have resulted from a less than adequate approach.

The research methods presented here demonstrating manuscript and text inventory, analysis and interpretation might constitute a new paradigm appropriate for further study which may be transferred, with appropriate caution, to other cultures and periods. If so, it would not only make it possible to approach the history of hospital therapeutics in a new and productive way, but also to confer on this field a new status within historical studies. Instead of being marginalized at the edges of other disciplines, therapeutics, as a research focus, could take its place at the center of an enquiry in a population's health history. This focus may reveal facts otherwise hidden.

Chapter 11

Medieval Monastic Customaries on *Minuti* and *Infirmi*

M.K.K. Yearl

Introduction

In the medieval religious communities of Western Christendom, all aspects of life were tightly regulated: eating, sleeping and dying, in addition to the spiritual exercises that were a focal point of a communal religious existence. In the early Middle Ages, rules were written down that provided the heads of monastic houses with a standard of expectation to follow in guiding their brethren. From the ninth century onwards, rules were supplemented by legislation containing even more details. Statutes and customaries served to ensure that established rules would be followed precisely, rather than be left to interpretation. These regulations covered not only the regimen of healthy religious (those who had devoted themselves to the ascetic Christian life), but also those who were excused from the rigors of regular life for reasons of ill health.

The religious who were suffering from some physical weakness and who therefore were not required to join their brethren in every aspect of the work of God included those who were infirm in old age, those who had been bled in order to prevent illness (*minuti*),[1] and those who complained of any sort of malady (*infirmi*). The chronically infirm, who could not be expected to regain the stamina required to fulfill the duties of a life of devotion, did not receive much attention in customaries or in any other monastic documents dealing with daily life. The vast majority of regulations were concerned with those for whom physical weakness was a temporary condition: *minuti* and *infirmi*. *Minuti* and *infirmi* had much in common, particularly that they experienced a transient infirmity, but there were fundamental differences between the two, and they were given distinct consideration in monastic regulations, so therefore merit separate, if comparative, examination.

---

1 *Minuti* was shorthand for those who had undergone regular bloodletting, which in most monastic texts was known as *minutio sanguinis*.

Defining Periodic and Prophylactic Bloodletting

Although *minuti* had undergone a medical procedure (phlebotomy, or the cutting of
a vein), the treatment they received did not follow the rules established in medical
texts.[2] Instead, monastic customaries and statutes commonly included a chapter that
described bloodletting as an event that in modern history writing merits its own
title: periodic bloodletting. Periodic bloodletting was specific to medieval religious
communities, where from at least the ninth through the sixteenth century, healthy
men and women were bled for reasons of physical and spiritual prophylaxis at
regulated intervals throughout the year.[3] Anecdotal evidence suggests that those who
were bled for reasons of illness may have had treatment that followed the rules laid
down in medical texts, but that the same rules, dictating when to bleed according to
elaborate calendars, did not apply to the healthy religious.[4] This is curious because

---

2   The most current considerations of periodic bloodletting appear in Angela Montford,
Health, Sickness, and the Friars in the Thirteenth and Fourteenth Centuries (Aldershot, 2004),
pp. 232–8; Megan Cassidy-Welch, *Monastic Spaces and Their Meanings: Thirteenth-century
English Monasteries* (Turnholt, 2001), pp. 133–65; Carole Rawcliffe, "'On the Threshold of
Eternity': Care for the Sick in East Anglian Monasteries," in *East Anglia's History: Studies
in Honour of Normal Scarfe*, ed. Christopher Harper-Bill, Carole Rawcliffe and Richard G.
Wilson (Woodbridge, 2002), pp. 41–72, and Barbara Harvey, *Living and Dying in England
1100–1540: The Monastic Experience* (Oxford, 1993; repr. 1996), pp. 96–9. The most extensive
work is that of Louis Gougaud, who includes a chapter on "La phlébotomie monastique" in
Anciennes coutumes claustrales, Moines et monastères, 8 (Vienna, 1930), pp. 49–68. The
latter is a later version of his article, "La practique de la phlébotomie dans les cloîtres," *Revue
Mabillon*, 14 (1924), 1–13.

3   The earliest written reference to this practice is in the decrees of the First Aachen
Synod of 816: J. Semmler, ed., "Synodi primae aquisgranensis decreta authentica," in *Initia
consuetudinis benedictinae: Consuetudines saeculi octavi et noni,* ed. Kassius Hallinger,
Corpus Conseutudinum Monasticarum, 1 (hereafter CCM) (Siegburg, 1963), pp. 459–60:
"X. Ut certum fleutomiae tempus non obseruent, sed unicuique secundum quod necessitas
expostulat concedatur et specialis in cibo et potu tunc consolatio prebeatur." The latest
references this author has seen come from seventeenth-century Carthusian General Chapter
pronouncements, and are cited in James Hogg, "Medical Care as Reflected in the Cartae of the
Carthusian General Chapter," in *Spiritualität Heute und Gestern*, 11, *Analecta Cartusiana*,
35(11) (Salzburg, 1991), 3–44.

4   There is, for instance, a story in Bede's *Ecclesiastical History* in which an abbess was
castigated because one of the nuns in her charge was bled at the time of the waxing moon;
Bede, *Ecclesiastical History of the English People*, cap. 5.3, trans. Leo Sherley-Price, rev.
R.E. Latham (London, 1955; repr. 1990), pp. 269–70. The author has taken this anecdote
to be about bleeding for illness; periodic bloodletting typically involved more than one
religious. Still, it is stories such as these that have led previous historians to assume that these
calendars dictated times of periodic bloodletting. Linda Voigts and Michael McVaugh wrote
that one of these texts, the *Epistola de phlebotomia*, "was probably a standard guide to the
bloodletting that was often a regular part of the cloister's annual routine"; Linda E. Voigts and
Michael R. McVaugh, "A Latin Technical Phlebotomy and its Middle English Translation," in
Transactions of the American Philosophical Society, 74(2) (Philadelphia, PA, 1984), 2.

periodic bloodletting, like the bleeding described in medical treatises, had its origins in the ancient Hippocratic and Galenic advice to bleed as a prophylactic those patients who were prone to diseases of plethora, or a superabundance of any one of the four humors: blood, phlegm, choler and melancholy.[5] This type of bloodletting was primarily a vernal affair, but could be employed any time it was considered necessary to preserve a patient's humoral balance and thus prevent illness.

In the Middle Ages, the ancient practice of preventative bleeding arguably evolved into two distinct, though closely related, forms of prophylactic bloodletting: that which was described in medical treatises, and periodic bloodletting, which was outlined in monastic documents. Medieval medical writings on bloodletting, prophylactic and therapeutic, placed a greater emphasis on seasonal and astral calendars than had their ancient predecessors. For example, it was not allowed during the "dog days" of summer (often defined as 1 August–9 September), when the moon was waxing, or at any of the other numerous occasions recorded on medical calendars when it was thought inauspicious to bleed.[6] This is not to say that Hippocratic and Galenic texts ignored the influence of seasons and stars, but the prominence given to these factors and the emergence of elaborate calendars to help practitioners determine when to bleed were medieval innovations. These calendars are hallmarks of medieval bloodletting: they are what distinguish it from the bloodletting described in the ancient texts from which they were descended. And it is the disregard for these calendars that in turn sets periodic bloodletting apart from the preventative bleeding described in medieval medical writings.

Periodic bloodletting was itself a medieval phenomenon, and its purpose was one of prophylaxis, but its application differed from the prophylactic bloodletting used by medical practitioners. There is potential for confusion in that the general term "prophylactic" is most strongly associated with medical writings; to attach those associations to periodic bloodletting is misleading. However, there are no specific terms to deal with the related types of medieval bloodletting that were carried out to prevent future afflictions, be they corporeal or spiritual. There is no room, and perhaps no need, to establish new terminologies here; suffice it to say that to contrast

---

5 Hippocrates, *Aphorisms* 6.47; 7.53, *Œuvres complètes d'Hippocrate*, trans. É. Littré, vol. 4 (Paris, 1844); Peter Brain, *Galen on Bloodletting* (Cambridge, 1986), p. 77. Galen, "Galeni de curandi ratione per venae sectionem," cap. 7, in *Claudii Galeni Opera Omnia, editionem curavit C.G. Kühn*, 11 (Leipzig, 1821–33; repr. Hildesheim, 1964), 270–71.

6 See, for instance, the work formerly attributed to Bede, "De phlebotomia," *Patrologiae cursus completus, series latina*, 90 (hereafter PL), ed. J.-P. Migne (Paris, 1844–91), cols 959–62, and also British Library Royal MS *Lat.* 15 B.19, Verses on phlebotomy, to Walannus, tenth century, fol. 126r. To give one example of these prohibitions, if a bleeder followed the advice of one calendar from the turn of the fourteenth century, he would have had to avoid bloodletting on five days in April: 10 and 20, which were "Egyptian days" (see below), and 6, 7 and 15, which were "perilous days." Whatever the subtle differences between Egyptian and perilous days, the message regarding bloodletting was the same: do not do it; Yale University Beinecke Rare Book and Manuscript Library MS 923, Folding calendar, Paris, *c.* 1290–1300, leaf 5.

periodic bleeding with prophylactic bleeding is not to suggest that the former was not prophylactic, the adjective, rather that it differed from the prophylactic practice as described in medical texts.

Although a line has been drawn between periodic and prophylactic bleeding in order to establish the periodic practice as unique, there are several similarities that reveal their common heritage. Periodic bloodletting was, like the prophylactic bloodletting of ancient and medieval medical treatises, an important part of a regimen. The latter was one element in a *regimen sanitatis*, or way of life that was aimed at maintaining a healthy balance within the body. So it was with periodic bloodletting, which was prophylactic at its core. However, the primary requirement for periodic bloodletting was arguably that it fit into a strict *regimen spiritualis*, the timing of which was dictated either by a liturgical calendar or by rota accounting for a few religious being bled each week. Finally, while treatises on traditional prophylactic bloodletting were concerned with when in an astrological calendar to bleed, writings on periodic bloodletting dealt with procedural matters: when in the religious calendar to bleed, how to ask permission to be bled, and what verses to recite in the days following the operation.

The regulations for *infirmi* do not challenge the existing vocabulary of medical history as do those for *minuti*; they do not refer to specific ailments in a way that allows for comparison with the works consulted by medical practitioners. Nor were they as elaborate as those for *minuti*. This is hardly surprising, given that illness was an individual and spontaneous occurrence that offered tremendous variety of circumstance, whereas periodic bloodletting was an orchestrated event in which all participated, though not necessarily at the same time. Regulations for *infirmi* consisted of generalizations that could apply to all who were ill: namely, how to ask permission to go to the infirmary for the duration of their illness, how they were to comport themselves when they were ill, and the procedure to follow when they were well enough to return to the regular pattern of life.

What is it to be "Medical"?

Other than that they were suffering from physical weakness, neither *minuti* nor *infirmi* fit easily into a category that can be described as "medical." In the case of *minuti*, it is not only the replacement of an astrological with a liturgical calendar for bleeding that raises questions. Also missing was the usual medical consideration of which veins to open.[7] Because bloodletting is a narrowly defined medical event, the aberration from normal medical treatises is far more apparent in the case of *minuti* than it is with *infirmi*, for whom one might not expect to read details of specific ailments.

What is clear is that extant monastic legislation makes it difficult to identify either of these groups of infirmary inhabitants as medical characters. The problem, however, may lie in modern conceptions of what was medical in the Middle Ages. Here the definition of "medical" is a narrow one, related to the prevention and cure of illness as described in texts written by and for those who administered to the care of the body. Medieval monasteries are known in medical history for their role in preserving and disseminating medical knowledge, particularly in the centuries prior to the rise of universities and the religious reforms that took hold in the twelfth century. What the current examination of monastic documents makes clear is that the religious did not necessarily experience medical care as described in the books that they themselves compiled and copied. This situation should not be regarded as anomalous, but does highlight the need for future scholars to revisit the definition of "medical" as it relates to the Middle Ages, and to consider the term as encompassing at once the spiritual and physical concerns that were so much a part of medieval life as to be indivisible.[8]

In addition to the need to establish a suitable definition of "medical," it is worthwhile to consider the attitude taken toward those religious who were in a state of physical weakness, and that taken toward the prevention of illness. The meaning of illness in the religious life is yet another area of enquiry that calls for further study, the care of ill brethren having been taken for granted in the past because it was a part of religious life from the outset.[9] A large proportion of the literature concerning the medieval religious and medicine deals not with the role played by illness in the religious life, but with the significance of the religious to medieval medicine and health care. Most of those works have looked either at health care offered by the religious as a form of charity, for which there is an abundance of sources relating to

---

7   There are indications that the bleeding was usually done from the arm, but this is not information that is forthcoming in most regulations. At Cluny, brethren were to uncover an arm and warm it by the fire. Udalric of Cluny, *Antiquiores consuetudines Cluniacensis monasterii*, cap. 21, "De minutione sanguinis," PL, 149, col. 709. In his eleventh-century *Constitutions*, Lanfranc advises that if a *minutus* be accused in chapter of improper conduct, then he should stand when responding to the prior, especially if he had been bled from a vein in the arm; Lanfranc, *The Monastic Constitutions of Lanfranc*, ed. and trans. David Knowles (New York, 1951), pp. 94–5.

8   Riccardo Cristiani has looked at the use of medical language in the *Rule of Saint Benedict*. In this context, medicine was metaphorical and was used to treat sin, and specifically to treat those who digressed from the Rule; "The semantic range of medical language in the Rule of Benedict," *American Benedictine Review*, 54 (March 2003), 20–29.

9   In his doctoral dissertation, Andrew Crislip includes a discussion of the health care systems of early monasticism; "The Monastic Health Care System and the Development of the Hospital in Late Antiquity" (PhD Dissertation, Yale University, 2002), p. 65.

England, or at monastics as preservers of ancient knowledge, including knowledge about the human body.[10] In the latter case, the focus has been on monastic medicine prior to the religious reforms that reached a summit in the twelfth century and the subsequent professionalization of secular medical practice.[11] There are exceptions, and recently historians have shown an interest in the rich and often complementary relationship between medieval medicine and religion.[12] What needs to be added to the emerging picture is a sense, offered by the work of sociologist Talcott Parsons and later commentators on his writings, of the importance to a monastic community of the sick role. Modern though Parsons' focus was, his ideas, particularly that illness was a form of deviance, resonate with the controlled environment of medieval monasteries.[13] The inclusion of this sociological approach in historical investigations would be particularly useful to those examining the functions played by the infirmary in religious communities.[14] As a place inhabited by those who were excused from normal services due to physical weakness, the infirmary had an essential role in ensuring that the healthy religious could continue to perform the work of God without being distracted by those who were unable to sustain the daily regimen; this was in addition to the imperative that it be a restful place where those who were

---

10 Works on religious charity include: Carole Rawcliffe, *Medicine for the Soul: The Life, Death and Resurrection of an English Mediaeval Hospital* (Stroud, 1999). On monastic healers, see James Hogg, note 3 above; Darrel W. Amundsen, *Medicine, Society, and Faith in the Ancient and Mediaeval Worlds* (Baltimore, MD, 1996). There is a brief discussion of this in the introduction to Hildegard of Bingen, *On Natural Philosophy and Medicine: Selections from Cause et cure*, trans. Margret Berger (Cambridge, 1999).

11 On later drives for professionalization see Michael R. McVaugh, *Medicine before the Plague: Practitioners and Their Patients in the Crown of Aragon, 1285–1345* (Cambridge, 1993). Both professionalization and religion in medicine are covered by Marie-Christine Pouchelle, *The Body and Surgery in the Middle Ages*, trans. Rosemary Morris (1983; English edn, New Brunswick, NJ, 1990).

12 Joseph Ziegler, *Medicine and Religion c. 1300: The Case of Arnau de Vilanova* (Oxford, 1998). Ziegler examines the medical and religious writings of the theologizing physician Arnald of Vilanova. See also the essays in *Religion and Medicine in the Middle Ages*, ed. Peter Biller and Joseph Ziegler (Suffolk, 2001), and Teresa M. Shaw, *The Burden of the Flesh: Fasting and Sexuality in Early Christianity* (Minneapolis, MN, 1998).

13 Talcott Parsons, "Social structure and dynamic process: The case of modern medical practice," in *The Social System* (London, 1951; rev. edn, 1991), 428–79.

14 The function of the infirmary in monastic life would be a worthwhile study. There are a few authors who have made brief comments about the inhabitants of the infirmary; see, for instance, Percy Flemming, "The Medical Aspects of the Mediaeval Monastery in England," in *Proceedings of the Royal Society of Medicine. Section of the History of Medicine*, 22 (1928), 772–3. More general information on the infirmary appears in Harvey, *Living and Dying*, pp. 72–111; E.A. Hammond, "Physicians in Mediaeval English Religious Houses," *Bulletin of the History of Medicine*, 32 (1958), 105–20; E.A. Hammond, "The Westminster Abbey Infirmarers' Rolls as a Source of Medical History," *Bulletin of the History of Medicine*, 39 (1965), 261–76.

in a weakened state would recover so that they could return without delay to their religious duties.[15]

Ill Health in Monastic Rules

The atmosphere of the infirmary, and more particularly the type of attention received by the *minuti* and *infirmi* who were recovering there, was in accordance with monastic rules on the care of the sick. The most widely known and followed of these was that written by Benedict of Nursia (480–547) for the monastery of Monte Cassino near Rome.[16] However, the experiences of those in the infirmary had roots in writings that pre-dated and also influenced St Benedict. Many early Christians expressed ambivalence about the place of physical methods of healing in spiritual life. Ambivalent though they may have been, the regulations adopted by religious communities consistently address the treatment of ill brethren. The primary concern conveyed in these passages is that those who were ill receive special care, food and other material comforts, to assist in their recovery. In the fourth century, Pachomius (died *c.* 346), often described as the father of monasticism, indicated that the ill should receive from monastic ministers "whatever is necessary" for their complete recovery.[17] Shortly afterward, near the end of the same century, Augustine of Hippo (354–430) was concerned that those who were unwell accept treatment that was deemed necessary even if, as he implied was often the case with baths, they did not want the treatment.[18] Equally, the demands of the ill were not to be met if they could harm the patient (in body or soul).

One exception to the attitude taken toward those who were unwell comes from the Rule of the Master, probably written in the early sixth century, and which apparently influenced Benedict of Nursia when he composed his famous Rule two or three decades later, *c.* 530. The Master opened the chapter on "The Sick Brethren" by advising that one ought not accuse those who claimed they could not work because of illness, but grant them only liquids and eggs or warm water, for this food "the really sick can hardly get down, so that if they are pretending, hunger will at least

---

15 While several authors have focussed on the infirmary as an administrative unit, there are only a few who have included a discussion of the experience of those who were ill. Perhaps the best source is Chapter 3, "Sickness and its Treatment," in Harvey, *Living and Dying*, 72–111. More on the infirmarian than those taken care of by him appears in Léo Moulin, *La vie quotidienne des religieux au Moyen Age Xe–XVe siècle* (Paris, 1978), pp. 217–20. For an older account, see *British Monachism; or, Manners and Customs of the Monks and Nuns of England*, 3rd edn (London, 1843), pp. 135; 233–7.

16 Benedict of Nursia, *St. Benedict's Rule for Monasteries*, trans. Leonard J. Doyle (Collegeville, MN, 1948).

17 Precepts of Pachomius, 40, *Pachomian Koinomia II, Pachomian Chronicles and Rules*, trans. Armand Veilleux, Cistercian Studies Series, 46 (Kalamazoo, MI, 1981), p. 151.

18 Augustine of Hippo, cap. V, *The Rule of Saint Augustine*, trans. Robert Russell, <http://www.geocities.com/Athens/1534/ruleaug.html>, updated 6 April 2000, viewed 27 September 2003.

force them to get up."[19] Those who arose for services but claimed to be too weak for manual work were to be offered less food and drink than healthy monks. The opinion of the Master was that if one were truly too ill to work, then one ought to be unable to eat.[20] Thus in his instructions on abstinence from food or drink during Lent, he warned that although wine should not be withdrawn from those who were ill, "let the abbot see to it that no one is lying and pretending to be sick."[21] This approach is in contradiction to other rules, which did not overtly question the motivations of the *infirmi* and were more inclined to adopt the view that those who were ill required special foods for the restoration of their strength.

St Benedict may have been influenced by the Master, but he, like Pachomius two centuries before, was more concerned with the treatment of the sick than with exposing suspected malingerers (who were, in any event, arguably suffering from a spiritual malaise).[22] In his Rule, he wrote: "Care must be taken of the sick, so that they will be served as if they were Christ in person."[23] In contrast to the lesser food that the Master was willing to provide for the sick, Benedict stipulated that the very weak be allowed to eat meat for strength.[24] In turn, *infirmi* had a responsibility to remember their position, being served "in honor of God," and were warned not to

---

19 *The Rule of the Master*, trans. Luke Eberle (Kalamazoo, MI, 1977), cap. 69, "The Sick Brethren"; *La Règle du Maître II*, trans. Adalbert de Vogüé, *Sources chrétiennes*, 106 (hereafter SC) (Paris, 1964), p. 296.

20 Eberle, cap. 69; de Vogüé, pp. 296–300.

21 Eberle, cap. 53, "Abstinence from Food and Drink during Lent," de Vogüé, p. 242.

22 That the spirit of care won out may be for reasons of practicality, but there was also a tradition that saw those monks who were struggling with the ascetic life as being ill in their own non-physical way. In the eremitic tradition, these religious were described as suffering from *acedia*, which would eventually turn into the sin of sloth, but which in Christian writings of Late Antiquity signaled a spiritual weariness. It is a common theme in the *Apophthegmata Patrum*, which were not written down until the fifth century even though they are set mostly in the fourth-century Egyptian desert. In fact, it is the subject of the first of the sayings of Antony (*c*. 250–355 AD), making it the first topic one encounters in the corpus of desert wisdom; *Patrologiae cursus completes, Series graeca*, 65, ed. J.-P. Migne (Paris, 1857–66), cols 71–440; *The Sayings of the Desert Fathers: The Alphabetical Collection*, trans. Benedicta Ward (London, 1975). For secondary source commentary, see G. Bardy, "Acedia," in *Dictionnaire de spiritualité ascétique et mystique*, 1 (Paris, 1937), cols 166–9; Siegfried Wenzel, *The Sin of Sloth: Acedia in Medieval Thought and Literature* (Chapel Hill, NC, 1960; repr. 1967).

23 *St. Benedict's Rule*, cap. 36, "On the Sick Brethren." The reason for this is given as being the biblical verse Mt 25:40. This is a common reference. See also the female rules reproduced in Jo Ann McNamara, *The Ordeal of Community*, 2nd edn, *Peregrine Translation Series*, 5 (Toronto, 1993), pp. 42, 93.

24 In fact, the question was raised whether the Carthusian refusal to offer meat to their ill was heretical. In the early fourteenth century, Arnald of Vilanova wrote a commentary in their favor, citing their ascetic piety, but this question illustrates the important association that arose between recovery from illness and meat; see Dianne Marie Bazell, "Christian Diet: A Case Study using Arnald of Villanova's *De esu carnium*" (PhD Dissertation, Harvard University, 1991).

"annoy their brethren who are serving them by their unnecessary demands."[25] In other words, Benedict's Rule imparts a sense of mutual responsibility on the part of both the ill and those who were charged with looking after them; this was a far cry from the Master's fundamental suspicion of the former.

In medieval religious life, it was the tone of Benedict that would prevail over that of the Master. The author of the late tenth-century *Regularis concordia* urged that all the wants of sick brethren be met.[26] The same message was given in the thirteenth-century Rule of St Clare. The extra comforts to be offered ill sisters included not only food, but also straw sacks and feather pillows for those who needed them.[27] Even where specifics differed, the outlook with regard to the ill was undeniably influenced by Benedict's instruction that provisions be made for the comfort of the sick male and female religious, but that those who were unwell had to act prudently and with honor in their position as transitory representations of Christ.

The message of monastic rules also governed the care given to those who, despite being otherwise healthy, had been weakened by bloodletting. The overarching tone of the regulations governing illness in religious rules was that of a careful concern (*cura*), and it was this attitude that would color the experience of not only the medieval *infirmi*, but also the *minuti*.

The Experience of *Minuti*: What the Regulations Said

Periodic bloodletting was a scheduled event, rather than a reaction to an immediate medical complaint; consequently, it could be regulated and made to conform to chronological and procedural limits at every stage. This contrast, between a planned and an unanticipated occurrence, is at the root of many of the differences between those who had been bled and those who were ill. The opportunity to regulate bloodletting was keenly taken, the event appearing as the subject of a chapter in nearly every medieval religious customary. There are variations between documents, but a basic pattern was followed in most religious communities. When a religious wanted to be bled, he would request in chapter license to leave choir for this reason.[28] Usually a few religious would go together to be bled, an obedientiary accompanying the more junior members to ensure that all behaved during the time of rest following

---

25 *St. Benedict's Rule*, cap. 36.

26 *Regularis Concordia: The Monastic Agreement of the Monks and Nuns of the English Nation*, trans. Thomas Symons (London, 1953), cap. 12.

27 Presumably it would have been only the very ill who would have needed such comforts; St Clare of Assisi, "The Rule of Saint Clare," in *The Life of Saint Clare*, trans. and ed. Paschal Robinson (Philadelphia, PA, 1910), 114–15.

28 This is the way that the chapters were written. The appearance of individual choice may be just that, an appearance. The abbot or prior was the ultimate authority determining who would be bled and when. Although the wording suggests that brethren could decline to be bled, the documentation indicates that bloodletting was an event in which all brethren would participate on a regular basis.

bloodletting, and to report any who did not.[29] Those who had permission to be bled would assemble in the infirmary, warming room or some other place appointed for the event, and they would be phlebotomized in the arm. After this operation, the *minuti* were afforded three days to recuperate, during which time they had to attend only limited services and they were to receive replenishing foods, often including meat. When the period of rest was over, the *minuti* were to return to the chapter house, where they would go through the formality of petitioning to be allowed back into the community. In a small number of houses, including the Benedictine abbey of Hirsau in Germany, they had to beg forgiveness in chapter as part of the petition for re-entry; however, this was an action that was much more commonly expected from those who were returning after a period of illness.[30]

The frequency of bloodletting depended on the preference expressed in a given institution's written regulations. The Carthusian brethren, whose customs were written in the early twelfth century, were bled communally five times per year: after the Octave of Easter, after the Solemnity of the Apostles Peter and Paul (29 June), in the second week of September, during the week preceding Advent and in the week before Quinquagesima.[31] In contrast, customs for the abbey of Oigny, written later in the same century, stated that the religious could be bled five times per year, but provided a list of times when it was not permitted to undergo bloodletting: at the time of harvest and haying, in Advent and Lent, for the first three days of the Nativity, during Easter and Pentecost, and for two or three days before either an important fast or Festival of Nine Lessons.[32] According to their fifteenth-century

---

29 At Barnwell (Austin canons), the reason given for bleeding in small groups was that it would ensure that there were enough to perform services; this would be a theme in some later English visitation records, where there were so many being bled that there would not be enough present at services; *The Observances in Use at the Augustinian Priory of Barnwell, Cambridgeshire* (henceforth Barnwell Customary), ed. and trans. John Willis Clark (Cambridge, 1897), p. 198. Similarly, at St Victor's Paris (Regular canons), between three and five would be bled together, designated by the abbot, and junior members were not to be bled without the presence of a senior member (generally an obedientiary); "De ordine minuendi," cap. 65 in *Liber ordinis Sancti Victoris Parisiensis*, ed. Lucas Jocqué and Ludovicus Milis, *Corpus christianorum continatio mediaevalis*, 61 (hereafter CCCM) (Turnholt, 1984). In the 1437 visitation to Peterborough Abbey, William Alnwick, Bishop of Lincoln, heard that out of 44 monks, only 10–12 were present at any given day to perform divine service. This he attributed to brethren being excused for various reasons, including infirmity and age, but he also noted that for at least two days in every week, seven were excused for bloodletting; *Visitations of Religious Houses in the Diocese of Lincoln*, Vol. 3(2), ed. A. Hamilton Thompson, *Canterbury and York Series*, 33 (Oxford, 1927), p. 273.

30 William of Hirsau, *Constitutiones Hirsaugienses*, cap. 59, "De minutione sanguinis, vel phlebotomare volentibus," PL, 150, col. 989.

31 Guigo, *Coutumes de Chartreuse,* cap. 39, "De minutione," SC 313 (Paris, 1984).

32 F. Lefèvre and A.H. Thomas, *Le coutumier de l'abbaye d'Oigny en Bourgogne au XIIe siècle, Spicilegium Sacrum Lovaniense Études et Documents*, 39 (Louvain, 1976), pp. 101–2. This list of prohibited times is nearly identical to that given by the Cistercians, provided below. The same list appears in the fifteenth-century customary for the Benedictine abbey of

customs, the Benedictines of Tegernsee were to be bled a modest four times evenly spaced throughout the year: the Feast Day of the Apostles Philip and James (1 May), the Feast of St Bartholomew (24 August), the Feast of St Martin (11 November), and the Feast of St Blaise (15 February).[33] Not all institutions referred to a liturgical calendar, however. The letters of Peter the Venerable (c. 1092–1156), Abbot of Cluny, show that he was bled bi-monthly, though the Cluniac customs do not actually stipulate how often the brethren could be bled.[34] Yet another timetable is given in the late thirteenth-century customs of the Augustinian priory at Barnwell in Cambridge, which permitted its canons to be bled every seven weeks.[35]

When there are distinct differences between the bleeding of members of the same order, it is not between male and female religious, as might be expected, but between those whose primary duty was the work of God, and lay brethren, whom many institutions utilized to perform necessary menial work. The men and women who looked after patients at the hôtels-Dieu were considered together in a single chapter on bloodletting, and were to be bled six times per year.[36] However, in the Carthusian statutes there were separate chapters concerning the bleeding of regular and lay brethren; the latter were bled four rather than five times per year (on or near the dates of 1 May, 15 July, 1 October and 1 February).[37]

Monastic Regulations Compared with Medical Advice

Regardless of how one interprets the frequency of periodic bloodletting, the fact that a bleeding timetable was given in so many customaries sets these chapters on bloodletting apart from medical treatises. Those treatises were likely to discuss the virtues or dangers of bleeding at various times of the year, but were unlikely to give much advice other than that it was good to bleed from the right in spring and from the left in autumn.[38] For the most part, prophylactic bloodletting was done on an

---

Kastl in Germany, which is unique in adding to this list the "dog days" (dies caniculares); Consuetudines Castellenses, ed. Petrus Maier, CCM, 14(1) (Siegburg, 1996).

33   Joachim Angerer, Die Bräuche der Abtei Tegernsee unter Abt Kaspar Ayndorffer (1426–1461), verbunden mit einer textkritischen Edition der Consuetudines Tegernseenses, Studien und Mitteilungen zur Geschichte des Benediktiner-Ordens und seine zweige 18 (Ottobeuren, 1968), p. 237.

34   Giles Constable, ed., The Letters of Peter the Venerable, 2 vols (Cambridge, MA, 1967), 1:247–51; 2: 379–83.

35   Barnwell Customary, p. 198.

36   Léon le Grand, Statuts d'hôtels-Dieu et de léproseries recueil de textes du XIIe au XIVe siècle (Paris, 1901). See the statutes for the Hôpital Comtesse, Lille, p. 73, and the Hôtel-Dieu de Pontoise, p. 137.

37   Coutumes de Chartreuse, cap. 54, "De minutione eorum." Interestingly, the dates given for the bleeding of lay brethren were based on a regular calendar, whereas those given for regular brethren were related to saints' days.

38   Mayno de' Mayneri, "Tractatus de fleubothomia secundum arnaldum de villa noua," in Regimen sanitatis (Lyon, [after 1500]), fol. 87; John Harrington, The School of Salernum,

individual basis depending on need, though spring was generally considered a good time to be bled in order to prevent the onset of plethoric ailments.

The differences between the prophylactic bloodletting of medical treatises and periodic bloodletting were not limited to timetable variations. An examination of the placement of chapters on the letting of blood bears some indication as to the context in which periodic bloodletting was considered (or rather, the context in which it was not considered). Interestingly, in the majority of cases *minuti* were considered separately from *infirmi*, a fact that raises questions about the way in which both of these groups were viewed. Out of a sample of 50 customaries, in only 20 per cent of cases did those chapters on bloodletting appear either immediately before or after a chapter concerning the sick or the infirmary more generally. The remaining 80 per cent were not dominated by any one subject, but consisted mostly of chapters on the religious calendar (for instance, what to do or not do in Lent). Also common were chapters on shaving and tonsuring.[39] While chapter placement is one signal that *minuti* and *infirmi* were thought of in different spheres, an analysis of the legislation dealing with bloodletting and illness is even more striking. It is uncommon to find references to *infirmi* in chapters on *minuti*, and vice versa. Moving from customaries to account rolls, one finds more evidence that the two had distinct roles in religious life, though future examination of Continental accounts may reveal whether this observation is limited to the English rolls examined in this study. There are more references to bloodletting in records of the pittancer and cellarer, both of which have to do with provision of food and drink, than in the infirmarian's rolls. In fact, it is rare to find any mention of periodic bloodletting in infirmary accounts, either for provisions or for money that would have been paid to an external bleeder had they called upon one. There do seem to be occasional references to bleeding in the rolls of almost every other monastic office, be it, for example, the sacrist, almoner, chamberlain or prior.

The account rolls are of further interest because some of them contain indications of the actual days on which the religious were bled. This is because *minuti* were entitled to a pittance (an additional allowance of food), and in some cases were even given money. *Infirmi* were also entitled to a pittance, but do not appear in account rolls in this way; they are covered in the infirmarian's rolls, and there is the occasional reference to money paid for an abbot or prior's illness, but nothing to the magnitude of coverage for *minuti*.[40] In the example of Ely in England, account rolls

---

Regimen sanitatis Salernitanum (New York, 1920), p. 178.

39 In the *Ancrene Wisse*, the author ties bloodletting to the cutting or shaving of hair: "You must have your hair cut, or, if you want, shaved, four times a year to lighten your head ... and let blood as often, or more often if need be"; *Anchoritic Spirituality. Ancrene Wisse and Associated Works*, trans. Anne Savage and Nicholas Watson (hereafter cited as *Anchoritic Spirituality*) (New York, 1991), p. 204.

40 Why there was this exchange of money is a mystery that merits further study. The geographical span of this practice also demands attention, as this author's examination of account rolls has been limited to English institutions, where it is often referred to as "seyny money." It may be that this was a type of internal system to account for the additional expense

indicate that in the year October 1335–September 1336, the Prior of Ely Cathedral was bled precisely every six weeks.[41] This information makes it possible to compare his dates of bleeding to several charts of Egyptian days, days thought dangerous on which to begin any new undertaking, but which came to be recognized as days on which it was perilous to administer any form of medicine, bloodletting in particular.[42] There is no chart according to which he avoided being bled on at least one prohibited day, and he was bled on four of the more commonly cited Egyptian days: 22 July, 22 October, 5 November and 4 February.[43] Similarly, of the seven Sundays from late September to early November 1336, the monks of that same priory were bled in rotation, again, every six weeks; two of those Sundays were commonly cited Egyptian days. Moreover, if a few monks were bled each week, it would have been impossible to avoid the waxing moon, and the waxing moon was considered at least as perilous for bloodletting as were Egyptian days.[44]

It is not that medieval religious went out of their way to be bled at these prohibited times; rather, their priorities lay elsewhere. It is evident from the customaries that their primary concern was to avoid disruption to monastic life, and if this meant that bloodletting occasionally coincided with a prohibited day, so be

---

of good food provided for the *minuti*. It is unlikely that this accounts for the fees paid for an external bleeder, as in many (though not all) instances the bleeding was done by a member of the house; moreover, if seyny money were used to pay an external bleeder, why not mention this in the records?

41 For these dates this author has relied on John Willis Clark's introduction to the Barnwell Customary, p. lxiv. The Ely Dean and chapter rolls are housed in the Manuscripts Room of the Cambridge University Library, but were away for preservation upon the author's last visit. Several of the rolls were transcribed by James Bentham, "Notitia Ecclesia Eliensis," Cambridge University Library MS Add. 2956 and MS Add. 2957.

42 Several of these lists came from Robert Steele, "Dies Aegyptiaci," in *Proceedings of the Royal Society of Medicine, Section of the History of Medicine*, 12 (1919), 108–21. For a description of perilous days, as well as a calendar listing both perilous and Egyptian days, see Yale University, Beinecke Rare Book and Manuscript Library, MS 923, dated to Paris, c. 1290–1300. Pseudo-Bede also lists Egyptian days, "De phlebotomia," PL, 90, cols 959–62.

43 Steele provides several lists of Egyptian days in his article (cited above); other lists come from Yale University Beinecke Rare Book and Manuscript Library Marston MS 213, a thirteenth-century Austrian missal, and Beinecke MS 923, a folding calendar from Paris created *c.* 1290–1300.

44 These dates also appear in Barnwell Customary, p. lxiv. An examination of printed accounts from Durham, Norwich, and Peterborough also indicates that bleedings occasionally coincided with Egyptian days; *Extracts from the Account Rolls of the Abbey of Durham, from the Original MSS*, Surtees Society 99; 100; 103, 3 vols (Durham, 1898–1901); E.C. Fernie and A.B. Whittingham, *The Early Communar and Pitancer Rolls of Norwich Cathedral Priory with an Account of the Building of the Cloister* (London, 1972); *Account Rolls of the Obedientiaries of Peterborough*, ed. Joan Greatrex (Northampton, 1984); *The Book of William Morton, Almoner of Peterborough Monastery 1448–1467*, transcribed by W.T. Mellows, ed. P.I. King (Oxford, 1954). See note 4 above for Bede's anecdote illustrating concern about the waxing moon.

it. It is not as if those desiring to be bled were on the brink of death. *Infirmi*, on the other hand, were in a far more delicate state of health, and they could not time illness according to the monastic calendar, a factor that may have influenced the way in which their needs were regulated.

Regulating *Infirmi*

Just as was the case for *minuti*, legislation described the experience of *infirmi* as beginning in the chapter house. There, those who were unwell were to request permission to go to the infirmary, if they were strong enough to make that request. Before the entire community, they were to beg forgiveness and show that they were ill.[45] This was to be repeated, usually after a couple of days, when again an *infirmus* would demonstrate his ill health and beg forgiveness. During his time in the infirmary, he would receive fortifying foods which, to a greater extent even than for *minuti*, often included meat, as permitted in Benedict's Rule.[46] Presuming the *infirmus* recovered, his stay in the infirmary would end with a visit to chapter where, once again, he would beg for mercy and explain, in simple words as at the Burgundian abbey of Cluny, "I was in the infirmary," to which the prior would respond, "May God be patient with you."[47]

Whereas chapters on bloodletting outline the logistics of an event all took part in several times a year, chapters on *infirmi* have more to do with the etiquette of illness. It was impossible to control the frequency or timing of poor health in the manner the religious controlled bloodletting, but they did control how the religious behaved when they were ill: this much is apparent in monastic regulations, which indicate how and when to beg forgiveness, and how to go about making special requests, such as for permission to attend services.

Because illness was individual and unscheduled, there was a burden of proof on *infirmi* that did not exist for *minuti*. There was the threat of feigning illness to avoid work, a concern that dominated the passage on the sick in the Rule of the Master, and to an extent the ritual deals with this by stipulating punishment for those who

---

45   The Cluniac chapter on illness begins: "Frater qui incoeperit ita infirmari ut conventum tenere non possit, petit veniam in capitulo, et monstrat quod sit infirmus"; Udalric of Cluny, *Antiquiores consuetudines Cluniacensis monasterii*, cap. 27, "De infirmis," PL, 149, col. 769.

46   *St. Benedict's Rule*, cap. 36.

47   "*Deus indulgeat vobis*," *Consuetudines Cluniacensis*, cap. 27, "De infirmis," PL, 149, cols 769–70. Similar words were passed between prior and *infirmus* at the Augustinian house of Marbach, whose twelfth-century regulations were influenced by Cluny; Josef Siegwart, *Die Consuetudines des Augustiner-Chorherrenstiftes Marbach im Elsass*, cap. 133, "De fratre, qui ceperit infirmari," in *Spicilegium Friburgense*, 10 (Freiburg, 1965). See also the customs for the Benedictine abbey of Kastl, which were revised in the early fifteenth century; *Consuetudines Castellenses*, ed. Petrus Maier, cap. 48, "De officio infirmarii et infirmis in infirmitorio manentibus," CCM 14(1) (Siegburg, 1996), p. 386.

were not as ill as they claimed. At Cluny, anyone in the infirmary who was guilty of "evacuating himself in idle talk" (and so presumably did not feel too ill) could expect to be denounced and receive corporal punishment, which usually entailed being beaten with a rod, in chapter.[48] Similarly, in the house for regular canons at Arrouaise in France, he who disturbed other *infirmi* while recovering would be corrected publicly, again in chapter.[49] Such suspicion of the sick extends back to early monasticism, where allowances had to be made for those who were ill, but where all were expected to adhere to a strict ascetic lifestyle. In that setting, sickness may well have been seen as a form of relief, in addition to weakness.

Given the contrast of the comforts afforded *infirmi* to the severity of the early monastic regime, such malingering must have been a real danger. It is possible that bloodletting first became a regular part of monastic life as an answer to this threat, and that it continued to evolve from that time until its demise in the early modern period. To explain further, if the religious knew that there would be a respite from the regimen at regular (and fairly frequent) intervals throughout the year, perhaps they would be able better to sustain their commitment to the life from one period of rest to the next. Bloodletting would have worked well in this capacity because it was considered necessary to prevent illness, but it was also thought crucial for a full recovery that bleeding be followed by a period of rest and replenishing food. Why not allow bloodletting at regular intervals throughout the year as a prophylactic not only against illness, but also against feigned illness? Thus by incorporating into the routine regular and regulated periods of rest, akin to the modern notion of a holiday, the religious would have preserved their physical health while maintaining within the community a high level of dedication and devotion, not to mention discipline. This interpretation may also help to explain why many medieval religious were bled prophylactically more frequently than were their secular counterparts, many of whom were bled in spring and autumn, but do not appear to have been bled regularly throughout the year.

The Governance of *Minuti* and *Infirmi*

Although there was a distinct concern about those enjoying the comforts of the infirmary, the view was not entirely negative. Both *minuti* and *infirmi* were governed by ideas in tune with the comments on sick brethren in the Rule of St Benedict, which, as noted above, begins: "Before all things and above all things, care must be taken of the sick, so that they will be served as if they were Christ in person."[50] There may have been differences in the way *minuti* and *infirmi* were kept in line, but the basic message was the same: care had to be taken because these religious were in a delicate state, physically and spiritually. No rule mentions bloodletting, but the

---

48 *Consuetudines Cluniacensis*, cap. 27, "De infirmis," PL, 149, cols 769–70.

49 *Constitutiones canonicorum regularium ordinis Arroasiensis*, ed. Ludovicus Milis, CCCM, 20 (Turnholt, 1970), sections 193–5.

50 *St. Benedict's Rule*, cap. 36.

writings on this practice in customaries refer, sometimes explicitly, to Benedict's instruction for the care of those who were ill. Equally present in legislation regarding *minuti* and *infirmi* is his admonition to the sick to recall that the care they were being shown was for the honor of God, and that they ought not pester those who were looking after them.[51]

When it came to principles of care, monastic documents treated *minuti* and *infirmi* in the same way. And why not? Both were in a delicate state, even if the former were weakened merely by bloodletting. One might even argue that both represented, to a degree, "Christ in person," *minuti* achieving this category by virtue of having been bled since Christ was bled on the Cross to heal humanity of the sins that the five senses had brought forth.[52] If *infirmi* and *minuti* had to remember that they were being treated with great care because in their weakened state they represented Christ's suffering, there was also the constant reminder that even if they stood for Christ, they were still human, and as such were weak and vulnerable. The Carthusian customs lump together "the sick, the infirm, and those who are in the test of temptations" as deserving special attention and forgiveness.[53] The forgiveness granted by the prior was itself a form of medicine, thus confirming the implication that physical and spiritual sicknesses were not mutually exclusive.[54]

The care shown *minuti* and *infirmi* was often in the form of guidance: make allowances for minor digressions they may follow in their precarious state, but watch over them, read to them or have them sing if they are able, so that their minds will be occupied with religious themes. In the *Ancrene Wisse*, the women were advised to do nothing that would tax their strength. They should occupy themselves by telling edifying stories; this they should do not only when they had been bled, but any time they felt ill or had thoughts of worldliness.[55] *Minuti* and *infirmi* at the Benedictine house at Fruttuaria in Italy were enjoined to occupy themselves during that time of day devoted to work, by singing prescribed songs and orations, which included the Lord's Prayer, a few psalms, and one of the Lenten orations, "Oh Lord, free us from the bonds of our sins."[56]

---

51 Ibid.

52 Ibid.; on the phlebotomizing of Christ, see *Anchoritic Spirituality*, pp. 90–91. The customary for the regular canons of Rolduc is one of the few to make an explicit link between body and spirit. The chapter on bloodletting begins: "Minutio etiam sanguinis, quae humanis non solum corporibus, sed etiam in quibusdam aliis remedio esse solet animabus …"; Helmut Deutz, *Consuetudines canonicorum regularium Rodenses, Die Lebensordnung des Regularkanonikerstiftes Klosterrath*, Vol. 1, cap. 39, "De minutione sanguinis," in *Fontes Christiani*, 11(1) (Freiburg, 1993), p. 408.

53 *Coutumes de Chartreuse,* cap. 38, "De cura infirmorum."

54 On medicine for body and soul, see Ziegler, *Medicine and Religion.*

55 *Anchoritic Spirituality*, p. 204.

56 "Absolve quaesumus domine nostrorum vincula peccatorum"; *Consuetudines Fructuarienses-Sanblasianae*, ed. Luchesius G. Spätling and Petrus Dinter, CCM, 12(1) (Siegburg, 1985), p. 50.

Explaining Away the Differences

In many instances, the experience of those who were ill included more reminders of spiritual failing than did that of *minuti*. It may be that *infirmi* had to beg forgiveness in many institutions because their illness was more likely to be an inconvenience to their brethren: that is, their absence from services and work was not pre-accounted for.

However, there may have been more at stake than inconvenience to one's brethren. Sickness itself, when sent by God, was a means of purification from sin. In the section on temptations, the author of the *Ancrene Wisse* makes the analogy between God and a goldsmith. The heat and pain of sickness purifies the soul just as with fire a goldsmith rids gold of its impurities: "Sickness is a hot flame to suffer, but nothing cleanses gold so well as it cleanses the soul."[57] The author listed six beneficial properties of sickness, among them that it washed away sins already committed. Further, it was a prophylactic against those that were imminent, and "makes the patient person equal to a martyr." The author continued: "In this way sickness is the soul's health, a salve for her wounds and a shield against receiving more."[58] Here, illness was positive for its relation to purification and martyrdom, and because it served as a powerful penance. While illness may have represented penance sent by God, the demonstrations of penance outlined by the legislation concerning illness were a reminder of why God sent this suffering. It should be little surprise, then, that this level of penance did not usually apply to *minuti*, whose treatment was not to cure, but to prevent illness (metaphorical and literal).

Bloodletting was clearly orchestrated to cause the least disruption to the monastic routine, and for this reason the language used in chapters on this subject is full of exception. Many chapters on bloodletting begin with a list prohibiting bleeding at times when the monks' services were most needed. The list in the Cistercian statutes is typical, forbidding bleeding at the time of the harvest; in Advent and Lent; for the three days of the Nativity, Easter and Pentecost, and when it was the second or third day preceding a Festival of Nine Lessons.[59] Only having established when not to bleed did the author list the four times when it was usual to be bled: in February, April, September, and near the feast of St John the Baptist (24 June)[60] – usual rather than mandated, because in the face of important religious services, bloodletting could

---

57 *Anchoritic Spirituality*, pp. 115–16.

58 Ibid.

59 P. Guignard, *Les monuments primitifs de la règle cistercienne* (Dijon, 1878), cap. 90. At Worcester, it appears that brethren were not bled in Lent or Advent, or in the weeks of Easter and Christmas; at least, they did not receive seyny money during this period; *Journal of Prior William More*, ed. Ethel S. Fagan (London, 1914), pp. v–vi.

60 *Les monuments primitifs*, cap. 90. These statutes are replicated with only minor variations in the following manuscripts, all located at Yale University's Beinecke Rare Book and Manuscript Library: Marston MS 233; MS 349; MS 386, and MS 635. The Oigny Customary is another example of one which begins instructions on bloodletting with a list of prohibited times (again those when the services of the religious were required). P.F. Lefèvre

be postponed. This much was true at Einsiedeln in Switzerland, where there was an opportunity for the monks to be bled on first day of every month; however, when the kalends preceded a feast, bloodletting would occur at another (unspecified) time.[61]

Concerns about when to bleed were common. At Barnwell Priory, the brethren were not to be bled when their presence was needed at important services. In addition, the late thirteenth-century customs stipulated that less than a handful of the canons were to be bled at once, lest too few be left to perform the work of God. Following this was added the allowance that "after seven weeks permission to be bled is not to be refused, except for a reasonable cause."[62] As was a common compromise, the privilege of being bled on a regular basis was granted, but under the condition that any "reasonable cause" would override that privilege. Similarly, at St Victor's in Paris, canons were not allowed more than five bleedings per year, unless required by grave necessity.[63] Normally strict rules governing the details of bloodletting were broken as needed. At Hirsau, which followed the common custom of requiring that *minuti* wear only their nightclothes for the duration of their recovery, there was an exception made for the occurrence of processions.[64] Although recuperation was considered important following bloodletting, abbots and priors evidently had no qualms about disrupting that repose when it interfered with the performance of the work of God.

This raises the question of what took precedence when bloodletting was deemed necessary at a time that did not fit into the normal schedule. These cases represent rare glimpses of how the religious were treated when they required bloodletting either to stave off imminent illness or to treat a condition that had set in.[65] For example, monks were not to be bled in Lent or when there was a fast that could not be broken,

---

and A.H. Thomas, *Le coutumier de l'abbaye d'Oigny en Bourgogne au XIIe siècle*, *Spicilegium Sacrum Lovaniense Études et documents*, 39 (Leuven, 1976), cap. 68.

61 "Consuetudines Einsidlenses," in *Consuetudines monasteriorum germaniae necnon S. Vitonis Virdunensis et Floriacensis abbatiae monumenta saeculi decimi continens*, ed. Bruno Albers, *Consuetudines Monasticae*, 5 (Monte Cassino, 1912), 84 : "Sanguinis minutio generaliter fiat in Kalendis, nisi forte occurrerit praecipua sollempnitas, pro qua re aut antecipanda erit aut differenda in postmodum." This text is also available in *Consuetudinum saeculi X/XI/XII monumenta non-Cluniacensia*, ed. Kassius Hallinger, CCM, 7(3) (Siegburg, 1984), p. 214.

62 Barnwell Customary, pp. 198–202.

63 What constituted "grave necessity" is left to the imagination; *Liber ordinis Sancti Victoris Parisensis*, p. 251: "Quinquies in anno fient generales minutiones, extra quas sine periculo grauis infirmitatis licentia minuendi nulli omnino conceditur."

64 *Constitutiones Hirsaugienses*, PL, 150, cols 989–90.

65 Other than references to "grave necessity," there is little indication that the regulation of *minuti* applied to those who were bled for curative reasons. The one exception I have found is from the twelfth century: "Consuetudines Portuensis," Ch. 24, "De usu balnearum, et sanguinis diminutione," begins: "Si quibus fratrum balnearum, vel minutionis usu pro conservatione, vel restauratione sanitatis necessarius fuerit ...." This chapter is unique in that it combines baths, commonly reserved for the ill, with bloodletting; *Vetus disciplina canonicorum regularium et saecularium ex documentis magna parte huiusque ineditis a*

unless it was a case of grave infirmity. In those cases, which came first: the food or the fast? The distinct impression given by the customaries is that unless death were imminent – unlikely in cases of periodic bloodletting but a real possibility in cases of illness – the fast was given priority. Einsiedeln's tenth-century customary stated that, if due to "the most grave necessity" one must be bled in Lent, this was to be done on a Saturday. For the night following the bleeding and the next day, monks were to follow the usual custom for *minuti*, except that they were not to eat eggs or cheese. On the third day at None, they were to rejoin their brethren in fast.[66] It may seem peculiar that the customary would specify that this bleeding, done out of the most grave necessity, be carried out on a Saturday. This was in fact quite common, and illustrates even further the need to adhere to the usual routine to the extent that this was possible. Saturdays were the preferred days for bleeding during Lent because the fast was generally broken on Sundays to celebrate the Resurrection. Thus one could be bled and enjoy for one day the rich diet normally given to those who were recovering, without violating the Lenten fast.[67]

Conclusion

The experiences of *minuti* and *infirmi* reveal little about the medical care that was offered to those who were in the monastic infirmary. What they do provide is a sense of how important it was to adhere to the established regimen. The regimen was a defining feature of the religious life, and to disrupt it was to undermine a fundamental aspect of the ascetic existence.

Periodic bloodletting was built into monastic regulations in such a way that it would not deprive the community of members during those times when they were needed most: for key liturgical events, and when all hands were needed for manual labor, as at the harvest. The possibility that some religious might be bled in order to avoid work was accounted for; those who claimed that they needed to be bled outside the regulated times were denied the very comforts that would have made bloodletting appealing to those who did not require it.[68]

---

temporibus apostolicis usque ad saeculum XVII, ed. Eusebio Amort, Vol. 1 (Venice, 1747; repr. Westmead, 1971), p. 363.

66 *Consuetudines Einsidlensis*, CM, 5, p. 87.

67 The question of whether and when one could be bled during Lent is the opening subject of the customary for the Benedictine abbey at Bury St Edmunds in England; *The Customary of the Benedictine Abbey of Bury St. Edmunds in Suffolk*, ed. Antonia Gransden, *Henry Bradshaw Society*, 99 (Chichester, 1973), p. 50. When to bleed during Lent is subject to comment in several other customaries.

68 As stated in Chapter 29 of the customs written for the regular canons at Aureil: "Si sine licentia sibi minuerint, non accipiunt que prenotata sunt." Jean Becquet, "Le coutumier des chanoines réguliers d'Aureil en Limousin au XIIIe siècle," in *Vie canoniale en France aux Xe–XIIe siècles* (London, 1985).

Infirmi appeared in chapters separate from *minuti* because they differed in at least one way that was critical given the tight control characteristic of the religious life: their absence was unplanned. The spontaneous nature of illness made it necessarily inconvenient to a community where every detail was spelled out. There was a natural suspicion of those who were excused from what was a demanding life. On one hand, there was the question of whether the illness were genuine; if it were, then what spiritual failings had brought about this display of inward corruption? There was a delicate balance to achieve between a fundamental suspicion of those who were ill (as characterized by the Rule of the Master), and the care that the Christian religion required be given to those who were weak (as is seen in the Rule of St Benedict). The confessional words of *infirmi* and the penitential gestures required of them before they were accepted back into the community following their convalescence were one answer to the dilemma. They emphasized the link between illness and sin and they served as a final reminder that the care they had received was not a reflection of the individual, but was only to satisfy the requirement that the ill be treated "as if they were Christ in person."[69] Most importantly, however, the confessional words of *infirmi* reaffirmed the distinction between them and *minuti*: illness was spontaneous and could not be manipulated, like periodic bloodletting was, to fit with minimum disruption into an intricate *regimen spiritualis*.

---

69 *St. Benedict's Rule*, cap. 36.

Chapter 12

Challenging the "Eye of Newt" Image of Medieval Medicine

Anne Van Arsdall

Introduction

An incident in a physician's office lies behind the title of this chapter. Hearing that his patient's research area was medieval medicine, the physician said knowingly: "Oh sure, eye of newt and tongue of toad, right?" By "eye of newt," he was thinking of something out of *Macbeth*: witchcraft, boiling cauldrons of nostrums, and incantations to keep elves and sorcerers at bay. Unfortunately, this image of medieval medicine is all too prevalent, and it is wrong. Indeed, much recent scholarly work judges the herbal remedies in medieval texts to be ineffective, and quickly turns to what is thought to be a more interesting aspect of the writings: superstition and magic. This focus can be found, for example, in studies by Stanley Rubin,[1] Charles Talbot[2] and Karen Jolly,[3] and in dissertations by Frieda Hankins and Barbara Olds.[4]

A fascination with the magical and superstitious aspects of medieval medicine, which actually make up quite a small part of the surviving texts, has helped shape an erroneous image of a system that is essentially botanical medicine as still practiced both as ethnobotany and by more scientific modern herbalists. It is a system of healing that has been in place and active since the beginning of written time. Records of one era in this long-lived system are in the medieval medical texts, all of them derived in part from classical works. Written witnesses of the system continue to this day. Thus it seems entirely reasonable that by studying various contemporary healing traditions that share in aspects of this system of healing, which is largely based on use of medicinal plants, modern scholars can gain an insight into how the medieval medical texts might be meaningfully interpreted. Few clues exist in the manuscripts

---

1   Stanley Rubin, *Medieval English Medicine* (New York, 1974).

2   Charles Talbot, *Medicine in Medieval England* (London, 1967).

3   Karen Louise Jolly, *Popular Religion in Late Saxon England: Elf Charms in Context* (Chapel Hill, NC, 1996). Although Jolly talks about a composite and partly unwritten medical tradition in Anglo-Saxon England, for some reason she entirely excludes the *Old English Herbarium* and similar texts from the realm of medicine as it was practiced in Anglo-Saxon England.

4   Barbara Olds, "The Anglo-Saxon Leechbook III: A Critical Edition and Translation" (PhD Dissertation, University of Denver, 1984); Frieda Richards Hankins, "Bald's Leechbook Reconsidered" (PhD Dissertation, University of North Carolina at Chapel Hill, 1991).

as to how a medieval practitioner might have made and administered the remedies that we find written down. For this reason, many modern readers have dismissed the texts as useless, blaming imprecision as a reason. The basis for reaching an opposite conclusion about them is presented in this chapter. It comes out of a close study of one major Anglo-Saxon medical work, the *Old English Herbarium*, and familiarity with two other Old English medical texts and with a variety of ancient and medieval Latin medical writings, complemented by several years of study in various types of practical botanical medicine.

Of the three Old English texts (all *c.* AD 1000), *Bald's Leechbook* and the *Lacnunga* were originally written in the vernacular. Both have received a good deal of interest, not because of their medical content, but rather to try to discover native Germanic lore behind or among the medicinal remedies. The *Old English Herbarium*, on the other hand, has prompted less interest largely because it is a translation into Anglo-Saxon of a fourth-century Latin treatise on medicinal plants. Because it is not a so-called native work, some have wrongly assumed that the *Herbarium* cannot be representative of healing in Anglo-Saxon England. Four manuscripts of the Anglo-Saxon translation of the *Herbarium* exist, as well as numerous Latin versions from the same time and earlier. The two other medical texts in Anglo-Saxon, the *Leechbook of Bald* and the *Lacnunga*, exist as unique copies. Both contain remedies similar to those in the *Herbarium* and derive largely from classical sources.[5] Their non-medical content, including prayers, charms and what is branded superstition, makes up a small percentage of the whole, but has received the lion's share of study until recently.

A New Look at the Old Texts

Not everyone, however, shares the view that medieval plant remedies are fanciful, and if not fanciful, useless, and that the magical aspects are more representative of the early medical tradition. In fact, quite a bit of interest is developing in using medieval herbal remedies as objects of scientific study for new cures. Scholars such as John Riddle, Linda Voigts, Jerry Stannard, M.L Cameron, Amalia D'Aronco and Bart Holland have done ground-breaking work in looking at the remedies and the herbs as possibly being efficacious.[6] Their approach is generally to assume that no

---

5   See M.L. Cameron, "The sources of medical knowledge in Anglo-Saxon England," *Anglo-Saxon England*, II (1983), 135–55.

6   See, for example, John Riddle, "Theory and Practice in Medieval Medicine," *Viator Medieval and Renaissance Studies*, 5 (1974), 157–84; Linda E. Voigts, "Anglo-Saxon Plant Remedies and the Anglo-Saxons," *Isis*, 70 (1979), 250–68, and Linda E. Voigts and Robert P. Hudson, "A drynke þat men callen dwale to make a man to slepe whyle men kerven him," in *Health, Disease and Healing in Medieval Culture*, ed. Sheila Campbell, Bert Hall and David Klausner (New York, 1992); Jerry Stannard, *Herbs and Herbalism in the Middle Ages and Renaissance* (London, 1999), and *Pristina Medicamenta: Ancient and Medieval Medical Botany* (London, 1999); M.L. Cameron, "Anglo-Saxon Medicine and Magic," *Anglo-Saxon*

part of the remedy is superstition or magic, but instead first to assume that it might have a practical reason for being included. For example, Cameron, a biologist, refuted the notion that directions to use a brass or copper vessel to prepare or store medicines for the eyes was for ritual/magical reasons. He explained: "It is significant that in all these recipes there is at least one ingredient with which copper would react to form copper salts. That the physician recognized the value of these salts is made clear in the last prescription of the chapter ....."[7] A prohibition against cutting or chopping a plant with iron has the same explanation: there is no magic involved, just chemistry. Cameron also suggested that *elf shot*, widely discussed as a native Anglo-Saxon belief in elves shooting an arrow to cause disease, was actually a witness to the Anglo-Saxons' awareness of communicable diseases.

A few scholars have been looking at the possible efficacy of medieval remedies apart from any non-medical aspects the remedy might contain. For example, Linda Voigts and Robert Hudson took seriously the claim in a widely circulated late medieval manuscript that a mixture called *dwale* would "make a man to slepe whyle man kerven him."[8] They researched the frequency of the prescription in fourteenth- and fifteenth-century vernacular collections in England and used some twentieth-century pharmacological knowledge to analyze the ingredients, with some older knowledge to temper it. (The authors note that "Older dispensatories provide details of pharmacognosy, medical indications, methods of preparation, warnings, dosages, and so on that no longer appear in current descriptions of highly standardized, often synthetic medicaments.")[9] The authors studied the ingredients and method of administration to try to ascertain whether *dwale* was effective, and they found it certainly could have worked. Along the same line of research, John Riddle devotes an entire book to studying the efficacy of ancient and medieval remedies for contraception and abortion.[10]

Bart Holland of the New Jersey Medical School believes that modern pharmacy can learn from the past if the ancient texts are examined and the ingredients carefully analyzed. In *Prospecting for Drugs in Ancient and Medieval Medical European Texts*,[11] Holland presents a selection of articles to bring home his point. Papers include John Riddle discussing the efficacy of medicines of antiquity, botanist James L. Reveal outlining how to approach the plants in pre-Linnaean botanical literature, and Thurman Hunt (also from the New Jersey School of Medicine) detailing how to test the efficacy of ancient medical lore. Holland asserts that ancient and medieval

---

England, 17 (1988), 191–215; Maria Amalia D'Aronco and M.L. Cameron, *The Old English Illustrated Pharmacopoeia*, (Copenhagen, 1998); Bart Holland, ed., *Prospecting for Drugs in Ancient and Medieval European Texts: A Scientific Approach* (Amsterdam, 1996).

7   Cameron, "Anglo-Saxon Medicine and Magic," 203.

8   Voigts and Hudson, "A drynke Þat men callen dwale to make a man to slepe whyle men kerven him."

9   Ibid., 36.

10   See John M. Riddle, *Contraception and Abortion from the Ancient World to the Renaissance* (Cambridge, MA, 1992).

11   (Amsterdam, 1996).

testimonies, such as "this remedy really works well," are no longer sufficient in this age of medical science, and that documented, systematic studies of yet unexamined ancient cures are called for.

Indeed, interest in, some might say governmental concern about, the increased popular acceptance of herbal medications, and often self-prescribed use of herbal remedies, is reflected in the USA in the creation of a National Center for Complementary and Alternative Medicine (NCCAM) under the National Institutes of Health. Mainstream health practitioners too are eyeing this form of treatment, and schools of public health and medical schools at many universities are giving complementary and alternative medicine serious attention.[12]

Long a part of mainstream medicine in Europe, phytotherapy (herbal or botanical medicine) was, for example, the subject of a 1999 Colloquium in Amsterdam on the place of herbal medicinal products in health care sponsored by the European Scientific Cooperative on Phytotherapy (ESCOP).[13] The journal *Fitoterapia* regularly reports the results of scientific studies on ethnobotanical remedies worldwide, many of them in Western countries.[14] Now all this may seem far afield from a discussion of medieval herbal remedies; however, the results of such studies and the information in NCCAM could be used to further knowledge of how, or whether, the medieval remedies worked, and to show that the remedies are not just "eye of newt."

Overwhelming evidence indicates that medications made with medicinal plants have actual therapeutic effects. Thus if medieval herbal remedies are read as witnesses to the actual practice of healing in the Middle Ages, and if all the elements in them are initially regarded as having added value of some kind, one's interpretation of them will be quite different than if magic or superstition is sought or assumed. It is also important to abandon the notion that herbal medicine is only to be found on some kind of lunatic fringe.

Consider instead that everything in a medieval herbal remedy might have a good reason for being there. The instruction to say a phrase, a charm or prayer a certain number of times after ingesting the remedy might have been there so that the patient would rest or wait a given amount of time, allowing the herb do its work in the body, not because the words were believed to have magical effects. And it might also have increased the patient's belief that the medication would work. Even modern medicine does not understand the placebo effect or the role of faith in healing.

In an age that demands instant cures from a pill, having to wait a time for medications to work is not generally accepted. The herbalist's instruction to drink a cup of warm chamomile tea, then to lie down for fifteen minutes on a pillow scented with lavender and rosemary has been proven to cure a headache as certainly as aspirin, but few today are willing to take the time for tea and herbs.

---

12 Please consult the NIH-sponsored Website of the National Center for Complementary and Alternative Medicine (NCCAM) at <http://nccam.nih.gov>.

13 As reported in *Fitoterapia*, 71 (2000), 343–345

14 The ESCOP provides a wealth of information about phytotherapy through its extensive Website: <http://www.escop.com>.

An instruction to harvest a medicinal plant on Midsummer's Day at sunrise probably means nothing other than this is the best time to harvest the plant, when its medicinal properties are strongest. In a day before calendars hung on every wall and a watch was on every wrist, the name of the day, the season and the general time of day for harvesting would have been much easier to remember. The point is that modern readers tend to interpret medieval instructions based on their own experiences with medicine, whose practice is far different now than then.

If medieval medical texts are read objectively as witnesses to a living tradition of *healing* (not magic), a different picture emerges, and any emphasis on superstition, charms, elves and dwarves is seen to be out of proportion to what was written down. Indeed, medieval medicine appears to have been quite different and more benign than is generally portrayed. (Surgery is a separate topic of discussion; in the early Middle Ages, when reliable anesthetics were unavailable, surgery was by necessity an emergency measure.)

Please note that no distinction is being made here between the Anglo-Saxon medical tradition and that on the European Continent. The evidence is overwhelming that they were essentially the same.[15] On the Continent, scores of similar texts were produced and traded throughout the West and England, as Augusto Beccaria's work on pre-Salernitan manuscripts attests.[16]

Particularly in Germany, the remedies in these many texts are being studied as an original early medieval type of medical writing which is generally termed *Rezeptliteratur*, a term coined by Henry Sigerist[17] in the 1920s, and now associated with Gundolf Keil and his colleagues in Würzburg.[18] *Rezeptliteratur* is a term describing texts that generally contain medicinal remedies, not theories of the causation of disease, and not medical explanations. These collections of remedies are not standard, and, for example, the Latin original of the *Old English Herbarium* changed, if slightly, over the centuries as remedies were altered or added. The situation was typical for this kind of medical remedy book for centuries, and it is not a flaw. Changes reflect use over time.

---

15 In a personal communication, John Riddle pointed out that Anglo-Saxon medical texts contain more non-medical content than the *receptaria* and *antidotaria* on the Continent, suggesting that a comparative study of similar texts might ascertain the reason why.

16 Augusto Beccaira, *I Codici di Medicina del Periodo Presalernitano: Secoli IX, X, e XI* (Rome, 1956).

17 Henry Sigerist, *Studien und Texte zur frühmittelalterliche Rezeptliteratur* (Leipzig, 1923); see also Ulrich Stoll, *Das Lorscher Arzneibuch: ein medizinisches Kompendium des 8. Jahrhunderts* (Stuttgart, 1992).

18 See, for example, Gundolf Keil and Paul Schnitzer, eds, *Das Lorscher Arzneibuch und die Frümittelalterliche Medizin* (Lorsch, 1991); Gundolf Keil, *Fachprosa-Studien: Beiträge zur mittelalterlichen Wissenschafts und Geistesgeschichte* (Berlin, 1982); H. Jansen-Sieben, ed., *Artes Mechanicae en Europe médiévale/en middeleeuws Europa* (Brussels, 1989).

Applying a Practical Approach to Manuscript Medicine

What made possible a common body of changing/dynamic medical texts throughout the West over many centuries was access to a common body of ingredients, including plants, either by being able to grow them in protected situations, being able to trade for them or being able to find equivalents in the wild. Also what made it possible was person-to-person instruction in how to prepare the remedies and treat sick people, information that is not totally reflected in the writings. As Riddle noted: "The texts of medieval pharmaceutical treatises generally are less descriptive of the herbs and minerals than classical texts, and thus require that the reader have some prior acquaintance with the subject before using the written texts."[19] How else would such seemingly imprecise instructions have been used, and why else would they have continued to be copied?

One tangible way to unlock the mysteries of terse medieval medical manuscripts is to ascertain whether they can be shown to make sense in practice. A year-long course on the Foundations of Herbalism offered by the North American College of Botanical Medicine provided training in herbalism and in making compounds out of medicinal plants.[20] The Foundations class and this author's study of the *Old English Herbarium* happened to coincide nicely. As the year unfolded, so did the medieval text. At the outset, the importance of knowing individual medicinal plants by sight and smell was stressed, including how to identify them at various times of the year and when to collect them. The class covered the medicinal properties of individual plants and herbs, how to prepare remedies using them, how to administer them to children (with great caution) and people of various ages and physical conditions. It gave instruction in standard doses of medicinal teas and how to brew them. The class treated how smells affect the reception of medicine, and how administering a remedy can affect the patient's response to it. The teaching herbalists stressed that one should look beyond what patients say, and sense other possible causes for disease than the obvious.

The scope of the training was extensive, most of it verbal and by repetition and hands-on practice, supplemented by texts, many of them quite like the medieval ones. Interpreted in the context of the modern healing system generally called herbalism, the medieval medical texts become to a large part comprehensible and useful. It is now plausible to view medieval medical texts as the written remains of a medical system whose legacy continues. (By this kind of herbalism is meant a practice based on learning how to administer medicinal plants, not the pre-packaged commercial so-called herbal products.)

The practice of herbal medicine being described here is, in fact, very much tapped into scientific studies on medicinal plants, and it uses modern medical knowledge

---

19 Riddle, "Medieval Medicine," 163.

20 The school became the North American College of Botanical Medicine, Albuquerque, New Mexico, and it offered a three-year program leading to a degree in botanical medicine. As of 2004, it ceased to exist. Other such schools can be found in the USA and abroad, most unaccredited, but the NCCAM may change this situation, for good or ill.

about human physiology and pathology. Modern herbalists are the first to advise going to a hospital or a mainstream physician for a scientific diagnosis of one's condition. However, the herbalist might offer an alternative method of treatment for a condition known to respond well to an herbal remedy. For many conditions, herbal remedies can be helpful and less caustic than pharmaceutical prescriptions.

In addition to investigations into the chemical properties of medicinal plants and the efficacy of medications compounded with them, how treatment is delivered is an important topic that is gaining increased attention in contemporary medicine. The topic includes the effect a practitioner and any kind of ritual might have on the patient. This effect might be the reason that charms and prayers are included in medieval medical texts. In fact, a spiritual or mind-calming element is an integral part of most systems of botanical medicine. (In this regard, it is interesting that the NCCAM is now calling for studies on "Research into Mind–body Interactions and Health" at its website.) Taken together, the chemistry of medicinal herbal remedies and the method of treatment are important to understanding how medieval medical remedies were intended to work, just as they are to knowing why herbal medicine is often quite effective.

General statements about the multitude of healing systems usually termed holistic (the object of the NCCAM's attention) are difficult and dangerous to make because each tends to be based on some kind of philosophical or religious footing, and the botanicals are only part of the picture. It seems obvious that when dealing with human beings, who have a mental facility that affects the physical, a chemical analysis alone will not give a true picture of why a remedy might work in some cases and not in others. The spiritual (mental, philosophical) aspect plays a role, just as it undoubtedly did in the early Middle Ages. Peter Biller and Joseph Ziegler have edited a book of collected papers on this subject titled *Religion and Medicine in the Middle Ages*,[21] in which the spiritual aspect of hospitals and healing is considered and demonstrated in some depth.

The same alliance of medicine, particularly botanical, and overt spirituality can be found in a living tradition close to the medieval world of medicine. The practice and the books used or written by Hispanic *curanderas/os* (folk healers) show remarkable similarities to the early medieval ones. Partly text-based, but mostly taught by apprenticeship, the *curanderas/os* brought their medieval healing arts with them from Spain to the New World. They came into unfamiliar territories, some brought plants and roots, some had to rely on what they found, and all began borrowing from the Native American healers. It is a situation so similar to the late classical and early medieval world that it begs to be applied to the transmission of medieval medical information.

The *curanderas/os* do not rely on medicine alone to treat their patients. A religious aspect is always part of it, whether that be in the form of an appeal to Roman Catholicism with its saints or to a native pre-Columbian tradition. To incorporate such an elusive topic as the spiritual aspects of folk healing in a scholarly paper on

---

21 (York, 2001).

medieval medicine is perhaps unusual, but it must not be forgotten that medicine has always dealt with complete human beings, not exclusively with the written history of how human beings have been treated. Thus if living traditions of healing can give an insight into how the medical texts of a bygone period might be interpreted, it seems justified and reasonable to use them.

Familiarity with *curanderismo*, as this healing tradition is called, coupled with classroom and hands-on workshops in modern botanical medicine, provides a unique perspective to bring to bear on medieval writings about healing herbs. Studies in botanical medicine, numerous related workshops and classes, and informal sessions with practicing herbalists and *curanderas* have revealed that seemingly imprecise, terse written instructions are typical for this kind of healing art. The inescapable conclusion is that the medieval texts were written by healers for healers who were steeped in this tradition of healing.

The medieval practitioners who used the texts must have served, or were serving, an apprenticeship; they knew their plants; they knew how to recognize illnesses, and how to treat wounds and bites and cuts. This method of instruction existed outside a traditional university setting, and was most likely based in an infirmary. As such, it required a familiarity with numerous medicinal plants, and must be much the same today as it was throughout the Middle Ages. Texts have never been the main part of it. Instead, hands-on experience with the plants and patients is primary. The texts serve only as reminders and references.

With all of the healers who use medicinal plants today, treatment is individualized to the patient, and the plant or plants used to effect a cure or an improvement will vary. This lack of dogma in choice of remedy may explain why several plants are listed both in medieval and modern herbal references as being good for the same thing. There is no such concept, for example, that betony is the *only* plant to be used for earache and yarrow for wounds. Quantities in the remedies tend to be imprecise because the person who would be prescribing and/or mixing the remedy already knows common proportions of plant to a given medium.

Most medieval medicinal remedies follow this pattern, or a slight variation of it: for this condition, take this plant, prepare it in a certain manner, administer it, this is the result you can expect. An example from the *Herbarium* is as follows:[22]

> If a person cannot keep food down and vomits when he swallows, take four coins' weight of the betony plant and boiled honey, then make four little pills from it. Eat one, take one in hot water, and then two in wine. Then swallow three cupfuls of water. (1)

These directions are fairly detailed compared to many; for example the following, also from the *Herbarium*:

---

22 Anne Van Arsdall, *Medieval Herbal Remedies: The Old English Herbarium and Anglo-Saxon Medicine* (New York, 2002). The number in parentheses following the remedy refers to a given section in the translated *Herbarium* (Chapter 5 in the book).

For stomach ache, take the comfrey plant and mix it with honey and vinegar. You will experience beneficial effects. (60)

How much comfrey? Fresh or dried? And when it is mixed with honey and vinegar, again, how much of each should be used? And then what is done next?

Modern directions to herbal healers are quite similar. The following quotation is taken from Michael Moore's *Los Remedios de la Gente: Traditional New Mexican Herbal Remedies and their Use*:[23]

> Mountain Mugwort, primary use, a cold and flu medicine, drunk cold to settle the stomach and hot to bring on and shorten the fever. A bitter tonic for stomach pains and acidosis from greasy and rancid foods. Secondary use, for diarrhea. Note: feverfew and tansy are substituted for it.

Influenced by the precision of prescribing drugs in today's mainstream medicine, many contemporary writers on medieval medicine see its imprecision and terseness as a flaw.

A Distorted Picture

Because herbology (or phytotherapy, as it is also called) is generally no longer highly valued, even called *alternative* medicine by the medical establishment, modern readers influenced by current medical thinking tend to consider the medieval remedies based on plants to be ineffective by their very nature. Since the mid-nineteenth century, in fact, the focus has been on what are considered to be magical aspects of the medieval writings on medicine. This emphasis is actually a focus on folklore rather than the healing arts of the time.

This distorted picture of medieval medicine, so prevalent in the English-speaking world, can be traced at least in part to 1864–66, when Oswald Cockayne translated the Anglo-Saxon medical texts and published them under the title *Leechdoms, Wortcunning and Starcraft of Early England*, a title that in itself connotes magic and superstition.[24] Cockayne was a trained classicist and teacher of Latin and Greek who turned to Anglo-Saxon rather late in life, and for reasons unknown, possibly out of morbid fascination with the childhood of the English race.[25] His translation style made what had been serious works on healing sound quaint and ridiculous, and he introduced certain erroneous notions in the prefaces to his translations that have been emphasized quite out of proportion to their importance and relative frequency in the actual texts.

Cockayne began his trilogy of translations/editions with the words: "It will be difficult for the kindliest temper to give a friendly welcome to the medical philosophy

---

23 (Santa Fe, 1977).

24 Oswald Cockayne, ed., *Leechdoms, Wortcunning and Starcraft of Early England*, 3 vols (1864; repr. London, 1965).

25 See Van Arsdall, *Medieval Herbal Remedies*, Chapter 1, on Cockayne.

of Saxon days" – hardly an endorsement of his chosen subject. His accounts of
Saxon medicine are contrasted with what he considered to be the clearly superior
classical tradition, and he reveled in demonstrating what he called the "darker side"
of the Saxon mind. But also in Cockayne is a desire to reach back beyond Christian
Anglo-Saxon England to the pagan world behind it.

This desire can be seen to grow in later scholars, notably Charles Singer and
Wilifrid Bonser (it was quite strong on the Continent too, with Jacob Grimm and his
followers, who sought to find vestiges of the pre-Christian Germanic past). Singer
used many of Cockayne's ideas, often not giving him full credit, and Bonser, his pupil,
repeated and intensified his ideas. They both published works about Anglo-Saxon
medicine, beginning in the 1920s and continuing through the 1950s, that are widely
cited.[26] Both men emphasized the magical and superstitious aspects of the tradition,
and it is Singer who seems to have introduced the idea that *Bald's Leechbook* and
the *Lacunuga*, both of which contain a number of charms and other elements that are
not strictly medical, were much more typical of the healing tradition in Anglo-Saxon
England than the *Old English Herbarium*, a translation from the Latin. Singer even
called the remedies in the *Herbarium* "scribal exercises that were unintelligently
copied," and said they were just elaborate displays of learning that were beyond
the skill of the leeches of the time.[27] This is a message Singer repeated in every
publication, and its echo is found in many subsequent writers.

In an effort to isolate what they believed to be purely Anglo-Saxon charms and
superstition, Singer, Bonser and their followers, having discounted any value in the
herbal remedies, focused on the *Lacnunga* and its allegedly non-medical content.
However, an objective look at the *Lacnunga* shows that its contents are largely
remedies based on plants, not charms, not magic, nor superstition. Of its 194 entries,
only 25 contain what might be called magic or superstition, and this is arguable.
Take away 22 Christian prayers, and that leaves 147 straightforward remedies based
on medicinal plants in a text widely cited as an example of Anglo-Saxon magic.
In emphasizing the importance of the *Lacnunga* and *Bald's Leechbook* while also
excluding the translated *Old English Herbarium* as being virtually useless to the
Anglo-Saxon healer, these studies present a biased interpretation about the medical
tradition in medieval England and abroad.

Conclusion

Most studies of early English medicine have focussed on medical texts that were
originally written in Old English. Fewer have dealt with the *Old English Herbarium*,
a translation from Latin to Old English. Furthermore, the major interest in studying

---

26 J.H.G. Grattan and Charles Singer, *Anglo-Saxon Magic and Medicine* (London,
1952); Wilifrid Bonser, *The Medical Background of the Anglo-Saxons: A Study in History,
Psychology, and Folklore* (London, 1963).

27 Charles Singer, *From Magic to Science: Essays on the Scientific Twilight* (1928; repr.
New York, 1958).

the original Old English works has been centered on their non-medical aspects, which make up only a small portion of their rich material.

If the gamut of medical texts in England and the Continent is assessed as a whole, it will be found that the remedies using a common body of medicinal plants prepared in much the same way can be found in Italy, France, England and into Scandinavia. These remedies are typical of the healing arts of the early Middle Ages, not the chants, and not the "eye of newt." Using living herbal healing traditions that are still viable in the United States and in many other countries, it is possible to understand and appreciate better what the medieval tradition really was, and to realize that many of the remedies in those old manuscripts actually help in preventing and treating illness

Section IV
The Monastic Connection

Chapter 13

De Domo Sancti Lazari milites leprosi: Knighthood and Leprosy in the Holy Land

Rafaël Hyacinthe

One of the most fascinating aspects of the crusades in the Latin East is the foundation of the Order of St Lazarus, which seems to have been a military order composed of *milites leprosi* ("knights with leprosy"). Past work differs in the approach taken to this order. Some authors have included it within in the context of military forces put together to defend the Holy Cross, without considering the consequences of an association between leprosy and knighthood.[1] Others have considered it in discussing what seems to be a development of an increasing tolerance towards leprosy, in contrast to attitudes in Europe, where this disease was a synonym for exclusion from society.[2] Still others prefer to say little, leaving the name of St Lazarus as an obscure part of crusading history, justifying the silence by a lack of documents.[3]

But sources do exist, and a reassessment of what can be called the myth of the so called "leper knights" (*milites leprosi*) is now possible.[4] The statutes of the Order of St Lazarus are a rich documentary source. They have survived in the form of a Rule kept in the archives of an ancient Lazarite house in Switzerland. In 1321, the preceptor of that house had the Rule copied into Middle German. This document, divided in three parts, covers the whole of the crusading period. The first part was composed "for the house in Jerusalem," that is, before 1187, when the city was under Christian rule. Some sections were added in Acre, where the order established its

---

1   Christopher Marshall, *Warfare in the Latin East (1191–1291)* (Cambridge, 1992), pp. 66–7.

2   Piers Mitchell, "An evaluation of the leprosy of King Baldwin IV of Jerusalem in the context of the medieval world," in Bernard Hamilton, *The Leper King and his Heirs* (Cambridge, 2000), 256–7.

3   Alan Forey, *The Military Orders from the Twelfth to the Thirteenth Century* (London, 1992), pp. 17, 19, 22 and 225.

4   Accounts may be found in recent works such as: Malcolm Barber, "The Order of Saint Lazarus and the Crusades," *Catholic Historical Review*, 80 (1994), 439–56, or, Shulamit Shahar, "Des lépreux pas comme les autres," *Revue Historique*, 267 (1982), 19–41. These include most of the relevant documentation, but nevertheless do not consider the statutes which are the focus of this present study.

headquarters from 1240 to 1291.[5] Even though these are separate document sections existing together in a single manuscript, taken together they give a more accurate idea of the evolution of the Order of St Lazarus, thereby allowing us to reconsider the case of the *milites leprosi*. By focussing on the role allocated to the sick as expressed in the twelfth and thirteenth centuries, it is possible to understand more accurately and appreciate the place of those with leprosy within the context of religious and crusading ideals of that time.

One must indeed consider the Order of St Lazarus of Jerusalem as a crusader institution, and its original religious development in relation to other military orders linked to the Holy Land. When considered in all aspects, the existence of these orders was not only dedicated to warfare, as the famous case of the Order of the Temple would suggest.[6] For the Order of St John, the Teutonic Order and the Order of St Thomas of Canterbury, an important goal in their foundation was to provide welfare.[7] Assistance to others was then to be given in a religious setting, according to a Rule. This took on an international scale, as with the need to support pilgrims going overseas. To give donations to such charitable institutions was seen as an act of faith that was widespread throughout Western Europe during the twelfth century.[8] Similarly, the work carried out by the knights of the Order of St Lazarus can be seen as another component of what can be called "practical spirituality."

Historically, the order appeared at the same time as many other crusading institutions, in the first half of the twelfth century as recorded in documents dating from 1130 onward.[9] However, compared to other orders, its function was much more specific. The order's appearance parallels the establishment of leprosaria in the West. Recent research has demonstrated that they were both an institutional expression of religious devotion and an institution to provide for medical segregation for the afflicted. Medieval perceptions of the disease help to explain this duality.[10] The physical changes to the face, hands, feet and skin give the sufferer a striking appearance, which at that time could easily be associated with the idea of divine punishment. As the Old Testament puts it, God who is offended by man's sins

---

5   An edition of the manuscript is included in P. Gall Morel, ed., "Die ältesten Statuten für die Lazaritenklöster Seedorf," in *Der Geschichtsfreund: Mittheilungen des historischen Vereins der fünf Orte Luzern, Uri, Schwyz, Unterwalden und Zug*, 4 (1847), 119–58 (hereafter cited as Morel). The last part of the manuscript, which will not be discussed here, was composed by the above-mentioned preceptor when the community was about to become a nunnery in the fourteenth century.

6   Malcolm Barber, *The New Knighthood* (Cambridge, 1994), pp. 38–50.

7   See Malcolm Barber, ed., *The Military Orders: Fighting for the Faith and Caring for the Sick* (Cambridge, 1994).

8   Joshua Prawer, *Histoire du royaume latin de Jerusalem* (Paris, 1975), pp. 489–91 (hereafter cited as Prawer).

9   Comte de Marsy, ed., "Fragment d'un cartulaire de l'Ordre de Saint-Lazare en Terre sainte," *Archives de l'Orient Latin*, 2 (1884), 123–4 (hereafter cited as Marsy).

10   Peter Richards, *The Medieval Leper and His Northern Heirs* (Cambridge, 1977) pp. 6–11.

will strike him down with leprosy. He is thereby forced into exile because of the supposedly contagious and incurable nature of the disease. This explains the basis for general medieval regulations that denied a person with leprosy a place in society, forcing him to withdraw outside the town walls in leprosaria.

The Gospels give a light of hope to this metaphor of "fallen humanity." Christ healed people with leprosy and absolved them from their sins. Christ also exhorted man to acts of charity by taking on the form of a sick man, begging for help and care. Such allusions are to be found in numerous lives of saints, in sermons, and in art.[11] These various sources help to explain the particular nature of leprosaria. More than hospitals for an incurable sickness, they were establishments that sheltered a community of sick people wishing to gain forgiveness for their sins, as well as a promise of salvation through constant prayer. The ill patients were sometimes assisted by the healthy, who served them compassionately, wishing to follow Christ's teaching and example (*imitatio Christi*). Some statutes of these institutions hence allude to a highly religious life. Their existence should be viewed in the context of the growth of monasticism in the twelfth century that aimed at including every element of society in a common movement toward God.[12]

The same phenomenon took place in the Latin Kingdom of Jerusalem. Men who developed leprosy gathered together in such a house, located outside the walls of Jerusalem, between Saint Stephen's Gate and the tower named after Tancred. In 1172, a pilgrim described it as a "church and dwelling for people afflicted with leprosy, beautiful and well arranged."[13] The first Rule of this community is especially informative when considered in more detail.[14] It cites different elements of a monastic complex composed of: a church, two dormitories, a refectory and a hospice.[15] On a map of the city drawn in the twelfth century, it is seen represented as a religious building, an element of the local ecclesiastical background.[16] Indeed, just as the ideals of knighthood were taken into a religious setting within the Order of the Temple, so here too a particular ideal of assisting the sick developed into the Order of St Lazarus, having a Rule, a master and an international reputation. The case of the Order of St Lazarus of Jerusalem is a very significant illustration of the religious seclusion of people with leprosy. The first house was located outside the town, within a convent. It was "their" convent, a fact attested to by most of the

---

11 François-Olivier Touati, *Maladie et Société au Moyen Age* (Paris, 1998), pp. 187–201; Nicole Beriou and François-Olivier Touati, eds, *Voluntate Dei Leprosus* (Spoleto, 1991).

12 Léon Le Grand, ed., *Statuts d'Hotels-Dieu et de léproseries* (Paris, 1901); Peter Kay Jankrift and Martin Uhrmacher, eds, "Leprosorien und ihre Statuten: Normiertes Leben zwischen Ideal, Vorstellung und Abbild," in *Proceedings of the Third Conference of the International Network for the History of Leprosy* (Trier, 2003).

13 John Wilkinson, ed., *Jerusalem Pilgrimage* (London, 1988), p. 301.

14 Morel, pp. 145–54; Peter Kay Jankrift, *Leprose als Streiter Gottes* (Münster, 1996), pp. 58–3.

15 Morel, pp. 146, 148, 151 and 154.

16 Cambrai, *Médiathèque municipale*, MS 466, fol. 1 r. Map reproduced in Prawer, (see note 8 above), p. 227.

donations of that period. The beneficiaries are indeed called the *frates leprosi Deo servientibus* ("brothers with leprosy serving God"), *fraternitas* ("the confraternity"), or *conventus infirmorum* ("the convent of the infirm") dwelling in the church or "the house" of St Lazarus, outside the walls of Jerusalem.[17] Together they form the nucleus, or center, of this religious community.

The statutes show clearly that its definition is linked to an organization quite different from that found by comparison in the Hospital of St John. As leprosy was considered to be incurable, the expression of the ideal of assistance had a specific form. When someone suffering from leprosy found shelter inside the monastery of St Lazarus, it was not to be a temporary arrangement as it would have been for patients in the other, more conventional healing hospitals. The person with leprosy was considered to be permanently sick, and thus would become a perpetual member of the community. This important difference which set this order apart from other hospitaller orders is well expressed in the image on the order's seal. For such institutions, seals often present on one side an image that serves as a sort of self-representation, and on the other side an image containing iconography linked to its religious devotion. As an example, the Order of St John did not regularly represent the poor or the sick it cared for in seal images. On the reverse of most seals, a body lying before a tabernacle is found, covered from head to foot by a shroud, and so can be seen more as a symbol of Christ's entombment, or universally of death expected by all humankind. The self-representation of the brothers of St John shows on the Seal's obverse side a monk kneeling before the Holy Cross.[18] The obverse side of the seal of the Order of St Lazarus depicts a man with leprosy whose face is disfigured, holding a clapper. The reverse has a portrait of Lazarus of Bethany, the first Bishop of Marseille (Fig. 13.1).[19] His cult is documented in the Rule, where he is mentioned as a holy patron of the house, a position he held in many leprosaria throughout medieval Europe.[20] It is significant that the obverse seal image is of a diseased person, suggesting an identity with the sufferer and the self-representation, the main focus of the order.

---

17 Marsy, pp. 123–48.

18 Edward J. King, *The Seals of the Order of Saint John of Jerusalem* (London, 1932), pp. 9–10.

19 The seal image is reproduced in Prawer, p. 495; Charles-Simon Clermont-Ganneau, "Un sceau des croisades appartenant à la léproserie de Saint-Lazare de Jérusalem," *Recueil d'archéologie orientale*, 4 (1901), 242–6.

20 Françoise Bériac, *Histoire des lépreux au Moyen Age* (Paris, 1988), pp. 101–10.

13.1a   Seal of the Lepers of St Lazarus of Jerusalem, reverse (Charles-Simon Clermont-Ganneau, "Un sceau des croisades appartenant à la léproserie de Saint-Lazare de Jérusalem", in Recueil d'Archéologie orientale, 4, 1901, Plate 1. 242–6).

13.1b   Drawing by Joshua Prawer (from *Histoire du royaume latin de Jerusalem*, Paris, 1975, p. 495).

It was the case. According to the Rule, the sick had to make the three monastic vows: chastity, poverty and obedience to a master.[21] They were full-time brothers who slept in a specific dormitory, separated from those healthy brothers who assisted them, and from the pilgrims or poor seeking shelter for the night.[22] But most important, they were to participate in all the religious activities of the monastery. This meant that they were to take part in performing the offices of the Church and to respect all the usual liturgical hours of a regular religious community from the canonical hours of matins to compline. If they were too sick to move, the healthy brothers were to help them on their way to Mass, or else a weekly procession came to the dormitory so that all the community could pray.[23]

Hagiography and the beliefs concerning conceptions of leprosy combined to form a unique, single religious expression. The devotion to Lazarus insisted on a belief in resurrection, on patience and prayer to lead from sin to salvation, from death to life.[24] Following in the saint's footsteps, the sick hoped to pass from an earthbound sickness into a state of celestial health. Through prayer and frequent fasting, the community looked forward to the afterlife as they waited and listened for Christ's call.[25] All the brothers prayed for the salvation of their souls, and also for their predecessors whose names were inscribed in the calendar of the convent and remembered annually in the offices. Further, the Office of the Dead was to be recited each Monday in the monastery's cemetery.[26] The central organization of this community was thus comparable to that of a traditional monastery. The isolation and the social destitution imposed by what was believed to be a contagious and incurable sickness were turned into a spiritual reclusion, providing a self-contained life behind the walls of the monastery in the form of religious vows. What was the case for brothers with leprosy also applied to healthy members of the order. The treatment employed in this setting had little to do with medical care. The statutes only allude to the help they were to provide the sick in dressing, eating and going to church.[27] The brothers committed themselves to a life-long service of charity, service being a synonym for penance and salvation as part of an altruistic zeal linked to a common conception of assistance in the Middle Ages.[28] That is, to take care of those with leprosy was to serve them as if they were Christ's representatives, thereby sacrificing oneself as Christ did for others in *imitatio Christi*. This was indeed a

---

21 Morel, p. 144.

22 Ibid., pp. 146–8.

23 Ibid., p. 152.

24 Touati (see note 11 above), pp. 380–85.

25 Morel, p. 150.

26 Ibid., p. 151.

27 Ibid., p. 146.

28 François-Olivier Touati, "Les groupes de laïcs dans les hôpitaux et les léproseries au Moyen Age," in *Les mouvances laïques des ordres religieux, troisième colloque international du CERCOR* (Saint-Etienne, 1996), 151–75.

widespread concept through most of Western medieval civilization.[29] In Jerusalem, there are outstanding examples recorded. One twelfth-century chronicle tells of three pilgrims who took part in this in an especially penitential way by performing those functions typically disseminated through hagiographic models. Carrying the leprosy patients unable to move, feeding them and washing their feet daily after Mass are the most popular examples. This way to holy redemption was especially followed by the brothers of the Order of St Lazarus, just as bearing of arms would have been by a Templar, or aiding needy pilgrims would have been by a knight of the Hospital Order of St John.[30]

Crusading was both physical and metaphysical.[31] This physical and spiritual practice was regarded as having special meaning since it took place in the Holy Land, near the Holy Sepulchre. Delaruelle and Dupront have written at length, analyzing concepts and ideals linked to the crusades. In the twelfth century, ideas were associated with the notion of religious conversion, of a union with Christ in a very eschatological way. Going to the Holy Land and fighting for it was associated with a promise of salvation, and provided a plenary indulgence. To these military and religious goals were added philanthropy and care of the sick, an activity adopted by many of the institutions concerned.[32] If "crusade society was a society of accomplishment," the leprosy sufferers of Jerusalem played their part in it.[33]

References to parallel military functions in other hospitaller orders are to be found in documents of the end of the twelfth century. The Hospital of St John mixed both activities, fighting for the faith and caring for the sick.[34] However, this was not the case of the House of St Lazarus. There was no mention of brothers, either sick or healthy, bearing arms this early. On the contrary, the similarities with a more traditional monastic model are emphasized in the regulations of the time. The Rule required that all brothers were to remain behind the walls of the monastery in prayer. The only member allowed to go out was the master, and then only to tend to the administration and affairs of the community. All were required to be, as the text goes, "one heart and one soul stretching towards God."[35] The brethren played their part in doing good deeds and acts of faith in Jerusalem. They did not take part in active military campaigning. They are *frates leprosi* ("brothers with leprosy"), not *milites leprosi* ("knights with leprosy").

---

29 François-Olivier Touati, "Lèpre et société au Moyen Age," *Sources – travaux historiques*, 13 (1988), 3–30.

30 Benjamin Z. Kedar "Gerard de Nazareth, a neglected twelfth century writer in the Latin East," *Dumbarton Oaks Papers*, 37 (1983), 72.

31 Etienne Delaruelle, *L'idée de croisade au Moyen Age* (Torino, 1980); Alphonse Dupront, *Le mythe de croisade* (Paris, 1997).

32 Barber, *The Military Orders.*

33 Dupront, *Le mythe de croisade*, p. 1 435.

34 Alan Forey, "The Militarisation of the Hospital of Saint John," *Studia Monastica* 26 (1984), 75–89; Alain Demurger, *Chevaliers du Christ – les ordres religieux-militaires au Moyen Age* (Paris, 2002), pp. 41–3.

35 Morel, p. 152.

One may wonder whether that association may not have been made possible by the end of the twelfth century through the example of King Baldwin IV, commonly known as the "leper king."[36] All the chronicles cite him as an example. Although the first signs of his illness had been noted when he was just 9, he was only diagnosed as having leprosy after he was crowned in 1174. His reign lasted until he died in 1185. During that time, he played a role in the government of the kingdom, leading his army into battle and sometimes commanding while lying on a stretcher. To his last breath, he managed to maintain the authority of the monarchy and the integrity of the kingdom.

Does this special case of a leprosy patient still living among others in society suggest a novel tolerance towards the disease? Interpretation must be done very carefully. Baldwin IV was the king. His segregation or his renouncing the crown would have led to a political disaster since he was the only heir of his father Amaury I. The barons of the Holy Land were aware of this dynastic fragility. His maintenance on the throne was more than necessary to hold together the unity of the Latin Kingdom of Jerusalem. However, the issues were still highly complex. For instance, the reaction of Pope Alexander III was definite. The disabled body of the new king was considered a sign of the sins of the Christians. He was the microcosm symbolizing his reign, so his leprosy represented the division of feudal society in the Holy Land.[37] His sickness was taken very seriously. The fact that he remained in society must be seen within a political and also a psychological context. No doubt, if he had not been king, he would have joined the brothers of St Lazarus behind the walls outside the Holy City. By contrast, Eustache III Grenier, heir of the Lordship of Cesarea, entered the leprosarium of Jerusalem some time between 1149 and 1160, leaving the political duty to his younger brother, Hugh Grenier.[38] It may be inferred that Baldwin also considered doing this by the fact that the king's entourage made donations to the leprosarium during the last years of his life. By 1183, the family of Constable Humphrey of Toron had given an annual rent on the customs of Acre.[39] As well, and especially revealing, in 1185 the regent Raymond III of Tripoli granted another rent in order to become a *frater exterior* of the monastery. This meant that he wished to sustain it financially from the outside by making regular donations. But he also promised to enter the order as a healthy brother, should he ever decide to finish out his life by taking religious vows.[40] Two events prevented him from doing so before his death: the battle of Hattîn, from which he managed to escape, and the conquest of Jerusalem by Saladin in 1187. Baldwin IV himself had not made donations to sustain the Order of St Lazarus as did the noblemen of the

---

36 Hamilton, *The Leper King.*

37 M.G. Pegg, "Le corps et l'autorité: la lèpre de Baudouin IV," *Annales ESC*, 45 (1990), 265–87.

38 Marsy, p. 136; Hans E. Mayer, "The Wheel of Fortune: Seignorial Vicissitudes under Kings Fulk and Baldwin III of Jerusalem," *Speculum*, 65 (1990), 876; John L. Lamonte, "The Lords of Cesarea in the Period of the Crusades," *Speculum*, 22 (1947), 148–9.

39 Marsy, pp. 146–7.

40 Ibid., p. 147.

court. However, this was the institution to which the court obviously associated him as he was slowly dying, the place where more common leprosy sufferers like him usually remained.

The way that the *Livre au Roi*, the jurisdictional code drawn up between 1198 and 1205, considered the common case of leprosy was unequivocal. If any nobleman developed leprosy, he was to join the Order of St Lazarus. His wife was to enter a convent, and their property should be bestowed upon their heirs or their lord. The text specified that substitutes for the sick man's military obligations should be found.[41] The orientation of the law was toward strict segregation. Attitudes to Baldwin IV do not appear as a sign of tolerance valid for all eastern Latin society in the twelfth century. Would his example have any influence on the existence of *milites leprosi* that appear some fifty years after his death? To answer this, the thirteenth-century evolution of the order must be considered and compared with the order's role in the century before.

The ideal of "the city of Jerusalem" was a spiritual goal, which had become a political and physical reality for almost a century since its conquest in 1099. When the city was lost in 1187, local organizations were to be re-established within the walls of Acre, to where most representative institutions of the Latin East had withdrawn after the Third Crusade conquered the city. As may be seen on maps found in the works by Matthew Paris in the second half of the thirteenth century, all these institutions had a place pictured in the urban landscape.[42] Among them was the House of St Lazarus. Some changes to it may be noted. The convent is still on the edge of the town, but not outside the walls. The different sketches show it as part of the city's fortifications. Moreover, the legend on the map alludes to a different function. It reads "house of the knights of St Lazarus going to war" (*Domus militum Sancti Lazari qui sunt in bello perambuli*).

These knights appear for the first time in documents giving notice of military engagements at the end of the first half of the thirteenth century. In 1244, Robert, the Patriarch of Jerusalem, sent a letter to the West which gave a detailed account of the recent battle between Ascalon and Gaza. There, the Egyptian army circled the Christian troops, killing all the Franks that day. Among them were members of military orders, organized into different sections. The main part of the army was formed of 312 Templars, 325 Hospitallers and the Turcoples. But the patriarch also alluded to a novelty. For the first time, a force formed of *de domo Sancti Lazari milites leprosi* ("knights with leprosy from the House of St Lazarus") is mentioned. They are added to the general enumeration of the victims of this encounter, known as the battle of la Forbie in the chronicles. This letter was copied from one court to

---

41 "Le Livre au Roi," in *Recueil des Historiens des Croisade: Lois*, 2 vols (Paris, 1841–43), 1:636–7.

42 Suzanne Lewis, *The Art of Matthew Paris in the Chronica Majora* (Cambridge, 1987), pp. 350, 360.

another, thus the knowledge that the House of St Lazarus existed among crusading forces was spread.[43]

Chronicles were indeed a means of relaying and spreading the latest news about events overseas. For example, in the Kingdom of England, the Benedictine monk and chronicler Matthew Paris alluded to the heavy losses of the Seventh Crusade. From 1248, King Louis IX of France was present in the East. After taking back the city of Damietta, he led his army in a march toward Cairo in order to confront the Sultan. To get to Cairo, the army first needed to take the stronghold of Mansourah, which was protected by the Bahr es-Seghir canal. When Louis was told that a ford across the canal existed, he undertook to make his whole army cross the water. In the force's vanguard was his brother Robert, Count of Artois, along with the military orders of the Temple and the Hospital. They were ordered to wait for the rest of the army before beginning the siege of the city. But the count preferred to rely on the effect of a surprise attack. Along with the other knights, he rushed toward the city. He devastated a military encampment before the city, but would not wait any longer, as was advised by the master of the Templars. He led the forces inside a city that was fortified and prepared to resist. By taking full advantage of the narrow streets, the Mameluks managed to kill all the crusaders, trapped as they were by barricades. In this vanguard were many famous crusaders and French noblemen, as well as the troops assembled by the Templars. According to Matthew Paris's chronicle, the Order of the Hospital, the Teutonic Order and "Brothers of St Lazarus" (*fratres Sancti Lazari*) fought alongside each other.[44] This is solid evidence that again in a military action they are included among general military units in the Latin States of the East.

This is also confirmed in Jean de Joinville's chronicle about the crusade of St Louis. He described almost from day to day the activities of the army overseas, as well as the king's intention to fortify most of the strongholds of the Latin East before going back to France. Between 1252 and 1253, the army was encamped in front of the city of Jaffa. At that time, while the military orders were present to give protection, the city walls were rebuilt. This text gives the most detailed account of the Brothers of St Lazarus. They were under the command of a master. While "holding no precise rank in the host," the master "would do as he wished." In one incident recorded by Joinville, those knights left without the king's permission to scavenge for booty, and fell into an ambush. The Saracens would have killed them all if Templar and Hospitaller knights, led by Joinville himself, had not come along to rescue the four of them that survived the Saracens' attack.[45]

These chronicled descriptions confirm the presence of soldiers of St Lazarus within the crusading army by the second half of the thirteenth century. But one question comes to mind: were they always leprosy sufferers, as the account of Gaza

---

43 MGH SS 32:177.

44 Matthew Paris, *Chronica Majora*, 7 vols (London, 1872–83), 5:196; Matthew Paris, *Historia Anglorum*, 3 vols (London, 1866–1869), 3:84.

45 Jean de Joinville, *Vie de Saint Louis,* ed. J. Monfrin (Paris, 1995), pp. 267–9.

described it in 1244? No precise details were given in other chronicles. Yet there is a petition presented to Pope Innocent IV in 1253 by the Brothers of St Lazarus that alluded to the fact that all their forces, along with the master, had lately been killed. By custom, the chapter elected a brother with leprosy as their master, and there now being no more sick brothers among the members of the community, they asked for permission to choose a master from among the healthy ones.[46] So, from these documents, there obviously had been sick brothers on the battlefield, at least from 1244 to 1253. For nine years, the crusading military forces clearly included leprosy patients. The lack of fighting power in the Holy Land, and the inability of the feudal host to mount an effective defense of the Latin East by the second half of the thirteenth century, may be presented as the reason behind this exception to the segregation noted in most common cases.[47] But how was this accepted? It can be inferred that this hint of tolerance had its limits. In 1253, the Brothers of St Lazarus in St Louis's army had "no specific place" in the army. Thus they were not considered regular and stable military troops. Instead, they composed an additional, maybe occasional, fighting force. A possible role as military scouts has been suggested by Jankrift.[48] This fact may illustrate the reaction of the rest of the army: the sick were accepted when they were far away and not intermingling with others. They had no part in the permanent organization of the crusading army. They were part of it, but were yet set aside, just as leprosaria were set outside medieval cities while remaining included within the social and religious life of the city.

The statutes and rules relating to other military orders clearly allude to this fact.[49] In no way did their regulations consider as acceptable the presence of a brother suffering from leprosy among the rest of the community. Those regulations date from the second half of the thirteenth century, at a time when the Order of St Lazarus was recognized as a military order. In regulations of the Hospital of St John of 1270, such a case of a brother with leprosy is to be resolved by an imposed isolation. He is to be fed perpetually, but set apart from the others. He was not considered to be a member of the community any longer, since it was ordered that he had to renounce his religious habit.[50] By 1265, the Rule of the Templars also included an additional element concerning such a case. It stated that, after giving up his habit, the brother with leprosy could either be isolated from the others, or he could enter of the Order of St Lazarus.[51] No leprosy patients were accepted as brothers in the other military orders. Instead, they were encouraged to gather together in a specific one. The Rule of the Temple states they must to go to the House of St Lazarus and therefore live

---

46 Vatican City, *Archivio Segreto Vaticano*, Reg. Vat. 22, fol. 230v; summary in Elie Berger, ed., *Registres d'Innocent IV*, 4 vols (Paris, 1884–1921), 3:153.

47 Marshall, *Warfare in the Latin East (1191–1291)*, p. 56.

48 Jankrift, *Leprose als Streiter Gottes*, p. 84.

49 Indrikis Sterns, "Care of the Sick Brothers by the Crusader Orders in the Holy Land," *Bulletin of the History of Medecine*, 57 (1983), 43–69.

50 Joseph-Marie-Antoine Delaville Le Roulx, ed., *Cartulaire général de l'Ordre des Hospitaliers de Saint-Jean de Jérusalem*, 4 vols (Paris, 1894–1906), 3:229.

51 Henri de Curzon, ed., *La Règle du Temple* (Paris, 1886), pp. 239–40.

according to its own Rule (*que il se rende a saint ladre, et que il preigne l'abit de frere de saint ladre*).

But is the link between Holy War and leprosy always valid? The fact that reference to leprosy is lacking in most of the documentation concerning the order calls for prudence. *Milites leprosi* there certainly were. But were all the knights leprosy sufferers? A close consideration of the diffusion of the first text alluding precisely to this point brings an unexpected answer. The letter mentioned before, sent by the Patriarch of Jerusalem to Europe and reporting on the battle of la Forbie in 1244, has been widely copied, given that there are many extant copies conserved in archives today. However, by comparing documents, it becomes clear that all copies were not based on the same original. As it sometimes happens, a word was omitted, and this omission has later been repeated. There were not only knights with leprosy, but to be more accurate, there were knights with leprosy and healthy knights. The original letter goes as follows: *de domo Sancti Lazari milites leprosi et sani.*[52] The Latin words *et sani* were forgotten. So forgotten, too, were the healthy brothers of St Lazarus.

Earlier in the twelfth century, statutes of the House of St Lazarus alluded to two categories of brothers: the leprosy patients, and the healthy brothers who assisted them. This bipartite division was still legitimate by the thirteenth century. Just as before, each one had a different role in the same institution, sharing a common name. A detailed account is documented in additions to the first Rule. These additions concern the House of St Lazarus, "as it is established in Acre," that is, from 1240 onward, when the master of the Templars authorized the Lazarites to built their convent in the quarter of Montmusard.[53] They may be dated in the last third of the thirteenth century, since they allude to a more clearly defined hierarchy, which can also be found in other documents dating from that period.[54]

These additions to the Rule clearly describe what it meant to be a Knight of the Order of St Lazarus for that time.[55] In order to enter the order, one was to be free from all social ties (marriage and debts). He then pronounced the vows of poverty, chastity and obedience, swearing on the Gospels to respect the Augustinian Rule and the master's authority. Precise details concerning behavior in military engagements were also given.[56] On all occasions, the Lazarite was to wear a cape with a green cross on the shoulder, which was the distinctive crusading sign then used by the order. Underneath, he was to wear a surplice with a belt. However, on the battlefield he was to change it for a coat of armor and a shield. The cape was then to be replaced by a leather coat. Attached shoes were indicated for those on horseback. This was

---

52 MGH SS 32:177, note g; MGH SS 31/1:516.

53 Marsy, p. 156.

54 Rafaël Hyacinthe, *L'Ordre de Saint-Lazare de Jérusalem au Moyen Age* (Millau, 2003), pp. 38–46.

55 Morel, pp. 125–45; Jankrift, *Leprose als Streiter Gottes*, pp. 121–50.

56 Morel, pp. 138–43.

the exact description of the "brothers of St Lazarus going to war" (*Domus militum Sancti Lazari qui sunt in bello perambuli*).

Other details are crucial in reconstructing the status of a knight of St Lazarus for that time. When swearing on the Gospels, the future Lazarite also had to testify that he had no disease, either hidden or visible, to be fully able to fight. At the end of the ceremony, he swore to serve the Holy Cross as well as the sick.[57] Thus it seems that the new initiate could not have been a leprosy patient. He was a healthy member, fighting for the faith, and caring for his sick brothers. These additions to the Rule deal only with an extension of the role of healthy brothers. The others were not mentioned in this more defined view of military action. The brothers with leprosy were only alluded to in the charge to assist the sick, entrusted to the healthy brother who was to be responsible for two beds, one for himself and one for a brother with leprosy, whom he was to assist when not at war.[58] Nothing else was said about welfare, which probably remained the same as it was in the twelfth century. This amended Rule did not replace the older one, as it only seems to clarify it, adapting it to changed circumstances that mark a later phase in the evolution of the order. Indeed, there are no other certain details concerning the inner life of the Order of St Lazarus in these additions, as if the military expansion was the only significant change to be taken into account.

How, then, did the Lazarites actually combine warfare and welfare? At the end of these additions to the Rule, there is an important text addressed to the brothers, recommending that for further guidance they were to refer to the Rules of the Templars and of the Order of the Hospital of St John.[59] The codification was limited, but the principle to imitate the other military and hospital orders was clearly established. The author of these additions was probably someone who did not belong to the order but may have been an external ecclesiastical official. It may have been the Bishop of Acre himself, since the order depended upon his authority until 1262.[60] This unknown author thus authorized the Lazarites to follow the examples of other crusading orders. Except for the Templars, all crusader military orders chose the Augustinian Rule which was most suited to a monastic life within the secular world. Additions appropriate to the aim of each order were then incorporated into the Rule. For regulations concerning military engagement, the Templar Rule was most influential. The Hospitaller Rule was the model for regulations concerning assistance. By the thirteenth century, each institution had its own Rule, often inspired by these two sources.[61] And so, in 1198, when an hospital in Acre became the military Teutonic Order, it adopted regulations taken from both the Templar and

---

57 Ibid., pp. 143–44.

58 Ibid., p. 139.

59 Ibid., pp. 144–5.

60 Vatican City, *Archivio Segreto Vaticano*, Reg. Vat. 26, fol. 53v; summary in Jean Guiraud, ed., *Registres d'Urbain IV*, 4 vols (Paris, 1901–1906), 2:60.

61 Demurger, *Chevaliers du Christ*, pp. 81–90.

the Hospitaller Rules.[62] According to their Rule, the Lazarites were also authorized to adopt regulations as needed.

Scarce but interesting information comes from making a comparison of these two principal Rules which echo each other. The Templars were to live a religious and a military life. When not praying in their convent – that is, when they were on campaign – they were to observe a strict discipline under a marshal's orders. The Lazarite Rule mentions such an officer as being the one responsible for obedience among the brethren.[63] It thus may be inferred that the brothers of St Lazarus could then also form a united force within the Latin armies for raiding expeditions under the authority of this officer designated to lead the campaign. However, it should be noted that since 1244, Christian military strategy had been based more on mounting an effective defense of the territory. In order to guard the frontiers, fortresses and towers were maintained. From this defensive perspective, a *tur Seynt Lazare* ("St Lazarus's Tower") is mentioned in Caesarea by 1265, where the Lazarites had maintained a house since 1234.[64] Here, they probably formed the regular garrison of this tower stronghold, being responsible, according to its purpose, for defensive duties. Lazarite headquarters in Acre were also rebuilt after 1257 so as to be a fortification for the kingdom's capital city.[65] At one point during St Sabas's Civil War, the master of the Templars even found refuge there, since it was the only place where he supposedly was completely protected from "engines of war."[66]

When not on campaign, the Lazarites were to care for their sick brothers as they had done in the twelfth century. This parallels the Rule of the Hospitallers, which states that some brothers had to stay permanently in the monastery in order to welcome and care for the needy. The healthy brothers of the Lazarite community were probably divided into two groups, with some carrying arms and the others caring for the sick with leprosy. The care of the sick was still part of the order's founding principle and its main reason for existence. Even if the Lazarites were regarded as a military order by the late thirteenth century, they were still hospitallers who cared for the sick. In 1248, the Italian crusader Stephen of Salerno is recorded to have donated a rent to the order because his son was to join it. This donation was not a military appointment, but given to provide a shelter for the son, who had contracted leprosy, forcing him to remain in the Holy Land as a sick Lazarite.[67] Two other

---

62 Indrikis Sterns, "The Teutonic Order in the Holy Land," in K.M. Setton, ed., *History of the Crusades*, 6 vols (Madison, WI, 1969–87), 5:323–4.

63 Morel, p. 149.

64 Marsy, p. 154; Henri-Victor Michelant and Gaston Raynaud, eds, *Itinéraires à Jérusalem et descriptions de la Terre sainte* (Geneva, 1882), p. 190.

65 Vatican City, *Archivio Segreto Vaticano*, Reg. Vat. 25, fol. 98; summary in Charles Bourel de la Roncière, ed., *Registres d'Alexandre IV*, 3 vols (Paris, 1902–53), 2:722.

66 Gaston Raynaud, ed. "Chronique du Templier de Tyr," in *Gestes des Chiprois* (Geneve, 1887), 153.

67 Marsy, p. 158.

donations (in 1261 and 1264) were addressed to those *leprosi Sancti Lazari.*[68] The documentary evidence is very descriptive. Instead of recording the transformation of a community of people with leprosy, the statutes deal with additional military obligations for those who assisted them. From at least that point in time on, the order was considered a military and hospitaller institution, but not an order composed only of *milites leprosi.* They had existed previously, but were not taken into account in this later redefinition.

By the end of the thirteenth century, the Order of St Lazarus had become an institution expressing several ideals at the same time. In addition to a devotion to people with leprosy, it had added a military involvement in the crusades. These ideals exist parallel to one another, not combined. This duality is expressed well in papal documents concerning the establishment of the order in the West dating from 1253 onward. The network of Lazarite houses that then began to spread across Europe represents not only a new warfare institution dedicated to the crusades, but also a new institutional element in the treatment of leprosy. This well illustrates the double nature that the Order of St Lazarus was to have until the fall of Acre in 1291.[69]

By the thirteenth century, thoughts and ideals had indeed changed along with the situation in the East. The "Holy Land" as an ideal had by then more to do with the notion of "Holy War" than with the fundamental ideal of becoming sanctified through doing good deeds beside the walls of the "Holy City." By then, this had been lost. More than being just a pilgrimage, crusading became a very sophisticated institution.[70] The Order of St Lazarus of Jerusalem adapted itself to social expectations and requirements.

Long after the loss of the Holy Land, the Order of St Lazarus clearly had not created as lasting an impression on society's imagination as did the stories of glorious deeds associated with the Templars and Hospitallers. By the eighteenth century, an official Lazarite historiographer, aware of the double existence and function of the order, took upon himself to make of it a unique, general attribution of his institution and thereby giving it greater presence. As he transcribed a text dated 1155, he added the word *milites* ("knight") to the word *leprosi* ("person with leprosy").[71] Added or forgotten words are thus responsible for the diffusion of what was to later become the myth of *milites leprosi* ("knights with leprosy") in the Holy Land. But this is a myth of modern times, and its diffusion must be understood within its proper context.[72]

---

68 Henri-François Delaborde, ed., *Chartes de Terre sainte provenant de l'abbaye de Notre-Dame de Josaphat* (Paris, 1880), p. 109; Delaville Le Roulx, ed. *Cartulaire général de l'Ordre,* 3:91.

69 Hyacinthe, *l'Ordre de Saint-Lazare,* pp. 47–92.

70 Christopher T. Maier, *Preaching the Crusades* (Cambridge, MA, 1994), p. 5.

71 Reprinted as Gautier de Sibert, *Histoire de l'Ordre militaire et hospitalier de Saint-Lazare de Jérusalem* (Geneva, 1983).

72 For modern commentary, see also Ray Bagdonas, *The Military and Hospitaller Order of Saint Lazarus of Jerusalem: Its History and Work* (Nottingham, 1989); Paul Bertrand de la Grassière, *L'Ordre militaire et hospitalier de Saint-Lazare de Jérusalem* (Paris, 1960); Lino Conti, *Lazaro sancti Lazari* (Pisa, 1999).

The history of the Order of St Lazarus and the special place granted to those with leprosy can be seen as a reflection of then contemporary ideals of *imitatio Christi* and Holy War. Thus the order represents an outstanding example of the Middle Ages' commitment to its religious convictions.

Chapter 14

The Infirmaries of the Order of the Temple in the Medieval Kingdom of Jerusalem

Piers D. Mitchell

Introduction

Current knowledge of the role of the hospital during the crusades and the resulting Frankish states in the Latin East is sketchy at best. While some fascinating discoveries have recently taken place regarding the hospitals of the Order of St John,[1] many other institutions remain poorly understood. Although it seems that most *hospitalia* in the Frankish states just provided accommodation to pilgrims and the poor in a religious setting, some also provided medical care for the sick.[2] Apart from the Order of St John, three orders are known to have provided medical treatment. These were: the Order of St Mary of the Germans, the English Order of St Thomas of Canterbury and the multinational Order of the Temple. The hospital activities of these organizations are still obscure, and very little work has been written at all about this aspect of St Thomas and the Templars.

Hospitals in Europe underwent tremendous change between the eleventh and fourteenth centuries. Not only were much larger hospitals founded, but also the emphasis shifted away from merely preparing the soul of the patient for death to

---

1 Benjamin Z. Kedar, "A twelfth century description of the Jerusalem Hospital," in *The Military Orders*, Vol. 2, *Welfare and Warfare*, ed., Helen Nicholson (Aldershot, 1998), 3–26; Susan Edgington, "The Hospital of St. John in Jerusalem," in *Medicine in Jerusalem Throughout the Age,* ed. Zohar Amar, Efraim Lev and Joshua Schwartz (Tel Aviv, 1999), ix–xxv.

2 Jean Richard, "Hospitals and hospital congregations in the Latin kingdom during the first period of the Frankish conquest," in *Outremer: Studies in the History of the Crusading Kingdom of Jerusalem*, ed. Benjamin Z. Kedar, Hans E. Mayer and Raymond C. Smail (Jerusalem, 1982), 89–100; Monique Amouroux, "Colonization and the creation of hospitals: The eastern extension of western hospitality in the eleventh and twelfth centuries," *Mediterranean Historical Review*, 14 (1999), 31–43; Nicholas Coureas, "The provision of charity and hospital care on Latin Cyprus," *Epeteris: Annual Journal of the Cyprus Research Centre*, 27 (2001), 33–50.

include medical treatment intended to actually cure them.³ It is still far from clear exactly why, when and how these changes took place. It has been suggested that a major trigger for this change was the experience gained by Europeans who traveled to the Frankish states of the eastern Mediterranean and saw the hospitals there.⁴ After all, the Islamic *bimaristan* and the Byzantine *xenon* were hospitals where medical treatment was of fundamental importance.⁵

While studies of infirmaries such as those of the Order of the Temple are fascinating in their own right, they also play a much wider role in the study of the medieval hospital. It is only through understanding the function of the hospitals of the military orders in the Latin East that the evolution of the hospital in Europe can be appreciated.

The Order of the Temple

The armies of the First Crusade took Jerusalem in 1099, and the territories they seized were divided into states that lasted until they were conquered in the late thirteenth century.⁶ About twenty years after the Frankish states were established, a small group of knights (Fig. 14.1) vowed to protect pilgrims traveling to religious sites from robbers, wild animals and enemy raids.⁷ These were genuine risks in the Latin East. Certain chronicles mentioned how human corpses were often left to rot by the side of certain roads as other pilgrims were too afraid to stay there long enough to bury them.⁸

---

3   John Henderson, "The hospitals of late mediaeval and renaissance Florence: a preliminary survey," in *The Hospital in History*, ed. Lindsay Granshaw and Roy Porter (London, 1989), 63–92.

4   Timothy S. Miller, "The knights of Saint John and the Hospitallers of the Latin west," *Speculum*, 53 (1978), 709–33.

5   D.M. Dunlop, "Bimaristan: Early Period and Muslim East," in *Encyclopaedia of Islam*, 2nd edn, ed. Hamilton, A.R. Gibb, J.H. Kramers, E. Levi-Provençal, J. Schacht, B. Lewis and C. Pellat (Leiden, 1960), 1(2):1 223–4; Timothy S. Miller, *The Birth of the Hospital in the Byzantine Empire*, 2nd edn (Baltimore, MD, 1997).

6   Kenneth M. Setton, ed., *A History of the Crusade*, 6 vols (Vol. 1, Philadelphia, PA; Vols 2–6, Madison, WI; 1955–89). Hans E. Mayer, *The Crusades*,. trans. J. Gillingham, 2nd edn (Oxford, 1988). Jonathan S.C. Riley-Smith, *The Oxford History of the Crusades*, (Oxford, 1999).

7   Peter Partner, *The Knights Templar and their Myth* (Rochester, NY, 1987) pp. 1–23; Malcolm Barber, *The New Knighthood: A History of the Order of the Temple* (Cambridge, 1994); Anthony Luttrell, "The earliest Templars," in *Autour de la Première Crusade*, ed. Michel Balard, *Série Byzantina Sorbonensia*, 14 (Paris, 1996), 193–202.

8   Saewulf, "A reliable account of the situation of Jerusalem, 1101–13," in *Jerusalem Pilgrimage 1099–1185*, ed. and trans. John Wilkinson, Joyce Hill and William F. Ryan (London, 1988), 94–116; see p. 100.

Figure 14.1   A very early illustration of two Templar knights (Corpus Christi College MS 26, fol. 220r; Matthew Paris, *Historia Major*, Vol. 1, written at St Albans before 1253; reproduced with the permission of Corpus Christi College, Cambridge).

The Templars established their headquarters on land given to them by King Baldwin II in the southern part of the former Jewish temple complex in Jerusalem, and this explains how they acquired their name. Originally attached to the regular canons of the Holy Sepulcher, as their numbers grew they evolved into an independent order by the 1130s, following a Rule based on that of the Cistercian order.[9] By the thirteenth century there are thought to have been about 600 knights and 2 500 sergeants in the order in the Latin East. They built numerous castles and other fortifications at key

9   Judith M. Upton-Ward, *Rule of the Templars* (Woodbridge, 1992), p. 3.

locations in Frankish territory, contributed to the garrisons of some of the major cities in the Latin East, and also provided troops for the Frankish armies. The order established a number of commanderies in Europe, which supported the activities of the Knights Templar in the Frankish states by providing not only money and food, but also troops. The Templars are known to have founded infirmaries to treat the sick and wounded soldiers of the order, and it is these infirmaries that are the subject of this discussion.

Sources of Evidence

A number of crusader chronicles mention the trauma sustained in battle by soldiers such as the Templars[10]. Typical injuries include penetrating wounds from arrows and lances, blade injuries from swords and axes, crush injuries from maces or stone projectiles, and burns from combustible substances such as Greek fire.[11] These chronicles also mention how the initial treatment of wounds often took place on the battlefield itself.[12] After the battle, the wounded were transported back to appropriate treatment facilities for further care if required.

Occasionally, Frankish chronicles mention the Templars caring for their sick. *The Continuation of William of Tyre* was a contemporary Frankish history covering the years 1184–97. This mentioned in passing that in 1187, the Templar castle of La Fève in the Kingdom of Jerusalem kept its sick together in the same room,[13] suggesting that it functioned as some kind of infirmary. Although the only detailed records of Templar infirmary life concern the Kingdom of Jerusalem, others are known to have existed. Records mention two Templar infirmaries in the Commandery of England, and another in the Commandery of Aragon.[14] This suggests that other commanderies in Europe may well have provided such medical facilities. It is interesting to speculate

---

10 John of Joinville, *Histoire de Saint Louis: Jean Sire de Joinville*, ed. Natalis de Wailly (Paris, 1874); Oliver of Paderborn, "Historia Damiatina," in *Die Scriften des Kölner Domscholasters, Spätern Bischofs von Paderborn und Kardinal-Bischofs von Sabina Oliverus*, ed. H. Hoogeweg (Tübingen, 1894) ; Richard de Templo, *Itinerarium Peregrinorum et Gesta Regis Ricardi*, in *Rerum Britannicarum Medii Aevi Scriptores, or Chronicles and Memorials of Great Britain and Ireland During the Middle Ages*, ed. W. Stubbs, *Rolls Series*, 38(1) (London, 1864).

11 Piers D. Mitchell, "War injuries," in *Encyclopedia of the Crusades*, ed. Alan V. Murray (Santa Barbara, CA, forthcoming).

12 Ralph de Diceto, "Decani Lundonensis: Opera Historica," in *Rerum Britannicarum Medii Aevi Scriptores, or Chronicles and Memorials of Great Britain and Ireland During the Middle Ages*, ed. William Stubbs, 2 vols, *Rolls Series*, 68 (London, 1876), 2:80–81. Benjamin Z. Kedar, "A twelfth century description of the Jerusalem Hospital." in *The Military Orders: Welfare and Warfare*, ed. Helen Nicholson, Vol. 2 (Aldershot, 1998), 3–26.

13 Peter W. Edbury, ed., "Old French Continuation of William of Tyre," in The *Conquest of Jerusalem and the Third Crusade* (Aldershot, 1996), 33.

14 Thomas W. Parker, *The Knights Templar in England* (Tucson, AZ, 1963). Alan Forey, *The Templars in the Corona de Aragon* (London, 1973), pp. 292–3.

whether the Templar complexes possessed infirmaries in other major cities in the Latin East outside the Kingdom of Jerusalem, such as at Antioch and Tripoli. The long, thin shape of the Frankish states adjacent to the Mediterranean coast means that logistically, this would have made sense.

There is some evidence that the order owned medical books that may have been useful in the treatment of the sick and wounded in such an infirmary. When the Templars were dissolved in 1308, a catalog of the books and manuscripts owned by the order in Aragon was sent to its ruler, King James II.[15] This confirmed that the order possessed a copy of the *Chirurgia* of Theodoric Borgognoni, written not in Latin, but in the vernacular. Unfortunately, it was not specified whether this surgical book was actually for use in the order's infirmary in Aragon. However, the presence of this practical text on the treatment of weapon injuries, held by a military order, written in the local language which would increase its accessibility, does raise the possibility that it may have been for use in the infirmary there. It is unfortunate that comparable lists for other commanderies have not yet come to light, as they might demonstrate whether such a practice was more widespread.

The Rule of the order was divided into seven main sections that were written over a 150-year period. While no original twelfth- or thirteenth-century manuscripts of the entire text survive today, a nineteenth-century edition based on three original manuscripts is available.[16] Statutes and other records are very illuminating with regards to the architectural and functional composition of its main centers. They show that the order's headquarters in twelfth-century Jerusalem contained: churches, a cloister, refectory, sleeping quarters, baths, granary, storehouses, armory, stables, garden and infirmary. The section discussing the infirmary is found in the hierarchical statutes, which date from *c.* 1165. The passage is entitled the "Retrais of the Infirmarer Brother," and gives valuable evidence for the diseases, treatments and general approach to healing employed there.[17]

Specific conditions mentioned that warranted admission to the infirmary ranged from weapon injuries to gastrointestinal diseases and fevers such as malaria.[18] Unlike other *hospitalia* run by military orders in the Latin East,[19] the Templar infirmary was not open to pilgrims or sick from the local population, but just to members of its own order. Templars who were sick for more than one day were obliged to enter the infirmary until well, with the exception of the master of the order, who could stay in his own room. On entry, the sick confessed their sins and received communion, while the dying received extreme unction from the chaplain. Most conditions were treated in the main infirmary hall, but those members with illnesses that made them

---

15 Joaquin L. Villanueva-Estengo, ed., *Viage Literario a las Inglesias de Espana*, 22 vols (Madrid, 1803–52), 5:200–202.

16 Henri de Curzon, ed., *La Règle du Temple* (Paris, 1886).

17 Ibid., pp. 138–41.

18 Examples of terms used in the Rule and referred to in this paper: weapon injury, *laide naffre*; diarrhoea, *malades de menoison*; vomiting, *geter par le goule*; quartan malaria, *malades de quartaine*; delirium, *frenesie*.

19 See note 2 above.

unsociable or disruptive were nursed separately in an adjacent room. Individuals kept separate included those with vomiting and diarrhea, those who were delirious, and those with serious wounds. Once patients had improved to the extent that "the other brothers could tolerate their presence,"[20] they were moved back into the main infirmary hall.

The majority of the statutes cover diet in the infirmary, and a number of foods were forbidden to the sick. The plant foods forbidden were lentils, beans and cabbage, while animal foods forbidden were beef, goat, mutton, veal, trout, eels and cheese. The infirmarian was to modify the diet of each patient by asking them what foods they could tolerate. It is interesting that the patients made this decision, rather than a medical practitioner recommending the diet based on his assessment of their humeral balance.

Drugs are mentioned in the statutes, and the master of the order was obliged to give the infirmarian "the means with which to buy the medicines they need."[21] Syrups made from sugar cane were given to those patients who asked for them. The infirmarian was in charge of the garden, but it is not clear from the statutes whether he grew medicinal plants for the preparation of drugs, or merely foods that were thought to be beneficial for the sick from a nutritional point of view.

Medical practitioners were contracted by the order to treat the sick in the infirmary. These were laymen, rather than members of the order. The master of each house was responsible for finding, "a doctor [le miege fesicie] for the sick brothers so that he may visit them and advise them on their illnesses."[22] The functions of the barber (bloodletting, shaving and basic surgery) were also mentioned in the Rule, although there is no specific reference to an actual barber in the statutes. The infirmarian could give permission for the patients to have their heads shaved or undergo bloodletting, but it was the master of the house who had to give permission before surgery could take place for a serious weapon injury. Bloodletting was performed both as a treatment for the sick in the infirmary and also as a prophylactic therapy to maintain the health of other members of the order. This was standard practice of the time in monasteries.[23] The healthy were allowed to eat three meals in total in the infirmary after undergoing bloodletting, but thereafter they had to return to eating the normal diet of the order. This suggests that the diet in the infirmary was perceived as more nourishing and desirable than that fed to the healthy members of the order.

Archeological evidence for the Jerusalem infirmary is limited, as it was founded on the same site as the Aqsa mosque. As this mosque is still in use today, excavation of the site is not permitted. However, past work from the early twentieth century identified a considerable amount of Frankish stonework that has allowed a basic plan

---

20 De Curzon, *La Règle du Temple*, p. 140.

21 Ibid., p. 141.

22 Ibid.

23 L. Gougaud, "La pratique de la phlébotomie dans les cloitres," *Revue Mabillon*, 14 (1924), 1–13.

of the Templar complex to be reconstructed.[24] Unfortunately, the exact location of the infirmary hall within this complex is not clear. Architecturally, Latin infirmaries were often built as vaulted halls, and in themselves often had few distinguishing features to suggest their function. However, they were almost invariably associated with a chapel or church. This was either located inside the infirmary or adjacent to it and connected by a door so that patients could hear religious services.[25] This means that the location of such an infirmary can usually be identified, as the plans of chapels are very distinctive. Chapels were typically constructed with an east–west alignment, and a rounded apse at the east end for the altar. However, a number of chapels and churches are known in the Jerusalem complex of the Templars. In consequence, on this occasion the position of the infirmary cannot be located accurately by this method.

When the headquarters of the order moved to the coastal city of Acre after Jerusalem was lost in 1187, the infirmary would have been located in the order's complex in the south-west of the old city. This site is marked on medieval maps of the city, such as that of Marino Sanuto.[26] While excavation of the nearby complex of St John is progressing well,[27] this is not possible for the Templars, as their complex has previously been razed to the ground. In consequence, knowledge of the finer details of the Templar infirmaries must still come from the textual evidence.

Excavation of human skeletal remains from Templar sites in the Latin East has provided good evidence for weapon injuries. This helps us to imagine the kinds of injuries that would have been sustained by those treated in the order's infirmaries. The castle of Jacobs Ford (Metzad 'Ateret) in Galilee contained a large number of Templar troops when Saladin destroyed it in 1179.[28] Research by the author has demonstrated a variety of sword injuries and arrow wounds in the Frankish garrison. Some were clearly fatal injuries, such as deep cranial wounds and limb amputations. Others were less severe, such as superficial sword blows. These less severe examples represent the kinds of wounds we would expect the survivors of such battles to sustain, later to be cared for in the infirmary.

---

24 Robert W. Hamilton, *The Structural History of the Aqsa Mosque: A Record of Archaeological Gleanings from the Repairs of 1938–1942* (London, 1949); Adrian J. Boas, *Jerusalem in the Time of the Crusades: Society, Landscape and Art in the Holy City Under Frankish Rule* (London, 2001), p. 91.

25 Roberta Gilchrist, *Contemplation in Action: The Other Monasticism* (London, 1995).

26 Oxford, Bodleian Library, MS Tanner 190 fol. 207r. *Secreta fidelium crucis*; early fourteenth-century manuscript.

27 Zeev Goldmann, *Akko in the Time of the Crusaders: The Convent of the Order of Saint John* (Akko, Israel, 1994).

28 Piers D. Mitchell, Yossi Nagar and Ronnie Ellenblum, "Weapon injuries in the 12th century crusader garrison of Vadum Iacob Castle, Galilee," *International Journal of Osteoarchaeology*, 16 (2006), 145–55.

The Infirmary in Context

In order to appreciate the evidence for the infirmaries of the Order of the Temple fully, they must be placed in context. This requires a comparison with medical practice and hospital institutions in the medieval world. Templar infirmaries shared many similarities with the monastic infirmaries of religious orders in twelfth- and thirteenth-century Europe. Typically, these monastic infirmaries were for those members of the order who became sick, and their main function was not to provide philanthropy to the local poor. Patients had to confess their sins on admission to the infirmary, and were then treated with a combination of spiritual care, nursing, dietary modification, medicines, bloodletting and surgery, where appropriate. The vital importance of the confession of sins prior to any medical treatment was highlighted in an edict of the Fourth Lateran Council of 1215.[29]

While basic medical care was coordinated by the infirmarian brother, local doctors from outside the order were employed to visit the sick if required. When a brother died in the infirmary, it was not regarded as a medical failure in any way, as it was presumed that they would have gone to heaven, which was a natural progression from their contemplative religious life on earth. This summary could apply just as easily to the Templars as to almost any large contemporary monastic community in Europe, such as the Benedictine abbey of Westminster in England.[30]

However, what sets the Templar infirmaries apart was their need to treat the wounded. Clearly, daily life in an Augustinian, Benedictine or Cistercian monastery in Europe did not usually include armed combat. This strongly contrasted with the military activities of the knights and brothers in the Order of the Temple. The order had special provision in their statutes regarding who should make the decision to operate on serious wounds. Such patients were nursed away from the main infirmary hall until their wounds had healed sufficiently. Those that remained delirious or whose wounds had an offensive odor due to infection were kept apart until they either started to improve or they died.

Influences on Medical Practice

Past assessment of the military orders in the Frankish states has concluded that the Salernitan School of Medicine was the dominant philosophy in determining medical practice in their hospitals.[31] This theory was largely based on comparison of the dietary advice in the *Regimen Sanitatis Salernitani* with that found in the statutes of

---

29 Norman P. Tanner, ed., *Decrees of the Ecumenical Councils*, 2 vols (London, 1990), 1:245.

30 Barbara F. Harvey, *Living and Dying in England, 1100–1540: The Monastic Experience* (Oxford, 1993).

31 Indrikis Sterns, "Care of the sick brothers by the crusader orders in the Holy Land," *Bulletin of the History of Medicine*, 57 (1983), 43–69; Jonathan S.C. Riley-Smith, *Hospitallers: The History of the Order of St. John* (London, 1999), p. 30.

these Eastern Latin orders. While it is true that there are many similarities between the approach found in the Salernitan regimen and the military orders' statutes, all medieval *regimen sanitatis* treatises are broadly similar, as they were all based on the fundamental teachings of Galen.[32] In consequence, it seems more sensible to look not for similarities, but for differences between these texts and the Eastern military order statutes to identify the dominant influences.

To investigate the influences on medical practice within Templar infirmaries the orders' statutes need to be compared with a number of dietary texts that specifically mention whether foods should be encouraged or forbidden to sick people. Many medieval texts on diet discuss the qualities of different foods, but only a few actually state whether particular foods should be encouraged or forbidden to the sick. However, four texts that do give such specific advice will be compared here.

The advice in the Templar statutes has been compared with two relevant medieval European works: that of the Regimen Sanitatis Salernitani[33] and also the appropriate sections of Theodoric Borgognoni's book of surgery.[34] To compare the Templar statutes with Eastern ideas on dietary modification, the recommendations were assessed against the dietary regimen of Maimonides, written in Cairo in the 1190s,[35] and the fourth-century Byzantine text of Oribasius.[36] Although this latter text was written before the medieval period, it exerted strong influence upon medical practice in the eastern Mediterranean for many centuries, especially among the local Greek-speaking medical practitioners who were widely employed by the crusaders.

There were 11 forbidden foods in the Templar regulations. Interestingly, there were no contradictions at all between the Templar dietary advice and that of either Eastern author, while there were three examples where the European texts flatly contradicted the advice in the Templar statutes. Both Theodoric and the Salerno regimen encouraged the sick to eat veal, while this was expressly forbidden in the Templar statutes. Similarly, the Salerno regimen encouraged the sick to eat trout, while the Templars forbade this in the infirmary. The dietary regulations in the statutes of the Order of the Temple appear to have more in common with the Eastern texts assessed here than with the European texts.

---

32 Pedro Gil-Sotres, "The regimens of health," in: Mirko D. Grmek, Bernardino Fantini and Antony Shugaar, eds, *Western Medical Thought from Antiquity to the Middle Ages* (Cambridge, MA, 1998) pp. 291–318; J. Mauron, "Food, mood and health: The mediaeval outlook," *International Journal for Vitamin and Nutrition Research*, 29 (1986), 9–26.

33 John Harington, ed., *The School of Salernum. Regimen Sanitatis Salerni* (Salerno, 1953).

34Theodorich Borgognoni, "The Surgery of Theodorich, ca. AD 1267," ed. and trans. Eldridge Campbell and James B. Colton, 2 vols (New York, 1955–60), 1:92–3.

35 Ariel Bar-Sela, Hebbel E. Hoff and Elias Faris, "Moses Maimonides' two treatises on the Regimen of Health," *Transactions of the American Philosophical Society*, 54 (1964), 3–50.

36 Oribasius of Pergamon, *Dieting for an Emperor: A Translation of Books 1 and 4 of Oribasius' Medical Compilations*, ed. and trans. Mark Grant (Leiden, 1997).

However, it could be argued that the rather limited number of examples where the advice contradicted might actually be coincidental, rather than proving a dominance of Eastern over Western ideas in the Templar infirmary. The absence of contradiction between statutes of this military order and advice in the Eastern medical texts might have occurred by chance. To reduce the likelihood of this possibility, it is necessary to substantially increase the sample size of military order statutes. Comparison between these four texts and all the relevant medical orders in the Frankish states (Order of the Temple, Order of St John and the Teutonic Order) should allow a conclusion to be reached with more confidence, given an increased sample size.

Such a study has been published recently.[37] The details of the regulations of each order are slightly different from each other, but none contradict any of the others. When amalgamated, this larger collection of dietary regulations has found agreement with Maimonides on 14 specific foods, and disagreement on none. There was agreement with Oribasius on 11 specific foods and also the safe time of year to eat pork, and disagreement on none. The Regimen Sanitatis Salernitani agreed with the military orders statutes on 13 specific foods, but crucially disagrees on 5, nor does it mention the safe time of year to eat pork. The advice in Theodorich is very similar to the Regimen Sanitatis Salernitani, but goes into a little less detail.

This larger study supports the preliminary findings using just the Templar regulations. The Eastern military orders' dietary regulations for the sick contradict the European texts on a number of points, but do not contradict the Eastern dietary texts on any of their recommendations. The individuals who drafted these dietary regulations for each of the Eastern military orders seem to have held opinions similar to those expressed in Eastern dietary texts such as Oribasius and Maimonides. One interpretation of this finding is that local Eastern medical practitioners may have exerted a significant influence upon treatment methods in Frankish infirmaries in the Latin East.

Conclusion

The infirmaries of the Templars were not the same as those already present in Europe in other religious orders. While they did follow the typical monastic infirmary pattern to a large degree, they did not just provide care for the soul together with basic medical interventions. It was important for the Templars to return their soldiers to health to continue their religious vocation, which was to defend pilgrims and the holy places from those they regarded as enemies. In consequence, it was not enough for the infirmary merely to provide spiritual care and relieve discomfort, as it was important to heal the soldier's wounds too. This fundamental step makes the Templar infirmaries distinctive. It took the medieval Latin hospital one step closer to the late medieval model, where medical treatment with the aim of curing the patient was just as important as medicine for the soul.

---

37 Piers D. Mitchell, *Medicine in the Crusades: Warfare, Wounds and the Medieval Surgeon* (Cambridge, 2004), pp. 99–103.

Chapter 15

The Benedictine Rule and the Care of the Sick: The Plan of St Gall and Anglo-Saxon England

Maria A. D'Aronco

The Rule and the Care of the Sick

Infirmorum cura ante omnia et super omnia adhibenda est, ut sicut revera Christo eis serviatur;[1] thus begins Chapter 36 of the *Regula Sancti Benedicti* dealing with the care of the sick. St Benedict in fact devotes this entire chapter, titled *De infirmis fratribus*, "to the care of sick brethren." Benedict is concerned not only with the moral aspect of treatment that sick should receive, "let them be served as if they were Christ Himself," but also indicates therapeutic measures, going into specific details. The sick should be allocated a separate area set aside for the purpose (*cella super se deputata*), and a God-fearing, diligent, solicitous nurse. The sick should not be denied baths when baths are deemed appropriate, and food should also be suited to their needs. The infirm were even to be allowed meat when necessary to build up their strength, although as soon as they are better, they must return to abstinence as usual.

As a matter of fact, no other Rule brings together in a single chapter such a complete program of treatment for the sick.[2] Although in the writings of St Basil, St Augustine, St Caesarius and others there is an occasional prescription and/or recommendation, it was St Benedict who tackled the subject with his customary wisdom, clear-headedness, sobriety and experience of the human heart. His affectionate Christian attention for the sick was in fact the inspiration behind an entire series of provisions that transformed Benedictine monasteries into some of the most important centers driving progress in medical science. Consequently, Benedictine monasteries became powerful driving forces for the advancement of medical science in Western Europe, and the most important centers in Europe

---

1 "The care of the sick should be put forward everything, let them be served as if they were Christ Himself."

2 See Anselmo Lentini, ed., *San Benedetto, La Regola* (Montecassino, 1980), p. 337. The *Regula Magistri* on the other side is very strict and somehow suspicious toward those monks who "claim" to be ill; see Chapters 69 and 70 in Adalbert de Vogüé, ed., *La Règle du Maître*, 3 vols (Paris, 1964), Introduction and 2:296–303.

where medicine was studied and practiced.[3] This role was of major significance in the diffusion of scientific knowledge, since European Western monasticism was essentially, and in large measure, Benedictine. Not only were libraries enriched with texts that reproduced classical medical knowledge, but the monasteries also provided appropriate places to care for the sick.

An outstanding example of how a Benedictine monastery organized the care of the sick is represented by a ninth-century document, the so-called Plan of St Gall. In it, the plan for a medium-sized monastery, of about eighty monks, is represented (Fig. 15.1).[4]

The Benedictine Monastery and its Health Provisions: The Plan of St Gall

The Plan was found in 1604 in the library of St Gall, whence its name.[5] However, its layout has nothing to do with the actual St Gall monastery or any other Carolingian monastery on the Continent. It is generally agreed that the Plan represents a blueprint for a Carolingian monastery that originated as part of a movement known as the Benedictine revival, fostered by St Benedict of Aniane in 816–17. Studies such as those by Bernard Bischoff have demonstrated that it is a copy made at Reichenau around 820 by Bishop Heito for Abbot Gozbert of St Gall.[6] However, the features of the monastery in the Plan are nowhere to be found in any Carolingian monasteries that were being organized according to Benedict of Aniane's instruction. Benedict's own monastery church at Inden near Aachen (Germany) bears neither the slightest structural resemblance to the imposing church of the Plan, nor many other particular features, both included and notably absent, are in agreement with Benedict of Aniane's reform. Examples include: a pretentious residence for the abbot with its own kitchen; an absence of lock-ups for disciplining monks (which, on the contrary, were customary in Carolingian monasteries); no provision for burying the monastery's dignitaries in the church (the provisions are only for burying the monks in the orchard), and there is no gate at the entrance which is kept free for the people. In particular, the absence of a gate is in sharp contrast to the program of Benedict of

---

3   John J. Contreni, "The Tenth Century: The Perspective from the Schools," in *Carolingian Learning, Masters and Manuscripts* (Aldershot, 1992), 379–87.

4   For full description and reconstruction of the Plan, see Walter Horn and Ernest Born, *The Plan of St Gall: A Study of the Architecture and Economy of, and Life in a Paradigmatic Carolingian Monastery*, 3 vols (Berkeley, CA, 1979) (hereafter cited as Horn and Born), and Lorna Price, *The Plan of St Gall in Brief* (Berkeley, CA, 1982).

5   St Gallen, Stiftsbiblliothek, cod. 1092.

6   Bernard Bischoff, "Die Entstehung des Sankt Galler Klosterplanes in palaögrapischer Sicht," in *Studien zum St. Galler Klosterplan* (St Gallen, 1962), 67–78, reprinted in his *Mittelalterliche Studien*, 3 vols (Stuttgart, 1966), 1:41–9; see esp. p. 42, note 7. See also Lawrence Nees, "The Plan of St Gall and the Theory of the Program of Carolingian Art," *Gesta*, 25 (1986), 1–8.

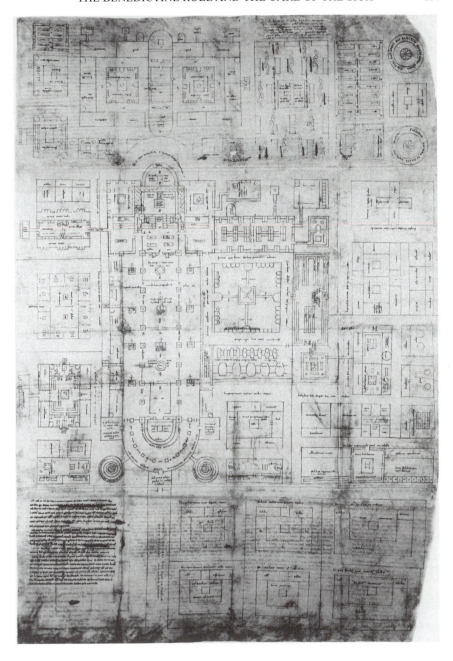

Figure 15.1   The Plan of St Gall (used by permission of the Stiftsbibliothek Skt. Gallen).

Aniane, who intended to introduce a strict ascetic life without any contact with the outside world. A final important point is this: nowhere in the Carolingian monasteries of Franconia are there churches arranged along a common axis, a characteristic that shows a rational attitude toward the monastic precinct's organization.[7]

The Structure of the Plan

The first feature that strikes the observer is the extreme lucidity and rationality of the layout (where the use and function of every building and part of it are carefully indicated), revealing an architectural consciousness of the highest order, carried out with a consistency unmatched in any other medieval cloister plan. The Plan can be divided roughly into two zones. First is the monastic precinct itself, composed of the church-cloister and the novitiate-infirmary complexes that exclude contact with the public. These buildings are therefore separated from the buildings in the second, western zone by continuous, unbroken walls, or fences. Buildings in this zone, such as the guests' and pilgrims' houses,[8] and the farm buildings are not strictly intended for use by the monks (see Fig. 15.2, nos 35–40). The main entrance to the monastery is located in this second zone as well. As Horn points out, this solution "established the monks on a site where they were neither exposed to contacts with worshipping laymen, nor to needless intercourse with their own serfs and workmen."[9]

---

7   For a thorough overview of the problem, see Nees, "The Plan of St Gall."

8   The house for distinguished guests, with private quarters for servants and horses, separate kitchen, cellar, bakery and brewery, is situated on the northern side of the church, below the abbot's residence (see Fig. 15.2, nos 10, 11 and 34); the hospice for pilgrims and the poor, with their own kitchen, bakehouse and brewhouse stands symmetrically on the south side of the church (see Fig. 15.2, nos 31 and 32).

9   Walter Horn, "On the Origins of the Medieval Cloister," *Gesta*, 12 (1973), 13–53, 47.

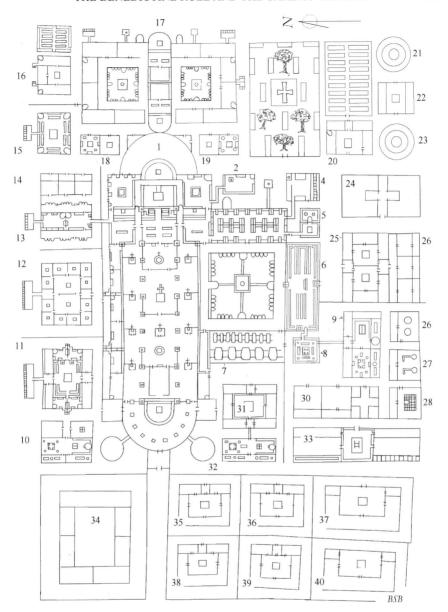

Figure 15.2   The Plan of St Gall with explanatory key (numbered according to W. Horn and E. Born, *The Plan of St Gall: A Study of the Architecture and Economy of, and Life in a Paradigmatic Carolingian Monastery*, 3 vols, Berkeley and Los Angeles, 1979; drawn from the plan by B.S. Bowers).

Key:

1. The church.
2. Annex for preparing sacred bread and oil.
3. Monks' dormitory above, warming room below.
4. Monks' privy.
5. Monks' bath and laundry.
6. Monks' refectory below, vestiary above.
7. Monks' cellar below, food stores above .
8. Monks' kitchen.
9. Monks' bakery and brewery.
10. Kitchen, cellar, bakery, and brewery for distinguished visitors.
11. Hostelry for distinguished visitors.
12. External school.
13. Abbot's house.
14. Abbot's kitchen, cellar and bath.
15. House for bleeding and purgation.
16. Physicians' house.
17. Novitiate and infirmary complex.
18. Infirmary kitchen and bath.
19. Novitiate kitchen and bath.
20. Gardener's house.
21. Goose yard.
22. House for keepers of chickens and geese.
23. Poultry yard.
24. Granary.
25. Workshops and artisans' lodgings.
26. Annex for artisans' lodgings.
27. Mill.
28. Mortars.
29. Drying kiln.
30. House for turners and coopers with threshing stage for grain for the brewery.
31. Hospice for pilgrims and the poor.
32. Kitchen, bakery, and brewery for pilgrims and the poor.
33. Cow stalls and stable with lodging for cowmen and stable boys.
34. House for the emperor's suite (identification uncertain).
35. Sheepfold and shepherds' lodging.
36. Goat stalls and lodging for goatherds.
37. Stable for dairy cows and lodging for dairymen.
38. House for farm workers and servants attached to the emperor's suite (uncertain, cf. no. 34).
39. Pigsty and lodging for swineherds.
40. Stable for mares and colts and lodging for stable boys.

The church-cloister complex, which makes up almost one third of the whole, stands in the medial zone of the Plan. At its center is an imposing church, which allows for direct access, on its southern side, to the monks' living quarters, with their own facilities, such as a furnace for heating the dormitories, privy, kitchen, baths and so on (see Fig. 15.2, nos 1–9). On its northern side, the church has the abbot's living quarters, kitchen and other special facilities (nos 13–14).

At the eastern end of the church-cloister complex is the novitiate-infirmary complex (see Fig. 15.3). This part of the Plan, although completely self-sufficient with respect to the monks' and abbot's living quarters, is closely connected to the inner monastic precinct. In fact, the chapel was made up of two separate, single-celled apsidal churches, one facing west for the sick monks, the other facing east for the novices. It stands between the infirmary cloister and that of the novitiate, and is disposed along an axis with the main church. No walls or fences isolate this section from the monastic enclosure. This rational disposition creates a setting in which the sick and the young are separated from the monks' living quarters. As such, it is perfectly attuned to St Benedict's dictates, the first Rule to suggest separating the sick, the old and the young. He outlined this concept in two chapters, 36 De infirmis fratribus and 37 De senibus vel infantibus, establishing the provisions that the abbot and the cellerarius[10] were to make for the weak and infirm. The young and the ill were not subjected to strict a monastic rule, and they were allowed meat and baths more frequently. For these reasons, the accommodations for sick monks and those for the novitiate could stand close to one another while still being separated and self-sufficient.[11] In the Plan, in fact, the two twin cloisters are housed in separate but identical quarters located on the north and south flanks of the double-apsed church. Axially aligned with the large church, these are partitioned transversely by a median wall into two separate chapels. Each cloister, moreover, is provided with its own separate kitchen and bath (see Fig. 15.3, nos 4, 4.1–4.3, 5, 5.1–5.3).

---

10 "Cellerarius monasterii … infirmorum, infantum, hospitum pauperumque cum omni sollicitudine curam gerat"; *Benedicti Regula* 31.9, in *La Regola di San Benedetto e le Regole dei Padri*, ed. Salvatore Pricoco (Verona, 1995), p. 198.

11 The novices, both oblates and *pulsantes*, were educated separately from the sons of the nobles, who were trained in the outer school, which in the Plan, is set between the abbot's living quarters and those for the distinguished guests, but separated from both by a wall or a fence; see Fig. 15.2, no. 12.

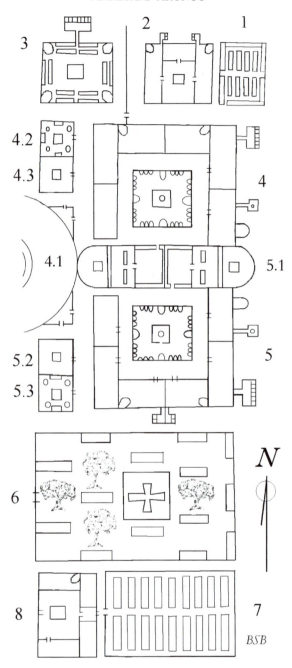

Figure 15.3   The Plan of St Gall medical facilities (drawn from plan by B.S. Bowers, explanatory key by the author).

Key:

1. Medicinal herb garden.
2. Physicians' house.
3. House for bloodletting and purging.
4. Monks' infirmary.
4.1 Chapel of the infirm.
4.2 Infirmary bath.
4.3 Infirmary kitchen.
5. Novitiate.
5.1 Novitiate chapel.
5.2 Novitiate kitchen.
5.3 Novitiate bath.
6. Cemetery and orchard.
7. Vegetables garden.
8. Gardener's house.

Medical Facilities

The alignment for installations of all kinds of medical facilities at the eastern edge of the monastery complex appears to have been purposeful, as it answers well to the need to take care of the sick and weak while providing for the necessity to keep them isolated, far from the healthy, although inside the inner monastic precinct. Starting from the north-east corner of the Plan, health facilities occupy almost one tenth of the monastic site. They comprise the physicians' house with its medicinal herb garden, the monks' infirmary, the sick ward in the novitiate, and the house for bloodletting (Fig. 15.3).

The so-called house for bloodletting and purging stands west of the physicians' house, and consists of a large, square house heated by a central fireplace and four additional corner ones. It is furnished with six tables or benches (*mensae*) where patients could be attended to.[12] As is well known, bleeding was used as a remedy for almost all kinds of disease, and was widely prescribed even for people in good physical health. Lorna Price points out that "monks and serfs needing medical attention could leave the church after the service and report to whichever medical facility they were assigned. The House for Bloodletting was probably used by both monks and serfs"[13] – and, one could add, by guests and their attendants, not to mention pilgrims or other visitors. The building stands outside the actual infirmary zone, being located just behind the abbot's quarters, divided by a wall or a fence from the physicians' house, while accessible through a gate (Fig. 15.3, no. 3). The physicians were therefore close enough to reach the building easily in order to conduct or oversee the bloodletting and administer purgings, also a widely used remedy. For this purpose, a suitable number of privies were provided. Also close at

---

12 A full description is in Horn and Born, 2:184–5; 3:52.

13 Price, *The Plan of St Gall in Brief*, p. 33.

hand were the infirmary bathing facilities and kitchen, for use by the sick and those who had been bled and needed to recover their strength.

The central building of the health complex set in the far north-east corner with easy access to the medicinal herb garden is the physicians' house,[14] or *domus medicorum* as the Latin caption reads. It is separated from the house for bloodletting by a wall, and has no direct access to the infirmary (Fig. 15.3, no. 2). It consists of a square building with four rooms. The central one is a kind of communal room, heated by an open, square hearth set in the middle. This central room is surrounded by three peripheral rooms. The one at the eastern side is designated the chief physician's lodgings (*mansio medici ipsius*). The one at the western side is intended for the critically ill (*cubiculum ualde infirmorum*). Both rooms are equipped with corner fireplaces and their own privies. The third room, on the north side, is the pharmacy where drugs and medicaments are to be kept and prepared (*armarium pigmentorum*).

In their reconstruction of the Plan, Horn and Born pointed out that the physicians' house is one of the few buildings on the Plan in which the main room with an open fireplace is directly accessible from the outside. They objected to the hypothesis that the room for the critically ill served primarily as an isolation ward for patients with communicable diseases, suggesting instead that it was "the place where the monastery's serfs and workmen were taken when their condition became critical, since laymen could not be admitted to the Monks' Infirmary."[15]

Among the physicians' chief duties was the preparation of remedies, most of which were made using simples,[16] among which, of course, an important place was given to herbal drugs. For this reason, the medicinal herb garden lies close to the physicians' house in the far north-east corner of the monastic complex. It is oriented north–south, protected from northern and eastern winds by the boundary walls of the monastery.

The herbs to be cultivated were selected carefully for their medicinal properties: *lilium, rosas, fasiolo, sata regia, costo, fena greca, rosmarino, menta, saluia, ruta, gladiola, pulegium, sisimbria, cumino, lubestico* and *feniculum*.[17] The beds are arranged orderly in a double set. Within the beds, the plants are not distributed at

---

14 The full description is in Horn and Born, 2:174–81; 3:53.

15 Ibid., 2:181.

16 A simple is one medicinal plant or one ingredient with medicinal properties, as opposed to a mixture of such ingredients, as in a medicinal remedy with multiple parts.

17 That is, according to Horn and Born: *Lilium candidum* L., *Rosa gallica* L., *Dolichos melanophtalmus* L., *Satureia hortensis* L., *Tanacetum balsamita* L., *Trigonella fenum graecum* L., *Rosmarinus officinalis* L., *Mentha spp.* L., *Salvia officinalis* L., *Ruta graveolens* L., *Iris germanica* L., *Mentha pulegium* L., *Mentha aquatica* L. (but, perhaps more correctly, either *Nasturtium officinale* R. Br. or *Mentha silvestris* or *M. viridis* L.; see Jacques André, *Les Noms de plantes dans la Rome antique* [Paris, 1985], s.v. *sisymbrium*), *Cuminum cyminum* L., *Levisticum officinale* L., *Anethum foeniculum* L. (or *Foeniculum vulgare* Gaertn.; see André, *Les Noms*, s.v. *feniculum*). A full description of the medical herb garden is in Horn and Born, 2:181–4; 3:88.

random. On the contrary, it seems they are arranged by families.[18] This proves that their names were not simply copied from the lists in Charlemagne's *Capitulare de villis*.[19]

The main complex of health facilities, of course, contains the building for the monks' infirmary and the novitiate cloisters. This is the largest single building represented in the Plan. The two cloisters are small replicas of the monks' cloister (each about two-thirds of its surface area), and together with the chapel they share, they lie between the physicians' house on the north and the monks' large cemetery and orchard on the south (see Fig. 15.3). As in the monks' cloister, dormitories are heated by hypocausts[20] with a firing chamber (*caminus*) and smoke stack (*exitus fumi*). Both buildings open to the west on either side of the apse of the chapel for the sick, but they do not allow for access: "since the apex of this apse touches the apex of the eastern paradise of the main church, it would have been impossible for any of the novices to stray onto the grounds of the infirmary, or for any of the sick to enter into the cloister of the novices."[21]

On the northern side of the double chapel lies the infirmary intended for sick monks: *Fratribus infirmis pariter locus iste paretur*, as the Latin caption reads.[22] On the east wing is the dormitory (*dormitorium*) with a six-seat privy (*necessarium*) and warming room (*pisal*), while the supply room (*camera*) and the refectory (*refectorium*) are set in the west wing. In the north wing, the room for the critically ill (*locus ualde infirmorum*) is set close to the lodgings of the Master of the infirmary (*mansio magistri eorum*).[23] While both rooms have a corner fireplace, they lack a privy; on the other hand, a privy is clearly indicated in the Plan for the corresponding novitiate rooms. This possible error is perhaps "one of the genuine oversights of the Plan and may be an inadvertent omission by the copyist."[24] It appears from this disposition that the dormitory was intended for monks afflicted with minor ailments, for the aged, or for the chronically ill who were permanently housed in the infirmary.

The novitiate lies symmetrically on the south side of the chapel, and its layout mirrors that of the monks' infirmary. Here too, all the rooms are separated from each other, while opening onto the cloister. A sick ward (*infirmorum domus*) is provided so that ill novices do not have to be in contact with the monks. The ward lies close to the master's lodgings (*mansio Magister eorum*); both rooms are heated with corner fireplaces and are provided with separate privies, each with two seats.

---

18 See Günter Noll, "The Origin of the So-called Plan of St Gall," *Journal of Medieval History*, 8 (1982), 191–240, 203–7.

19 *Capitulare de Villis*, in *Capitularia Regum Francorum*, MGH, LL 2 (Hanover, 1940), 82–90.

20 Each hypocaust is made up of several parts, including the firing chamber, the smoke stack and the under-floor piping to distribute the heat generated in the firing chamber.

21 Horn and Born, 1:311.

22 "For the sick brethren similarly this place should be established"; ibid., 1:313.

23 Ibid., 1:314.

24 Ibid.

The Benedictine Rule and Anglo-Saxon England

The origin of the Plan of St Gall and reason for its creation are still obscure; perhaps some pertinent information will come from new archeological research at the sites of Anglo-Saxon and Carolingian monasteries. Lawrence Nees has demonstrated Horn and Born's theory that the Plan was the model for the layout of a Benedictine monastery and possibly used as a guide throughout France. However, this idea is not thoroughly consistent with the present state of research.[25]

Nevertheless, there are some points that are not usually taken into consideration by researchers. As Günther Noll pointed out in a widely discussed paper that appeared in 1982,[26] one of the main features of the Plan is the way heating is provided. In addition to the open central square fireplaces and/or corner fireplaces, there are three hypocaust systems to warm the monks' dormitory, the dormitories of the infirmary and the novitiate. It is clear that the heating structures depicted in the Plan, along with the types of herbs and trees to be grown in the gardens, suggest a mild climatic zone, although not necessarily a Mediterranean one. Not only are no plants such as pomegranates, olive trees or grapes for winemaking mentioned, but the plants are arranged in such a way as to lie fully in the sun, far from the shadows of buildings and trees, protected from both cold northern and eastern winds and strong south-westerlies. Moreover, the presence of breweries[27] suggests a location north of the Alps, but not Germany. In Germany, the winters are too cold to grow the plants indicated, and too cold for a heating system based on open fireplaces, like the one shown in the Plan. Only the monastery of Reichenau has a similar heating system, which, however, by the tenth century, was found insufficient since the monks had to build an extra furnace to warm their scriptorium.[28]

In Noll's opinion, the climatic zone that best answers all these requirements is the peninsula of Kent in the south-east corner of England. Here, the climate is mild, there are no harsh winters, the chalky soil is fertile, and two of the most outstanding monasteries of Anglo-Saxon England stand: Christ Church and St Augustine, Canterbury. However, there are more coincidences. The Plan's peculiar arrangement within a single monastery of two churches aligned on a common axis is one of the most significant distinguishing features of early Anglo-Saxon monasteries. In England, according to John Blair, "the tradition of twinned or multiple churches (general throughout early Christendom on sites of any importance) often took the form of two or more churches aligned on a west-east axis."[29] This disposition is known from

---

25 Nees, "The Plan of St Gall," p. 18.

26 See Noll, "The Origin."

27 There are several in the Plan, often together with the bakeries. See Fig. 15.2: no. 9, Monks' bakery and brewery; no. 10, Kitchen, cellar, bakery, and brewery for distinguished guests; no. 30, House for turners and coopers with threshing stage for grain for the brewery; no. 32, Kitchen, bakery, and brewery for pilgrims and the poor.

28 See Noll, "The Origin," pp. 202–9.

29 John Blair, "Monastic Sites", in *The Blackwell Encyclopaedia of Anglo-Saxon England*, ed. Michael Lapidge, John Blair, Simon Keynes and Donald Scragg (Oxford, 1999),

excavations in Canterbury St Augustine's,[30] Glastonbury, Monkwearmouth-Jarrow,[31] Lindisfarne and Wells, but it can also be found on the Continent in Anglo-Saxon monastic foundations, such as Fulda.

The rational disposition of all elements marks the St Gall Plan as the first instance of a classic Benedictine layout, with the cloister arranged to the south, in front of the nave of the monastic church, around which all the buildings are grouped. It is also the first example of a Benedictine monastery with organized health facilities to comply with the dictates of the Rule of St Benedict.

This rational disposition is even more apparent if one considers how intelligently the health facilities were planned. The whole complex is grouped and organized as a coherent structure which is united with, although existing separately from, the other buildings. This complex extends from the bloodletting and purging house set on the north-eastern side of the convent, separated from the physicians' house by a wall or a fence on the opposite south-eastern corner, to where the monks' orchard, the house for the gardener and the one for the poultry-keeper are located.

There are no descriptions of what a hospital, or an infirmary, was like in an Anglo-Saxon or Carolingian Benedictine monastery in those early centuries.[32] The organized practice of medicine, and the consequent organization of assistance to the sick, would begin later on after the Conquest, when medicine first began to be taught at medical schools (such as the school of Salerno) and then later at the universities. However, there are enough surviving documents to know that in Anglo-Saxon England, the practice of medicine was mentioned as early as the second half of the seventh century. In 669, Theodore of Tarsus arrived in England as Archbishop of Canterbury. Theodore, along with Hadrian, the abbot of the monastery of SS Peter and Paul (later St Augustine's), was the founder of the school at Canterbury whose most renowned pupil was Aldhelm. The medical arts were not taught formally at Canterbury, at least according to Aldhelm, who described its syllabus in a letter,[33] but Bede mentions Theodore's reputation as an expert in medicine. There exist remedies attributed to Theodore that continued to be handed down for centuries in medieval England.[34] From the end of the ninth century, there also began to appear

---

322–4, 323.

30 See Horn and Born, 1:298.

31 See Rosemary Cramp, "Monkwearmouth and Jarrow in their European Context," in *"Churches Built in Ancient Times": Recent Studies in Early Christian Archaeology*, ed. Kenneth Painter (London, 1994), 279–94.

32 Monastic foundations must have had an infirmary; see Audrey Meaney, "The Practice of Medicine in England about the Year 1000," in *The Year 1000: Medical Practice at the End of the First Millennium*, ed. Peregrine Horden and Emilie Savage-Smith, *Journal of the Society for the Social History of Medicine*, 13(2) (2000), 221–37.

33 *Aldhelmi Opera*, Rudolf Ehwald, ed. MGH, Auct. Antiq. 15, Berlin 1919, 476 (Epist. i); English trans. by Michael Lapidge and Michael Herren, *Aldhelm: The Prose Works* (Cambridge, 1979), p. 152.

34 See Michael Lapidge, "The School of Theodore and Hadrian," *Anglo-Saxon England*, 15 (1986), 45–72, 50–51. Theodore may have studied medicine at Constantinople, see Michael

medical compendia in Old English, similar to the Latin *dynamidia*. One example is the *Læceboc*.[35]

It is not known who rationally designed the two distinct cloisters: the one for sick monks (situated close to the chief physician's residence and the herb garden so that he could tend and have control over it), and the other one for the novices with its own infirmary. Nor is it known who planned the three gardens: the herb garden close to the physicians' house (Fig. 15.3, no. 1); the orchard where fruit trees were grown among the monks' sepulchers (Fig. 15.3, no. 6); and further south the garden where the gardeners grew all the vegetables for the monastery (Fig. 15.3, no. 7). However, according to Noll, there was only one man who had the culture, the experience and the breadth of mind to imagine such a complex: Theodore of Tarsus, whose native Greek culture may have prompted him to make another small innovation, the arrangement of plants according to plant families in the vegetable garden. This kind of disposition was utterly unknown, not only to the medieval world but also to the Classical Roman one, where the economic aspects of agriculture were considered more important than the scientific study of botany. However, as early as the fourth century BC in Greece, Theophrastus outlined in his *Natural history of plants* a theoretical classification of different plants according to their leaves, flowers, roots and tastes, as well as by shape, color and firmness of their seeds.

Noll's hypothesis has been harshly challenged, largely on the grounds that there is no direct evidence to connect the St Gall Plan with Canterbury, or indeed with England, and that his arguments are too often based upon unconvincing evidence or upon erroneous assumptions about early Canterbury.[36] Nevertheless, Noll's suggestion about the Plan and Anglo-Saxon monasteries is rather intriguing. There are no similarities between Christ Church Monastery and the monastery on the Plan, as there are none whatsoever between the Plan and Continental Carolingian monasteries. Nor are there proofs that the Plan was a product of the Carolingian Monastic Reform. There are, however, some features of the Plan that place it closer to the late antique period than to the Carolingian epoch. The exemplary clarity of the carefully planned architectural complex is reminiscent of the structure of the Roman villa, a rural dwelling with annexes, yard, garden and orchard. Evidence is to be seen in the complicated and autonomous structure of the Plan, with its systematic,

---

Lapidge, "The Career of Archbishop Theodore," in *Archbishop Theodore. Commemorative Studies on his Life and Influence*, ed. Michael Lapidge (Cambridge, 1995), pp. 1–29, 17–19, and *Biblical Commentaries from the Canterbury School of Theodore and Hadrian*, ed. Bernard Bischoff and Michael Lapidge (Cambridge, 1994), 253–5.

35 First published by Oswald Cockayne, *Leechdoms, Wortcunning and Starcraft of Early England, Rerum Britannicarum medii aevi scriptores*, 35, 3 vols (London, 1864–66): 2. For its relationship with classical and Late Antique medicine, see Malcom L. Cameron, "Bald's Leechbook: Its Sources and their Use in its Compilation," *Anglo-Saxon England*, 12 (1983), 153–82.

36 "The evidence is not handled in a way which inspires confidence"; Lapidge, "The School of Theodore and Hadrian," 52. See also *A History of Canterbury Cathedral*, ed. Patrick Collison, Nigel Ramsay and Margaret Sparks (Oxford, 1995), esp. p. 59.

architectural integration of buildings and their functions so as to be able to meet both the spiritual needs of monastic life and the practical needs of the monks' daily life. Moreover, the layout of the infirmary-novitiate complex on the eastern part of the Plan is "more Roman in spirit than any other building of the Plan, and is without antecedent in either Early Christian or early medieval architecture having its roots in Roman imperial audience halls and luxurious Roman villas."[37] To be able to conceive of a plan with the buildings having such a degree of complexity and perfect architectural and functional relationships, the designer must have been brought up in a classical Roman or late antique cultural milieu. In addition, the rational and meticulous arrangements in the Plan for medical provisions point to a man well versed in medical learning.

The refusal to admit that the Plan could have been conceived in Anglo-Saxon England as early as the seventh or the eighth century is also based on a negative conception about early medieval medicine, in particular in Anglo-Saxon times. It must, however, be stressed that such a modern misconception is the result of opinions expressed by scholars such as Oswald Cockayne and Charles Singer. To quote M.L. Cameron's words: "There has been an unfortunate and widely held belief that all ancient medicine, with the exception of that of the Hippocratic school, of Galen and some early Byzantine physicians, was filled with superstitious and magical practices and with generally worthless remedies, practices and theories."[38] Only in the last forty years has this trend undergone a drastic change. Medieval medicine, and Anglo-Saxon medicine in particular (the first treatises to appear in a European vernacular were written in Old English), is now studied as rational components. Consideration is now taken of the medical value of the remedies[39] and of the relationship of early medieval medicine to late antique Greek and Roman medical knowledge. Thanks to these studies, we now know that Anglo-Saxon medicine developed from that of the Greeks and Romans, taking "some of the best they had to offer,"[40] and attained a remarkable level of quality, not inferior to the highest Continental standards.[41]

---

37 Price, *The Plan of St Gall in Brief*, p. 31. An example is the Roman summer residence in Trier, Konz (*Contionacum*), whose "perfect bisymmetry bears striking resemblance to the layout of the Novitiate and Infirmary complex of the Plan of St Gall, except that in the villa at Konz the open courts were not colonnaded"; *The Plan of St Gall*, 1:294. Horn and Born have indicated a whole list of similar examples of Roman buildings showing the same characteristics; see Horn and Born, 1:256, 1:293–7, 1:315–16.

38 Malcolm L. Cameron, *Anglo-Saxon Medicine* (Cambridge, 1993), p. 2.

39 Ibid., pp. 117–29.

40 Ibid., p. 186.

41 Besides the already quoted works by Malcolm L. Cameron, see his "The Sources of Medical Knowledge in Anglo-Saxon England," *Anglo-Saxon England*, 11 (1983), 135–55. For the relationship of Anglo-Saxon England with the Continent, and the monastery of Montecassino in particular, see Maria A. D'Aronco, "Le conoscenze mediche nell'Inghilterra anglosassone: il ruolo del mondo carolingio," in *International Scandinavian and Medieval Studies in Memory of Gerd Wolfgang Weber*, ed. Michael Dallapiazza, Olaf Hansen, Preben Meulengracht Sorensen and Yvonne S. Bonnetain (Trieste, 2000), 129–46; Maria A.

A final consideration: there is no direct evidence that any Anglo-Saxon monastery in Canterbury (as well as at any other place in England) followed a strict Benedictine Rule before the mid-tenth century. Nevertheless, Michael Lapidge has been able to prove that the Benedictine Rule was known in Canterbury at a very early stage.[42] In fact, glosses to the *Regula* are preserved in the *Leiden Glossary*[43] and in two other Continental manuscripts belonging to the same family of glossaries.[44] From a comparison of these glosses *(lemmata* plus *interpretamenta)* to the text of the Rule, it appears that the *lemmata* preserved in the Leiden family glossaries "are drawn unmistakably from the *textus interpolatus.*"[45] This recension is preserved in five principal manuscripts, the oldest of which is also the oldest extant manuscript of the *Regula*, now at Oxford's Bodleian Library, Hatton 48, written in England *c.* 700.[46] But the evidence is that the author of the glossed text did not utilize it, as there are no known connections of this manuscript with a Canterbury location. Conversely, the author seems to have used an exemplar which shares peculiar readings with the other four principal manuscripts belonging to the *textus interpolatus* recension, and with one in particular, an early ninth-century manuscript now at the Stiftsbibliothek in St Gallen, ms. 916.[47] According to Michael Lapidge, the Leiden family glossaries preserve materials from the "original English collection," or *glossae collectae,* which originated in England and were compiled in Canterbury under Theodore and

---

D'Aronco, "Il ms. Londra, British Library, Cotton Vitellius C. iii dell'erbario anglosassone e la tradizione medica di Montecassino," in *Incontri di popoli e culture tra V e IX secolo. Atti delle V giornate di studio sull'età romanobarbarica. Benevento, 9–11 giugno 1997*, ed. Marcello Rotili (Naples, 1998), 117–27; Maria A. D'Aronco, "Introduction," *The Old English Illustrated Pharmacopoeia: British Library Cotton Vitellius C iii*, ed. Maria A. D'Aronco and Malcolm L. Cameron, *Early English Manuscripts in Facsimile*, 27 (Copenhagen, 1998), 26–43. For an up-to-date and thorough assessment of the present state of research on medieval medicine, and herbals in particular, see esp. Anne Van Arsdall, *Medieval Herbal Remedies: The Old English Herbarium and Anglo-Saxon Medicine* (New York, 2002), 1–100.

42 Lapidge, "The School of Theodore and Hadrian."

43 MS Leiden, Bibliothek der Rijksuniversiteit, Voss. Lat. Q. 69, fols 20r–36r, printed in *A Late Eighth-century Latin–Anglo Saxon Glossary Preserved in the Library of the Leiden University*, ed. Jan H. Hessels (Cambridge, 1906).

44 The two MSS are: Fulda, Hessische Landesbibliothek, Aa. 2, fols 129r–139r, and Paris, Bibliothèque Nationale, lat. 2685, fols 47r–56r. Both MSS are unprinted; see Lapidge, "The School of Theodore and Hadrian," pp. 68, 70.

45 There are two principal recensions of the *Regula Sancti Benedicti*: the *textus purus*, deriving from St Benedict's original (best preserved in a Carolingian copy of a MS from Montecassino, now St. Gallen, Stiftsbibliothek 914 [s. ix[1]]), and the *textus interpolatus*, probably originated in Rome c. 600; see Ludwig Traube, "Textgeschichte der *Regula S. Benedicti,*" *Abhandlungen der königlich bayerischen Akademie der Wissenschaften, phil.-hist. Klasse*, 21 (1898), 601–731, and Paul Meyvaert, "Towards a History of the Textual Transmission of the *Regula S. Benedicti,*" *Scriptorium*, 17 (1963), 83–110.

46 Facsimile edition by David H. Farmer, *The Rule of St Benedict, Early English Manuscripts in Facsimile*, 15 (Copenhagen, 1968).

47 Lapidge, "The School of Theodore and Hadrian," p. 63.

Hadrian. It seems evident that a copy of the Benedictine Rule was among the books that Theodore and Hadrian had brought together in their libraries at Canterbury.

The question of where and by whom the Plan was conceived must still be left open, as certainty remains elusive. Nevertheless, the classical elements of the Plan point to a connection with a highly cultivated and Roman-oriented milieu, and it is impossible not to remember the outstanding level of scholarship achieved in the seventh and eighth centuries by what was arguably "the most brilliant school of studies during the entire Anglo-Saxon period,"[48] along with its fundamental role in conserving the great heritage of classical culture and re-elaborating it, handing it down to new generations.

---

48 Ibid., p. 67.

Index

(References to illustrations are in **bold**).